Educating the Other America

Educating the Other America

Top Experts Tackle
Poverty, Literacy, and Achievement
in Our Schools

edited by

Susan B. Neuman, Ed.D.
University of Michigan
Ann Arbor

·P A U L·H·
BROOKES
PUBLISHING Co.®

Baltimore • London • Sydney

Paul H. Brookes Publishing Co.
Post Office Box 10624
Baltimore, Maryland 21285-0624
USA

www.brookespublishing.com

"Paul H. Brookes Publishing Co." is a registered trademark of
Paul H. Brookes Publishing Co., Inc.

Typeset by Maryland Composition, Inc., Laurel, Maryland.
Manufactured in the United States of America by
Sheridan Books, Inc., Chelsea, Michigan.

The individuals described in this book are composites based on the authors' experiences. In all instances, names and identifying details have been changed to protect confidentiality.

Library of Congress Cataloging-in-Publication Data

Educating the other America : top experts tackle poverty, literacy, and achievement in
  our schools / edited by Susan B. Neuman.
    p.   cm.
  Includes bibliographical references and index.
  ISBN-13: 978-1-55766-906-3 (pbk.)
  ISBN-10: 1-55766-906-6 (pbk.)
    1. Children with social disabilities—Education—United States.   2. Poor children—
Education—United States.   3. Educational equalization—United States.   4. Poverty—
United States.   I. Neuman, Susan B.   II. Title.
LC4091.E343 2008
371.826′9420973—dc22   2008023727

British Library Cataloguing in Publication data are available from the British Library.

2012   2011   2010   2009   2008
10   9   8   7   6   5   4   3   2   1

Contents

About the Editor

Susan B. Neuman, Ed.D., Professor, University of Michigan, 610 East University Avenue, Ann Arbor, Michigan 48109

Dr. Neuman is a professor in educational studies specializing in early literacy development. Previously, she served as the U.S. Assistant Secretary for Elementary and Secondary Education. In her role as Assistant Secretary, she established the Reading First program and the Early Reading First program and was responsible for all activities in Title I of the Elementary and Secondary Act of 1965 (PL 89-10). She has directed the Center for the Improvement of Early Reading Achievement (CIERA). Her research and teaching interests include early childhood policy, curriculum, and early reading instruction for prekindergarten through Grade 3.

About the Contributors

Marilyn Jager Adams, Ph.D., Research Professor, Cognitive and Linguistic Sciences Department, Box 1978, Brown University, Providence, Rhode Island 02912. Dr. Adams served as the chief scientist of Soliloquy Learning, Inc., and is internationally regarded for her research and applied work in the area of cognition and education. She is the recipient of the American Educational Research Association's Sylvia Scribner Award for outstanding research. She is Senior Literacy Advisor for Instruction for PBS's *Between the Lions,* as well as senior author of *Fox in a Box,* an award-winning, standards-based literacy assessment kit. Dr. Adams has also written/designed three empirically proven instructional programs: on thinking skills for middle school students, on reading and writing for elementary school students, and on linguistic awareness for emergent readers and students with special needs.

Daniel R. Anderson, Ph.D., Professor of Psychology, University of Massachusetts at Amherst, 135 Hicks Way, Tobin Hall, Amherst, Massachusetts 01003. Dr. Anderson's general area of research is children and media, particularly television. His research has focused on a cognitive analysis of children's television viewing as well as the impact of television on cognitive development and education. In addition to his research, Dr. Anderson and his students frequently do research and consulting for children's educational television programs. Dr. Anderson advised on the development of *Blue's Clues, Dora the Explorer,* and *Bear in the Big Blue House,* among many other programs, and has also been a consultant for *Sesame Street.*

Adriana G. Bus, Ph.D., Professor of Education and Child Studies, Leiden University, Wassenaarseweg 52, 2333 AK Leiden, The Netherlands. Dr. Bus is a former reading specialist and teaches courses in reading, writing, and learning problems. She is a leading scholar on the impact of attachment theory on children's emergent literacy development and on developmental changes in storybook reading among parents and children. Dr. Bus's recent research examines the impact of multimedia storybooks on children's reading skills, and she has published many articles in the field of education, educational psychology, and child development.

Sandra L. Calvert, Ph.D., Chair and Professor, Department of Psychology, Georgetown University, 37th and O Streets NW, Washington, D.C. 20057. Dr.

Calvert is Director of the Children's Digital Media Center, a multisite interdisciplinary research center funded by the National Science Foundation. Her current research focuses on the effects of media on very early development and on the effects of interactive media and food marketing on children's diets and health. Dr. Calvert authored *Children's Journeys Through the Information Age* (McGraw-Hill, 1999) and coedited *Children in the Digital Age: Influences of Electronic Media on Development* (with Amy B. Jordan & Rodney R. Cocking, Greenwood Publishing Group, 2002) and the *Handbook of Children, Media, and Development* (with B.J. Wilson, Wiley-Blackwell Publishing, 2008). She has served on two committees for the National Academies, leading to two committee coauthored books: *Food Marketing to Children and Youth: Threat or Opportunity* (2006) and *Youth, Pornography, and the Internet* (2002).

Bette Chambers, Ph.D., Vice-President for Research, Success for All Foundation, 200 West Towsontown Boulevard, Baltimore, Maryland 21204. Dr. Chambers is Vice-President for Research at the Success for All Foundation, where she oversees foundation research and directs the development and dissemination of the early childhood education and technology embedded programs. She is also a professor in the Institute for Effective Education at the University of York and at the Center for Research and Reform in Education at the Johns Hopkins University. She has authored and coauthored numerous articles, books, and practical guides on cooperative learning, technology infusion in literacy, and early childhood education.

Mary Corcoran, Ph.D., Professor of Political Science, Public Policy and Women's Studies, University of Michigan, Gerald R. Ford School of Public Policy, 5223 Weill Hall, 735 South State Street, Ann Arbor, Michigan 48109. Dr. Corcoran's research focuses on the effects of gender and race discrimination on economic status and earnings and on welfare and employment policies. She has published articles on intergenerational mobility, the underclass, and sex-based and race-based inequality. Dr. Corcoran teaches seminars on poverty and inequality and on women and employment. She received her doctorate from the Massachusetts Institute of Technology.

Holly K. Craig, Ph.D., Professor of Education, University of Michigan, 1111 East Catherine Street, Ann Arbor, Michigan 48109. Dr. Craig is a research professor at the Institute for Human Adjustment. Her interest areas are normal language processes in children and language differences and disorders across the life span. She serves as Director of the University Center for the Development of Language and Literacy (formerly the Communicative Disorders Clinic). Her current research focuses on the role of language skill in academic underachievement, particularly to the contribution of the black–white test score gap.

Sandra K. Danziger, Ph.D., Professor of Social Work and Research Professor of Public Policy, School of Social Work, University of Michigan, 735 South State Street, Ann Arbor, Michigan 48109. Dr. Danziger is Director of the Michigan Program on Poverty and Social Welfare Policy at the University of Michigan. Her primary research interests are the effects of public antipoverty and social service programs and policies on the well-being of disadvantaged families. Her current research examines barriers to employment among single mothers making the transition from welfare to work and the implementation of employment and training programs for welfare recipients in Michigan. She was Principal Investigator on the Women's Employment Survey.

Sheldon H. Danziger, Ph.D., Henry J. Meyer Distinguished University Professor of Public Policy and Director of the National Poverty Center, Gerald R. Ford School of Public Policy, Weill Hall, 735 South State Street #5132, Ann Arbor, Michigan 48109. Dr. Danziger is also Research Professor at the Population Studies Center at the University of Michigan. His research focuses on the effects of economic, demographic, and public policy changes on trends in poverty and inequality. He is a fellow of the American Academy of Arts and Sciences, a John Simon Guggenheim Foundation Fellow, and a member of the MacArthur Foundation Research Network on Transitions to Adulthood. Dr. Danziger is the coauthor of *America Unequal* (with Peter Gottschalk, Russell Sage Foundation, 1995) and *Detroit Divided* (with Reynolds Farley & Harry J. Holzer, Russell Sage Foundation, 2000) and numerous edited volumes and articles.

Matthew J. Davis, M.S., Doctoral Student, Graduate Research Assistant, Texas A&M University, College of Education and Human Development, Department of Educational Psychology, 4225 TAMU, College Station, Texas 77843. Mr. Davis is pursuing a doctoral degree in counseling psychology at Texas A&M University with a focus in public health. He works as a graduate research assistant on a currently funded Institute of Education Sciences grant examining methods to accelerate vocabulary and language development among preschool children at risk for reading difficulty. His research roles on this project include observational methods and analyses of adult–child interactions during shared book reading. His career goal is the study of risk behaviors and related intervention research in the public health sector.

Maria T. de Jong, Ph.D., Assistant Professor, Leiden University, Wassenaarseweg 52, 2333 AK Leiden, The Netherlands. Dr. de Jong received her doctorate in educational psychology from Leiden University. Her research focuses on the use of electronic media in early literacy and includes first and second language learners. She published about her research in leading journals such as

Journal of Educational Psychology and *Reading Research Quarterly.* She teaches courses in reading, writing, and learning problems.

Barbara R. Foorman, Ph.D., Director, Florida State University's Florida Center for Reading Research, 227 North Bronough Street, Suite 7250, Tallahassee, Florida 32301. Dr. Foorman is the Francis Eppes Professor of Education at Florida State University. In 2005, Dr. Foorman served as the Commissioner of Education Research in the Institute of Education Sciences in the U.S. Department of Education. Her research focuses on early reading interventions, scaling assessment-driven instruction, and literacy development in Spanish-speaking children. In addition, her centers have provided professional development and technical assistance to school districts in Texas, Florida, and the eastern seaboard receiving Reading First funds.

Claude Goldenberg, Ph.D., Professor of Education, Stanford University, 3840 Fir Circle, Seal Beach, California 90740. Dr. Goldenberg is the author of *Successful School Change* (Teachers College Press, 2004) and coauthor of *Promoting Academic Achievement for English Learners* (with Rhoda Colema, Corwin Press, forthcoming). Dr. Goldenberg's research focuses on literacy and academic achievement among English language learners, particularly those from Spanish-speaking homes. He was a member of the Committee on the Prevention of Reading Difficulties in Young Children and the National Literacy Panel. Dr. Goldenberg received the Albert J. Harris Award (with Ronald Gallimore) from the International Reading Association in 1993.

Jorge E. Gonzalez, Ph.D., Assistant Professor of School Psychology, Texas A&M University, College of Education and Human Development, Department of Educational Psychology, College Station, Texas 77843. Dr. Gonzalez received his doctorate in school psychology from the University of Nebraska–Lincoln. He works closely with Drs. Deborah C. Simmons and Sharolyn D. Pollard-Durodola on issues related to language, literacy, and early reading for Spanish-speaking low-income children. Together, they examine the impact of instructional design and instructional features, and home literacy environment on school achievement for children at-risk or with disabilities.

Charles R. Greenwood, Ph.D., Senior Scientist, Juniper Gardens Children's Project, Schiefelbusch Institute for Life Span Studies, University of Kansas, 650 Minnesota Avenue, Second Floor, Kansas City, Kansas 66101. Dr. Greenwood is Professor of Applied Behavioral Science at University of Kansas and Senior Scientist in the Schiefelbusch Institute for Life Span Studies, serving as Director of the Juniper Gardens Children's Project. His research areas include development of evidence-based instructional and behavioral intervention practices, special education research, formative evaluation, and continuous progress monitoring. He is the author of ClassWide Peer Tutoring, listed at the What Works Clearinghouse web site as a program that promotes beginning reading achievement. Dr. Greenwood is the recipient of APA–Division 25's Fred S. Keller award for distinguished contributions to the field of education.

Heather L. Kirkorian, Ph.D., Postdoctoral Research Associate, Department of Psychology, Tobin Hall, University of Massachusetts, Amherst, Massachusetts 01003. Dr. Kirkorian received her doctorate in developmental psychology from the University of Massachusetts–Amherst, where she is currently a postdoctoral research associate. Her research focuses on the impact of television on children and the cognitive processes involved in television viewing. With respect to media impact, Dr. Kirkorian studies the effects of background television exposure on very young children's solitary play and social interactions. Other research focuses on the extent to which infants and toddlers understand and can learn from video.

Nancy A. Madden, Ph.D., President and CEO, Success for All Foundation, 200 West Towsontown Boulevard, Baltimore, Maryland 21204. Dr. Madden is President and Co-founder of the Success for All Foundation, a professor at the University of York, and a professor in the Center for Research and Reform in Education at the Johns Hopkins University. As a research scientist at the Johns Hopkins University, Dr. Madden directed the development of the reading, writing, language arts, and mathematics elements of Success for All. An expert in literacy and instruction, Dr. Madden is the author or coauthor of many articles and books on cooperative learning, mainstreaming, Chapter 1, and students at risk, including *Effective Programs for Students at Risk* (with Robert E. Slavin & Nancy L. Karweit, Allyn & Bacon, 1989) and *One Million Children: Success for All* (with Robert E. Slavin, Corwin Press, 2001).

Vonnie C. McLoyd, Ph.D., Stephen Baxter Distinguished Professor of Psychology, Department of Psychology, University of North Carolina, CB# 3270, Davie Hall, Cameron Boulevard, Chapel Hill, North Carolina 27599. Dr. McLoyd is the director of the National Institute of Mental Health–funded Training Program in Research on Black Child Development. Her work focuses on the impact of economic stress and work-related transitions on family life and children's development, the mediators and moderators of these impacts, and implications of this research for practice and policy. Dr. McLoyd also has a longstanding interest in how race, ethnicity, and culture shape child socialization and development. Her research has been supported by the National Institute of Mental Health, the National Institute of Child Health and Human Development, the William T. Grant Foundation, and the Rockefeller Foundation.

Louisa C. Moats, Ed.D., Consultant, Moats Associates Consulting, Inc., 411 Mother Lode Loop, Hailey, Idaho 83333. Dr. Moats is Consulting Advisor on Literacy Research and Professional Development with Sopris West. Formerly, she was a site director for the National Institute of Child Health and Human Development Early Interventions Project in Washington, D.C. Dr. Moats specializes in reading and writing instruction, teacher education, and the identification and treatment of dyslexia and has worked as a consulting psychologist with individuals, schools, and state boards of education. Author of several books and numerous journal articles dealing with language and literacy, she has been an adjunct assistant professor of psychiatry at Dartmouth Medical School and a clinical associate professor of pediatrics at the University of Texas, Houston.

Allan Paivio, Ph.D., Professor Emeritus of Psychology, University of Western Ontario, Department of Psychology, Social Science Centre, Location: SSC 7418, London, Ontario, Canada N6A 5C2. Dr. Paivio is the author of a general theory of cognition called *dual coding theory*, which assumes that all human cognition entails the cooperative activity of multimodal verbal and nonverbal (especially imagery) processing systems. The theory has guided his research for more than 40 years on problems related to memory, language, and other aspects of cognition. The theory and research have been described in more than 100 publications of a total to date of about 200 research articles and chapters, as well as 6 books. Dr. Paivio received his doctorate from McGill University in 1959.

Julia Parkinson, M.A., M.D.P., Doctoral Candidate, School of Education, University of Michigan, 610 East University Avenue, Ann Arbor, Michigan 48109. Ms. Parkinson is a doctoral candidate at the University of Michigan in quantitative methods in education. Her research interests center on issues connected to improving the educational outcomes of children in poverty. She is currently investigating the effects of interventions designed to counteract children's risk factors, such as mental health problems. Specifically, Ms. Parkinson's research examines the efficacy of interventions targeting mental health, alone and in combination with academic interventions, to improve the education outcomes of children at risk.

Sharolyn D. Pollard-Durodola, Ed.D., Assistant Professor, Bilingual Education Program, Department of Educational Psychology, College of Education and Human Development, Texas A&M University, 107G Harrington Tower, MS 4225, College Station, Texas, 77843. Dr. Pollard-Durodola's research interests are in the area of early literacy in Spanish and English, with an emphasis on vocabulary acquisition and early reading interventions. She specifically focuses on developing intervention curricula that build on empirically validated instructional design principles and evaluating their impact on the language and reading development of second language learners by attending to both oral language (vocabulary) and comprehension needs. Dr. Pollard-Durodola worked for 14 years as a public school teacher and school administrator.

Kelly M. Purtell, Doctoral Student, Department of Psychology, University of North Carolina at Chapel Hill, CB# 3270, Cameron Boulevard, Chapel Hill, North Carolina 27599. Ms. Purtell is currently pursuing a doctoral degree in developmental psychology with a concentration in quantitative methods at the University of North Carolina at Chapel Hill. Her research interests center around the impact of economic hardship on child and adolescent development. Her current work focuses on understanding psychological mediators of the effects of poverty on academic achievement and adolescent employment. She is also interested in the impact of public policies, such as welfare and educational reform, on children and families.

Gabrielle Rappolt-Schlichtmann, Ed.D., Research Scientist, Center for Applied Special Technology, 40 Harvard Mills Square, Suite 3, Wakefield, Massachusetts 01880. Dr. Rappolt-Schlichtmann is currently a research scientist at the Center for Applied Special Technology focusing on the development of universally designed instructional practices and learning technologies that support students' achievement motivation and affective experiences in school. In her research, she has concentrated on studying the relationship between emotion and cognition in applied settings. Dr. Rappolt-Schlichtmann has expertise on the impact of stress experiences like poverty, stigmatization, and abuse on the development of cognition and emotion in early childhood. She received her Ed.D. in human development and psychology from the Harvard Graduate School of Education.

David H. Rose, M.A.T., Ed.D., Chief Education Officer, Center for Applied Special Technology, 40 Harvard Mills Square, Suite 3, Wakefield, Massachusetts 01880. In 1984, Dr. Rose helped to found Center for Applied Special Technology (CAST) with a vision of expanding opportunities for all students, especially those with disabilities, through the innovative development and application of technology. He specializes in developmental neuropsychology and in the universal design of learning technologies. Dr. Rose lectures at the Harvard Graduate School of Education and is the principal investigator of two national centers created to develop and implement the National Instructional Materials Accessibility Standard. He has also developed such award-winning literacy programs as *WiggleWorks* and *Thinking Reader* (Scholastic).

Kathleen A. Roskos, Ph.D., Professor of Education, John Carroll University Graduate School, 20700 North Park Boulevard, University Heights, Ohio 44118. Dr. Roskos is a Professor of Education at John Carroll University in Cleveland, Ohio, teaching courses in reading instruction and reading diagnosis. She recently completed 2 years of public service as the director of the Ohio Literacy Initiative at the Ohio Department of Education, providing leadership in preschool through Grade 12 literacy policy and programs. Dr. Roskos studies early literacy development, teacher cognition, and the design of professional education for teachers and has published research articles on these topics in leading journals. She served as a member of the e-Learning Committee and the Early Childhood Commission of the International Reading Association and is a leader in the Literacy Development for Young Children special interest group of that organization.

Brian Rowan, Ph.D., Burke A. Hinsdale Collegiate Professor in Education, Research Professor, Institute for Social Research, and (by courtesy) Professor of Sociology, University of Michigan, 610 East University Avenue, Room 3117A SEB, Ann Arbor, Michigan 48109. Dr. Rowan is a sociologist whose scholarly interests lie at the intersection of organization theory and school effectiveness research. Over the years, he has written on education as an institution, on the nature of teachers' work, and on the effects of school organization, leadership, and instructional practice on student achievement. His current work involves studying the design, implementation, and effectiveness of a variety of school improvement initiatives, including Comprehensive School Reform programs, formative assessment interventions, school leadership interventions, and federally sponsored technical assistance programs. Dr. Rowan is a member of the National Academy of Education, received the William J. Davis award for contributions to research in educational administration, and, with Heinz-Dieter Meyer, is editor of *The New Institutionalism in Education* (State University of New York Press, 2006).

Deborah C. Simmons, Ph.D., Professor, Texas A&M University, 4225 TAMU, College Station, Texas 77843. Dr. Simmons is a professor of special education in the Department of Educational Psychology at Texas A&M University. She is a former speech language specialist and conducts research on the prevention and intervention of reading disabilities in the primary grades and response to intervention. She was the recipient of the Jeanette Fleischner Award for outstanding contribution to the field of learning disabilities from the Division for Learning Disabilities of the Council for Exceptional Children.

Leslie E. Simmons, Project Coordinator, Texas A&M University, 4225 TAMU, College Station, Texas 77843. Ms. Simmons is a project coordinator for two federally funded research grants at Texas A&M University. She received her bachelor of arts degree in fine and applied arts and her bachelor of arts degree in geography from the University of Oregon. Her research interests are in the areas of early reading and language assessment and curriculum development. She is currently part of a research team evaluating the impact of shared book reading on preschool children's vocabulary development.

Robert E. Slavin, Ph.D., Chairman and Co-founder, Success for All Foundation, 200 West Towsontown Boulevard, Baltimore, Maryland 21204. Dr. Slavin is Director of the Center for Research and Reform in Education at the Johns Hopkins University and Director of the Institute for Effective Education at the University of York. He has authored or coauthored more than 200 articles and 20 books, including *Educational Psychology: Theory into Practice* (Allyn & Bacon, 2003), *Cooperative Learning: Theory, Research, and Practice* (Allyn & Bacon, 1995), and *Show Me the Evidence: Proven and Promising Programs for America's Schools* (with Olatokunbo S. Fashola, Corwin Press, 1998). Dr. Slavin received the American Educational Research Association's (AERA) Raymond B. Cattell Early Career Award for Programmatic Research in 1986, the Palmer O. Johnson award for the best article in an AERA journal in 1988 and again in 2008 with coauthors Nancy A. Madden and Bette Chambers, the Charles A. Dana award in 1994, the James Bryant Conant Award from the Education Commission of the States in 1998, the Outstanding Leadership in Education Award from the Horace Mann League in 1999, and the Distinguished Services Award from the Council of Chief State School Officers in 2000.

Verna A.C. van der Kooy-Hofland, M.A., Doctoral Student, Leiden University, Wassenaarseweg 52, 2333 AK Leiden, The Netherlands. Mrs. van der Kooy-Hofland, a former teacher and staff developer in primary education, is a Ph.D. student at Leiden University in the Netherlands. Her dissertation research focuses on the efficacy of computer programs to stimulate alphabetic knowledge in groups of young learners at risk for reading impairments.

Marian J.A.J. Verhallen, M.A., Leiden University, Wassenaarseweg 52, 2333 AK Leiden, The Netherlands. Mrs. Verhallen, a lecturer at the Center for Learning Problems and Impairments of Leiden University, investigates the effects of multimedia features in digitized storybooks on visual attention, mental effort, and language development of young second language learners.

Foreword

As the Director of Title I at the U.S. Department of Education, I saw firsthand the face of poverty in our American neighborhoods and schools. At one end of the poverty pendulum, I visited towns where families live in homes with dirt floors and no running water, where they have few basic services because they lack the literacy skills needed to access these services. I visited drug-infested neighborhoods and communities with large numbers of families with young children who were homeless, who were from migrant families, who were recent immigrants, and who lacked sufficient English language skills to enable them to function effectively in our society. On the other end of the pendulum, I talked to families who, for the first time, were unable to put food on the table or pay their rent or mortgage. But I was also able to see the impact that high-quality, effective programs can have on these same children regardless of the difficult or even desperate circumstances in which they live.

Based on one's experiences, the term *poverty* means different things to different people. For some, it means believing that poor people don't want to work; they have too many children, abuse alcohol and drugs, and are violent. Others understand that as a group, people living in poverty are as diverse as any other group. When you realize that at any given time about 40% of Americans will fall into or are on the brink of being in this category, it is possible to conceive that as you interact with your neighbors, colleagues, and friends, anyone could be one paycheck or a divorce or health emergency away from being part of that 40%. Sometimes it only takes an unforeseen incident to change the patterns of our life. While non-whites are disproportionately represented, poverty crosses all races, all ethnic groups, and all religions.

Most advocates for persons experiencing poverty agree that that the calculation that the federal government uses to determine poverty is outdated. In recent times, the U.S. economy has taken a downturn and the outsourcing of jobs and cost of food, energy, and health care have contributed to the fact that many more families are living in poverty than we publicly acknowledge.

Poverty is invasive. It invades all aspects of a family's life—housing, nutrition, health, and education—and limits their options. You cannot run away from it; you cannot hide from it. You have to live with it every day, every hour, every minute. The longer a child lives in poverty, the more likely he or she will drop out of school, become a teen parent, and/or develop health problems.

We are once again at a crossroads. It has been a long time since there have been so many organizations and prominent individuals focused on making the elimination of poverty a priority for the nation. There has even been a call by some to have a federal-level cabinet position established that would focus on the elimination of poverty. The time is ripe for immediate action to be taken. We need to take this opportunity to finally deal with the wide range of issues and problems that cause poverty.

Public and private organizations have to agree to work together for a common good. Once we agree, we can stand on one side of the road, hold hands, and try to figure out a way to ensure that all of us make it across safely. We have to be firm in our resolve. There are many ideas about the best way to cross the road. But we have to select and implement the best ideas because this is too important of an issue to choose the wrong approach.

The solutions to poverty are like the pieces of a puzzle, and those pieces include education, housing, health and nutrition, employment, child care, and community support services, to name a few. Getting one piece right does not solve the poverty puzzle; only all the pieces put together in some coherent and cohesive way can create a lasting solution.

One critical piece of the puzzle that I would like to discuss is education. Education is the glue that can help keep the other pieces in place. Research shows that the more education that people have the less likely they will live in poverty, and if they do they can more easily escape it. We know that there is a direct correlation between improving the education of poor children and solving the problems of poverty.

Forty-four years ago, President Lyndon B. Johnson declared a "War on Poverty." In 1965, the Elementary and Secondary Education Act (PL 89-10) and especially its centerpiece, Title I, was created to provide greater educational opportunities for children living in poverty. Specifically, Title I was designed to help educate those who are economically and educationally disadvantaged and to close the achievement gap between poor and affluent children. Although the linkage between family income and student achievement is well documented, a strong body of evidence indicates that a concentration of poverty in a school exerts a strong independent influence on how well children perform academically. Over the years Title I has been amended but has always stayed true to its core principle of supporting the education of children attending high poverty schools. Title I funding goes to nearly every school district and to over half of the public schools in the nation.

While education is a state's responsibility, the federal government has a role in assuring that all children have an equal opportunity to learn. In 1983, a landmark report, *A Nation at Risk,* called out attention to the decline of educational achievement among high school graduates and the sobering consequences of poverty, poor health care, and discrimination. Many high-poverty schools continue to have low expectations and a mediocre curriculum that teaches basic and not advanced skills despite a federal law that requires high standards, aligned assessments, and an accountability system. If Title I is to have a stronger impact on helping children living in poverty to achieve, then it will have to ensure that the funds are being used for research-based, high-quality, intensive, and effective programs.

The focus of this book is literacy. Why literacy? Because literacy is the cornerstone of all learning and is fundamental to a student's success in school and in life. *Educating the Other America: Top Experts Tackle Poverty, Literacy, and Achievement in Our Schools* was created to present current and relevant research in a way that nonresearchers can understand and use. It seeks to help practitioners and policy makers understand what needs to be done to improve the literacy of children living in poverty.

This book adds to the body of knowledge about teaching children living in poverty how to read. Literacy and the importance of teaching children to read have been in the forefront of American educational policy. This book touches on every aspect of what it takes to develop a viable reading program. Section I describes the problem and explores public policy options. It also discusses the most recent research on literacy achievement for high-poverty children. Section II focuses on raising achievement levels through instruction, especially for children in poverty who are English learners and African American children. Section III explores other tools that can help improve children's literacy, such as the use of technology, improvements in the design of school facilities, and the use of innovative learning media.

When President Johnson signed the Elementary and Secondary Education Act, he declared, "Education is the only valid passport from poverty." Johnson's war on poverty began nearly half a century ago. But despite valiant efforts, the war is not yet won. The effect of poverty, still on the faces of thousands of American children, is a cruel reminder that our work is still cut out for us. We cannot as a nation turn a deaf ear to the needs of our disadvantaged children. We must renew our belief in an America in which there is no discernable difference in achievement among students of diverse economic backgrounds, ethnicity, race, social class, language background, or gender.

My vision is an America in which all our children are equally likely to excel in advanced skills largely based on their proficiency as readers, graduate from high school, and are equally likely to become lifelong learners. This is a tall order, but I am optimistic. It is my hope that this book will give you some of the tools to achieve this vision.

Jacquelyn C. Jackson, Ed.D.
Former Director, Title I
Student Achievement and School Accountability Programs
Office of Elementary and Secondary Education
U.S. Department of Education

Preface

It is virtually indisputable. Poverty rates are on the increase among American children, rising more than one third higher than they were 2 decades ago and 1.5–4 times higher than for children in Canada and Western Europe. According to the latest report from the Small Area Income and Poverty Estimates, a division of the U.S. Census Bureau that calculates annual income for states, counties, and school districts, the number of children living in poverty has increased from 13 million to 13.4 million since 2004, with the most striking increases for children under the age of 5. This means greater food insecurity, greater residential instability, and greater educational mobility. This also means that families will be hard-pressed, more than ever, to provide the kinds of early language and literacy experiences central to children's success for reading achievement.

These material hardships will affect nearly every aspect of children's lives—from parental responsiveness to parental teaching, from the quality of the physical environment to the level of stimulation for learning. The seriousness of the problem for the life chances of these children cannot be overestimated. Poverty will exert a heavy tool on children's cognitive, social, and emotional development. Born poor, children are likely to stay poor unless we are determined to change the predictable trajectory of low achievement.

But while the adverse outcomes associated with poverty have been widely recognized, what to do about it is much less understood. It is this central question that brought top experts in poverty research, instructional design, technology, and intervention together for an historic gathering at the University of Michigan in Ann Arbor in the fall of 2007. Sponsored by the Ready to Learn program, through the Corporation for Public Broadcasting, and the Public Broadcasting System and funded by the U.S. Department of Education grant program, experts addressed the question: How do we fashion language and literacy experiences that could potentially mediate the ill-effects of poverty and, in turn, affect children's literacy outcomes?

During the 2-day meeting, rich with conversations and active discussions, a convergence of research began to form around a number of central themes. These include

1. The size and the number of children involved suggests that the reading problems for poor children may require a different mediational path than the current reading methods for struggling readers.

2. Instructional design features can significantly bootstrap children's learning, promoting both content knowledge and skill-based instruction to occur simultaneously, providing a greater dosage of instruction and subsequent learning.

3. Technology can make a difference.

This book is organized around these key themes. It begins by describing the extent of poverty and the policies that have put children at tremendous risk of low achievement. It is designed not to discourage but to help people understand how fragile our systems of supports are for those who live in the "other America." With this background in mind, we then turn to interventions that have changed the odds for children through high-quality instruction. Though varied, these programs show remarkable consistencies in their attention to quality instructional features that make a difference. They describe strategies that are more explicit, more intentional, more sustained, and more accountable for outcomes than previous models of interventions. The last section of the book highlights the many new technological supports that are available which, when constructed with these features in mind, can strongly influence learning. Together, these technologies along with school learning create a *360-degree surround*—a powerful coalition of services that embrace the needs, interests, and motivational supports for children who are poor.

This book is the first of its kind to address the needs of an underrepresented group: children who live in poverty. It argues that to understand the solution for improving student achievement, we must first understand the problem. By doing so, we can move more aggressively to design powerful interventions for poor children that break down these barriers to help them succeed and achieve in literacy. This book, therefore, represents an important first step along what should be an exhilarating ride on the road toward educating the other America.

Acknowledgments

I wish to sincerely thank Dr. Jayne James, Executive Director of Ready to Learn, and Peggy O'Brien, former Senior Vice President of Educational Programming and Services at the Corporation for Public Broadcasting, for their tremendous support and their vision in recognizing the importance of scientifically based evidence for the construction of media tools that support children's learning. They brought together a true coalition of talent from the public broadcasting community, along with cutting-edge technology and highly innovative strategies to reach out to diverse communities. Their efforts and commitment to ensure that all children are ready to learn have been extraordinary, and we could not do the work that we do without them.

In addition, all of the researchers and producers on the Ready to Learn project have benefited from the wisdom, support, and direction of Cheryl Petty Garnette, Director of Education Programs in the Office of Innovation and Improvement at the U.S. Department of Education. We thank her for her continuing support and active involvement.

I must also thank Jeanne Friedel for putting the conference together and organizing logistics, as well as many committed students and colleagues who helped organize and attend to the details of this venture. They are Serene Koh, Sarah Tucker, Julie Dwyer, Tanya Wright, and Colleen Neilson. Finally, I wish to thank my colleagues for contributing to this volume and for participating so actively throughout their careers to make a difference for children who are economically disadvantaged. Hopefully, their expertise and enthusiasm for their mission will encourage others to follow in their wonderful footsteps.

Introduction

The Mediating Mechanisms of the Effects of Poverty on Reading Achievement

Susan B. Neuman

This book is about educating the other America: the children who fail to read, not because of cognitive impairments but because they are poor. Their numbers are sizable. According to the latest census, nearly one in every five children in the United States live in families whose income falls below the poverty threshold (Rhode Island KIDS COUNT, 2005). The percentage of young Americans defined as *poor* is higher in 2008 than at the bottom of the 2001 recession. But that is not the worst of it. An additional 21% of children live in working poor families between the 100%–200% poverty line and experience many of the same material hardships as children in families defined as poor (Guo & Harris, 2000). They, too, suffer from less access to resources and services, less access to potentially enhancing experiences, and greater exposure to potentially debilitating substances and experiences.

Predictably, poor children, on average, do not perform well in school. In an analysis of the Early Childhood Longitudinal Study–Kindergarten (ECLS-K) cohort, for example, Lee and Burkam (2002) reported that the average cognitive scores of children at age 4 in the lowest socioeconomic groups were 60% below those of children from middle- and upper middle–income families. If previous studies are prescient, this gap is likely to persist throughout children's schooling (Juel, Griffith, & Gough, 1986). The National Assessment of Educational Progress (Perie, Moran, & Lutkus, 2005) reports that children who are economically advantaged score at or above the basic level of reading at nearly twice the rate of children who are economically disadvantaged. In fact, despite a decade-long emphasis on lifting the achievement of all children, the latest reading report card (National Assessment of Educational Progress, 2004) shows no substantial changes in overall achievement or in the gap between middle-class students and students from low-income families, a gap that has become a disturbing and defining fixture of American schooling for at least 40 years.

The size of the gap and the numbers of children involved suggest a reading problem of far greater magnitude than has previously been acknowledged in reading research. The picture only gets bleaker for students at the 8th- and 12th-grade levels. Students who trail other students academically continue to stay behind, but their decline continues at an accelerated rate. There is cumulative disadvantage. The gap that sharply defines students around Grade 4, according to the report card, gathers speed at an alarming rate as subject matter materials become more difficult (Stanovich, West, & Harrison, 1995). The precipitous decline known as the 4th-grade slump too often leads to the 9th-grade dropout.

The high probability of negative outcomes for poor children, however, suggests a reading problem of a different nature than that of children who may fall behind because of a learning disability. Although poor children in inner cities may perform no better than children in the suburbs who have dyslexia, it is unlikely that the two groups have the same set of reading impairments. It seems clear that some of the causes of failure to achieve for poor children must relate to impediments in the environment—the complex set of conditions that influence reading, such as print exposure, language experiences, and differential teaching strategies. Yet, professionals in the field of reading have no answer to the question of what to do about healthy children who come from poor environments who fail to learn to read.

The impact of this problem on children's life opportunities cannot be overestimated. Because education is the chief avenue for social mobility, this massive failure to learn to read reifies and intensifies social inequality. It is the primary mechanism that creates the great differentials in employment, health longevity, and quality of life between the poor and middle class in the United States.

The failure to understand the causes of limited achievement for children in economically distressed environments has impeded progress in teaching these students how to read successfully. This chapter highlights the central thesis of this book: By understanding the problem, researchers can begin to build solutions. These solutions relate not only to a more comprehensive approach to reading instruction but also to a better understanding of the environmental supports that can contribute to children's reading success.

BEING POOR

Twice per month, Tonetta Jones of Philadelphia sits at her kitchen table, turns on some music, and practices what some might call creative arithmetic, what others might call trying to get blood from a stone. Jones makes $8 per hour working as a child care provider 35 hours each week. Frequently she finds herself having to choose between which bills to pay in full, which ones to pay partially, and which ones to let slide until the next paycheck.

"I'm living week to week, paycheck to paycheck," she says. "It takes all I got to get groceries and to make ends meet, and sometimes I just don't see a way out."

Although Jones, her husband William, and their two children live on a salary of just $16,000 per year, they are not, according to the latest Census Bureau figures (U.S. Census Bureau, 2000), part of the 12.6% of the population living in poverty in 2006.

Originally dubbed the *thrifty food plan,* the federal poverty line was established in 1963. It was set by statisticians who developed the threshold at three times the annual cost of feeding a family of three, or about $3,100 at the time. Despite the fact that this is considered a conservative underestimate of poverty, this equation has been used as the official yardstick since President Lyndon Johnson's War on Poverty.

This poverty line, unfortunately, does not match the income needed to survive in the modern world. In 2006, the poverty line ranged from $9,800 for an individual to $23,400 for a family of five (Barbour, 2006). This official measure examines only whether a family has enough pretax income plus cash benefits from the government to pay for the bare necessities. It is essentially a holdover from a time when food represented a third of household costs and child care was not an issue. The actual number of people living in poverty is much larger than the official yardstick. For example, in 2007, the Census Bureau released 12 alternative measures of poverty: All but one sets the poverty line higher than the official rate. These alternative measures call for adding in the value of noncash government benefits such as food stamps and for subtracting expenses such as out-of-pocket medical costs and work-related outlays, including child care expenses. These estimates also take into account geographical differences in the cost of living, which makes poverty relative. A family of four living in New York City, for example, incurs radically different expenses than a family of four in Amarillo, Texas.

According to the National Research Council (Rank, 2004), 41.3 million Americans would fit the Census Bureau's measures of living in poverty—4.4 million more than are officially counted. This figure indicates a far more starkly divided nation of "haves" and "have nots" than previously has been reported.

Says Tonetta Jones, "I've been so close to losing the house so many times. It's been a real balancing act."

Such experiences are not unusual. Studies (e.g., Guo, 1998) indicate that 60% of Americans between the ages of 20 and 75 will live at least 1 year below the poverty line, and 75% of Americans will live the life of Tonetta Jones for at least 1 year of their lives.

MECHANISMS MEDIATING THE EFFECTS OF POVERTY

Family circumstances such as those of Tonetta Jones are important influences in children's lives. Numerous studies (Brooks-Gunn & Duncan, 1997) have documented the devastating consequences of living in poverty—dropping out of school, low academic achievement, teenage pregnancy and childbearing, poor mental and physical health, delinquent behavior, and unemployment in adolescence and early adulthood. Further, these studies (Huston, 1994) confirm a long-term negative trajectory: The longer children live in poverty, the lower their educational achievement and the worse their social and emotional functioning.

Nevertheless, poverty itself appears to have no direct effect on children's intellectual functioning and social and emotional development. That is, the relationship between poverty and child outcomes is not causal (Mayer, 1998). Instead, the effects of poverty are complicated and mediated by factors other than income alone. Several studies, for example, have begun to untangle the critical pathways through which economic deprivation operates to disadvantage children who are poor. According to a large corpus of research (Duncan & Brooks-Gunn, 1997), poverty or lack of income affects intervening factors; these factors, in turn, affect child outcomes. Three essential pathways help to explain the mediating process.

Materials and Resources

Poor children are resource poor. Family income influences the quantity and quality of books, newspapers, and magazines in the home. Studies (Purcell-Gates, 1995) show the scarcity of typical tools of literacy in these homes, such as paper for children's drawing, large pencils, markers, crayons, magnetic letters, and stencils among other educational resources.

Income may have an impact on the overall level of cognitive stimulation in the home. There will likely be fewer trips the family can afford, such as visiting the zoo or local museums, and fewer resources in the immediate environment. Children are also less likely to participate in organized activities, such as sports, social, and recreational programs. In fact, family material resources influence choices for many activities and educational services—anything that may be purchased with money. Studies (Brooks-Gunn & Duncan, 1997; Neuman & Celano, 2001) suggest that children growing up with fewer resources are less likely to do well in educational environments and other aspects of life.

Because so many families are cloistered in unsafe neighborhoods, quality child care is another institutional resource that too often eludes families who are poor. For example, in their study of family child care in three U.S. cities, Galinsky, Howes, Kontos, and Shinn (1994) rated about half of the home-based settings they observed as being of only "fair" quality or worse, reporting that children experienced significantly less nurturance and sensitivity than in other settings. In the Growing Up in Poverty project, Fuller, Kagan, Loeb, and Chang (2004) showed that among families receiving welfare, children in home settings displayed significantly lower rates of cognitive and language growth than children in center-based care. In the absence of government subsidies or interventions, families suffering, both psychologically and economically, are more likely to use poorer quality care.

Language Supports

The ravages of poverty also may be catastrophic for children's language and vocabulary development. A half century's worth of literature on language (Snow,

Baines, Chandler, Goodman, & Hemphill, 1991) indicates that children who are poor hear a smaller number of words with more limited syntactic complexity and fewer conversation-eliciting questions, making it difficult for them to quickly acquire new words and to discriminate among words. In our studies (Neuman & Roskos, 1993), for example, my colleague and I found that the 4-year-olds had difficulty discriminating among common objects such as a pad, stationery, a letter, and an envelope, referring to each of them as *mail*.

Often, poor children are highly competent in narrative structure, demonstrate syntactic sophistication, and have strong inferencing skills, as demonstrated by the complex world of inner-city dialects that are heard throughout the country (Labov, 1970). Nevertheless, as an instant signifier of class and educational level, these children are still deprived of the language, background knowledge, and the conventions they need to understand what is being said by teachers and in books. They may lack experience in the uses of language for abstraction.

"What breaks my heart is their talk," says Joann McCall, a middle school teacher of 20 years. "They almost seem to grope for words, using phrases, 'Like, like, you know.'" Children who live in poor communities are likely to hear many *nos* and *don'ts*—prohibitions that serve to restrict rather than elicit the habits of seeking, noticing, and incorporating new and more complex experiences. In their study of language, Hart and Risley (1995) found that whereas the average child in the professional home was accumulating 32 affirmatives and 5 prohibitions per hour, the average child in a welfare home was accumulating 5 affirmatives and 11 prohibitions per hour, which in 1 year would work out to 26,000 encouragements and 57,000 discouragements. Feeling out of control themselves, parents who are poor may attempt to overly control their children's behavior (sometimes through harsh punishment, restricting, and disapproving) instead of redirecting or extending their children's capacities for categorizing and thinking about new experiences. Multiply these daily experiences by the number of days and years before formal schooling begins, and it becomes evident why many of these students require intensive language supports.

Human and Social Capital

Raising children involves an enormous investment in resources in a community. Social scientists (Putnam & Feldstein, 2003) use the expressions *human capital* and *social capital* to describe and quantify these resources. *Human capital* refers to the basket of skills, education, and qualifications that individuals bring to the marketplace—the capacity to deal with abstractions, to recognize and adhere to rules, and to use language for reasoning. *Social capital*, coined by sociologist James Coleman (1987) as "the norms, the social networks, the relationships between adults and children that are of value for the children's growing up" (p. 245), refers to the benefits of strong social bonds and works somewhat the same way as human capital. Just like other forms of capital, human and social capital accumulate over generations; they are part of the culture of achievement that children successfully bring and deploy in school.

In poor communities where many institutions have disintegrated, parents face tremendous obstacles in their attempts to acquire human capital. They often experience life crises more often and with greater intensity than do parents in middle-class communities. Lacking human and social capital often leads to a feeling of powerlessness, especially when attempting to deal with complex bureaucracies, whether they be clinics, emergency rooms, or schools. As Lareau (2003) described, middle-class parents' superior levels of education give them vocabularies that can help them deal with institutional settings. Trained in the rules of the game, they can take over or dominate interactions. Poor families and working-class parents, however, may not be familiar with the key terms professionals use, such as *tetanus shot* at the doctor's office or *stanines, percentages,* and *norms* in schools, and generally are hesitant to ask. They may just accept the actions of a person in authority.

Poverty-generated stressors contribute to parenting styles, low levels of parent involvement, and inattention to children's educational endeavors (McLoyd, 1990), all of which negatively influence children's cognitive development and press for achievement. In the past, programs have attempted to "control" for these key mediating factors through socioeconomic status, parent education, and language proficiency. Intervention programs have sought to ignore poverty, suggesting there are no excuses for the lack of achievement of children who are poor. In contrast, I argue that by identifying the multiple pathways by which poverty may influence children, professionals will be better able to intervene effectively. Based on a conceptual framework that addresses the mediating mechanisms of poverty's effects on reading development, studies indicate that learning proceeds more rapidly once the problem is well defined.

CONCEPTUAL FRAMEWORK FOR UNDERSTANDING THE EFFECTS OF POVERTY ON READING DEVELOPMENT

Figure I.1 depicts the main features of a conceptual model of reading development that takes into account the ravages of poverty. The variables in the center box are mediating mechanisms, without which there would be a conventional regression line. Typically, the effects of poverty are estimated with controls for other family and child characteristics. Much of the research summarized in synthesis reports of reading development (National Institute of Child Health and Human Development [NICHD], 2000; Snow, Burns, & Griffin, 1998), for example, follows this approach, attempting to eliminate the variance associated with poverty, disadvantage, and limited opportunity.

In the theoretical model proposed in Figure I.1, however, poverty affects each of the mediating mechanisms, which in turn affect reading development. This model makes clear that many of the causes of failure to achieve literacy are

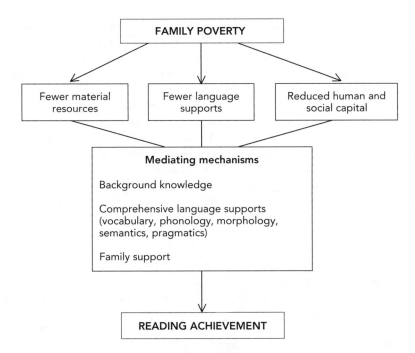

Figure I.1. The mediating mechanisms of the effects of poverty on reading achievement.

environmental influences that are subject to intervention. In other words, once a comprehensive set of mediating mechanisms is taken into consideration, there is no theoretical reason why poverty should affect reading development alone.

Figure I.1 makes it evident that the pathways for explaining the effects of poverty on children's reading success are themselves mediated by other factors. For example, material resources are an important consideration not because cognitive stimulation is expensive. Books and magazines, after all, are freely available at public libraries. Rather, material resources are a proxy for experiences through print and other activities that provide a rich source of *background knowledge*, the first mediating mechanism. This means having a solid conceptual and information base is vital to becoming a skilled reader. Such knowledge deficiencies, unfortunately, are already evident in preschool (Neuman, 2006). For example, 4-year-old Tanya is already behind her peers when she cannot participate in retelling the story of the Three Little Pigs or other classics assumed to be part of her background knowledge.

Reading with comprehension requires children to make inferences that depend on prior knowledge—knowledge of concepts, facts, and specialized vocabulary. To make constructive use of the words they hear, readers or listeners need a threshold of knowledge about a topic. Someone new to the world of tennis, for example, might understand each of the individual words in the sentence "Williams lobbed but lost the game at love" but may have little clue as to the meaning of the sentence. Words have multiple purposes and meanings across different knowledge domains. Comprehension, then, requires children to gain access to their background knowledge and to do it with relative speed.

Background knowledge allows readers to make rapid connections between new and previously learned content. Studies by Anderson and his colleagues (Anderson & Pearson, 1984), for example, have shown that students use background knowledge to construct a coherent understanding of a text. Expert readers do it quickly, activating schema to interpret a text. Those who lack relevant knowledge and a well-structured knowledge base take more time, only slowly make connections, and often fail to comprehend the text.

Knowledge accretion is a gradual and cumulative process. It is acquired through day-to-day activities that include being read to and talked to as well as through a variety of activities that immerse children in word and world knowledge. Limited experiences with print and limited opportunities for cognitive stimulation place children who are poor at a serious disadvantage in school. The high-performing kindergartner who has been read to 1,000 hours knows words and ideas with very different degrees of complexity and precision than the child who may have been read to 25 hours prior to kindergarten. Without intentional and powerful knowledge-rich interventions, students from low-income families will already demonstrate a dramatic knowledge gap compared with their middle-income peers by fourth grade (Neuman & Celano, 2006).

A large literature links poverty with deficiencies in *comprehensive language supports*, the second mediating mechanism. Numerous studies (Hart & Risley, 1995; Huttenlocher, Haight, Bryk, Seltzer, & Lyons, 1991) have shown that low-income homes on average expose young children to far fewer words and far simpler sentence structures than middle-class homes. Graves, Brunetti, and Slater (1982), for example, estimated that a high-performing first grader will know about 3 times as many words as a low-performing first grader, with differentials only magnifying in later years. Some estimate that by 12th grade, high performers will know about 4 times as many words as low performers (Hirsch, 2003).

Much of the research that was reviewed in the National Reading Panel report (NICHD, 2000) focused on language impairments associated with phonological and phonemic awareness and their linkages to reading success. Although these skills are important, there is now considerable evidence that, in the developing child, language ability is not rigidly restricted to these categories alone. Scarborough (2001), for example, in an elegant meta-analysis of the impact of oral language on subsequent reading abilities, concluded that successful predictors of future reading abilities have not been confined to a single linguistic domain. Instead, children draw on a *language system,* with abilities encompassing vocabulary, syntax, and academic discourse. The language needed to question, explain, and problem-solve is central to the formation of higher mental functions related to reading with comprehension.

Vocabulary and oral language skills form the foundation of reading comprehension and are integrally related to background knowledge. Yet, as with content knowledge, one does not just learn a word's meaning and instantly store it into an existing lexicon. Rather, growth of vocabulary is incremental, requiring multiple exposures and multiple interactions with words. Children will need opportunities to use language in many situations, allowing them to refine the semantic representations of words already in their vocabulary while acquiring additional words and determining the relationships among them.

It is said that academic language—the language of ideas—is ultimately decontextualized (Snow, 1983). That is, to be successful in school, children must be able to articulate ideas and abstract concepts in the absence of the immediate concrete objects or events. For this skill to develop, children need frequent experiences that engage them in producing and comprehending sentences. Sharing books interactively is an obvious source of decontextualized language; however, there are other powerful sources of language interaction that involve children in abstract language—sharing time, mealtime conversations, and dramatic play. For instance, the use of props in dramatic play (Roskos, 1988) makes it possible for children to represent experiences, feelings, and ideas, similar to what they do when they listen to storybooks. With many opportunities, children's symbolic transformations become increasingly elaborate as they engage in more complex and abstract language. As their proficiency grows, children develop metalinguistic skills that use language in play, enhance their thinking, and analyze ideas from multiple perspectives.

Language proficiency, then, is not confined to a single linguistic domain (Dickinson, McCabe, Anastasopoulos, Peisner-Feinberg, & Poe, 2003). In fact, Scarborough's (2001) meta-analysis makes it clear that the skills tied to reading proficiency take on different forms at different points in children's development. Although phonological sensitivity is an important correlate in learning to read, children need multiple language abilities to be successful in early and later literacy. These and other considerations mean that students should be immersed for extended periods of time in the sorts of coherent experiences that are most conducive to accelerating receptive and expressive language.

The third mediating mechanism is *family support*. There is a long history of research indicating that economic hardship affects nearly every aspect of children's home lives, from parental responsiveness and teaching to the quality of stimulation for learning and the exposure to developmentally enriching materials and experiences (Bradley, Corwyn, McAdoo, & Coll, 2001). Failing to ignore the critical role of families in children's literacy development, however, only hampers success in helping children learn to read.

Conventional parent involvement interventions, unfortunately, have shown only modest success. In a meta-analysis, White, Taylor, and Moss (1992), for example, found little support for the impact of these interventions on children's achievement. In addition, parent-oriented prevention and family literacy programs including Even Start, Parents as Teachers, and the Home Instruction Program for Preschool Youngsters (HIPPY), which attempt to provide children with school readiness skills and to support parent–child reading activities, have had little to no effect on children's language and literacy outcomes (St. Pierre, Layzer, & Barnes, 1995).

More targeted interventions designed to enhance children's access to books and increase their storybook reading behaviors have demonstrated more promising results. For example, a training program on dialogic reading developed by Whitehurst and colleagues (1994), in essence, has been successful in reversing the roles between adult and child. This intervention, which parents can use while sharing a book with their child, shows parents how to use one-to-one dialogue to help the child become the teller of the story. A corpus of studies has shown that children who participated in this intervention made significant gains in their language skills and concepts of print.

Similarly, our studies on parent book clubs (Neuman, 1996) reported significant improvements in children's language skills and print awareness. Books differentiated by genre (predictable; episodic predictable; narrative), available in English or Spanish, were provided to parents. Parents were taught to engage in reading strategies that enhanced interaction with the child. One part of the intervention included parent groups; the other part involved parents reading the books to their children. By the time the book club was over, parents had accumulated a 12-book library for their child and had engaged in a variety of interactional supports with them. Using this inexpensive 12-week intervention, we demonstrated significant language increases and concepts of print. This project proved to be an important value-added component to the children's early childhood experience.

Both the dialogic reading program and the book club program resulted in a strong increase in mothers' rich language input. Mothers across time demonstrated the ability to label pictures and give explanations and extensions related to their children's life. The mothers' increased interactions resulted in greater increases in children's word use and questioning strategies. In addition, the combined influence of quality parental support with quality early childhood experience optimally improved children's functioning.

In addition to the positive effects already discussed, there was another serendipitous effect across these and other targeted programs. Involving parents collectively in the school, each program began to build social capital; the strategies helped parents feel more comfortable in the school setting, more able to communicate closely with teachers about their children's programs, and better connected to what goes on in the school and related social functions. For example, we found in our study that parents were milling around the media center, looking at books together, and acting like welcomed members of the school community.

We might all take a lesson from Head Start, which has elevated the role of parent education and involvement, thereby creating real leadership opportunities among parents much to the benefit of their children's learning and development. Visitors to Head Start find a homey atmosphere in many of the parent rooms. Parents are encouraged to visit the school and volunteer in different ways. In some of my visits, I have found parents working on crafts together, getting ready for a tag sale, or listening to a speaker from the local community. Although they are not able to reverse all of the ill effects of a starkly disadvantaged status in society, these programs demonstrate that parents can collectively accumulate social capital, gaining a better sense of control over their lives and the lives of their children.

EFFECTS OF POVERTY ON CHILDREN'S LITERACY DEVELOPMENT

The conceptual model described previously specifies three overriding mechanisms that mediate the effects of poverty on children's literacy development. It recognizes that background knowledge and language and its interrelationships among vocabulary, pragmatics, and print in addition to skill-based instruction are central to children's development of reading readiness skills. Moreover, it argues that parent interactions around books and parental support in conjunction with quality instruction—especially early on—are essential if we are to enhance young children's literacy growth and development.

In an ideal pedagogical situation, we would use this knowledge to introduce rich background knowledge and intensive language interactions that include phonology but are not restricted to this skill alone, adding content-rich instruction that would allow children to catch up and catch up quickly. But too often in this situation early education has come to have a remedial flavor, focusing on a skill set that is a far cry from meaningful instruction. Children are taught the five essentials of literacy—phonemic awareness, phonics, fluency, vocabulary, and comprehension—without compensating for initial experiences of knowledge, language, and the kinds of interactions that build critical dispositions for learning that have left the young learners behind in the first place.

To paraphrase E.D. Hirsch (2003), imagine young children who are disadvantaged being introduced to a new story along with their more advantaged peers. The children who are advantaged are well-versed in stories and rich in background knowledge; they will likely understand about 90% of the meaning of the text, and, because they understand, they will also develop pretty accurate inferences for the 10% that is new to them. Those who do not come with this background knowledge and do not know 90% of the words will now be even further behind on both fronts: They will miss the opportunity to learn the content of the text and to learn more words. What results is a growing knowledge gap that becomes a huge challenge to overcome throughout the school years.

Now imagine a different scenario, one that does not attempt to control for the effects of poverty but that recognizes its concomitants and provides instruction designed to fill in these gaps. In this scenario, instructional environments are consciously constructed to promote learning. They include features that almost appear to "coerce" certain behaviors, such as language interactions and decontextualized talk. Further, they include instructional features designed to engage children in intensive interactions around print, such as quick pacing, repetition, and corrective feedback. They also use other forms of instruction such as multimedia to help students develop mental models and concepts that enhance synergy and redundancy. This kind of instructional environment wraps all instruction in content that is meaningful to the child and important to grasp as instruction moves from learning to read, to reading to learn.

This is the kind of instruction that poor children need (Neuman & Roskos, 2005). It is this knowledge–vocabulary nexus that establishes the foundation of understanding from which all the skills of reading (e.g., phonics, fluency) are applied. Skills taught in isolation of content will never significantly improve reading achievement. Without a solid content base, children may learn to be *word callers* but may not understand the meaning of the words.

CREATING A 360-DEGREE EARLY LEARNING SYSTEM

Although the adverse effects of poverty on children have been documented widely, we have not used what we have learned about the mechanisms through which poverty affects disadvantaged children. In this chapter, I have attempted to fill this void by articulating the multiple pathways by which poverty might influence children's reading achievement.

This is only a first step, however. This theory needs to be translated into action. Despite knowledge of the detrimental effects of poverty on reading achievement, efforts to address the problem often have involved a one-shot intervention approach: Establish a parent involvement program, provide a more academic focus in early care and education, supervise and support a child's informal learning after school, *or* give children access to books and other print materials through library programs. Each of these individual efforts, by itself, has focused on only part of the solution.

Careful research documenting years of evidence (Snow et al., 1998), however, clearly indicates a very different strategy: If we are serious about reducing the incidence of poor reading achievement, we need a more comprehensive system of support—a 360-degree surround to ensure that children start school ready to learn and succeed in reading. This requires a convergence of efforts, working together to build a more potent coalition of quality instructional interventions that systematically and fundamentally change the conditions in which children who are disadvantaged grow up. Such a 360-degree surround would include quality instruction in school but also would provide out-of-school resources that could powerfully affect children's opportunity, motivation, and support for learning to read.

Consider, for example, the following 360-degree literacy surround: 1) Children receive high-quality, content-rich instruction in informal early care settings and make the transition to quality instruction in preschools and elementary schools; 2) children receive parental support that is carefully aligned with learning in school; 3) children receive breakthrough scientifically based literacy content from outside sources, such as television, online formats, and other multimedia resources; and 4) communities use new distribution platforms and a focused engagement plan to help children, teachers, and parents implement the full program for helping children learn to read.

Schools alone, therefore, cannot be the sole source of reading education. Research and past experience combine to explode the myth that a simple solution will work. There are not enough hours in the day, days in the week, or weeks in the year to overcome disadvantage. Instead, we need to involve other people, institutions, and resources to help support children's learning, recognizing that there is little time to waste.

CONCLUSION

No doubt, understanding of the science of reading has increased exponentially in the last decade of the 20th century. Much of this knowledge has been attained from the study of children who have failed to learn to read because of specific cognitive impairments. These studies have been extremely important in establishing the fundamental skills that children need to become good readers; however, the large numbers of children who live in poverty require more intense scrutiny than they have received in the past. These children need to learn more than the basic skills of reading; they need to acquire world knowledge because every text takes for granted the readers' familiarity with background concepts. In addition, to become motivated readers, they need parental support to extend their learning time and to help them see the rewards of reading. Children who are poor also need to be surrounded more intensely by environments that support quality opportunities to learn. The more these children can be surrounded with quality instruction, the greater the impact of the interventions. It is the synergy of learning opportunities that will produce the most powerful long-term and beneficial effects for children who live in poverty.

REFERENCES

Anderson, R.C., & Pearson, P.D. (1984). A schema-theoretic view of basic processes in reading comprehension. In P.D. Pearson (Ed.), *Handbook of reading research* (pp. 255–291). New York: Longman.

Barbour, C. (2006). *Redrawing America's poverty line.* Detroit, MI: Detroit Free Press.

Bradley, R., Corwyn, R., McAdoo, H.P., & Coll, C.G. (2001). The home environments of children in the United States Part I: Variations by age, ethnicity, and poverty status. *Child Development, 72*, 1844–1867.

Brooks-Gunn, J., & Duncan, G. (1997). The effects of poverty. *The Future of Children, 7*, 55–71.

Coleman, J.S. (1987). Families and schools. *Educational Researcher, 16*, 32–38.

Dickinson, D., McCabe, A., Anastasopoulos, L., Peisner-Feinberg, E.S., & Poe, M.D. (2003). The comprehensive language approach to early literacy: The interrelationships among vocabulary, phonological sensitivity, and print knowledge among preschool-aged children. *Journal of Educational Psychology, 95*, 465–481.

Duncan, G., & Brooks-Gunn, J. (Eds.). (1997). *Consequences of growing up poor*. New York: Russell Sage Foundation.

Fuller, B., Kagan, S., Loeb, S., & Chang, V. (2004). Centers and home settings that serve poor families. *Early Childhood Research Quarterly, 19*, 505–527.

Galinsky, E., Howes, C., Kontos, S., & Shinn, M. (1994). *The study of children in family child care and relative care: Highlights of findings*. New York: Families and Work Institute.

Graves, M., Brunetti, G., & Slater, W. (Eds.). (1982). The reading vocabularies of primary-grade children of varying geographic and social backgrounds. In J.A. Harris & L.A. Harris (Eds.), *New inquiries in reading research and instruction* (pp. 99–104). Rochester, NY: National Reading Conference.

Guo, G. (1998). The timing of the influences of cumulative poverty on children's cognitive ability and achievement. *Social Forces, 77*, 257–287.

Guo, G., & Harris, K. (2000). The mechanisms mediating the effects of poverty on children's intellectual development. *Demography, 37*, 431–447.

Hart, B., & Risley, T. (1995). *Meaningful differences in the everyday experiences of young American children*. Baltimore: Paul H. Brookes Publishing Co.

Hirsch, E.D., Jr. (2003). Reading comprehension requires knowledge—of words and the world: Scientific insights into the fourth-grade slump and the nation's stagnant comprehension scores. *American Educator, 27*, 10–13, 16–22, 28–29, 48.

Huston, A. (Ed.). (1994). *Children in poverty*. New York: Cambridge University Press.

Huttenlocher, J., Haight, W., Bryk, A., Seltzer, M., & Lyons, T. (1991). Early vocabulary growth: Relation to language input and gender. *Developmental Psychology, 27*, 236–248.

Juel, C., Griffith, P.L., & Gough, P. (1986). Acquisition of literacy: A longitudinal study of children in first and second grade. *Journal of Educational Psychology, 78*, 243–255.

Labov, W. (1970). The logic of non-standard English. In F. Williams (Ed.), *Language and poverty: Some perspectives on a theme* (pp. 153–187). Chicago: Markham.

Lareau, A. (2003). *Unequal childhoods*. Berkeley: University of California Press.

Lee, V., & Burkam, D. (2002). *Inequality at the starting gate*. Washington, DC: Economic Policy Institute.

Mayer, S. (1998). *What money can't buy: Family income and children's life chances*. Cambridge, MA: Harvard University Press.

McLoyd, V. (1990). The impact of economic hardship on black families and children: Psychological distress, parenting, and socio-emotional development. *Child Development, 61*, 311–346.

National Assessment of Educational Progress (NAEP). (2004). *Percentage of students by reading level, Grade 4*. Retrieved June 15, 2005. Washington, DC: National Center for Education Statistics.

National Institute of Child Health and Human Development. (2000). *Report of the National Reading Panel. Teaching children to read: An evidence-based assessment of the scientific research literature on reading and its implications for reading instruction: Reports of the subgroups* (NIH Publication No. 00-4754). Washington, DC: U.S. Government Printing Office.

Neuman, S.B. (1996). Children engaging in storybook reading: The influence of access to print resources, opportunity, and parental interaction. *Early Childhood Research Quarterly, 11*, 495–514.

Neuman, S.B. (2006). The knowledge gap: Implication for early literacy development. In D. Dickinson & S.B. Neuman (Eds.), *Handbook of early literacy research* (Vol. II, pp. 29–40). New York: Guilford Press.

Neuman, S.B., & Celano, D. (2001). Access to print in middle- and low-income communities: An ecological study of four neighborhoods. *Reading Research Quarterly, 36*, 8–26.

Neuman, S.B., & Celano, D. (2006). The knowledge gap: Implications of leveling the playing field for low-income and middle-income children. *Reading Research Quarterly, 41*, 176–201.

Neuman, S.B., & Roskos, K. (1993). Access to print for children of poverty: Differential effects of adult mediation and literacy-enriched play settings on environmental and functional print tasks. *American Educational Research Journal, 30*, 95–122.

Neuman, S.B., & Roskos, K. (2005). Whatever happened to developmentally appropriate practice in early literacy? *Young Children, 60*, 22–26.

Perie, M., Moran, R., & Lutkus, A. (2005). *NAEP 2004 trends in academic progress: Three decades of student performance in reading and mathematics.* Washington, DC: National Center for Educational Statistics.

Purcell-Gates, V. (1995). *Other people's words.* Cambridge, MA: Harvard University Press.

Putnam, R., & Feldstein, L. (2003). *Better together.* New York: Simon & Schuster.

Rank, M. (2004). *One nation, underprivileged: Why American poverty affects us all.* New York: Oxford University Press.

Rhode Island KIDS COUNT. (2005, February). *Getting ready: Findings from the National School Readiness Indicators Initiative. A 17 state partnership.* Providence, RI: Author.

Roskos, K. (1988). Literacy at work in play. *Reading Teacher, 41*, 562–567.

Scarborough, H. (2001). Connecting early language and literacy to later reading (dis)abilities: Evidence, theory, and practice. In S.B. Neuman & D. Dickinson (Eds.), *Handbook of early literacy research* (pp. 97–110). New York: Guilford.

Snow, C. (1983). Literacy and language: Relationships during the preschool years. *Harvard Educational Review, 53*, 165–189.

Snow, C., Baines, W., Chandler, J., Goodman, I., & Hemphill, L. (1991). *Unfulfilled expectations: Home and school influences on literacy.* Cambridge, MA: Harvard University Press.

Snow, C., Burns, M.S., & Griffin, P. (1998). *Preventing reading difficulties in young children.* Washington, DC: National Academies Press.

St. Pierre, R., Layzer, J., & Barnes, H. (1995). Two-generation programs: Design, cost, and short-term effectiveness. *The Future of Children, 5*, 76–93.

Stanovich, K., West, R., & Harrison, M. (1995). Knowledge growth and maintenance across the life span: The role of print exposure. *Journal of Educational Psychology, 31*, 811–826.

U.S. Census Bureau. (2000). *U.S. census 2000.* Retrieved from http://www.census.gov/main/www/cen2000.html

White, K., Taylor, M., & Moss, V. (1992). Does research support claims about the benefits of involving parents in early intervention programs? *Review of Educational Research, 62*, 91–125.

Whitehurst, G., Arnold, D., Epstein, J., Angell, A., Smith, M., & Fischel, J. (1994). A picture book reading intervention in day care and home for children from low-income families. *Developmental Psychology, 30*, 679–689.

I

Poverty and
Its Consequences

Susan B. Neuman

Poverty takes a terrible toll on young children and families. Section I includes chapters that address the broad problem of poverty and its consequences on achievement. These chapters describe the extent of poverty and recent public policies that have put poor children at tremendous risk, affecting their well-being, educational achievement, and social-emotional functioning. As subsequent chapters in this section clearly indicate, these factors cannot be ignored but must be addressed through carefully designed interventions that work to improve children's literacy achievement.

In Chapter 1, Sandra and Sheldon Danziger provide an historical analysis of poverty-reduction strategies since the 1960s. Though designed to help "level the playing field," these strategies have failed to ameliorate the devastating effects for children. Despite antipoverty initiatives begun as early as President Johnson's War on Poverty, we still know more about poverty's pernicious influences on children than we do about effective policies designed to prevent the harm it does to them.

In Chapter 2, Mary Corcoran examines race-based inequality in income. Using estimates of multiyear poverty, she argues that the distributions of income are far more unequal by race than that of single-year estimates. She paints a dismal portrait of children's quality of life during the childhood years and children's future economic attainments, indicating that race and parental income each predict children's futures. The "rags to riches" myth, unfortunately, is indeed a myth.

In Chapter 3, Vonnie C. McLoyd and her colleague Kelly M. Purtell highlight what these expansive bodies of research tell us about children's cognitive functioning and school achievement. Recognizing that lack of income places severe constraints on cognitive and academic functioning for disadvantaged children, they argue for out-of-home experiences, such as quality child care and adult-supervised after-school programs, to serve as potent mediators for improving the opportunities for children who live in difficult life circumstances.

Julia Parkinson and Brian Rowan in Chapter 4 begin to address the critical question of how we can turn things around. In a provocative series of "thought experiments" using the Early Childhood Longitudinal Study, they examine what it would take to enable our most at-risk students to achieve success and close the reading gap. Their conclusions build a strong foundational support for a 360-degree surround, indicating that children need not only educational supports, as in school learning, but family supports and parent involvement to more effectively reach the ambitious goals of literacy achievement for all.

A critical turn-key is the role of the teacher. Louisa C. Moats and Barbara R. Foorman in Chapter 5 focus on the teacher, his or her background knowledge of reading development, and the use of effective teaching strategies to improve student outcomes. Using evidence from a 5-year National Institute of Child Health and Human Development (NICHD) study, the authors argue that professional development of teachers must be more than an afterthought if we are going to improve children's odds for success in reading. There are skills and strategies that teachers must know in order to be effective. Reforms in teacher education must take into account the long-range development of teacher professional knowledge that is required for skillful teaching of the essential components of good instruction.

Charles R. Greenwood in Chapter 6 describes a program of research that emphasizes both the measurement and the impact of interventions on children's social and academic achievement. Based on work in high-poverty settings, Greenwood's findings point to alterable variables that support early literacy achievement. Furthermore, Greenwood provides empirical support for the ecological-interactional-developmental theoretical framework that threads throughout all of the chapters in this book.

These chapters, together, focus on the problems we face for educating children who live in poverty. Despite our increasing knowledge base of the skills and strategies predictive of literacy achievement, previous research has not effectively grappled with these issues. Until we do, we are likely to remain a nation of haves and have-nots.

1

Childhood Poverty in Economic and Public Policy Contexts

Sandra K. Danziger and Sheldon H. Danziger

Compared with children who are not poor, children who grow up in poverty, particularly if their families are poor for many years during their childhood, are at greater risk for many negative outcomes. They are less likely to enter school ready to learn, more likely to have health and behavior problems, and more likely to drop out of school and become teen parents (see Corcoran, 2001; Duncan & Brooks-Gunn, 1997). Parents who have difficulty making financial ends meet are more likely to have emotional problems that increase stress and negatively affect their parenting styles. These families are more likely to live in neighborhoods that are dangerous and have lower-quality child care facilities and schools and less healthy environments than families who are not poor. In testimony to Congress, Holzer, Schanzenbach, Duncan, and Ludwig (2007) concluded that children who grow up in persistently poor households have reduced earnings as adults and are more likely to participate in criminal activities and to have health problems. Since the 1970s, policy makers in the United States have not made reducing child poverty a priority; however, Holzer and colleagues (2007) conclude that "the investment of some significant resources in poverty reduction might be more socially cost-effective over time than we previously thought" (p. 31).

This chapter begins by reviewing changes in the economy and public policies since the mid-1960s that have affected the extent of child poverty. Then, selected poverty-reduction strategies are discussed and suggestions are made for what can be done to level the playing field for children who are poor and provide them with greater opportunities for economic success. We conclude that poverty will remain high unless, as a nation, we muster the political will to attack poverty. President Johnson rallied Congress and the country to support the War on Poverty and Great Society in the mid-1960s; such political leadership and popular support are absent today. Although fighting poverty is no longer a national priority, the U.S. experience with antipoverty policies and research in subsequent decades provides effective examples for reducing poverty. In fact, in 1999, the United Kingdom launched a major initiative to reduce child poverty that borrowed heavily from U.S. programs and policies. If policy makers and the public could find the political will to launch a new antipoverty initiative, the United States could "reimport" some of these successful policies.

ECONOMIC CHANGES FROM THE WAR ON POVERTY TO THE PRESENT

The U.S. economy experienced two decades of sustained economic growth, rising real wages, and low unemployment rates following World War II. The benefits of prosperity were widely shared among most of the poor, the middle class, and the wealthy. Even though poverty rates had been falling, concerns were raised in the late 1950s to early 1960s that many families, especially those headed by less-educated workers, minorities, and women, were not benefiting from the prosperous economy (Galbraith, 1958; Harrington, 1962; Lampman, 1959). Policy analysts called for the government to target policies and programs at those being left behind.

President Johnson responded by declaring a War on Poverty in 1964: "We cannot and need not wait for the gradual growth of the economy to lift this forgotten fifth of our Nation above the poverty line" (U.S. Council of Economic Advisers, 1964, p. 15). Johnson and his economic advisors predicted that income poverty, as officially measured, could be eliminated by 1980; they assumed that stable economic growth would continue for the subsequent two decades much as it had for the prior two decades and that the benefits of economic growth would continue to be shared among most workers. That is, if macroeconomic policies kept the economy growing, then real wages would increase steadily for workers throughout the wage distribution. The additional resources that would be devoted to new antipoverty initiatives would further reduce poverty, for example, by raising the marketable skills and employment of those who previously had been left behind.

New employment and training programs would enhance students' skills and launch their graduates into an economy with low unemployment and growing wages. Human capital programs, from Head Start for preschool children to Pell Grants for college students, would prevent the children of the poor from becoming poor workers in the next generation. Together, macroeconomic and antipoverty policies would sustain economic performance, raise the productivity of the poor, and remove discriminatory barriers to participation in the education system and the labor market.

Poverty in America was not eliminated in the next generation. Indeed, four decades later, the vision of the War on Poverty planners remains unfulfilled, primarily because the optimistic economic forecasts of the 1960s turned out to be wrong due to fundamental economic changes that began in the early 1970s and continue today (see Danziger, 2007; Danziger & Gottschalk, 2005). The labor market no longer provides rising real wages to workers across the skill distribution. Instead, wages have fallen for the least-educated workers, barely kept up with inflation for the typical worker, and zoomed ahead for professionals. A rising tide stopped lifting all boats after the oil price shock of the 1970s. The following decades have been an era of rising inequality (Danziger & Gottschalk, 1995, 2005).

Many factors contributed to this transformation of the economy, including labor-saving technological changes that favored the most-skilled workers, the globalization of markets, and deterioration of labor market institutions that help less-educated workers, such as declines in the value of the inflation-adjusted minimum wage and declines in the percentage of workers covered by union contracts. Unemployment rates were high for most years between the early 1980s and the mid-1990s. Also, since the mid-1970s, growth in median earnings (adjusted for inflation) has been very slow, and wages and access to employer-provided health insurance and pensions have fallen for many workers.

Men who left high school before graduating or only completed a high school degree lost the most ground. For example, inflation-adjusted annual earnings of male high school dropouts were 23% lower in 2002 than in 1975, and earnings of male high school graduates were 13% lower. In contrast, by 2002, men who were college graduates or had higher degrees earned 62% more than they did in 1975.

As a result of these labor market changes, progress against poverty has been very slow. The poverty rate remains high for many groups of children, especially racial and ethnic minorities, those who do not live with both parents, and those whose parents have completed no more than a high school degree.

Child poverty in the United States is higher than it is in many industrialized countries, even though U.S. living standards on average are higher than living standards in most other countries. In part, this is due to the labor market problems mentioned previously; however, poverty is also higher here because our social safety net provides smaller benefits to fewer low-income families. We spend a smaller share of our gross domestic product (GDP) on social welfare programs than do most other industrialized countries. Smeeding (2006a) showed that the United States spends only about 3% of its GDP on social expenditures for individuals who are not elderly, compared with about 12% in the Scandinavian countries and more than 6% in Australia, Canada, and the United Kingdom.

Smeeding (2006b) compares the U.S. poverty rate around the year 2000 with that in eight other advanced economies by converting each country's currency into U.S. dollars and utilizing a poverty line that is similar to the official U.S. Census Bureau measure. According to his calculations, the U.S. per capita GDP in 2000 was about 20% higher than that in the other countries, but the U.S. child poverty rate, 12.4%, was higher than the other countries' 9.1% average. The rate in Canada, for example, was 9.0%; in Sweden, it was 5.8%.

Demographic factors that contribute to a higher child poverty rate in the Unites States include increases since the mid-1960s in divorce, separation, and nonmarital childbearing. Children raised in single-parent families have lower incomes and higher poverty rates than those raised in two-parent families. In part, this is because the number of two-earner families has increased among married-couple families over the last several decades, and, in part, it is because it is difficult for single parents with young children to work year round full time.

TRENDS IN POVERTY BY AGE: THE ROLE OF ECONOMIC AND POLICY CHANGES

Trends in the poverty rates of different age groups have greatly diverged. The economic status of older adults has increased relative to that of children and adults ages 18–64. Figure 1.1 shows poverty trends for these three groups and highlights the dramatic reduction in poverty among the elderly compared with that among adults and children.[1]

In 1959, the poverty rate for older adults was 37.1%, more than twice the 17.4% rate for adults ages 18–64. By 1999, the poverty rate of the elderly had fallen to 7.0%, lower than the adult rate, 9.1%, and the child poverty rate of 13.9%.

Poverty declines were significant for children, adults, and older adults in the 1960s. Yet, between 1969 and 1999, there was little progress against poverty for children and adults because of the labor market difficulties discussed previously. In addition, government support for children whose parents did not work eroded after the early 1970s. Cash welfare payments for families with children did not keep up with inflation, and the 1996 welfare reform led to a major reduction in the welfare rolls. Also, a smaller percentage of unemployed workers receive unemployment insurance today compared with the 1970s (Levine, 2006). In addition, the minimum wage fell relative to the average wage and failed to keep up with inflation. For example, the minimum wage was raised to $5.15 per hour in September 1997 and remained at that level until July 2007, when it was raised to $5.85 per hour. In the 1960s and early 1970s, the minimum wage was about half of the average wage of private nonsupervisory workers; by 2006, it had fallen to only 31% of this average (Bernstein & Shapiro, 2006).

---

[1]The poverty rates shown in Figures 1.1 and 1.3 are taken from Danziger and Gottschalk (2005) and differ somewhat from the official poverty lines used by the U.S. Bureau of the Census (2006), which are shown in Figure 1.4. The primary difference is that the Census poverty threshold is updated each year to reflect changes in the cost of living using the Consumer Price Index for Urban Consumers (CPI-U). Danziger and Gottschalk use the Consumer Price Index Research Series (CPI-U-RS), which has grown more slowly than the CPI-U. For example, in 2002, the official poverty threshold for a family of three was $14,348, whereas the corresponding CPI-U-RS threshold was $12,307. A lower threshold used by Danziger and Gottschalk yields poverty rates that are lower than official census rates.

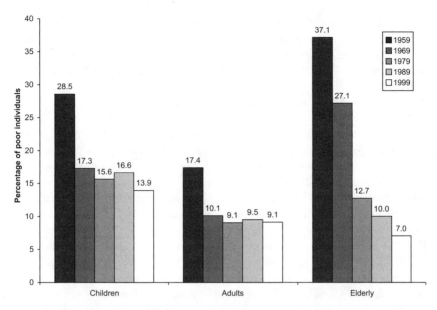

Figure 1.1. Trends in poverty by age, 1959–1999. (Danziger, Sheldon and Peter Gottschalk. Figure 8, "Poverty Rate by Age, 1959–1999." In *The American People: Census 2000.* © 2005 Russell Sage Foundation, 112 East 64th Street, New York, NY 10021. Reprinted by permission.)

The primary exception to this story of declining government support for the incomes of parents who are poor is the dramatic increase in the earned income tax credit (EITC), which was enacted in 1975. The value of the EITC is not included in the poverty rates shown in Figure 1.1; if it were, poverty rates for children and adults would be somewhat lower than the 1999 rates shown.

Since the mid-1970s, the EITC has provided a significant increase in income to working poor and near-poor parents at the same time that cash welfare has declined. Unlike a welfare program that provides benefits to nonworkers, EITC payments are zero for nonworkers and reach a maximum for minimum wage workers who work year round full time. EITC payments rise with earnings until the maximum benefit is reached and then fall as incomes rise beyond some amount before phasing out at income levels about twice the poverty line. The EITC avoids the social stigma associated with welfare receipt because parents receive payments from the Internal Revenue Service if the credit due exceeds their income tax owed. The EITC is available to both one- and two-parent families with children and provides a benefit level that is constant across the nation. (A number of states have supplemented the federal EITC with their own EITC.) The maximum federal EITC for a family with two or more children was $400 in 1975, $550 in 1986, $953 in 1991, and $4,204 in 2003.

The EITC was increased during the Reagan, George H.W. Bush, and Clinton administrations. For the most part, it has had broad, bipartisan Congressional support and has been mostly invisible to the public, even though the numbers of recipients and the total costs have increased substantially. The number of families receiving credits increased from between 5 million and 7.5 million families per year between 1975 and 1986 to about 11 million by 1988 and 17 million by 2001.

In 1975, a family with one parent working full time for a full year at the minimum wage received an EITC payment that was about 10% of his or her annual earnings; by 1990, the EITC reached 15% of his or her earnings. By 2003, because of a large expansion promoted by the Clinton administration in 1993, the EITC was 40% of the annual earnings of a parent of two children earning minimum wage. Compared with the value of cash welfare benefits and the minimum wage, which tends to remain constant, the EITC increases each year with inflation. In 2002, federal expenditures for the refundable portion of the EITC were about $28 billion for about 17 million families, more than twice the $13 billion combined spending of the federal and state governments on about 2 million families who received Temporary Assistance to Needy Families (TANF; i.e., cash welfare).

In contrast to the experience of nonworking families with children, government assistance for older adults increased dramatically after the War on Poverty, has not been reduced, and is the major reason poverty rates of the elderly have fallen so much. Between 1965 and 1973, there were seven across-the-board increases in Social Security benefits (Derthick, 1979). In 1973, Congress passed the automatic inflation-indexation of Social Security benefits to begin in 1975. Because the earnings of workers failed to keep up with inflation after the mid-1970s, Social Security benefits increased relative to earnings, relative to the poverty line, and relative to the government benefits available to adults and children.

The Supplemental Security Income Program (SSI), enacted in 1972, provides a minimum monthly cash payment to all poor older adults (as well as people with disabilities who are poor and people who are blind). SSI is available to older adults who did not work enough to qualify for Social Security benefits; it also supplements those who had very low earnings and hence have low Social Security benefits. As a result, all older adults who are poor, but not all children or adults who are poor, are eligible for cash assistance.

Economic progress since the 1970s for families with children has been uneven. Figure 1.2 (Congressional Budget Office, 2005) compares average after-tax income (including the value of the EITC) for households with children in each quintile of the income distribution and the top 1% of all households in 1979 and 2003 (in constant 2003 dollars). These data document that the last quarter of the 20th century was an era of rising inequality—the percentage increase in income is largest for the highest-income groups and lowest for the poorest fifth of households. Income in the poorest fifth increased by only 7%, from $18,500 to $19,800, whereas it increased by 63.5% for the richest fifth, from $109,900 to $179,700. The wealthiest 1% of families with children increased their after-tax income by 145% to $930,800. In 1979, the richest fifth of households with children

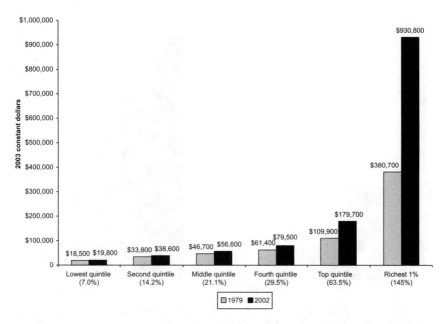

Figure 1.2. After-tax income, households with children 1979 and 2003. (Reprinted from Congressional Budget Office. [2005]. *Historical effective federal tax rates: 1979–2003.* Retrieved February 18, 2008, from http://www.cbo.gov/ftpdocs/70xx/doc7000/12-29-FedTaxRates.pdf)

had about 6 times the after-tax income of the poorest fifth ($109,900/$18,500); by 2003, their incomes were about 9 times as high ($179,700/$19,800).

TRENDS IN CHILD POVERTY BY LIVING ARRANGEMENTS

As mentioned previously, another reason that child poverty has remained high is the decline in the percentage of all children living in married-couple families, which have low poverty rates compared with other types of families with children. Between 1959 and 1999, the percentage of all children living in married-couple families fell from 91% to 71%, as marital fertility declined, the divorce rate increased, and the rate of nonmarital childbearing increased.

Figure 1.3 shows that the poverty rate for children in married-couple families fell from 24.8% to 6.9% between 1959 and 1999 and that the rate for children in other living arrangements fell from 66.2% to 31.4%. Danziger and Gottschalk (1995) found that the shift in children's living arrangements away from two-parent families between 1973 and 1991 led the child poverty rate to be about 4.5 percentage points higher than it would have been if family structure had stayed as it was in 1973. The percentage of children living outside of married-couple families has not changed much since the 1990s. As a result, Nichols (2006) found that over the period from 1993 to 2004, "changes in the share of

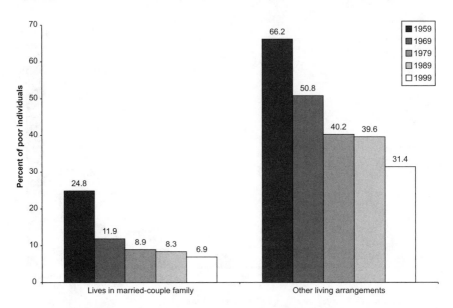

Figure 1.3. Trends in child poverty, by family status, 1959–1999. (Danziger, Sheldon and Peter Gottschalk. Figure 9, "Child Poverty Rate by Family Status, 1959–1999." In *The American People: Census 2000.* © 2005 Russell Sage Foundation, 112 East 64th Street, New York, NY 10021. Reprinted by permission.)

families headed by single parents seem to have played almost no role" (p. 1) in explaining the trend in child poverty.

Child poverty would be lower if a greater percentage of children lived in two-parent families; however, many single mothers with low incomes do not marry the fathers of their children because these men have poor labor market prospects—their wage rates are low and they frequently are unemployed (Edin & Kefalas, 2005). To reduce child poverty in these families requires higher employment and earnings as well as increased marriage.

Children living in married-couple families have benefited since 1973 from the increased work effort and wage rates of married mothers. Children in other living arrangements primarily live with single mothers. Even though work hours and earnings for single mothers increased after the 1996 welfare reform, they remain low enough on average to continue to place their families at high risk of poverty (Danziger, Heflin, Corcoran, Oltmans, & Wang, 2002).

DIFFERENCES IN CHILD POVERTY BY RACE AND ETHNICITY

Figure 1.4 shows trends in the official U.S. Census Bureau (2006) child poverty rates for all children between 1959 and 2005 and for white non-Hispanic, African American, Hispanic, and Asian children starting at different years. The

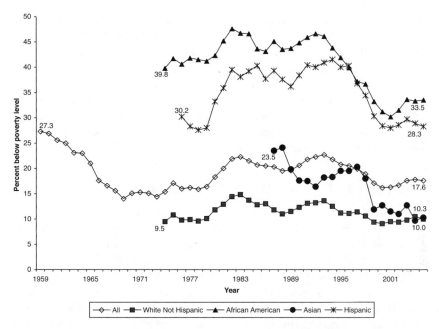

Figure 1.4. Child poverty, 1959–2005. (Reprinted from U.S. Census Bureau. [2006]. *Historical poverty tables*. Retrieved February 18, 2008, from http://www.census.gov/hhes/www/poverty/histpov/hstpov3.html)

Census Bureau did not gather information on large enough numbers of families to publish a rate for Hispanic children until the early 1970s or a rate for Asian children until the mid-1980s.

For all children, poverty fell from 27.3% in 1959 to 14.4% in 1973. After that year, economic growth faltered, and in 1983, the national unemployment rate reached its highest levels since the Great Depression of the 1930s—about 10%. As a result, child poverty rose to 22.3% in 1983. During the economic boom of the late 1980s, poverty fell a bit but rose again to 22.7% in 1993, as the economy then went into recession. The economic boom of the 1990s led the poverty rate to fall to 16.2% in 2000 before rising to 17.6% in 2005. Note that the official child poverty rate in 2005 was about the same as it was in 1966, just after the War on Poverty was declared. If the value of noncash transfers and the EITC are included as income sources (data not shown), the child poverty rate in 2005 would have been about 14%, the same as the official rate in 1973.

The patterns of child poverty rates since the 1970s are similar for children of each race/ethnic group. White non-Hispanic children and Asian children have much lower poverty rates than African American and Hispanic children in every year. All of the rates were highest during the recession of the early 1980s and fell substantially during the economic boom of the late 1990s. The poverty rate for white non-Hispanic children rose from 9.5% in 1974 to 14.8% in 1983 and then fell to 10% in 2005. The rate for Asian children fell from 23.5% in 1987 to 10.3% in 2005, just about the same level as that of white non-Hispanic children. In contrast, even though poverty fell dramatically for African American and Hispanic children in the 1990s, they remain 3 times as likely to be poor as white and Asian children. For African Americans, child poverty peaked at 47.6% in 1982 and fell to 33.5% in 2005; Hispanic child poverty peaked at 41.5% in 1994 and fell to 28.3% in 2005. Race and ethnic disparities in the likelihood of experiencing poverty as a child remain high.

TOWARD A NEW ANTIPOVERTY AGENDA

As other chapters in this book demonstrate, children who are poor are at high risk for a wide range of negative outcomes that begin at birth and extend into early adulthood. Policies to reduce child poverty can be of several types. Some aim to reduce financial hardship directly by raising family incomes. Examples include cash welfare, food stamps, school lunch, the minimum wage, and the EITC. Other policies seek to reduce the social consequences of poverty, for example, by expanding access to health care and by subsidizing child care or placing children who are poor in Head Start. Our focus in this chapter is on several policies that would increase family income and reduce the number of children who lack health insurance (see Currie, 2006, for a comprehensive analysis of safety-net programs for poor children).

Income-tested programs, commonly called *welfare programs*, provide benefits only to those whose incomes (and for some programs, whose assets) from other sources are below an eligibility threshold. The Congressional Research Service (Burke, 2003) reports more than 80 programs that provide cash or noncash benefits to individuals with limited income. These include cash assistance, food stamps, school nutrition aid, Medicaid, and programs that fund education, employment and training, housing, and social services. The largest cash welfare programs today are TANF, which replaced the Aid to Families with Dependent Children (AFDC) program in 1996; SSI for older adults, blind people, and people with disabilities (including children with disabilities); and the EITC for the working poor and near poor.

Reform of cash welfare programs has generated intense public and policy debates on the nature and goals of antipoverty policy for more than 30 years. Welfare reform proposals in the late 1960s were considered antipoverty proposals. They sought to reduce income poverty by extending welfare eligibility and raising cash benefit levels. Later, as public dissatisfaction with rising welfare rolls and government spending increased, greater attention was paid to constraining budgetary costs and to promoting work incentives and, since the 1990s, adding work requirements. These requirements came to be applied to mothers with children at increasingly younger ages. By the mid-1990s, reforming welfare had little to do with reducing poverty; the goal was to reduce reliance on welfare and increase work among the poor, independent of the policy's effect on poverty (Weaver, 2000).

The Personal Responsibility and Work Opportunity Reconciliation Act of 1996 (PRWORA; PL 104-193) decisively ended welfare as we knew it. The act eliminated the entitlement to cash assistance for single mothers that had been in place for 60 years. A single mother is no longer allowed to reject a job offer and remain on welfare; a recipient who refuses to search for work or cooperate with the welfare agency is sanctioned by having her benefits reduced or ended. Together, welfare reform and the economic boom of the late 1990s contributed to a dramatic decline in welfare caseloads and a substantial increase in the employment of single mothers. In a single decade, the national welfare rolls declined by almost 70%.

Although the extent of work has increased and the poverty rate has fallen since the mid-1990s, poverty among children living with single mothers and poverty among African American and Hispanic children remains very high. Less-skilled workers face frequent spells of nonemployment and continuing economic hardship even when the economy is growing. In addition, welfare reform produced a small but increasing group of mothers who are disconnected from regular sources of economic support—they have no work, no cash assistance, and do not live in households that have other earners. If our nation is to further reduce poverty in a post–welfare reform world, additional public policies are needed to supplement low earnings of former welfare recipients and other less-educated workers.

Many reasonable policy changes could be adopted that would increase the likelihood that women making the transition from welfare to work and millions of other low earners could move out of poverty. We focus on four examples—raising the minimum wage, subsidizing health insurance for low-income families not covered by Medicaid, reforming the unemployment insurance program to cover a greater percentage of low-wage laid-off workers, and providing transitional jobs of last resort for those who want to work but cannot find steady employment.

Raising the minimum wage is the simplest example. The federal minimum wage was raised in 2007 after a decade, last raised in 1997. The minimum wage had been about 50% of the average wage from the early 1950s to the early 1970s; however, it is now only about one third of the average. In inflation-adjusted terms, the minimum wage was above $6.00 per hour in every year between 1962 and 1983, reaching a maximum of $7.44 in 2006 dollars in 1968. Raising the minimum wage to about $7.50 in 2008 and indexing it so that it would increase in the future as average wages increase would represent an important antipoverty policy for low-skilled workers.

A second example is the State Child Health Insurance Program (SCHIP) enacted in 1997. Together with a series of Medicaid expansions from the late 1980s to the mid-1990s, all children who are poor or near poor now have guaranteed access to subsidized health care coverage. Between 1987 and 2004, the lack of insurance for children fell from 12.9% to 11.2%; in contrast, for all individuals, it rose from 12.9% to 15.7%. In 2004, the uninsurance rate was 11.2% for children, 31.4% for those ages 18–24, and 25.9% for those 25–34. Wisconsin, under Republican Governor Tommy Thompson, adopted Badger Care, a program that allows low-income adults to purchase SCHIP coverage at a subsidized rate. This experience shows that government can do more to help offset the fact that fewer firms today offer subsidized insurance to workers. Lack of insurance has fallen for children because government has done more to help them; at the same time, lack of insurance has increased for adults because of labor market changes.

The third example is that labor market changes, especially the increase in part-time and low-wage employment, has reduced the likelihood that unemployed workers receive unemployment insurance (UI) benefits. In the 1950s, about half of unemployed individuals received UI benefits; about three fourths received UI benefits during the recession of the mid-1970s when Congress provided a federal extension of UI for up to 39 weeks in addition to the traditional 26 weeks of coverage. In the mid-2000s, only about one third of the unemployed received UI benefits. One solution is to mandate that all states provide UI coverage to part-time workers; less than half the states now do so. Another is to raise the UI replacement rate for low-wage workers. A minimum-wage worker who is laid off from a 30-hour per week job, for example, would, if he or she met other eligibility requirements, receive only about $75 per week in most states (National Employment Law Project, 2004).

A fourth, more ambitious example of a policy to help those being hurt by the changing economy is transitional jobs of last resort. Many individuals who are poor want to work and are willing to take minimum wage jobs but do not have the skills that firms now demand. This is especially important for single mothers who have been terminated from welfare. The federal government, for example, might pay 80% of the total costs of providing the transitional job, and the non-profit or community-based organizations or local governmental agencies administering the jobs would cover the remaining costs. Workers would be expected to perform socially beneficial tasks for which there is little effective labor demand. For example, they might provide labor-intensive public services in impoverished areas that are generally provided in affluent communities, such as monitoring of playgrounds, neighborhood maintenance, and assisting older adults.

Wages for transitional jobs would be lower than the minimum wage, providing an incentive to individuals in transitional jobs to take an available private sector job. Employees who did not meet performance standards would be dismissed. Those hired might be limited to a 1–2 year "term" at the transitional job, after which time they should have acquired the experience and skills needed to get a private sector job. Transitional jobs of last resort would provide a social safety net to individuals who are poor who want to work but cannot find a regular private or public sector job. They are particularly needed now that welfare reform has placed time limits on cash assistance.

SUCCESSFUL POLICIES: THE UNITED KINGDOM CASE

In contrast to the erosion of the antipoverty goal in U.S. policy since the 1970s, U.K. Prime Minister Tony Blair made a Johnson-esque War on Poverty pledge in 1999: "Our historic aim will be for ours to be the first generation to end child poverty, and it will take a generation. It is a 20 year mission but I believe it can be done" (Blair, 1999, p. 1). The antipoverty policies put into place by the Blair government are based to a significant extent on the U.S. experience with antipoverty policies. Significant new programs were established and existing programs were expanded to promote "work for those who can, security for those who cannot," (p. 12) and to increase investments in children and expand opportunity and intergenerational mobility. For example, the Blair government implemented a minimum wage in April 1998 and has increased it each year since. By October 2006, it was about 50% higher than it was 8 years earlier.

In response to the Blair initiative, child poverty in the United Kingdom has fallen dramatically (Hills & Waldfogel, 2004). As this experience demonstrates, if there is a political will to reduce poverty, there are many public policies that could be put in place to achieve the goal that President Johnson proclaimed in 1964—to eliminate income poverty within a generation.

REMAINING POVERTY PROBLEMS: RACIAL AND ETHNIC DISPARITIES

Even if the nation was willing to spend the money to adopt or expand these policies, the concentration of poverty would remain very high in our inner cities, where many poor African American and Hispanic families reside (Jargowsky, 1997, 2003; Wilson, 1987, 1996). It is easier to support family income than it is to implement policies to deconcentrate and desegregate poverty—to spread people who are poor out of high-poverty neighborhoods—because such policies would be place-specific and race-specific. The United States has had relatively limited success with place-specific policies, even though a key focus of the War on Poverty was to deconcentrate poverty in Appalachia, a region still characterized by high poverty rates.

The programs that have had some promising results, such as the Movement to Opportunity Program or other housing voucher programs, such as Section 8 housing vouchers, typically face resistance from predominantly white communities (Yinger, 2001). Most white people report that they do not want more than a small number of African Americans to move into their neighborhoods; in addition, many among the poor prefer to live in areas where they are not socially isolated from friends and relatives. Desegregation of middle- and upper-income African Americans has proceeded only slowly since the 1960s (Logan, Stults, & Farley, 2004). As more middle-class African Americans move from highly segregated inner cities to inner-ring suburbs, middle-class whites tend to move further out.

CONCLUSION

The antipoverty policy reforms we have suggested in this chapter aim to "lift all boats" by increasing the incomes of those who work for low wages and receive few fringe benefits. They would be particularly beneficial for groups with high poverty rates—single parents, African Americans, Hispanics, and those who live in inner-city impoverished neighborhoods.

Although a combination of economic, demographic, and policy trends have kept rates of child poverty high, effective policies to reduce economic disparities of children are available and are common in other countries. What remains absent is the political leadership and public support to take bold actions to commit the public funds needed to confront poverty and inequality. As long as public opinion polls suggest that the public considers poverty to be due primarily to a failure of the poor to avail themselves of existing opportunities (Ladd & Bowman, 1998) and as long as government is viewed as wasteful and unable to effectively combat poverty (Pew Research Center, 2005), it is unlikely that these initiatives, no matter how effective they might be, will soon be implemented.

In the early 1960s, the "paradox of poverty amidst plenty" troubled President Kennedy and led him to instruct his Council of Economic Advisers to plan the antipoverty initiatives that would become the foundation for the War on Poverty declared by President Johnson in 1964. The next few chapters provide compelling evidence that poverty amidst plenty should again come to be viewed as unjustifiable and unnecessary in this rich nation. We know more about its pernicious and wide-reaching effects, and we have evidence that effective policies can prevent and correct the harm poverty does to children.

REFERENCES

Bernstein, J., & Shapiro, I. (2006). *Nine years of neglect: Federal minimum wage remains unchanged for ninth straight year, falls to lowest level in more than half a century.* Washington, DC: Center on Budget and Policy Priorities. Retrieved February 18, 2008, from http://www.cbpp.org/8-31-06mw.htm.

Blair, T. (1999). Beveridge revisited: A welfare state for the 21st century. In R. Walker (Ed.), *Ending child poverty: Popular welfare for the 21st century?* (pp. 7–18). Bristol, UK: Policy Press.

Burke, V. (2003). *Cash and noncash benefits for persons with limited income: Eligibility rules, recipient and expenditure data, FY2000–FY2002* (Order code RL3223). Washington, DC: Congressional Research Service.

Congressional Budget Office. (2005). *Historical effective federal tax rates: 1979–2003.* Retrieved February 18, 2008, from http://www.cbo.gov/ftpdocs/70xx/doc7000/12-29-FedTaxRates.pdf

Corcoran, M. (2001). Mobility, persistence, and the consequences of poverty for children: Child and adult outcomes. In S. Danziger & R. Haveman (Eds.), *Understanding poverty* (pp. 127–161). Cambridge, MA: Harvard University Press.

Currie, J.M. (2006). *The invisible safety net: Protecting the nation's poor children and families.* Princeton, NJ: Princeton University Press.

Danziger, S. (2007). *Fighting poverty revisited: What did researchers know 40 years ago? What do we know today?* Retrieved February 18, 2008, from University of Wisconsin–Madison, Institute for Research on Poverty web site: http://www.irp.wisc. edu/publica tions/focus/pdfs/foc251a.pdf

Danziger, S., & Gottschalk, P. (1995). *America unequal.* Cambridge, MA: Harvard University Press.

Danziger, S., & Gottschalk, P. (2005). Diverging fortunes: Trends in poverty and inequality. In R. Farley & J.J. Haaga (Eds.), *The American people: Census 2000* (pp. 49–75). New York: Russell Sage Foundation.

Danziger, S., Heflin, C., Corcoran, M., Oltmans, E., & Wang, H. (2002). Does it pay to move from welfare to work? *Journal of Policy Analysis and Management, 21*(4), 671–692.

Derthick, M. (1979). *Policy making for Social Security.* Washington, DC: Brookings Institution.

Duncan, G.J., & Brooks-Gunn, J. (1997). *Consequences of growing up poor.* New York: Russell Sage Foundation.

Edin, K., & Kefalas, M. (2005). *Promises I can keep: Why poor women put motherhood before marriage.* Berkeley: University of California Press.

Galbraith, J.K. (1958). *The affluent society.* New York: New American Library.

Harrington, M. (1962). *The other America: Poverty in the United States.* New York: MacMillan.

Hills, J., & Waldfogel, J. (2004). A "third way" in welfare reform? Evidence from the United Kingdom. *Journal of Policy Analysis and Management, 23*(4), 765–788.

Holzer, H.J., Schanzenbach, D.W., Duncan, G.J., & Ludwig, J. (2007). *The economic costs of poverty in the United States: Subsequent effects of children growing up poor* (Working paper series 07-04). Ann Arbor: Michigan National Poverty Center.

Jargowsky, P.A. (1997). *Poverty and place: Ghettos, barrios, and the American city.* New York: Russell Sage Foundation.

Jargowsky, P.A. (2003). *Stunning progress, hidden problems: The dramatic decline of concentrated poverty in the 1990s.* Washington, DC: Brookings Institution, Center on Urban and Metropolitan Policy, Living Cities Census Series.

Ladd, E., & Bowman, K. (1998). *Attitudes toward economic inequality.* Washington, DC: American Enterprise Institute.

Lampman, R. (1959). *The low-income population and economic growth* (U.S. Congress, Joint Economic Committee, study paper no. 12). Washington, DC: U.S. Government Printing Office.

Levine, P. (2006). Unemployment insurance over the business cycle: Does it meet the needs of less-skilled workers? In R. Blank, S. Danziger, & R. Schoeni (Eds.), *Working and poor: How economic and policy changes are affecting low-wage workers* (pp. 366–395). New York: Russell Sage Foundation.

Logan, J.R., Stults, B.J., & Farley, R. (2004). Segregation of minorities in the metropolis: Two decades of change. *Demography, 41*(1), 1–22.

National Employment Law Project. (2004). *Changing workforce, changing economy: State unemployment insurance reforms for the 21st century.* Retrieved February 18, 2008, from http://www.nelp.org/docUploads/ChangingWorkforce.pdf

Nichols, A. (2006). *New federalism series A: No. A-71. Understanding recent changes in child poverty.* Washington, DC: Urban Institute. Retrieved February 18, 2008, from http:// www.urban.org/UploadedPDF/311356_A71.pdf

Personal Responsibility and Work Opportunity Reconciliation Act of 1996, PL 104-193, 42 U.S.C. §§ 211 *et seq.*

Pew Research Center for the People and the Press. (2005). *Katrina relief effort raises concern over excessive spending, waste.* Retrieved February 18, 2008, from http://people-press.org/reports/display.php3?ReportID=260

Smeeding, T.M. (2006a). Government programs and social outcomes: Comparison of the United States with other rich nations. In A.J. Auerbach, D. Card, & J. Quigley (Eds.), *Poverty, the distribution of income, and public policy* (pp. 149–218). New York: Russell Sage Foundation.

Smeeding, T.M. (2006b). Poor people in rich nations: The United States in comparative perspective. *Journal of Economic Perspectives, 20*(1), 69–90.

U.S. Census Bureau. (2006). *Historical poverty tables.* Retrieved February 18, 2008, from http://www.census.gov/hhes/www/poverty/histpov/hstpov3.html

U.S. Council of Economic Advisers. (1964). *Economic report of the President.* Washington, DC: U.S. Government Printing Office.

Weaver, R.K. (2000). *Ending welfare as we know it.* Washington, DC: Brookings Institution.

Wilson, W.J. (1987). *The truly disadvantaged: The inner city, the underclass, and public policy.* Chicago: University of Chicago Press.

Wilson, W.J. (1996). *When work disappears: The world of the new urban poor.* New York: Knopf.

Yinger, J. (2001). Housing discrimination and residential segregation as causes of poverty. In S. Danziger & R. Haveman (Eds.), *Understanding poverty* (pp. 359–391). Cambridge, MA: Harvard University Press.

2

Childhood Poverty, Race, and Equal Opportunity

Mary Corcoran

Equality of opportunity is highly valued in the United States. The color of a child's skin or the poverty of his or her parents should not be barriers to future achievements. But equal opportunity can conflict with another strongly held value—the right of parents to help their children get ahead (Jencks, 2002). Because some parents are more economically advantaged than other parents and can more easily afford to help out their children, many critics claim that the playing field is not level. This is further complicated by the fact that white parents are more likely than African American parents to have high incomes and to have assets and less likely to be long-term poor. Many argue that racial background and poverty can and do handicap children in the contest for success.

In this chapter, I address three questions:

1. How many children grow up in long-term economic need? On average, how different are the economic resources available to children born to white parents from the economic resources available to children born to African American parents?

2. How much do childhood economic resources matter for children's current and future material well-being?

3. How comparable are the mobility experiences of African American and white children raised in comparable economic circumstances?

I begin by documenting race-based inequality in children's access to economic resources using single-year income and poverty measures. I then discuss how using multiyear income and poverty measures, including measures of wealth, and assessing resources available from extended family members change estimates of race-based inequality in children's access to economic resources. This is followed by a review of research studies examining the associations between parents' economic circumstances, children's quality of life during the childhood years, and children's future economic attainments. I conclude with an overview of what is known about the extent to which educational interventions might be useful in lessening the effects of parents' economic circumstances on children's economic futures.

RACE-BASED DIFFERENCES IN CHILDREN'S ACCESS TO ECONOMIC RESOURCES

Racial and ethnic differences in annual childhood poverty rates and in 1-year income rates are large. The bar graph in Figure 2.1 shows child poverty rates and the percentages of families in the bottom income quintile, the top income quintile, and the top 5 income percentiles for the year 2005. African American and Latino children were 2–2.5 times as likely as white children to be poor and to live in families in the bottom income quintile. For instance, 14.4% of white children were poor, but 34.5% of African American children and 28.3% of Latino children were poor. White families are correspondingly overrepresented relative to African American and Latino families at the upper end of the income distribution: 23.5% of white families were in the top income quintile, whereas only 9.2% of African American families and 8.5% of Latino families were in the top income quintile. Whites were 4 times more likely as either African Americans or Latinos

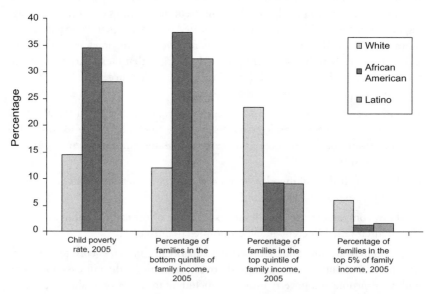

Figure 2.1. One-year child poverty rates and one-year family income quintiles from 2005. (*Note:* The child poverty rate was taken from Table POV01 and the family income distribution data were taken from Table FINC-06 in the U.S. Census Bureau's *Current Population Survey 2006 Annual Social and Economic Supplement.* Available online at http://www.census.gov/cps/)

to live in very affluent families (those in the top 5 income percentiles)—6% for whites versus 1.4% for African Americans and 1.6% for Latinos.

Because 1-year poverty measures are affected by transitory fluctuations in income, they only imperfectly measure families' long-term economic resources and may understate race-based inequalities in children's long-term experiences of poverty. Hertz (2005) tracked the poverty experiences of white and African American children from birth to 5 years for the 10 years between 1987 and 1996 (see Figures 2.2 and 2.3.) The majority of white children (75%) were never poor during those 10 years and long-term poverty was rare: Only 5% of white children were poor for 6 or more years, and a mere 1% were poor for 9 or 10 years. The 10-year poverty experience patterns of African American children are the mirror opposite of those for white children. The majority of African American children (69%) were poor at some point, and long-term poverty was common: More than one in five African American children were poor for 9 or 10 years and one in three were poor for 6 or more years.

Corcoran and Matsudaira (2005) investigated race differences in 3-year income by estimating the distributions of white and African American children across 3-year income quintiles from ages 15 to 17 years (see Figure 2.4). Over these 3 years, 55.3% of African American children but only 15% of white children were in the bottom income quintile. From ages 15 to 17, hardly any (1.2%) African American children, but 22.8% of white children, were in the top income quintile.

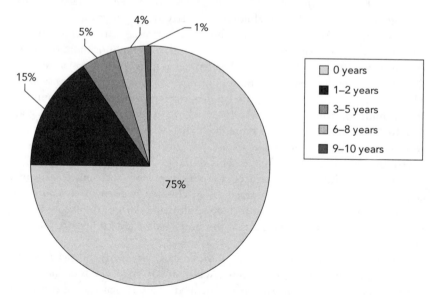

Figure 2.2. Years poor from 1987 to 1996 for non–African American children ages 0–5. (*Note:* Data from U.S. Department of Health and Human Services. [2003]. *Indicators of welfare dependence: Annual report to Congress 2003* [Table ECON 6, p. 13]. Available online at http://aspe.hhs.gov/HSP/indicators03/)

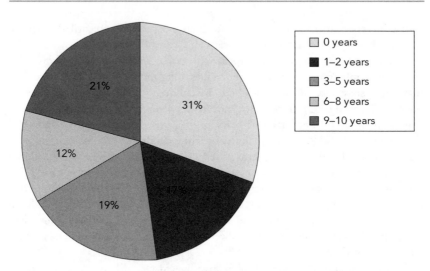

Figure 2.3. Years poor from 1987 to 1996 for African American children ages 0–5. (*Note:* Data from U.S. Department of Health and Human Services. [2003]. *Indicators of welfare dependence: Annual report to Congress 2003* [Table ECON 6, p. 13]. Available online at http://aspe.hhs. gov/HSP/indicators03/)

Multiyear poverty rates are considerably more racialized than 1-year poverty rates, and the distribution of multiyear income is more unequal by race than that of single-year income. Annual childhood poverty rates are typically 2–3 times higher for African Americans than for whites, but African American children were 7 times more likely than white children to be poor during 6 or more of the 10 years between 1987 and 1996. In 2005, 2.5 times as many African American families as white families were in the bottom income quintile and 2.6 times as many white families as African American families were in the top income quintile. When childhood family income was measured over 3 years instead of over 1 year, African Americans were 4 times more likely than whites to be in the bottom 3-year income quintile and whites were 18 times more likely than African Americans to be in the top 3-year income quintile.

As large as these race differences in multiyear poverty and multiyear income are, they still understate race differences in children's access to economic resources. Income measures do not include wealth, and African American parents have fewer assets than white parents at the same income level (Oliver & Shapiro, 2006).

Two commonly used measures of wealth are *net worth* and *net financial worth* (Gittleman & Wolff, 2004, 2007; Wolff, 2006). *Net worth* is defined as assets minus debts. *Net financial worth* is defined as assets that can be converted readily to cash minus debts. The difference between the two measures is that home equity is included as an asset when computing net worth but not when computing net financial worth.

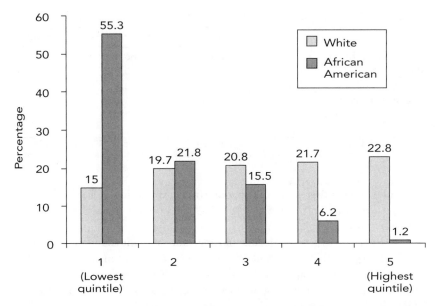

Figure 2.4. The distribution by race of children born between 1962 and 1969, across 3-year income quintiles at ages 15–17. (From Corcoran, M., & Matsudaira, J. [2005]. Is it getting harder to get ahead? Economic attainment in early adulthood for two cohorts. In R.A. Setterstein, F.F. Furstenberg, & R.G. Rumbaut [Eds.], *On the frontier of adulthood* [Table 11.8, p. 382]. Chicago: University of Chicago Press; reprinted by permission. Copyright © 2005 by University of Chicago Press.) (*Note:* Analyses are based on Panel Study of Income Dynamics, 1977–1996.)

The distribution of net worth is far more unequal than is the distribution of income. In 2001, households who were in the top income quintile held 60% of all income, whereas those in the bottom two income quintiles held 10% of all income (Wolff, 2006). In contrast, the families who were in the top net worth quintile in 2001 held 84% of all net worth, and those in the bottom two net worth quintiles held three tenths of 1% of all net worth (Wolff, 2006). The distribution of net worth is so unequal because many individuals have a zero or negative net worth. Wolff estimates that 18% of all U.S. households had zero or negative net worth in 2001. Further, because many households' only asset is their house, an even larger percentage of minority families will have a zero or negative net financial worth.

Wolff's (2006) estimates of the net worth and net financial worth of African American and white families are compared in Table 2.1. Three patterns jump out. First, medians are much lower than means because the distributions of net worth and net financial worth are highly skewed. Second, many African American families have little or no wealth. The median net worth is $10,700 for African Americans. Their median net financial worth is only $1,100, and more than 30% of African American families have a zero or negative net worth. Third, white families have more wealth than African American families. The median net

Table 2.1.   Net worth and financial wealth in 2001 by race

	White	African American	Ratio
Mean net worth	465,800	66,300	.14
Median net worth	106,400	10,700	.10
Mean financial wealth	369,700	43,200	.12
Median financial wealth	42,160	1,100	.03
Percentage with zero or negative net worth	13.1	30.9	2.35

From Wolff, E.N. (2006). Changes in household wealth in the 1980's and 1990's in the U.S. In *International perspectives on household wealth* (p. 35). Cheltenham, UK: Edward Elgar Publishing; reprinted by permission.

worth of white families is 10 times that of African American families, and the median net financial worth of white families is almost 40 times that of African American families.

The gap in assets between African American and white families is not solely due to the fact that African American families have lower incomes than white families. Oliver and Shapiro (2006) showed that whites have more wealth than African Americans even among families with comparable incomes, occupations, education, work experience, and family configurations.

Why African American families accumulate less wealth than white families with comparable incomes is a matter of much debate. Oliver and Shapiro (2006) proposed two explanations: 1) race differences in inheritance and intergenerational transfers and 2) race differences in access to housing and mortgage markets. Others speculate that information, financial demands from relatives, risk averseness, and investment strategies may differ by race (Charles & Hurst, 2003; Gittleman & Wolff, 2004, 2007; Wolff, 2006). Whatever the causes, these wealth gaps mean that African American children have fewer resources and live in more economically precarious circumstances than do white children raised in families with similar incomes. This could have negative repercussions for children's immediate and future well-being.

Parental assets or lack thereof are not the only familial economic resources available to children. Heflin and Pattilo (in press) hypothesized that members of one's extended family (e.g., grandparents, aunts and uncles) are potential sources of both economic supports and economic strains. Middle-class siblings can provide financial assistance, role models, and information and links to good jobs and educational opportunities. Relatives with low incomes, on the other hand, can impose financial obligations and a sense of guilt in their more financially secure relatives.

Heflin and Pattilo (in press) used the National Longitudinal Survey of Youth to map out the sibling networks of young adults ages 33–41 years. They report that controlling for social class, sibling networks of African Americans are more likely to engender economic obligations and less likely to engender economic supports than those of whites. Middle-class African Americans were more likely to have a sibling who is poor than were middle-class white Americans (40% for African Americans versus 16% for whites), and African Americans with low incomes were less likely than whites with low incomes to have a middle-class sibling (50% versus 66%).

Chiteji and Hamilton (2002) used the Panel Study of Income Dynamics (PSID) to compare the sibling and parental networks of adults in middle-class white and African American families (see Table 2.2). Like Heflin and Patillo (in press), they found that middle-class African American adults are more likely than middle-class white adults to have relatives who are poor and less likely to have high-income or wealthy relatives. Middle-class African Americans are 4.5 times more likely than middle-class whites to have parents who are poor (36% versus 8%). The average income of the siblings of middle-class whites is 2 times higher than that of the siblings of middle-class African Americans, and the average net worth of the siblings is more than 4 times higher.

DO PARENTAL ECONOMIC RESOURCES PREDICT CHILDREN'S CURRENT WELL-BEING?

Children born to African American parents have fewer economic resources on multiple dimensions than do children born to white parents. One concern about these race differences is that economic resources matter for children's current quality of life. For instance, very low income and no assets are associated with higher rates of material hardships. As Table 2.3 illustrates, rates of material hardships—eviction, disconnected telephone, utility service suspension, housing problems, hunger, lack of food security, unpaid bills, unmet medical and dental needs—are higher among families who are poor and families with few or no assets than among middle-class families and families with some assets (Beverly, 2001; Ouellette, Burstein, Long, & Beecroft, 2004). For instance, 32% of households with incomes below the poverty line compared with only 5.4% of households with incomes more than twice the poverty line experienced food insecurity in the previous 4 months (Ouellette et al., 2004). Similarly, 23% of households with $100 or less in liquid assets compared with only 6.5% of households with more

Table 2.2. Mean income, mean net worth, and percent poor for parents and siblings of middle-class families by race

	Parents		Siblings	
	White	African American	White	African American
Mean income	$48,667	$22,267	$50,599	$24,337
Mean net worth	$266,397	$47,385	$98,324	$22,099
Percent poor	8%	36%	8%	34%

Source: Chiteji & Hamilton (2002).

Table 2.3. Availability of basic needs and food security by income and assets

	Did not pay rent or mortgage	Evicted for failure to pay rent or mortgage	Did not pay gas, oil, or electricity bill	Lost gas, oil, or electricity for failure to pay	Telephone disconnected for failure to pay	Needed to see doctor or go to hospital but did not	Needed to see dentist but did not	Food insecure	Food insecure with hunger
Household income relative to federal poverty line									
Under 100%[a]	18.2%	1.1%	29.4%	6.0%	15.1%	14.9%	16.8%	32.0%	12.6%
100%–200%	13.0%*	0.4%*	21.6%*	3.2%*	10.4%*	11.1%*	16.0%	19.5%*	7.6%*
Over 200%	4.5%*	0.2%*	8.7%*	1.0%*	2.9%*	4.4%*	6.9%*	5.4%*	1.7%*
Liquid assets									
< $100[a]	14.6%	0.7%	24.6%	4.5%	12.3%	12.5%	16.1%	23.0%	9.0%
≥ $100	4.7%*	0.2%*	9.0%*	1.0%*	2.9%*	4.4%*	7.1%*	6.5%*	2.2%*
All households	8.3%	0.4%	14.4%	2.2%	6.2%	7.3%	10.2%	12.2%	4.6%

Reprinted from Ouellette, T., Burstein, N., Long, D., & Beecroft, E. (2004). *Measures of material hardship: Final report* (Exhibit 4.3). Washington, DC: U.S. Department of Health and Human Resources.

[a]Reference category

*Statistically significantly different from reference category, $p < 0.01$

than $100 in liquid assets experienced food insecurity in the previous 4 months.

Parental assets can improve children's immediate material well-being by providing a cushion for families during periods of economic crisis. Assets can smooth consumption, for instance, when family income drops due to a job loss or a marital breakup or when family expenses rise due to unexpected medical costs. Oliver and Shapiro (2006) explored the capacity of families to deal with such financial stresses by estimating the number of months a family could support themselves at the poverty level using only their net financial assets. Their results are displayed in Figure 2.5. Seventy-three percent of African American children and forty percent of white children reside in families who do not have sufficient assets to support themselves at the poverty level for even 1 month. Forty-four percent of white children but only eleven percent of African American children live in families whose assets can support them at the poverty level for 3 months or more. African American families are not as well positioned financially as white families to deal with emergencies.

A third way in which parents' economic resources can improve children's material well-being is by giving parents the wherewithal to subsidize sons and daughters as they leave home and set up independent households (e.g., by subsidizing living costs, buying computers, providing loans for house down payments, paying for health insurance). These subsidies can ease children's transitions from school to work. Schoeni and Ross (2005) used the PSID and the National

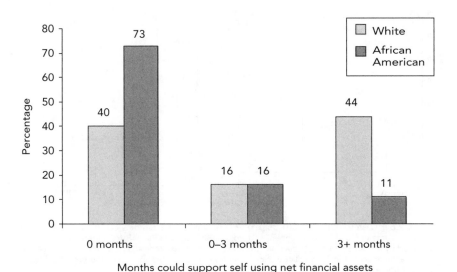

Figure 2.5.   Months of support at the poverty level for children by race. (*Source:* Oliver & Shapiro, 2006.) (*Note:* Oliver and Shapiro used 1987 Survey of Income and Program Participation data.)

Postsecondary Student Aid Study (NPSAS; National Center for Educational Statistics, 2003) to examine the extent to which parents provide financial assistance to young adults ages 18–34. Schoeni and Ross (2005) estimated that the average young adult received $17,909 in interhousehold cash transfers from parents between the ages of 18 and 34. Interhousehold cash transfers from parents differed by race and by parents' income quartile (see Figure 2.6). White children averaged $22,338 in cash assistance from parents between the ages of 18 and 34, whereas African American children averaged only $5,678 in cash assistance between the same ages.[1] Children from the bottom income quartile received $9,458 in cash transfers from parents between the ages of 18 and 34, whereas children from the top income quartile received $33,194 in direct cash transfers.

DO PARENTAL RESOURCES PREDICT CHILDREN'S FUTURE ECONOMIC WELL-BEING?

Probably the biggest concern about long-term childhood poverty is that the parents' economic disadvantages will be passed on to the children. If income inequality were highly intergenerational or highly racialized, this would violate strongly held U.S. norms about equal opportunity and fairness.

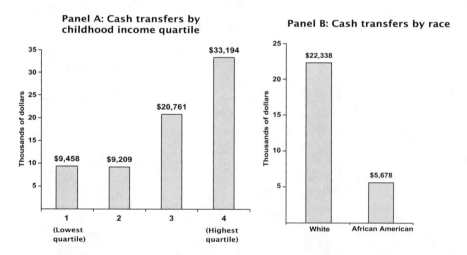

Figure 2.6. Cash transfers (in 2001 dollars) from parents to children between the ages of 18 and 34 years. (Data in Panel A from Schoeni and Ross (2005). Data in Panel B from unpublished tables provided by Robert Schoeni.) (*Note:* Cash transfers equal all cash received between ages 18 and 34. Cash transfers do not include college expenses and the value of housing and food received while living at home.)

[1]Robert Schoeni provided this unpublished data.

Many researchers have used intergenerational income and wealth correlations to measure the persistence of economic inequality from parents to children. Estimates of the correlation between parents' and children's multiyear logged incomes are typically 0.4 or higher (Corcoran, 2002; Hertz, 2005; Mazumder, 2005; Solon, 1999, 2002). Charles and Hurst (2003) reported a correlation of 0.37 between parental wealth and children's wealth as adults.

Another way analysts have examined the intergenerational persistence of income inequality is by the extent to which individuals switch income positions—for example, income quartiles—between childhood and adulthood. If there is no change in income quartiles between childhood and adulthood, then this indicates complete immobility: Economic origins perfectly predict economic destinations. In contrast, if one's adult income quartile is different from one's childhood income quartile, then this indicates complete mobility: Economic destinations are completely independent of economic origins.

Mobility researchers typically pose one or both of the following two questions: 1) How many children who are poor remain poor as adults? and 2) To what extent does being raised in a rich family guarantee that one becomes a rich adult? Many mobility analyses focus on mobility into and out of the top and bottom ends of the income distribution (see, e.g., Hertz, 2006). The percentage of children from the bottom income quartile who are still in the bottom income quartile as adults indicates the extent to which low income persists across generations—"rags to rags." The percentage of children from the bottom income quartile who reach the top income quartile as adults indicates the extent to which low-income children make it to the top—"rags to riches." The percentage of children from the top income quartile who remain in the top quartile as adults indicates the extent to which high income persists from parents to children—"riches to riches." The percentage of children from the top income quartile who drop all the way to the bottom income quintile indicates the extent of extreme downward mobility—"riches to rags."

Hertz (2006) used the 1968–2001 PSID to compare the childhood and adulthood income quartiles of individuals who were children in families who participated in the PSID. Childhood income was computed over the 5 years between 1967 and 1971, whereas adult income was measured over the 5 years between 1996 and 2000. The average age at which adult income was measured was 33. The bar graphs in Panel A of Figure 2.7 report Hertz's findings on the mobility experiences of white and African American children raised in families with low incomes (i.e., families in the bottom income quartile), whereas the bar graphs in Panel B of Figure 2.7 reflects Hertz's findings on the mobility experiences of children raised in families with high incomes (i.e., families in the top income quartile). Within-race comparisons across Panels A and B provide information on the associations between childhood income and adult income. Cross-race comparisons within a panel provide information on whether rates of upward and downward mobility differ by race for children raised in the same income quartile.

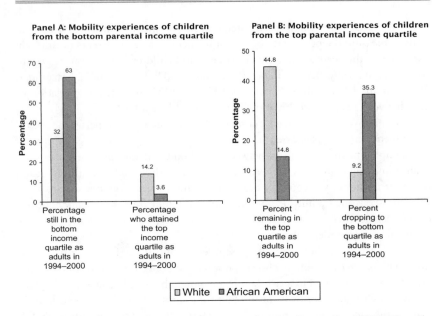

Figure 2.7. Mobility experiences of children by parental income. (*Source:* Hertz, 2005.) (*Note:* The average age at which parental income was measured was 43. The average age at which children's adult income was measured was 33.)

One message from Hertz's (2006) results in Figure 2.7 is that childhood income predicts adult income for both white and African American children. Children raised in families with low incomes (bottom quartile) are more likely than children raised in families with high incomes (top quartile) to have low incomes as adults and are less likely than children raised in families with high incomes to achieve high incomes as adults. First look at white children. Thirty-two percent of white children from low-income families but only approximately nine percent of white children from high-income families have low incomes as adults. Approximately 45% of white children from high-income families but only about 14% of white children from low-income families are in the top income quartile as adults. The same pattern holds for African American children: Sixty-three percent of African American children from low-income families but only about thirty-five percent of African American children from high-income families have low incomes as adults. Approximately 15% of African American children from high-income families but only 3.6% of African American children from low-income families have high incomes as adults.

The second message in Figure 2.7 is that upward mobility is more common for white children, and downward mobility is more common for African American children (Hertz, 2006). Most white children raised in low-income families are upwardly mobile: 68% escape having low incomes as adults and about 14% go from "rags to riches," that is, are in high-income families as adults. Rates of upward mobility are lower for African American children raised in low-income families: Only 37% of African American children from low-income families escape having low incomes as adults, and only 3.6% of African American children from low-income families go from "rags to riches." Many African American children raised in high-income families are downwardly mobile: About 85% of high-income African American children do not have high incomes as adults and approximately 35% go from "riches to rags." Downward mobility is less common for white children raised in high-income families: about 45% are in high-income families as adults and only about 9% go from "riches to rags."

Race and parental income each predict children's futures. Within a racial group, children from high-income families are more likely than children from low-income families to be high-income adults (Hertz, 2006). Within an income quartile, African American children are less likely to be upwardly mobile and more likely to be downwardly mobile than are white children. African American children from low-income families are twice as likely as white children from low-income families to have low incomes as adults (63% versus 32%). African American children from high-income families are one third as likely as white children from high-income families to remain in the top income quartile as adults (14.8% versus 44.8%) and are almost 4 times more likely to drop down into the bottom income quartile (35.3% versus 9.2%). In fact, African American children from high-income families are more likely than white children from low-income families to have low incomes as adults. These race differences in mobility are distressing in light of the facts that African American children are several times more likely than white children to live in low-income families and are much less likely than white children to live in high-income families (see Figure 2.4).

One issue is whether these large associations between parental income and children's adult income are due to differences in parental attributes that are correlated with income (e.g., parental education, family structure, parental personality traits, parents' expectations for their children). That is, do the same attributes that cause parents to have high incomes also enable them to raise successful children? Analysts typically explore this by regressing a measure of children's adult economic status on parental income and race, with and without controlling for parental attributes such as family structure and parents' education levels, language skills, assets, disabilities, occupations, union memberships, personality traits, and expectations for children (Brooks-Gunn & Duncan, 1997; Corcoran, 2002; Corcoran & Kunz, 2007; Duncan & Brooks-Gunn, 1997, Mayer 1998). These researchers typically find the associations between parental income and children's adult economic status drop by one quarter to one half when controls are added but remain moderate to large in size.

A second issue is what processes explain the transmission of income inequality across the generations parental advantages are controlled for. How and why does growing up in a poor (or rich) family affect children's adult incomes? One prominent argument is the investment model: Poor parents invest less in children's education than do more affluent parents because poor parents devote all or most of their time and money to meeting basic consumption needs (Corcoran, 2002). Brooks-Gunn and Duncan (1997) and McLoyd (1998), for instance, hypothesized that parents who are poor are more stressed, more likely to have authoritarian parenting styles, more likely to live in unsafe neighborhoods with poorly funded schools, and less likely to provide cognitively stimulating home environments. There is some empirical support for the investment model. Parental income is positively correlated with children's years of schooling, and children's years of schooling strongly predict their adult incomes (Brooks-Gunn & Duncan, 1997; Corcoran, 2002; Hertz, 2005, 2006).

CONCLUSION

Millions of children experience long-term poverty. Roughly 1 in 20 white children and 1 in 3 African American children lived in poor families for 6 or more of the 10 years between 1987 to 1997. More than 1 in 5 African Americans were poor for 9 or 10 of those years. Long-term poverty has negative consequences for these children's quality of life during childhood and the transition from school to work and for their economic futures.

Race differences in children's economic resources are high. African American families have higher long-term poverty rates, lower long-term incomes, and less wealth than white families. African American children are several times more likely than white children to be at the bottom of the income distribution, whereas white children are many times more likely than African American children to be at the top of the income distribution. Among families with the same family structure, incomes, and parental education, African American families have fewer assets than white families, and African American families are more likely to have poor relatives and less likely to have middle-class relatives than white families. These childhood resource disparities mean that African American children are more likely than are white children to experience material hardships as they grow up, are less likely than white children to receive financial help from parents as they leave home and set up independent households, and will have lower adult incomes, on average, than will white children.

But even when African American children are raised in similar economic conditions as white children, they are less likely than whites to be upwardly mobile and more likely to be downwardly mobile. Upward mobility is common for low-income white children but not for low-income African American children. Downward mobility is common for high-income African American children but not for high-income white children. African American children are handicapped both by race and class in the contest for adult economic success.

How might we improve the life chances of children, especially minority children, raised in long-term poverty? A commonly proposed solution is to use the public education system to level the playing field. After all, one role of education is to facilitate economic mobility. Rouse and Barrow (2006) cited Martin Luther King, Jr. as having written that "the job of the school is to teach so well that family background is no longer an issue" (p. 100).

Barnett and Belfield (2006) review the research on the extent to which preschool programs affect children's short-term and long-term developmental and socioeconomic outcomes. They conclude that "U.S. programs are effective across a wide set of outcomes" (p. 100) and cite two programs—Abecedarian and the Perry Preschool Program—as being particularly effective. Barnett and Belfield argued that one educational strategy for improving the mobility chances of children from low-income families would be to invest more in intensive preschool education programs for disadvantaged children, like Abercedarian and Perry Preschool. They warn that successful programs are expensive and are long term, typically having highly qualified, well-paid teachers and low student–teacher ratios and providing many hours of service over multiple years.

A second strategy to improve opportunities for children from low-income families is by reforming elementary and secondary public education. Rouse and Barrow (2006) reviewed research on the effectiveness of schools in promoting mobility and on popular educational interventions and reforms including charter schools, vouchers, school accountability programs, summer school, grade retention, smaller schools, and class-size experiments. Rouse and Barrow concluded that as currently constituted, U.S. schools are more likely to replicate the status quo than to equalize opportunity. According to Rouse and Barrow, "Children from well-to-do families attend better schools than children from poor families. As a result, rather than encouraging upward mobility, U.S. public schools tend to reinforce the transmission of low economic status from parents to children" (p. 78). They identify smaller schools and class sizes, summer school programs, and grade retention as promising strategies that could improve the quality of schooling available to poor children. They do not recommend vouchers or charter schools based on the research evidence but are cautiously optimistic that institutional accountability systems could provide small improvements for children from low-income families.

REFERENCES

Barnett, W.S., & Belfield, C.R. (2006). Early childhood development and social mobility. *The Future of Children, 16*(2), 73–98.

Beverly, S.G. (2001). Measures of material hardship: Rationale and recommendations. *Journal of Poverty, 5,* 23–41.

Brooks-Gunn, J., & Duncan, G. (1997). The effects of poverty. *The Future of Children, 7,* 55–71.

Charles, K., & Hurst, E. (2003). Intergenerational wealth correlations. *Journal of Political Economy, 11*(6), 1155–1182.

Chiteji, N., & Hamilton, D. (2002). Family connections and the black/white wealth gap. *Review of Black Political Economy, 30*(1), 9–27.

Corcoran, M. (2002). Mobility, persistence and the consequences of poverty for children: Child and adult outcomes. In S.D. Danziger & R.H. Haveman (Eds.), *Understanding poverty* (pp. 127–161). Cambridge: Harvard University Press.

Corcoran, M., & Kunz, J. (2007). Do black and white students start out on an equal footing in the race for success? In M. Kim (Ed.), *Race and economic opportunity in the twenty-first century* (pp. 187–204). New York: Routledge.

Corcoran, M., & Matsudaira, J. (2005). Is it getting harder to get ahead? Economic attainment in early adulthood for two cohorts. In R.A. Settersteim, F.F. Furstenberg, & R.G. Rumbaut (Eds.), *On the frontier of adulthood* (pp. 356–395). Chicago: University of Chicago Press.

Duncan, G., & Brooks-Gunn, J. (1997). (Eds.). *Consequences of growing up poor.* New York: Russell Sage Foundation.

Gittleman, M., & Wolff, E.N. (2004). Racial differences in patterns of wealth accumulation. *Journal of Human Resources, 39*(1), 193–227.

Gittleman, M., & Wolff, E.N. (2007). Racial and ethnic differences in wealth. In M. Kim (Ed.), *Race and economic opportunity in the twenty-first century* (pp. 29–49). New York: Routledge.

Heflin, C., & Pattilo, M. (in press). Crossing class boundaries: Race, siblings and socio-economic heterogeneity. *Social Science Review.*

Hertz, T. (2005). Rags, riches, and race: The intergenerational economic mobility of black and white families in the United States. In S. Bowles, H. Gentes, & M. Osborne Groves (Eds.), *Unequal chances: Family background and economic success* (pp. 165–191). New York: Russell Sage Foundation.

Hertz, T. (2006). *Understanding mobility in America.* Washington, DC: Center for American Progress.

Jencks, C. (2002, Winter). Does inequality matter? *Daedalus, 131*(1), 49–65.

Mayer, S. (1998). *What money can't buy: Family income and children's life chances.* Cambridge, MA: Harvard University Press.

Mazumder, B. (2005). The apple falls even closer to the tree than we thought: New and revised estimates of the intergenerational inheritance of earnings. In S. Bowles, H. Gentes, & M. Osborne Groves (Eds.), *Unequal chances: Family background and economic success* (pp. 80–99). New York: Russell Sage Foundation.

McLoyd, V. (1998). Social disadvantage and child development. *American Psychologist, 53,* 185–204.

National Center for Educational Statistics. (2003). *National postsecondary student aid study.* Washington, DC: Author.

Oliver, M., & Shapiro, T.M. (2006). *Black wealth, white wealth.* New York: Routledge.

Ouellette, T., Burstein, N., Long, D., & Beecroft, E. (2004). *Measures of material hardship: Final report.* Washington, DC: U.S. Department of Health and Human Resources.

Rouse, C.E., & Barrow, L. (2006). U.S. elementary and secondary schools: Equalizing opportunity or replicating the status quo? *The Future of Children, 16*(2), 99–124.

Schoeni, R., & Ross, K. (2005). Material assistance from families during the transition to adulthood. In R.A. Settersteim, F.F. Furstenberg, & R.G. Rumbaut (Eds.), *On the frontier of adulthood* (pp. 396–416). Chicago: University of Chicago Press.

Solon, G. (1999). Intergenerational mobility in the labor market. In O. Ashenfelter & D. Card (Eds.), *Handbook of labor economics* (Vol. 3, pp. 1761–1800). Amsterdam: Elsevier Science.

Solon, G. (2002). Cross-country differences in intergenerational earnings mobility. *Journal of Economic Perspectives, 16,* 59–66.

U.S. Department of Health and Human Services. (2003). *Indicators of welfare dependence: Annual report to Congress 2003*. Available online at http://aspe.hhs.gov/HSP/indicators 03/

Wolff, E.N. (2006). Changes in household wealth in the 1980s and 1990s in the U.S. In E.N. Wolff (Ed.), *International perspectives on household wealth* (pp. 1–18). Cheltenham Glos, UK: Elgar Publishing.

3

How Childhood Poverty and Income Affect Children's Cognitive Functioning and School Achievement

Vonnie C. McLoyd and Kelly M. Purtell

The sharp rise in childhood poverty during the early 1980s and persistently high rates of childhood poverty through the late 1990s generated intense scholarly interest in the cognitive and social development of children who are poor. This interest is manifested most strikingly by the publication of numerous edited volumes and special issues of journals devoted to the topic. In addition to bringing fresh perspectives to the study of childhood poverty, this research, almost exclusively correlational in nature, yielded several important insights. Scholars focused attention for the first time on the dynamics and contexts of childhood poverty, producing evidence that 1) most poor children are only temporarily poor, 2) ethnic disparities in persistent poverty are much larger than ethnic disparities in poverty at single points in time, 3) poor African American children are much more likely than poor European American children to live in poor neighborhoods, and 4) persistent poverty compromises children's development, especially in the cognitive domain, to a much greater degree than does transitory or occasional poverty (Duncan, 1991; Duncan & Brooks-Gunn, 1997; Duncan & Rodgers, 1988).

Other issues around which scholarship of this era coalesced included the effectiveness of various antipoverty programs (e.g., Barnett, 1995; Olds & Kitzman, 1993), the application of research on children who are poor and their families to welfare policy and practice (Danziger & Danziger, 1995), and the processes that mediate and temper the adverse effects of poverty and economic stress on child development (e.g., Duncan & Brooks-Gunn, 1997; Huston, Garcia Coll, & McLoyd, 1994; Korbin, 1992). Scholarly interest in these topics

53

has remained high (e.g., Arnold & Doctoroff, 2003; Bradley & Corwyn, 2002; Mistry, Biesanz, Taylor, Burchinal, & Cox, 2004).

Relatively new to the landscape of poverty research is a generation of experimental studies assessing the effects of welfare reform and different welfare and employment policies on child well-being (e.g., Chase-Lansdale et al., 2003; Gennetian et al., 2002; Gennetian & Miller, 2002; Morris, Bloom, Kemple, & Hendra, 2003; Morris, Huston, Duncan, Crosby, & Bos, 2001). The impetus for these experimental studies was the Personal Responsibility and Work Opportunity Reconciliation Act of 1996 (PL 104-193)—popularly known as *PRWORA* and *welfare reform*—and federal waivers granted to states to implement and test welfare reform policies in anticipation of federal welfare reform legislation.

In this chapter, we highlight what these expansive bodies of research tell us about the relationship between poverty and variations in income and children's cognitive functioning and school achievement and the common processes that appear to mediate these relations. We begin with a brief discussion of findings from correlational research, including work published since the late 1990s. We then turn to experimental studies of the effects of different welfare and employment policies on these domains of child functioning, contrasting the effects of interventions that provided income supplements to the effects of interventions that did not. Two issues are of special interest: first, whether findings from interventions that provided income supplements generally converge with those from correlational studies linking economic disadvantage and child functioning and, second, whether correlational research and experimental studies point to similar mediating influences. On the basis of our review and analyses, we conclude that 1) these disparate bodies of research provide strong evidence that high levels of income facilitate cognitive and academic functioning in children who are economically disadvantaged, 2) out-of-home experiences (e.g., quality day care; adult-supervised, organized after-school activities) may be as potent a mediator of income effects as home-based cognitive stimulation and parental child rearing behavior, and 3) because of the potential implications for policy and practice, the search for processes that explain the effects of poverty and low income on children's cognitive and academic functioning needs to be expanded well beyond the home and family context.

CORRELATIONAL RESEARCH ASSESSING POVERTY AND FAMILY INCOME IN RELATION TO CHILDREN'S COGNITIVE FUNCTIONING AND SCHOOL ACHIEVEMENT

Family income and poverty status are significant predictors of preschoolers' cognitive-linguistic performance (e.g., intelligence quotient [IQ] scores, verbal comprehension, expressive language), even after accounting for maternal education, family structure, ethnicity, and other differences between low- and high-income families. Moreover, poverty status at 3 years of age predicts children's cognitive ability scores at age 5, even with IQ scores at age 3 controlled (Duncan, Brooks-Gunn, & Klebanov, 1994; Linver, Brooks-Gunn, & Kohen, 2002; Mistry et al., 2004; Yeung, Linver, & Brooks-Gunn, 2002). Numerous studies have now documented that the effects of between-group differences in the income-to-needs ratio on young children's cognitive-linguistic performance are nonlinear, with positive effects being substantially larger among children in families at the lower end of the income distribution (Duncan & Brooks-Gunn, 1997; Smith, Brooks-Gunn, & Klebanov, 1997) and virtually nonexistent among children in very affluent families (Mistry et al., 2004).

Findings from analyses of rates of change in the income-to-needs ratio within families—a more rigorous approach to estimating income effects—are in line with evidence of nonlinear effects found in between-group analyses. In particular, studies examining *patterns of change in income over time within individual families* and associations between these patterns and child outcomes report that change in the family's income-to-needs ratio is of considerable importance for cognitive-linguistic development among children who are poor but of markedly diminished significance for children from nonpoor families (Dearing, McCartney, & Taylor, 2001; Mistry et al., 2004). Among 3-year-old poor children, decreases in their family's income-to-needs ratio during the first 3 years of life are associated with worse outcomes (e.g., poor school readiness, less receptive language, less expressive language), whereas increases in their family's income-to-needs ratio are associated with better outcomes. Indeed, when 3-year-olds who are poor experience gains in their family's income-to-needs ratio of 1 standard deviation above the mean, their cognitive-linguistic performance matches that of children from nonpoor families (Dearing et al., 2001).

Poverty's link to decreased cognitive-linguistic functioning during the preschool years foreshadows its association to diminished school achievement in primary and secondary school. On average, children who are poor or from low socioeconomic status (SES) families perform significantly less well than nonpoor and middle-class children on various indicators of academic achievement, including emergent literacy and math skills, achievement test scores, grade retention, course failures, placement in special education, high school graduation rate, high school dropout rate, and completed years of schooling (for reviews of this research, see Arnold & Doctoroff, 2003; Bradley & Corwyn, 2002; McLoyd, 1998b). This economic disparity begins very early in children's school careers. For example, national survey data indicate that only 38% of children whose mothers had the least education entered kindergarten able to recognize letters, compared with 86% of children whose mothers had the most education (Arnold & Doctoroff, 2003). Consistent with associations found in between-group analyses, longitudinal research documents a link between within-family, over-time increases in income-to-needs and improvements in academic competence among third graders (Ackerman, Brown, & Izard, 2004). Like cognitive functioning during the preschool years, school achievement typically declines with increases in the duration of poverty (McLoyd, 1998b), although this persistence-of-poverty effect is greatly attenuated when child cognitive ability and maternal education are taken into account (Ackerman et al., 2004).

Both timing of poverty and timing of increases in family income appear to moderate the effects of income on children's school achievement. Although differences in the timing of poverty *within* the preschool period appear to have no effects on achievement scores or classroom placement (Pagani, Boulerice, & Tremblay, 1997; Smith et al., 1997), there is evidence that poverty during the first 5 years of life is far more detrimental to completed years of schooling than poverty during middle childhood and adolescence (Duncan, Yeung, Brooks-Gunn, & Smith, 1998). This timing effect likely reflects the influence of school readiness and, in turn, teachers' affective responses and expectancies, both of which predict later school achievement (Duncan et al., 1998; McLoyd, 1998b). The timing of increases in family income during the primary school years also appears to matter. Longitudinal analyses suggest that within-family increases in income between first and third grade are associated with much larger increases in children's academic functioning than are within-family increases in income between third and fifth grade. Deficits in cognitive skills at school entry and the consolidation of deficiencies early in elementary school appear to progressively constrain the extent to which children's academic performance changes in response to changes in their family's income-to-needs ratio (Ackerman et al., 2004). These findings also may point to a more generalized decrease with child age in the influence of family characteristics on achievement and conversely, an increase in importance of extrafamilial factors and settings (e.g., school and classroom characteristics) for children's learning and achievement.

Physical Health Status as a Mediator of Family-Level Income and Poverty Effects

Impairment of children's physical health status at birth and diminution of children's access to resources that buffer the negative effects of perinatal complications are major pathways by which socioeconomic disadvantage hinders cognitive development during the early years. Because of inadequate nutrition and substandard, delayed, or total lack of prenatal care, poor infants are overrepresented in samples of infants born prematurely (i.e., gestational age of 36 weeks or less and birth weight of less than 2,500 g) (Crooks, 1995). Prematurity, especially extremely low birth weight (less than 1,250 g), increases infants' risk for a series of respiratory, neurological, and cognitive problems, including birth asphyxia, apnea, cerebral palsy, seizure disorders, visual and motor coordination problems, intellectual disabilities, and learning disabilities (Bradley et al., 1994; Crooks, 1995). Increased severity of illness during the perinatal period predicts lower performance on IQ tests and tests of verbal skills (Sameroff, 1986; Siegel, 1982). Early first trimester initiation of prenatal care is associated with a reduction in low birth weight (Frank, Strobino, Salkever, & Jackson, 1992).

The health status of poor infants also is hampered by higher rates of prenatal exposure to drugs, both illegal (e.g., cocaine) and legal (e.g., nicotine, alcohol). This exposure increases perinatal complications such as reductions in birth weight, head circumference, and length of gestation, all of which are risk factors for delayed cognitive development, especially if infants are poor (Hawley & Disney, 1992; Korenman, Miller, & Sjaastad, 1995; Meisels & Plunkett, 1988; Siegel, 1982). Children who have been exposed to drugs, for example, show impaired organizational skills (e.g., the ability to complete test items that require the child to attend to several objects simultaneously or to structure the task) and language skills during the early years of life, although they are still generally within the normal range (Hawley & Disney, 1992).

Poverty and low SES increase the probability that perinatal complications will result in longer-term developmental problems. An interaction between birth status and SES is a common finding, particularly in studies of cognitive development, and reflects the fact that children who are economically disadvantaged are afforded fewer social, educational, and material resources that buffer the negative effects of perinatal complications (e.g., Escalona, 1984; Sameroff, 1986; Werner & Smith, 1982). Premature children who are born into poverty but are resilient at 3 years of age (i.e., functioning well in terms of cognitive competence, behavioral competence, health status, and growth status) have significantly more protective agents in their home environments (e.g., lower density and safer play environments, higher levels of acceptance by their caregivers, increased availability of learning materials, and more variety) than do their counterparts who are less resilient (Bradley et al., 1994).

Lead poisoning appears to be another significant pathway whereby the cognitive functioning of poor children is undermined. Children who are poor, especially those from ethnic minority backgrounds and those living in inner-city areas, have markedly higher levels of lead in their blood than do children who are not poor. This disparity results from higher rates of residence in older housing that contains lead paint (resulting in lead dust) and lead-soldered pipes (resulting in lead in drinking water) and to increased exposure to industrial and automobile air pollution and lead-contaminated soil near homes. Furthermore, lead poisoning is more prevalent among African American children than white children, irrespective of poverty status, a disparity traceable to longstanding housing discrimination that has relegated African Americans in disproportionate numbers to poor, urban neighborhoods where inadequate housing units and local-level industrialization are concentrated (Crooks, 1995; Dilworth-Bart & Moore, 2006; Massey, 1994). Income disparities in lead exposure among both pregnant women and women of childbearing age mirror those found among young children. Lead exposure can be transmitted from mother to child (and indeed across multiple generations) by crossing the placenta during pregnancy and via breast milk, risks that appear to be especially high under conditions of persistent poverty (Dilworth-Bart & Moore, 2006).

Although controversy persists regarding whether lead exposure in early life is a *cause* of lower cognitive functioning in children (for a discussion of this controversy, see Dilworth-Bart & Moore, 2006), it is indisputable that early lead exposure is negatively associated with later IQ scores after controlling for confounding variables, a finding replicated in studies of children in different countries and studies with American samples of different racial and ethnic composition. This association exists even at blood lead levels below the level considered by the federal government to be of concern (i.e., 10 ug/dl) (Dilworth-Bart & Moore, 2006). Lead exposure is also associated with lower school achievement and long-term impairment of neurological function (Needleman, Schell, Bellinger, Leviton, & Allred, 1990).

It is likely that elevated exposure to other harmful substances besides lead also contributes to the link between poverty and lower cognitive functioning. Reviews present overwhelming evidence that children who are poor or from low-income families, especially those from ethnic minority groups, face an overabundance of physical conditions beyond lead contamination that pose risks to development, including elevated exposure to pesticides, ambient air pollution, noise, poorer indoor air quality, crowding, and substandard housing (Dilworth-Bart & Moore, 2006; Evans, 2004). Achieving a deeper, more ecologically grounded understanding of the pathways through which poverty and low income adversely affect child development will require empirical tests of more complex, multilevel mediation models that incorporate cumulative exposure to a confluence of psychosocial and physical environmental risk factors (Evans, 2004; Evans & English, 2002)—work that requires a range of competencies more likely to be found in interdisciplinary teams of researchers.

Researchers have undertaken comparatively few direct tests of the extent to which health-related factors contribute to income-group differences in school achievement; however, given poverty's link to both children's physical health status and early cognitive functioning, the association between early cognitive functioning and school achievement, and the association between physical health and school achievement, it is highly probable that impaired physical health status partially mediates the link between poverty and lower school achievement (Crooks, 1995). Children who were low birth weight and who had various perinatal illnesses as infants experience greater school failure and more school-loss days (McGauhey, Starfield, Alexander, & Ensminger, 1991). Because school readiness and cognitive skills during the preschool years predict later school achievement, mediators of the impact of poverty and low SES on early cognitive functioning are also likely to be implicated in income-group differences in school achievement.

Mediating Influences of Home-Based Cognitive Stimulation

During the 1960s and 1970s, a panoply of interview and laboratory studies documented the relationship between children's cognitive functioning and countless indicators of mothers' knowledge of child development, childrearing attitudes, and childrearing practices (e.g., level of maternal stimulation of child, such as playing, talking, and elaborating on the child's activities; provision of appropriate play materials; abstractness of the mother's speech). During this era, researchers also catalogued social class differences in children's home and family environments (e.g., maternal teaching strategies, maternal speech patterns) and, on the basis of parent–child correlational data or developmental theory, inferred that these differences accounted for social class variation in children's cognitive and academic functioning. Poverty, low levels of maternal education, and other indicators of low social status were identified as predictors of both lower cognitive/ academic functioning in children and lower levels of various indicators of maternal behavior associated with children's cognitive and academic functioning (e.g., verbal and cognitive stimulation in home environment, emotional support of child, positive reinforcement) (for a discussion of these studies, see Clarke-Stewart & Apfel, 1978; McLoyd, Aikens, & Burton, 2006).

Research conducted during the 1990s and thereafter on parenting and home environmental factors as determinants of cognitive functioning in poor children diverges from 1960s-era research in that it tends to 1) emphasize social structural, rather than cultural deficiencies, as causal factors in poverty; 2) focus on income poverty rather than social class; and 3) directly assess parenting behavior, especially provision of stimulating experiences in the home, as a mediator of the relationship between family income and children's development. Another striking difference is that contemporary researchers tend to interpret links between family income and home environment within an investment model (i.e., the notion that income is associated with children's development because it enables families to invest in the human capital of their children by purchasing materials, experiences, and services that benefit the child's development and well-being) rather than within a cultural deficit model (e.g., Linver et al., 2002; Yeung et al., 2002). In short, they assume a direct link between income and home-based stimulation rather than an indirect one mediated through parenting knowledge and attitudes.

Researchers have documented a plethora of linkages between family income and children's home learning environment or the provision of cognitively stimulating experiences in the home (e.g., presence of cognitively stimulating toys, reading to child, helping child learn numbers and alphabet). Children who are poor have less home-based exposure and access to books and educational toys and experiences (e.g., shared reading), less access to a home computer or the Internet, and poorer-quality computer technology when it is available. It is estimated that children from low-SES families receive, on average, a total of only 25 hours of one-to-one picture book reading by school entry, compared with 1,000–1,700 hours for middle-class children. Income disparities also exist in the amount and quality of verbal stimulation children receive. Mothers from lower-SES families, compared with mothers from higher-SES families, talk less, provide fewer object labels, sustain conversational topics for a shorter period of time, elicit less talk from their children, and respond less contingently to their children's speech (for a review of relevant studies, see Arnold & Doctoroff, 2003; Evans, 2004; National Research Council and Institute of Medicine, 2000).

Provision of cognitively stimulating experiences in the home is a strong mediator of the relationship between family income and children's cognitive functioning and academic achievement (Duncan et al., 1994; Duncan & Brooks-Gunn, 2000; Klebanov, Brooks-Gunn, McCarton, & McCormick, 1998; Lee & Croninger, 1994; Linver et al., 2002; Yeung et al., 2002), although it appears to play a smaller role in mediating the effects of *across time, within-family income changes* on young children's cognitive performance than mediating the effects of average income (Dearing et al., 2001). Other variables such as maternal sensitivity appear to play a much weaker role in mediating the link between family income and children's cognitive functioning (Mistry et al., 2004). Further, these studies have yielded strong, consistent evidence that the relationship between family income and quality of home environment is nonlinear, such that the home environments of children in low-income households are particularly sensitive to income and income changes. The quality of children's home environment decreases as families' income-to-need ratios decline and as duration of poverty increases. Moreover, improvements in family income have the strongest effects on the quality of children's home environment if children were born poor (versus not born poor) or spent more time in poverty (Dubow & Ippolito, 1994; Garrett, Ng'andu, & Ferron, 1994).

In response to concerns that the reported income–home environment link and the home environment–child functioning link are spurious (i.e., that they reflect unmeasured individual differences or omitted variables related to income, income changes, home environment, and child outcomes), Votruba-Drzal (2003) used a longitudinal, fixed-effects model to control for stable omitted differences between individuals (e.g., mother and child cognitive abilities) by comparing individuals to themselves over time, an analytic strategy that holds these characteristics constant. This more rigorous test revealed nonlinear relations that parallel those reported previously (Dubow & Ippolito, 1994; Garrett et al., 1994). In particular, Votruba-Drzal's analyses of the level of cognitive stimulation children received in their homes during the transition to school (ages 3–4 years and 7–8 years) indicated that household income is positively related to cognitive stimulation and, more importantly, that over-time improvements and reductions in family income have much stronger impacts on cognitive stimulation in the home environments of children from low-income families than those of children from middle-income families.

Linver and her colleagues (Linver et al., 2002; Yeung et al., 2002) compared the explanatory power of an *investment model* (as noted previously, the notion that low family income hinders children's development because it severely limits families' ability to invest in the human capital of their children by purchasing materials, experiences, and services that benefit child development and well-being) with that of a *family stress model* (i.e., the notion that low family income is detrimental to children's development because of its association with parents' nonmonetary resources, such as their emotional well-being and interactions with their children) (Conger et al., 2002; Elder, Nguyen, & Caspi, 1985; Gutman, McLoyd & Toyokawa, 2005). These comparisons, based on correlational data, indicate that income effects on young children's cognitive functioning are better explained by an investment model than a family stress model, whereas a family stress model better accounts for income effects on children's socioemotional functioning (e.g., externalizing and internalizing behavior) (Linver et al., 2002; Yeung et al., 2002). Subsequent analyses demonstrating that maternal sensitivity and depressive symptoms are much weaker mediators of the family income–cognitive/linguistic link than the family income–social competence link are consistent with this conclusion (Mistry et al., 2004).

Although correlational research points to home-based cognitive stimulation as a robust mediator of income effects, other parental factors (e.g., parents' involvement in children's schooling, beliefs and attitudes about learning) and extrafamilial factors (e.g., quality of preschool, kindergarten, and grade school; teacher expectancies and behavior) have been implicated in income disparities in children's cognitive functioning and school achievement (Arnold & Doctoroff, 2003; Bradley & Corwyn, 2002; Hess & Holloway, 1984; McLoyd, 1998b). It is likely that as children age, home environment and parental factors diminish in their potency as proximal mediating influences, whereas extrafamilial factors and settings increase in importance as proximal mediators of income effects. In the next section, we consider the issue of mediating processes in more detail. We discuss findings from experimental studies of welfare and employment policies, giving focal attention to points of convergence and divergence between these findings and findings from correlational research discussed in the first section of this chapter.

EXPERIMENTAL TESTS OF EMPLOYMENT-BASED WELFARE AND ANTIPOVERTY POLICIES

The core goals of the 1996 federal welfare reform law (PRWORA) are to reduce long-term welfare dependency, increase employment-based self-support, encourage marriage, and discourage out-of-wedlock childbearing—not to directly enhance the well-being of poor children. The law voided the longstanding principle of federal entitlement to assistance for poor children and adults alike (i.e., Aid to Families with Dependent Children [AFDC]). It also 1) replaced AFDC and several related programs with state block grants known as Temporary Assistance for Needy Families (TANF); 2) mandated that recipients of public assistance be working within 2 years of the time they start to receive assistance; 3) lowered to 12 months the-age-of-child criterion for exempting parents' work requirements (in prior provisions, mothers of children under 3 years old were exempt from mandatory work-related activities); 4) imposed a 5-year lifetime limit on assistance in the form of cash aid, work slots, and noncash aid such as vouchers to children and families who are poor, regardless of whether parents can find employment; and

5) required states to have a certain proportion of their welfare caseloads meet work requirements (Greenberg et al., 2002). The law granted states numerous options and discretionary powers—for example, the option to require work of parents with children under 12 months of age, impose caps so that payments do not increase if recipients have additional children, and require recipients of public assistance to be working sooner than 2 years from the time they start to receive assistance (Morris et al., 2001; Zaslow, McGroder, & Moore, 2000).

Although sweeping in its changes, PRWORA was the denouement of a more gradual process begun during the 1960s to push welfare recipients toward higher levels of employment-based self-support (Morris et al., 2001). States' efforts to promote employment and reduce welfare gained full momentum during the mid- to late 1980s, and by the early 1990s, a large number of states had been granted waivers of AFDC rules to experiment with changes in welfare provisions (Morris et al., 2001). States' receipt of waivers from the federal government to experiment with changes in welfare provisions was conditional on use of a *random assignment design* and evaluation of the program (Gennetian & Morris, 2003). States mixed and matched several kinds of welfare and employment policies, and the resulting diversity of programs provided an opportunity to assess the comparative effects of different program features on child well-being.

Because some of these experimental programs provided income supplements to families, whereas others did not, a comparison of these categories of programs offers clues about how additional income might affect the development of children who are poor. Findings from any single program with an income supplement require tenuous statements about the effects of income per se because benefits and services within a program typically were offered as a package, making it impossible to identify the separate effects of different components of the program. However, consideration of findings across multiple programs whose common feature is income supplements (with a mixture of other program services) increases confidence in the *causal* effects of income supplements.

Direct Effects

Morris and colleagues (2001) examined the findings from five large-scale studies that together assessed the effects on preschoolers and elementary school age children of 11 different employment-based welfare and antipoverty programs aimed primarily at single-parent families. Morris and colleagues classified the programs on the basis of three features: earnings supplements, mandatory employment services, and time limits on welfare receipt. Four of the programs offered *earnings supplements* to compensate for some of the shortcomings of the labor market and to make work more financially rewarding. Some programs provided supplements outside of the welfare system (e.g., New Hope program) (Bos et al., 1999), whereas others provided earnings supplements within the welfare system by raising the earnings disregard—that is, the amount of earnings that were not counted as income in calculating the amount of a family's welfare benefit. Earnings disregards allowed welfare recipients to keep more of their welfare dollars as their earnings increased, whereas under AFDC, welfare recipients experienced sharp reductions in welfare dollars as their earnings rose. These programs differed in a number of respects, however. Some made earnings supplements contingent on full-time employment (at least 30 hours per week), whereas others provided earnings supplements for any amount of work. Some programs included additional components (e.g., child care subsidies, as in the New Hope program), but provision of supplements was the sole feature that the four programs in this category shared.

Six of the programs provided *mandatory employment services* (e.g., education, training, immediate job search) in which parents were required to participate to receive cash welfare benefits. These programs were generally successful in increasing employment rates but did not provide earnings supplements or institute time limits on family's eligibility for welfare benefits.

One of the programs put *time limits* on families' eligibility for welfare benefits. Receipt of cash assistance was limited to 24 or 36 months (depending on parents' level of disadvantage) in any 60-month period. Time limits were combined with mandatory employment services and a small earnings supplement in the form of an enhanced earnings disregard (Morris et al., 2003).

In all of these studies, parents were randomly assigned to either a *program group*, which had access to the new services and benefits and was subject to the new rules, or a *control group*, which received welfare benefits and were subject to rules governing welfare receipt that existed in the locale where the study was conducted. In most instances, control group members were eligible for cash assistance through AFDC. Children were assessed 2–4 years after random assignment and ranged in age from approximately 5 to 12 years at the time of assessment. For the synthesis of child effects, Morris and colleagues focused on a subset of measures that were similar across studies.

Morris and colleagues' synthesis identified a clear-cut pattern of effects. Programs that included earning supplements increased both parental employment and income. Moreover, these programs had modest, positive effects on a range of child behaviors. All of these programs had overall positive effects on children's school achievement (by approximately 10%–15%, as compared with children in the control groups) and some also reduced behavior problems, increased positive social behavior, or improved children's overall health. None of the programs, it is important to note, had overall negative impacts on children's behaviors. Some programs, such as New Hope, had effects primarily on boys, whereas others had stronger effects for girls. There is no clear pattern of gender differences when looking across different experiments (Morris et al., 2001).

Overall, programs with mandatory employment services successfully increased parental employment rates and reduced welfare receipt but generally left family income unchanged because participants lost welfare benefits as their earnings increased. These programs had few effects on children, and the effects found were mixed in direction. The pattern of effects among these programs appeared to be more closely linked to particular sites than to program characteristics (Morris et al., 2001). The program with time limits produced an increase in parental employment and a modest increase in income but had no consistent pattern of effect on child outcomes. Because this program was combined with mandatory employment services and a small earnings supplement, it is impossible to sort out the impact of time limits (Morris et al., 2001).

Findings from the evaluation of the New Hope program are illustrative of the effects of programs that offered earnings supplements. As expected, 2 years after random assignment, the New Hope program increased the economic resources of program group members. Program group members reported working more quarters of the year, working more total hours, and having a higher total income. The average total income for the 2 years after random assignment was $28,100 for program group members compared with $25,895 for control group members. In addition, program group members were less likely to report periods without health insurance. Two years after random assignment, teachers (who were unaware of whether the child was in the experimental group or control group) reported that boys in the New Hope program showed more academic skills in the classroom compared with boys in the control group. In addition, compared with their control group counterparts, boys in the New Hope program were more likely to expect that they would attend and complete college and aspired to higher prestige managerial and professional occupations. There were no program impacts on girls (Huston et al., 2001).

At the 5-year follow-up (2 years after families left the program), most of the economic impacts of the New Hope program had faded. There was no significant difference between program group parents and control group parents in the number of quarters per year that they were employed; however, the New Hope program participants had more stable jobs that paid slightly higher wages than did their control group counterparts. It is also notable that the average annual income of parents in the program group during the full 5-year period increased by 7% (Huston et al., 2003).

A direct assessment of children's academic skills at the 5-year follow-up revealed positive effects. Children in the New Hope program scored significantly higher than children in the control group on the Broad Reading component of the Woodcock-Johnson Tests of Achievement (Woodcock & Johnson, 1990). They also received higher overall achievement scores, although the effect was just short of statistical significance. Both male and female children in the New Hope program scored higher than their peers in the control group, but the effect was stronger for boys. Teachers still rated boys in the New Hope program significantly higher on academic abilities than their control group counterparts, but the program had no impact on girls' academic abilities as rated by teachers. Compared with parents in the control group, parents in the program group reported higher reading and literacy skills among both their sons and daughters (Huston et al., 2003, 2005).

Mediating Processes

All of the earnings supplement programs that Morris and colleagues reviewed had in common one result—an increase in employment and income—but no one mechanism appeared to be responsible for the beneficial effects of these programs on children. Within the corpus of relevant studies, none of the outcomes considered to be possible mediators of effects (i.e., family relations, child care, home environment, parenting practices, parental well-being) was affected across all of programs (Morris et al., 2001). Child-rearing practices, parents' psychological functioning, and children's home environment were thought to be key pathways through which earnings supplement programs would affect children, but, overall, programs had remarkably few effects on these factors (Gennetian & Miller, 2002; Huston et al., 2001; Morris et al., 2001).

Child care effects were more prominent in a relative sense, though as already indicated, effects were not uniform across programs. Some programs increased the use of formal and stable child care and children's participation in after-school activities, whereas others did not (Gennetian & Miller, 2002; Huston et al., 2001; Morris et al., 2001; Morris & Michalopoulos, 2003). For example, almost half of the parents in the experimental group of the New Hope evaluation used the child care subsidy, and at 24 months post random assignment, children ages 3–12 in the experimental group had spent almost twice as many months in center-based care (for preschool and school-age children) and more than twice as many months in school-based extended day care as children in the control group. Moreover, among the 9- to 12-year-olds, children in the program group spent more time in adult-supervised, organized after-school activities (e.g., lessons, sports, clubs, youth groups) than did children in the control group (Huston et al., 2001). It is notable that in the case of the New Hope program, in order to receive a subsidy to help cover the cost of child care for children age 13 or younger, parents had to enroll their children in child care homes or centers that were either state-licensed or county-certified.

There is evidence that center-based care, on average, is more likely than home-based care to enhance cognitive, academic, and social skills (Lamb, 1998; Loeb, Fuller, Kagan, & Carrol, 2004). Loeb and colleagues' (2004) longitudinal study of the effects of type, quality, and stability of child care suggests that when poor children are enrolled in high-quality center care, they accrue more benefits from such care than their advantaged counterparts. These researchers also found that among children from low-income families who were between 12 and 42 months old when their mother entered welfare-to-work programs, those in center-based child care programs had higher levels of performance on several indicators of cognitive functioning than children who remained with individual kith and kin providers (controlling for income and numerous maternal and child background factors). Quality of care (based on half-day observations of centers and home-based care settings) as well as stability of care were associated with higher school readiness and cognitive functioning, but even taking these factors into account, center care predicted more positive cognitive outcomes. Likewise, extended child care for elementary school children has been linked to higher school achievement; this appears to be due partly to tutoring and help with homework received by children in this setting (Pierce, Hamm, & Vandell, 1999; Posner & Vandell, 1999).

Taken as a whole, the pattern of findings across the three categories of experimental programs is consistent with evidence from correlational research suggesting that income can have salutary effects on the development of children who are poor; however, contrary to findings from correlational studies, home-based cognitive stimulation did not emerge as a prominent or core mediator of the experimental effects on children. Rather, these studies suggest that increases in family income enhance children's achievement less through changes in parental behavior and home environment and more through changes in out-of-home experiences. They also challenge poverty researchers conducting correlational field studies to expand the search for mediating processes beyond the home and family context and to give special attention to extrafamilial factors that can be readily regulated through public policy.

CONCLUSION

The research reviewed in this chapter suggests that raising the incomes of poor families is likely to enhance children's early cognitive functioning, school readiness, and academic achievement. Higher levels of income allow parents to increase human capital in their children by providing more learning experiences outside and inside the home. Raising the incomes of poor families can be achieved through a variety of strategies, including earnings supplements and earnings disregards that are part of government-supported work programs of the sort discussed in this chapter and the provision of more generous earnings supplements under the Earned Income Tax Credit (Smeeding, Rainwater, & Burtless, 2001; Wilson, 1996). Compared with universal social insurance policies that operate in many European countries (e.g., universal child allowances, universal health care, free or inexpensive child care), these "make work pay" strategies are more in keeping with America's strong capitalistic values, belief in individualistic explanations of economic inequality, and perception of current social and economic conditions as equitable (McLoyd, 1998a).

The acute need for income supports is underscored by evidence that America's exceptionally high rate of child poverty, compared with the rates in other Western industrialized countries, is partly due to a comparatively high incidence of low-paid employment. A substantial proportion of variance in cross-national poverty rates is accounted for by cross-national variation in the prevalence of low-paid employment, defined as the proportion of a nation's full-time workers who earn less than 65% of national median earnings on full-time jobs. In the 1990s, of 14 industrialized countries, the United States had the highest proportion of such workers (Smeeding et al., 2001).

Findings from the experimental tests of employment-based welfare and antipoverty policies reviewed here do not point to use of formal child care as a consistent mediator of the positive effects of these policies on children's school achievement. Nonetheless, a compelling case can be made that any "make work pay" strategy that purports commitment to the well-being of children who are poor should encompass substantial child care subsidies and increases in the availability of high-quality, formal, center-based child care; after-school activities; and other opportunities for supervised structured activities for children. There is ample evidence from a diverse array of field studies that these resources boost the cognitive functioning, literacy skills, and school readiness of poor children (e.g., Lamb, 1998; Loeb et al., 2004; National Institute of Child Health and Human Development [NICHD] Early Child Care Research Network, 2000; Pierce et al., 1999; Posner & Vandell, 1999).

The nonlinear effects of income on cognitive and academic functioning documented in numerous studies are consistent with the view that "reducing poverty is associated with improved outcomes for children, whereas increasing affluence is not" (Garbarino, 1992, p. 233). They bolster the assertion that targeting primarily families who are poor, rather than middle- and upper-income families, for income subsidies and tax relief, overall, will have a more salutary impact on children's development. Barring income increments for all poor families, Duncan et al.'s (1998) research on the differential effects of the timing of poverty argues for welfare policies that give highest priority to the elimination of deep and persistent poverty during children's early years of life. It also strengthens the case for expansion of Early Head Start, an intervention established in 1994 for children from low-income families from birth to age 3 and their families (Administration for Children and Families [ACF], 2002). The national longitudinal evaluation of Early Head Start, which used a random assignment experimental design, found that at 36 months of age, program children, compared with control children, scored higher on standardized measures of cognitive and language development, engaged their parents more, and were more attentive to objects during play. In addition, compared with control parents, Early Head Start parents provided more stimulating home environments and more support for language and learning than control parents and were more likely to read to their children daily (ACF, 2002). Unfortunately, however, as with Head Start, the positive effects of Early Head Start on child functioning are unlikely to be sustained because of poor-quality schooling subsequent to the intervention and the tangle of environmental risk factors and their multiplicative adverse effects that is the lot of too many poor children in the United States.

Owing to a confluence of factors, the daily life of Americans increasingly has become part of the monetarized economy (e.g., relying on professions rather than kith and kin for child care and help with mental health problems), and as a consequence, meeting children's needs has become increasingly more dependent on parents' ability to generate cash income (Garbarino, 1992). For this reason, combined with the fact that many of the causes of poverty and the difficult life conditions confronting poor families in America are structural in nature (e.g., historic and contemporary racism in the labor market), significant progress toward closing the achievement gap between children who are poor and children who are not poor is likely to require substantial reductions in income equality in America, combined with improvements in the living conditions, nutritional status, and health care of the poor and the major institutions with which the poor interact in their daily lives.

REFERENCES

Ackerman, B.P., Brown, E.D., & Izard, C.E., (2004). The relations between contextual risk, earned income, and the school adjustment of children from economically disadvantaged families. *Developmental Psychology, 40*(2), 204–216.

Administration for Children and Families. (2002). *Making a difference in the lives of infants and toddlers and their families: Vol. 1. Impacts of Early Head Start: Final technical report.* Washington, DC: U.S. Department of Health and Human Services. Retrieved October 23, 2004, from http//www.acf.hhs.gov/programs/opre/ehs/ehs_resrch/reports/impacts_vol1/impacts_vol1.pdf

Arnold, D.H., & Doctoroff, G.L. (2003). Early education of socioeconomically disadvantaged children. *Annual Review of Psychology, 54,* 517–545.

Barnett, W.S. (1995). Long-term effects of early childhood programs on cognitive and school outcomes. *The Future of Children, 5,* 25–50.

Bos, J.M., Huston, A.C., Granger, R.C., Duncan, G.J., Brock, T.W., & McLoyd, V.C., (1999). *New hope for people with low incomes: Two-year results of a program to reduce poverty and reform welfare.* New York: Manpower Demonstration Research Corporation.

Bradley, R., & Corwyn, R. (2002). Socioeconomic status and child development. *Annual Review of Psychology, 53,* 371–399.

Bradley, R., Whiteside, L., Mundform, D., Casey, P., Kelleher, K., & Pope, S. (1994). Early indications of resilience and their relation to experiences in the home environments of low birthweight, premature children living in poverty. *Child Development, 65,* 346–360.

Chase-Lansdale, P.L., Moffitt, R.A., Lohman, B.J., Cherlin, A.J., Coley, R.L., Pittman, L.D., et al. (2003). Mothers' transitions from welfare to work and the well being of preschoolers and adolescents. *Science, 299,* 1548–1552.

Clarke-Stewart, K.A., & Apfel, N. (1978). Evaluating parental effects on child development. In L.S. Shulman (Ed.), *Review of research in education* (Vol. 6, pp. 47–119). Itasca, IL: Peacock.

Conger, R.D., Ebert-Wallace, L., Sun, Y., Simons, R.L., McLoyd, V.C., & Brody, G.H. (2002). Economic pressure in African American families: A replication and extension of the family stress model. *Developmental Psychology, 38,* 179–193.

Crooks, D. (1995). American children at risk: Poverty and its consequences for children's health, growth, and school achievement. *Yearbook of Physical Anthropology, 38,* 57–86.

Danziger, S.K., & Danziger, S. (1995). Child poverty, public policy, and welfare reform. *Children and Youth Services Review, 17*(112), 1–10.

Dearing, E., McCartney, K., & Taylor, B.A. (2001). Change in family income to needs matters more for children with less. *Child Development, 72*(6), 1779–1793.

Dilworth-Bart, J.E., & Moore, C.F. (2006). Mercy mercy me: Social injustices and the prevention of environmental pollutant exposures among ethnic minority and poor children. *Child Development, 77,* 247–265.

Dubow, E., & Ippolito, M.F. (1994). Effects of poverty and quality of the home environment on changes in the academic and behavioral adjustment of elementary school-age children. *Journal of Clinical Child Psychology, 23,* 401–412.

Duncan, G. (1991). The economic environment of childhood. In A. Huston (Ed.), *Children in poverty: Child development and public policy* (pp. 23–50). New York: Cambridge University Press.

Duncan, G., & Brooks-Gunn, J. (Eds.). (1997). *Consequences of growing up poor.* New York: Russell Sage Foundation.

Duncan, G.J., & Brooks-Gunn, J. (2000). Family poverty, welfare reform, and child development. *Child Development, 71*(1), 188–196.

Duncan, G., Brooks-Gunn, J., & Klebanov, P. (1994). Economic deprivation and early childhood development. *Child Development, 65,* 296–318.

Duncan, G., & Rodgers, W. (1988). Longitudinal aspects of childhood poverty. *Journal of Marriage and the Family, 50,* 1007–1021.

Duncan, G., Yeung, W., Brooks-Gunn, J., & Smith, J. (1998). How much does childhood poverty affect the life chances of children? *American Sociological Review, 63,* 406–423.

Elder, G., Nguyen, T., & Caspi, A. (1985). Linking family hardship to children's lives. *Child Development, 56,* 361–375.

Escalona, S.K. (1984). Social and other environmental influences on the cognitive and personality development of low birthweight infants. *American Journal of Mental Deficiency, 88,* 508–512.

Evans, G. (2004). The environment of childhood poverty. *American Psychologist, 59*(2), 77–92.

Evans, G., & English, K. (2002). The environment of poverty: Multiple stressor exposure, psychophysiological stress, and socioemotional adjustment. *Child Development, 73*(4), 1238–1248.

Frank, R., Strobino, D., Salkever, D., & Jackson, C. (1992). Updated estimates of the impact of prenatal care on birthweight outcomes by race. *Journal of Human Resources, 27,* 631–642.

Garbarino, J. (1992). The meaning of poverty in the world of children. *American Behavioral Scientist, 35,* 220–237.

Garrett, P., Ng'andu, N., & Ferron, J. (1994). Poverty experiences of young children and the quality of their home environments. *Child Development, 65,* 331–345.

Gennetian, L.A., Duncan, G.J., Knox, V.W., Vargas, W.G., Clark-Kauffman, E., & London, A.S. (2002). *How welfare and work policies for parents affect adolescents: A synthesis of research.* New York: Manpower Demonstration Research Corporation.

Gennetian, L.A., & Miller, C. (2002). Children and welfare reform: A view from an experimental welfare program in Minnesota. *Child Development, 73*(2), 601–620

Gennetian, L.A., & Morris, P.A. (2003). The effects of time limits and make work pay strategies on the well being of children: Experimental evidence from two welfare reform programs. *Children and Youth Services Review, 25,* 17–54

Greenberg, M.H., Levin-Epstein, J., Hutson, R.Q., Ooms, T.J., Schumacher, R., Turetsky, V., et al. (2002). The 1996 welfare law: Key elements and reauthorization issues affecting children. *The Future of Children, 12*(1), 27–57.

Gutman, L., McLoyd, V.C., & Toyokawa, T. (2005). Financial strain, neighborhood stress, parenting behaviors, and adolescent functioning of urban African American boys and girls. *Journal of Research on Adolescence, 15*, 425–449.

Hawley, T., & Disney, E. (1992). Crack's children: The consequences of maternal cocaine abuse. *Social Policy Report, 6*, 1–22.

Hess, R., & Holloway, S. (1984). Family and school as educational institutions. In R.D. Parke (Ed.), *Review of child development research* (Vol. 7, pp. 179–222). Chicago: University of Chicago Press.

Huston, A.C., Duncan, G.J., Granger, R., Bos, J., McLoyd, V.C., Mistry, R., et al. (2001). Work-based antipoverty programs for parents can enhance the school performance and social behavior of children. *Child Development, 72*(1), 318–336.

Huston, A.C., Duncan, G.J., McLoyd, V.C., Crosby, D.A., Ripke, M.N., Weisner, T.S., et al. (2005). Impacts on children of a policy to promote employment and reduce poverty for low-income parents: New Hope after 5 years. *Developmental Psychology, 41*, 902–918.

Huston, A.C., Garcia Coll, C., & McLoyd, V.C. (Eds). (1994). Children and poverty [Special Issue]. *Child Development, 65*(2).

Huston, A.C., Miller, C., Richburg-Hayes, L., Duncan, G.J., Eldred, C.A., Weisner, T.S., et al. (2003). *New Hope for families and children: Five-year results of a program to reduce poverty and reform welfare.* New York: Manpower Demonstration Research Corporation.

Klebanov, P.K., Brooks-Gunn, J., McCarton, C., & McCormick, M.C. (1998). The contribution of neighborhood and family income to developmental test scores over the first three years of life. *Child Development, 69*(5), 1420–1436.

Korbin, J.E. (1992). The impact of poverty on children. *American Behavioral Scientist, 35*, 13–39.

Korenman, S., Miller, J., & Sjaastad, J. (1995). Long-term poverty and child development in the United States: Results from the NLSY. *Children and Youth Services Review, 17*, 127–155.

Lamb, M.E. (1998). Non-parental child care: Context, quality, correlates, and consequences. In W. Damon (Series Ed.), I. Sigel, & K.A. Renninger (Vol. Eds.), *Handbook of child psychology: Vol. 4. Child psychology in practice* (5th ed., pp. 73–133). New York: Wiley.

Lee, V., & Croninger, R. (1994). The relative importance of home and school in the development of literacy skills for middle-grade students. *American Journal of Education, 102*, 286–329.

Linver, M.R., Brooks-Gunn, J., & Kohen, D.E. (2002). Family process as pathways from income to young children's development. *Developmental Psychology, 38*(5), 719–734.

Loeb, S., Fuller, B., Kagan, S., & Carrol, B. (2004). Child care in poor communities: Early learning effects of type, quality, and stability. *Child Development, 75*, 47–65.

Massey, D. (1994). America's apartheid and the urban underclass. *Social Service Review, 68*, 471–487.

McGauhey, P., Starfield, B., Alexander, C., & Ensminger, M. (1991). Social environment and vulnerability of low birth weight children: A social-epidemiological perspective. *Pediatrics, 88*, 943–953.

McLoyd, V.C. (1998a). Children in poverty: Development, public policy, and practice. In W. Damon (Series Ed.) & I. Sigel, & K.A. Renninger (Vol. Eds.), *Handbook of child psychology: Vol. 4. Child psychology in practice* (5th ed., pp. 135–208). New York: Wiley.

McLoyd, V.C. (1998b). Socioeconomic disadvantage and child development. *American Psychologist, 53*, 185–204.

McLoyd, V.C., Aikens, N.L., & Burton, L.M. (2006). Childhood poverty, policy, and practice. In W. Damon (Series Ed.) & I. Sigel, & K.A. Renninger (Vol. Eds.), *Handbook of child psychology: Vol. 4. Child psychology in practice* (5th ed., pp. 700-775). New York: Wiley.

Meisels, S.J., & Plunkett, J.W. (1988). Developmental consequences of preterm birth: Are there long-term effects? In P.B. Baltes, D.L. Featherman, & R.M. Lerner (Eds.), *Life-span development and behavior* (Vol. 9, pp. 87–128). Hillsdale, NJ: Lawrence Erlbaum Associates.

Mistry, R.S., Biesanz, J.C., Taylor, L.C., Burchinal, M., & Cox, M.J. (2004). Family income and its relation to preschool children's adjustment for families in the NICHD study of early child care. *Developmental Psychology, 40*(5), 727–745.

Morris, P., Bloom, D., Kemple, J., & Hendra, R. (2003). The effects of a time-limited welfare program on children: The moderating role of parents' risk of welfare dependency. *Child Development, 74*(3), 851–874.

Morris, P.A., Huston, A.C., Duncan, G.J., Crosby, D.A., & Bos, J.M. (2001). *How welfare and work policies affect children: A synthesis of research.* New York: Manpower Demonstration Research Corporation.

Morris, P., & Michalopoulos, C. (2003). Findings from the self-sufficiency project: Effects on children and adolescents of a program that increased employment and income. *Applied Developmental Psychology, 24*, 201–239.

National Institute of Child Health and Human Development (NICHD) Early Child Care Research Network (2000). The relation of child care to cognitive and language development. *Child Development, 71*, 960–980.

National Research Council and Institute of Medicine, Committee on Integrating the Science of Early Child Development. (2000). *From neurons to neighborhoods: The science of early childhood development.* Washington, DC: National Academies Press.

Needleman, H.L., Schell, A., Bellinger, D., Leviton, A., & Allred, E. (1990). The long-term effects of low doses of lead in childhood: An 11-year follow-up report. *New England Journal of Medicine, 322*, 83–88.

Olds, D., & Kitzman, H. (1993). Review of research on home visiting for pregnant women and parents of young children. *The Future of Children, 3*, 53–92.

Pagani, L., Boulerice, B., & Tremblay, R. (1997). The influence of poverty on children's classroom placement and behavior problems. In G. Duncan & J. Brooks-Gunn (Eds.), *Consequences of growing up poor* (pp. 311–339). New York: Russell Sage Foundation.

Pierce, K.M., Hamm, J.V., & Vandell, D.L. (1999). Experiences in after-school programs and children's adjustment in first-grade classrooms. *Child Development, 70*, 756–767.

Posner, J.K., & Vandell, D.L. (1999). After-school activities and the development of low-income urban children: A longitudinal study. *Developmental Psychology, 35*, 868–879.

Sameroff, A. (1986). Environmental context of child development. *Journal of Pediatrics, 109*, 192–200.

Siegel, L. (1982). Reproductive, perinatal, and environmental factors as predictors of the cognitive and language development of preterm and full-term infants. *Child Development, 53*, 963–973.

Smeeding, T.M., Rainwater, L., & Burtless, G. (2001). U.S. poverty in a cross-national context. In S. Danziger & R. Haveman (Eds.), *Understanding poverty* (pp. 162–189). New York: Russell Sage Foundation.

Smith, J., Brooks-Gunn, J., & Klebanov, P. (1997). Consequences of living in poverty for young children's cognitive and verbal ability and early school achievement. In G. Duncan & J. Brooks-Gunn (Eds.), *Consequences of growing up poor* (pp. 132–189). New York: Russell Sage Foundation.

Votruba-Drzal, E. (2003). Income changes and cognitive stimulation in young children's home learning environments. *Journal of Marriage and Family, 65*, 341–355.

Werner, E., & Smith, R. (1982). *Vulnerable but invincible: A study of resilient children.* New York: McGraw-Hill.

Wilson, W.J. (1996). *When work disappears: The world of the new urban poor.* New York: Knopf.

Woodcock, R.W., & Johnson, M.B. (1990). *Woodcock-Johnson Psycho-Educational Battery—Revised.* Allen, TX: DLM Teaching Resources.

Yeung, W.J., Linver, M.R., & Brooks-Gunn, J. (2002). How money matters for young children's development: Parental investment and family process. *Child Development, 73*(6), 1861–1879

Zaslow, M.J., McGroder, S.M., & Moore, K.A. (2000). *The national evaluation of welfare to work strategies: Impacts on young children and their families two years after enrollment: Findings from the child outcomes study summary report.* Retrieved May 11, 2004, from http://www.aspe.hhs.gov/hsp/NEWWS/child-outcomes/summary.htm

4

Poverty, Early Literacy Achievement, and Education Reform

Julia Parkinson and Brian Rowan

The American education system, like education systems in most other nations, is characterized by significant differences in reading proficiency among children who live in poverty and those who do not. In the United States, these differences are present when children enter school and persist as children move through later grades. The National Assessment of Educational Progress (NAEP; 2004), for example, shows that only 14% of children who receive federal lunch subsidies (i.e., America's poorest children), compared with 42% of fourth-grade students who do not receive lunch subsidies, are proficient readers by the time they reach fourth grade. The NAEP data also show differences in reading proficiency among fourth graders from different racial and ethnic groups in the United States. For example, only 13% of black children and 16% of Hispanic children are proficient readers by fourth grade, compared with 41% of white children at this grade level. Finally—and perhaps most discouragingly—NAEP data show that the differences in reading achievement that exist in the fourth grade continue to exist as students move to 8th and 12th grades, demonstrating that early differences in reading achievement among social groups are not reduced as students move through the U.S. school system.[1]

This chapter takes a closer look at children's early development as readers using data from the Early Childhood Longitudinal Study–Kindergarten Class of

[1]The NAEP data can be obtained through the NAEP data explorer (http://www.ed.gov/nation-sreportcard/). In addition to documenting trends in reading achievement, the NAEP data show gaps in achievement among social groups in curricular areas other than reading.

Work on this chapter was supported by grants from the William and Flora Hewlett Foundation and the University of Michigan (through the Center for Advancing Research and Solutions for Society, David L. Featherman, Director). The authors also thank Stephen W. Raudenbush and Yu Xie for helpful comments on earlier drafts of this work.

1998–1999 (ECLS–K). ECLS–K is a large, ongoing, longitudinal study of the academic development of roughly 22,000 children who passed from kindergarten to fifth grade in U.S. schools between the years 1998 and 2003 (Rathbun & West, 2004). Sponsored by the National Center for Education Statistics of the U.S. Department of Education, ECLS–K data allow us to chart the academic development of school-age children with some precision and to examine how academic development varies for students from different family and social backgrounds attending schools of different quality. Using these data, we ask the following questions:

1. What are the current patterns of literacy achievement for students in U.S. elementary schools? In particular, how do students in poverty (who face many risk factors) fare in terms of measured reading achievement compared with children who grow up in far more privileged circumstances?

2. What targets for the achievement of children in poverty should we adopt, especially during the early years of schooling? Should we want children in poverty to achieve at the levels of the average student in American schools, or might we be bolder yet and aspire for these children to achieve at the level of our most privileged students?

3. What steps might we take to produce higher levels of reading proficiency among students in poverty? In addition, how close to achieving our goals for poor children's achievement might these steps bring us?

EXISTING APPROACHES TO IMPROVING ACHIEVEMENT FOR POOR CHILDREN

Three approaches to improving the reading achievement of students in poverty are being debated. One approach, best exemplified in Richard Rothstein's (2004) book *Class and Schools: Using Social, Economic and Educational Reform to Close the Black–White Achievement Gap*, calls for broad social and economic changes in society that directly address the underlying risk factors associated both with poverty and children's development as readers. In this chapter, we consider a variety of such factors, each of which has been shown in previous research to be associated with poverty *and* to negatively affect students' achievement. These include 1) students' ethnicity, which for complex reasons in the United States is associated with both poverty and children's achievement (Cook & Evans, 2000; Hedges & Nowell, 1998; Jencks & Phillips, 1998; Neal, 2005; Rothstein, 2004); 2) students' physical health and nutritional status, which in the United States is also associated with poverty and ethnicity (Currie, 2005; Evans, 2004; Kagan, Moore, & Bredekamp, 1995; Rothstein, 2004); 3) student behavior problems, which are sometimes symptomatic of underlying mental health disorders and which are especially prevalent in U.S. schools among black males from lower-income families (Arnold, 1997; Gutman, Sameroff, & Cole, 2003; McLeod & Kaiser, 2004; Spira & Fischel, 2005; Trzesniewski, Moffitt, Caspi, Taylor, & Maughan, 2006); and 4) students' home environment and family resources, which vary along income and ethnic lines in the

United States (Brooks-Gunn, Duncan, & Aber, 1997; Brooks-Gunn & Markman, 2005; Dauber & Epstein, 1993; Feuerstein, 2000; Foster, 2002; Garrett, Ng'andu, & Ferron, 1994; Henderson & Berla, 1994; Jackson, 2003; Klebanov, Brooks-Gunn, McCarton, & McCormick, 1998; McLoyd, 1998; Scott-Jones, 1995).[2]

One purpose of this chapter is to present data showing just how much these underlying risk factors, in fact, affect students' reading achievement at different points in elementary school. Rather than examine the effects of each risk factor alone, however, we provide an illustration of what happens to achievement when students experience multiple risks simultaneously—a situation faced by many children living in the deepest poverty in the United States.[3] Such data, we argue, provide useful information about two of the questions we asked earlier—1) How do students in the deepest poverty fare in terms of reading achievement compared with their more advantaged peers? and 2) What levels of reading achievement might we want poor children to achieve as they move through schools?

A second approach to improving the reading achievement of students in poverty involves an expansion of preschooling—especially to students in high-poverty settings. It is known from previous research, for example, that children of lower socioeconomic and minority status enter kindergarten with reading achievement scores well below those of their more advantaged peers and that a child's incoming level of achievement is highly predictive of his or her later achievement (Brooks-Gunn, Klebanov, Smith, Duncan, & Lee, 2003; Duncan & Magnuson, 2005; Jencks & Phillips, 1998; Lee & Burkam, 2002; Phillips, Crouse, & Ralph, 1998; Stipek & Ryan, 1997; West, Denton, & Reaney, 2001; Zill, 1999). As a result, many states are now working actively to expand access to high-quality early childhood education programs, especially for children in poverty. Of course, in today's education system, a wide variety of early childhood programming exists, including public and private preschool, day care, and child care, programs that operate for different lengths of time and with varying intensity and quality. Research shows that the effectiveness of such programs is highly dependent on the program type and characteristics, although many programs have significant, immediate short-term effects on children's academic achievement and several high-quality early childhood programs have been shown to promote significant long-term effects in achievement and other outcomes as well (Barnett, 1995, 2002; Ramey & Ramey, 1992).

---

[2]Many specific policy changes have been proposed to address these risk factors. These include providing poor families with direct income supports; increasing their access to health and mental health care (i.e., through expanded health insurance, better distribution of health care across geographic settings, or direct provision of health and mental health care in high poverty schools); and implementing school, family, and community intervention programs designed to improve parenting resources for low-income households.

[3]In this chapter, for example, we create a simple index that classifies children into three risk profiles: 1) a "high-risk" profile, in which students are living in poverty and show several other risk factors; 2) a "low-risk" profile, in which students come from more affluent circumstances and have low values on other risk factors; and 3) an "average-risk" profile, in which students are at the national average on both socioeconomic and other risk factors. For a discussion of the advantages and disadvantages to looking at risk factors in this way, see Burchinal et al. (2000).

In this chapter, we illustrate just how important entry levels of reading achievement are for the reading achievement of poor children at later grades in elementary schools. In particular, using data from ECLS–K, we examine the achievement trajectories of high-risk students who enter kindergarten with differing levels of reading achievement at entry. We then compare later levels of achievement for these students to the achievement levels of average and low-risk students to get a sense of just how much early childhood intervention might improve the reading achievement of students living in poverty.

A final approach to improving the academic achievement of students living in poverty involves working to improve school quality. Modern concerns with school quality date to the Coleman report (Coleman et al., 1966), but the evolution of this body of research can be traced through the 1980s literature on effective schools (e.g., Edmunds, 1979; Purkey & Smith, 1983; Rowan, Bossert, & Dwyer, 1983), through various whole-school reform programs (Borman, Hewes, Overman, & Brown, 2002), to today's emphasis on value-added models of school effectiveness (Raudenbush, 2004; Rowan, Correnti, & Miller, 2002). What this evolving literature demonstrates is that students living in poverty *in fact* attend schools of varying quality and that many school-level practices and intervention strategies can improve the quality of schools serving children in poverty. Past research, for example, shows that better patterns of resource allocation, many different dimensions of school climate and culture, and a variety of curricular and instructional interventions can improve early reading outcomes for students at risk (see, e.g., Hedges, Laine, & Greenwald, 1994a, 1994b; Slavin, Karweit, & Madden, 1989).

This chapter explores the importance of school quality to the reading achievement of children in poverty. In particular, using data from ECLS–K, we classify elementary schools into high, medium, and low levels of quality and then examine the achievement trajectories of high-risk students who attend these schools. We also compare later levels of achievement for high-risk students in schools of differing quality to the later levels of achievement attained by average and low-risk students to get a sense of just how much increasing school quality might work to improve the reading achievement of students living in poverty.

In presenting these data analyses, we illustrate three fundamental points about school reform. First, poverty and its associated risks have large and sustaining effects on children's development as proficient readers, with students living in poverty showing much lower levels of reading proficiency than their more privileged peers throughout the elementary years. This point, we argue, suggests a need for broader social and economic reform as a means to improving the reading proficiency of students living in poverty. Second, when students living in poverty enter schools ready to learn (i.e., with higher levels of reading proficiency), they experience greater learning gains in subsequent years. Third, even when students enter schools ready to learn, their continuing development as readers depends on the quality of the schools they attend. As a result, the general argument of this chapter is that improving the reading achievement of students living in poverty requires a multidimensional approach to education reform—one that seeks to address the underlying risk factors associated with poverty, that ensures students enter school ready to learn, and that works to improve the subsequent quality of the schools students attend.

MULTIDIMENSIONAL APPROACH TO EDUCATIONAL REFORM

To illustrate the previous points, we analyzed data from ECLS–K. The ECLS–K study sampled approximately 22,000 kindergarten children, attending more than 1,000 schools, and tracked their early school experiences from kindergarten through fifth grade. For this chapter, we analyzed data collected in the fall and spring of kindergarten, fall of first grade for a 30% subsample of children, and spring of first and third grades for all children. The data we analyzed came from questionnaires that the ECLS–K researchers administered to parents and teachers of the children in the study as well as results from achievement tests administered to the children at each data collection point.

Our data analysis focused, first of all, on the reading achievement of children as it developed from kindergarten to third grade. ECLS–K researchers used an adaptive testing procedure to administer reading achievement tests and then scored these tests using Bayesian approaches to Item Response Theory (IRT). The Bayesian paradigm can be seen in some ways as an extra step in the modeling world by attempting to infer about some unknown aspect through confidence intervals or hypothesis testing (Berger, 1999). The adaptive testing procedure produced high test reliabilities (hovering around .95 at each testing point), whereas the IRT scaling allowed reporting of growth in reading achievement on a common scaling metric across all grades (Pollack, Atkins-Burnett, Rock, & Weiss, 2005).

For the analyses that follow, we examined three types of scores derived from these reading assessments. First, we charted growth in reading achievement for children using the IRT scale scores. It is important to understand, however, that although these scales have the desirable property of making gains in achievement comparable at all time points (because scores are on a uniform scale at these time points), the scale score itself does not tell us what students know and can actually do. To better understand the kinds of reading proficiencies that children with different scale scores attained, we also reported proficiency scores.[4] These scores

---

[4]ECLS–K, for example, reports eight proficiency scores for students: 1) *letter recognition*, identifying uppercase and lowercase letters of the alphabet by name; 2) *beginning sounds*, associating letters with sounds at the beginning of words; 3) *ending sounds*, associating letters with sounds at the end of words; 4) *sight words*, recognizing words by sight; 5) *comprehension of words in context*, understanding words in context; 6) *literal inference*, making inferences using cues that were directly stated with key words in the text; 7) *extrapolation*, identifying clues used to make inferences; and 8) *evaluation*, demonstrating understanding of the author's craft and making connections between a problem in the narrative and similar life problems (Pollack et al., 2005). The proficiencies listed first (e.g., letter recognition) are usually attained first by students—and thus correspond to lower scale scores—whereas the latter proficiencies (e.g., evaluation) are attained later and correspond to higher scale scores.

were determined by grouping test items into clusters representing specific reading skills and then using a cutoff point for number of items correct to measure a child's proficiency in these skills dichotomously. Finally, on occasion, we represented students' achievement as standardized scores; student scores were rescaled to have a mean of 50 and standard deviation of 10 at each round, allowing comparisons of individual or group performance relative to other individuals or groups. If the standardized scores for a group increased (or decreased) over time, for example, this reflected an increase (or decrease) in the relative ranking of group members' test scores with respect to other groups.

An important purpose of this chapter is to compare the reading achievement of students with different risk profiles. These risk profiles summarize students' background status in terms of gender, race and ethnicity, socioeconomic status (SES), health status, social skills and behavior, and parental expectations for a student's educational attainment.[5] For the following analyses, for example, we were especially interested in examining the reading proficiency of high-risk students, which we then compared to average-risk and low-risk students. For our analysis, *high-risk students* were defined as being nonwhite males whose SES score was at or below the 25th percentile in the ECLS–K data set *and* who were at or below the 33rd percentile on at least two of the health, behavior, or parental expectation measures. Thus, these were students whose family income was low and who also had at least four other risk factors shown in previous research to be negatively associated with academic achievement. In the ECLS–K data, 19% of students had such a profile. The achievement of these 19% of students was then compared with the achievement of *low-risk students*, defined as white female students whose SES score was at or below the 75th percentile with at least two other risk measures at or above the 66th percentile. These were students whose family income was relatively high, whose parents were well educated and held good jobs, and who also had higher levels of health, better social behavior, and increased parental support. In the ECLS–K data, about 23% of students had this risk profile. The final group, for comparison purposes, was *average-risk students*. These were the

---

[5]*Gender* is coded simply as male/female, in which male is the risk factor. *Socioeconomic status* is a composite variable combining measures of parental income, education, and occupational prestige, in which lower SES is a risk factor. *Health status* was measured at kindergarten using three variables: premature birth (yes/no) as reported by the parent, body mass index (ratio of height and weight) as measured by a trained assessor, and general health (five-category scale ranging from "poor" to "excellent") as reported by the parent, in which premature birth, higher body mass index, and worse general health are risk factors. A child's *social skills and behavior* were drawn from both parent and teacher reports. The parent measure is simply an average of parental ratings of a student's self-control, sadness/loneliness, and impulsiveness at the beginning of kindergarten. The teacher measure is an average of ratings of the student's self-control, interpersonal behavior, and externalizing and internalizing problem behavior at the beginning of kindergarten. In both cases, children with more reported problem behaviors are considered at risk. The final measure included in the risk profile was *parental expectations for a student's educational attainment* (assessed in terms of six categories ranging from less than high school to Ph.D. or other higher degree), in which lower expectations were considered a risk factor.

hypothetical group of students who scored at the average on all measures of SES and other risk factors (and whose achievement trajectory was represented as the population average for the ECLS–K sample).

The figures and tables presented in the following pages show the achievement of these groups of children at the different points in time and under different assumptions about "readiness to learn" and school quality. The data in the figures and tables were derived from a series of Hierarchical Linear Model (HLM) regression analyses that we used to estimate growth in students' achievement across the time points under study. An HLM has a nested structure that allows effects to vary from one context to another. For example, in educational research, an HLM is often used to analyze data about student reading achievement. Here, students are nested within schools, and the model permits the investigation of the relationship between student socioeconomic status and reading achievement by school and allows the investigation of school-level factors that affect this relationship. Readers interested in the technical details of the analysis can consult the authors. For now, we simply note that the statistical model used in the analysis was a three-level, piecewise, linear growth model as described by Raudenbush and Bryk (2002). In this model, the achievement of individual students was modeled as a function of time, student risk characteristics, and school variables including region of the country and school composition (i.e., average SES of students, percentage of nonwhite enrollment). Using the results from these statistical models, we simply examined the model-based estimates of the achievement status for students with different risk profiles under the different assumptions discussed in the following sections.[6]

Illustration 1: Patterns of Early Literacy Achievement

We begin by showing the expected growth in reading achievement for our groups of high-, average-, and low-risk students as estimated in the HLM analysis. Figure 4.1 shows the growth trajectories for these three groups of pupils using the IRT scale scores. We can see from the figure that students' growth in reading achievement progressed at a relatively slow rate in kindergarten, decelerated over the summer period, accelerated markedly in the first grade, then slowed again through the second and third grades. Figure 4.1 also shows that students in the high-risk group showed the slowest growth rates over time, especially from first grade onward, producing a widening gap in achievement scale scores among high- and low-risk students over the total time period.

---

[6]It should be noted that our analytic sample only includes students who attended the same school across all rounds of data collection, bringing our sample of students down to 12,000; however, there were no noticeable difference in the background and family characteristics of children who attended the same school over time versus children who did not attend the same school. Detailed characteristics of the sample are available from the authors.

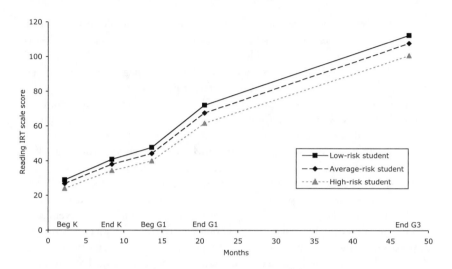

Figure 4.1. Early Childhood Longitudinal Study–Kindergarten Class of 1998–1999 reading trajectories based on child risk profiles. (Reprinted from Pollack, J., Atkins-Burnett, S., Rock, D., & Weiss, M. [2005]. *Early childhood longitudinal study, kindergarten class of 1998–99 [ECLS-K]: Psychometric report for the third grade* [NCES 2005–062]. Washington, DC: National Center for Education Statistics.) (*Key:* Beg G1, beginning of first grade; Beg K, beginning of kindergarten; End G1, end of first grade; End G3, end of third grade; End K, end of kindergarten; IRT, Item Response Theory.)

The problem with Figure 4.1, of course, is that the scale scores do not communicate a very clear sense of just how big the gaps in reading achievement are among students from the different risk groups under study. To combat this problem, we present some additional ways of looking at the same data. In Table 4.1, for example, we translated the data in Figure 4.1 from scale scores into two other metrics. The first metric (shown in the "*SD*" columns) places the scale scores for each group onto the standard normal curve. This column shows that students in our high-risk group entered kindergarten with test scores a third of a standard deviation below the average-risk group and two thirds of a standard deviation below the low-risk group. As students progressed through school, the size of this the gap remained fairly stable for 1–2 years; however, by the end of third grade, high-risk students ended up falling almost one half of a standard deviation below the average student and three fourths of a standard deviation below their low-risk peers.

In Table 4.1, we also translated the gaps in Figure 4.1 into the additional months of instruction that would be required for the high-risk students to catch up to the average- or low-risk students (shown in the "Months" columns). This was done simply by determining the number of scale score points per month that students were gaining over a given time period of instruction and then dividing the scale score gap by this number. These numbers showed that at entry into kindergarten, high-risk students were about 1.6 months behind the average student in their learning, but by the end of third grade, they fell behind by about 4.7 months.

Table 4.1. Gaps in reading achievement by child risk profile

	High-risk versus average-risk		High-risk versus low-risk	
	SD	Months	SD	Months
Beginning of kindergarten	0.36	1.6	0.64	2.8
End of kindergarten	0.32	2.1	0.55	3.6
End of first grade	0.34	1.8	0.61	3.2
End of third grade	0.45	4.7	0.74	7.8

Adapted from Pollack, J., Atkins-Burnett, S., Rock, D., & Weiss, M. (2005). *Early childhood longitudinal study, kindergarten class of 1998–99 (ECLS-K): Psychometric report for the third grade* (NCES 2005–062). Washington, DC: National Center for Education Statistics.
Key: SD, standard deviation.

Table 4.1 also shows that at the beginning of kindergarten, high-risk students were nearly 3 months behind the low-risk group and that by the end of third grade, this gap had widened to nearly 8 months—almost an entire school year.

Although Table 4.1 is informative (and certainly more intuitive than simply looking at scale points), we think Figure 4.2 is an even more informative way to look at the data. Figure 4.2 presents data on the percentages of students in the high- and low-risk groups that had mastered different reading proficiencies at the various points at which reading achievement was measured in ECLS–K. More than 50% of high-risk students entered kindergarten without having mastery of any of the proficiencies defined by ECLS–K, whereas more than 50% of low-risk children entered kindergarten already able to recognize letters and identify the be-

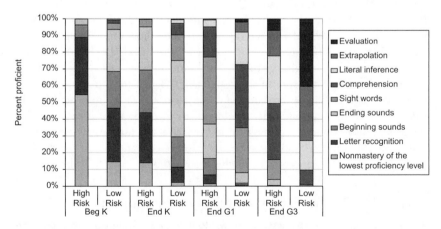

Figure 4.2. Early Childhood Longitudinal Study–Kindergarten Class of 1998–1999 reading proficiencies over time by child risk profiles. (Reprinted from Pollack, J., Atkins-Burnett, S., Rock, D., & Weiss, M. [2005]. *Early childhood longitudinal study, kindergarten class of 1998–99 [ECLS-K]: Psychometric report for the third grade* [NCES 2005–062]. Washington, DC: National Center for Education Statistics.) (*Key:* Beg K, beginning of kindergarten; End G1, end of first grade; End G3, end of third grade; End K, end of kindergarten.)

ginning or ending sounds of words. By the end of first grade, many high-risk students had gained solid mastery of word reading skills, but many low-risk students were beginning to master the comprehension and inference skills that are involved in successfully reading connected text. Figure 4.2 shows that high-risk students were only beginning to master these skills by the end of third grade, whereas their low-risk peers had moved on to higher level reading skills; in fact, about 40% of the low-risk group had mastered evaluation—the highest level of proficiency in the test battery.

These data are interesting on several counts. First, we can ask ourselves if we are satisfied with the level of reading proficiency shown by high-risk students in the data. For example, are we satisfied with the fact that half of all high-risk students enter kindergarten unable to identify their letters and that most have only mastered the most basic of reading proficiencies—being able, at best, to make only the most literal inferences from text—by the end of third grade? Or, would we rather see high-risk students enter kindergarten with the same reading skills as our most advantaged students and have solid mastery of the reading process by the end of third grade?

We think the answer is obvious and that we should want for our least advantaged students what our most advantaged students already have. If that is our goal, then the data in Table 4.1 begin to tell us just how powerful our interventions will need to be to attain this goal. At entry into kindergarten, for example, the ECLS–K data suggest that a few additional months of instruction would allow high-risk students to attain the reading skills already possessed by their low-risk peers but that nearly a year's worth of additional instruction would be required by the end of third grade. Alternatively, we can use data from Table 4.1 to suggest the kind of standardized effect sizes that interventions would need to produce for high-risk students to catch up with their more privileged peers. If we assume that the low-risk students continue to receive the kind of instruction they already get and then imagine giving high-risk students a one-time intervention at any given point in time, we can see from Table 4.1 that this one-time intervention would have to have a standardized effect size of 0.6 or 0.7 to bring high-risk students up to the level of achievement of their low-risk peers at the next time point. By today's standards of intervention effectiveness, that is a very large effect size, especially considering that the average effect of educational and psychosocial interventions to date appears to be on the order of 0.30 (Lipsey & Wilson, 1993).

Illustration 2: The Promise of Early Intervention

The preceding discussion suggests the wisdom of intervening early to attempt to improve the reading proficiency of young children. In fact, this is the reason so many education researchers and policy makers now support expanding preschool educational opportunities for high-risk students. In this section, we used the ECLS–K and our HLM regression models to simulate what would happen to high-risk children's achievement if they actually entered school with higher levels of achievement. In this simulation, we defined a child as having a *high start* if that child entered kindergarten with a reading test score of about 0.5 standard deviations above what the average high-risk student typically scores. Thus, our illustration assumes that the high-start student has had some form of early childhood intervention that produced an effect size on the order of 0.50.

Figure 4.3 shows that a high-risk kindergarten student who entered the average school with this kind of high start would have a beginning ECLS–K test score about 0.10 standard deviations above the average U.S. kindergarten student; this slight advantage in achievement would persist through first grade. Our model-based estimates, however, show that, in the average school, that same high-risk student (with a high start) would drop back down to the same level as the average student by the end of third grade. The point, of course, is that by providing high-risk students with an early childhood intervention with an effect size on achievement of around 0.50, we should, based on our estimates, be able to bring high-risk students up to the average level of achievement by third grade. However, as Figure 4.3 shows, this still leaves us short of our most ambitious goal for high-risk students— to bring them up to the level of achievement experienced by low-risk children. In fact, using our model-based estimates, high-risk students would require an intervention that had an effect size of 0.64 in order for them to have a level of third-grade achievement equal to that achieved by low-risk students.

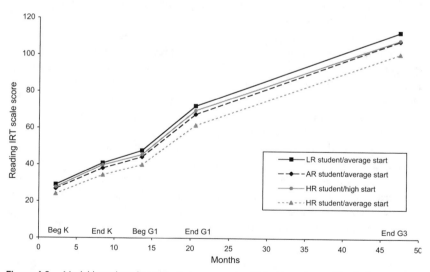

Figure 4.3. Model-based reading trajectories comparing high-risk students with a high start to average- and low-risk students with average starts. (Reprinted from Pollack, J., Atkins-Burnett, S., Rock, D., & Weiss, M. [2005]. *Early childhood longitudinal study, kindergarten class of 1998–99 [ECLS-K]: Psychometric report for the third grade* [NCES 2005–062]. Washington, DC: National Center for Education Statistics.) (*Key:* AR, average-risk; Beg G1, beginning of first grade; Beg K, beginning of kindergarten; End G1, end of first grade; End G3, end of third grade; End K, end of kindergarten; HR, high-risk; LR, low-risk.)

In summary, this simulation provides some evidence that if high-risk students entered schools more ready to learn, they would experience accelerated learning trajectories over time and could (under some scenarios) end up achieving the levels of reading proficiency now achieved by average- and low-risk students; however, it also is important to recognize that the scenarios we presented assume that we can produce effect sizes on high-risk students' achievement above what existing early childhood intervention programs actually have been shown to produce. Several reviews of research (Barnett, 1995; Magnuson & Waldfogel, 2005), for example, suggest that early childhood program effects on student achievement typically vary from 0 to about 0.30, well below the effect sizes we assumed in our most optimistic scenarios. Thus, under current conditions, working on early childhood intervention alone does not appear to be able, by itself, to raise high-risk students' achievement to our most ambitious target.

Illustration 3: Working to Improve School Quality

This brings us to our third illustration. Here, we used the ECLS–K data and our regression models to examine the effects of school quality on high-risk students' learning trajectories. The basic question here is whether high-quality schooling alone can accelerate the learning trajectories of high-risk students in ways that enable them to achieve our most ambitious targets or whether we might need to combine such high-quality schooling with especially effective preschool programming to achieve the desired results.

Our illustration used the same approach to measuring school quality as that used in value-added modeling (Goldstein, 1997; Heck, 2006; Luyten, Visscher, & Witziers, 2005; McCaffrey, Lockwood, Koretz, & Hamilton, 2003; McCaffrey, Lockwood, Koretz, Louis, & Hamilton, 2004; Rowan et al., 2002). In essence, after entering all of the student-level risk factors and the school-level variables discussed previously into our HLM models, we found that schools still vary in average levels of achievement and in average growth trajectories. Combining the school deviations for both achievement status and achievement growth after adjustment for student and school covariates creates a random distribution of errors centered around zero. In our simulation, we considered schools that scored one half of a standard deviation above the mean on this distribution to be high-performing schools and schools that scored one half of a standard deviation below the average on this distribution to be low-performing schools.[7]

---

[7]We computed the variances for these distributions at each time point using procedures discussed by Tate (2000) and Raudenbush and Bryk (2002). We should point out, however, that in our piecewise linear growth model, no single school was "effective" at all time points using the criteria just discussed. As a result, what we are presenting in this section is a simulation of what would happen if a student were in a school that met such criteria, a simulation that is derived from using the distributions at each time point, rather than a simulation derived from the observed effects of an actual set of schools.

Figure 4.4 shows the results of this simulation—what would happen if the average high-risk student attended a school consistently one half of a standard deviation above the average in school effectiveness, a school at the average in effectiveness, or a school one half of a standard deviation below the average in school effectiveness. The simulation showed that if the high-risk student attended a high-performing school, that student would have an achievement trajectory that was roughly similar to that of the average student but not to the level of the low-risk student (e.g., compare the growth trajectories for average and low-risk students in average schools as shown in Figure 4.1 to the growth trajectory shown in Figure 4.4 for a high-risk student in a high-performing school). In point of fact, even this result—which still falls short of our most ambitious goals for school reform—seems beyond the capacity of current school reform initiatives. For example, although our simulation assumed an effect size of 0.50, Borman and colleagues (2002) found that existing Comprehensive School Reform programs produced an average effect on student achievement of about 0.10, though several programs did show bigger effect sizes. Thus, there is nothing in the school reform literature that we know of that comes close to having the effect size necessary to raise the achievement of high-risk children to even the level of the average child in the average school; these data suggest that it is not feasible to rely solely on school reform to raise the trajectories of high-risk students to our desired targets.

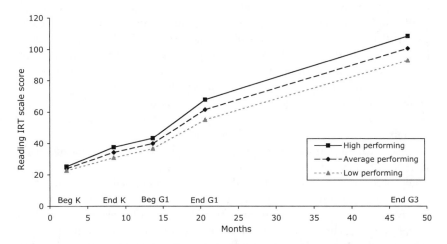

Figure 4.4.   Model-based estimates of reading trajectories for high-risk students in differently performing schools. (Reprinted from Pollack, J., Atkins-Burnett, S., Rock, D., & Weiss, M. [2005]. *Early childhood longitudinal study, kindergarten class of 1998–99 [ECLS-K]: Psychometric report for the third grade* [NCES 2005–062]. Washington, DC: National Center for Education Statistics.) (*Key:* Beg G1, beginning of first grade; Beg K, beginning of kindergarten; End G1, end of first grade; End G3, end of third grade; End K, end of kindergarten; IRT, Item Response Theory.)

WHAT IS WITHIN REACH?

To this point, we have shown that, under current conditions, high-risk students have levels of reading achievement far below both their average- and low-risk peers and that working only to improve student achievement at entry into schooling (the "ready-to-learn" strategy) or working only to improve the quality of K–3 schooling will not allow us to achieve our most ambitious learning objectives for high-risk students. So, should we just throw up our hands and declare our goal unreachable, at least for the foreseeable future? Our final simulation suggests that this is not necessary; if we follow early childhood intervention with high-quality schooling, the achievement of high-risk students should improve to the desired levels.

As a final step in our analysis, we developed a simulation more in line with the limitations that currently exist in the effectiveness of early childhood interventions and in the effectiveness of whole-school reform programs. In this last simulation, for example, we lowered our definition of high-performing schools to include those that were consistently 0.25 standard deviations better than the average school based on the school error distributions, and we defined a high start for high-risk students as being 0.25 standard deviations above the average starting level they currently attain.

Using these parameters in our simulation, we found that high-risk children who entered school with a high start but attended a low-performing school experienced lower academic growth rates from the start, negating all of the benefits of their high start by the end of third grade. By contrast, high-risk students who entered school with a high start and attended high-performing schools began kindergarten slightly below the average child in the average school but quickly made gains, ending third grade with achievement levels *above* that of the average student in the average schools (though still behind the low-risk student in the average school). The results from this simulation suggest that it is within our grasp to educate high-risk students to levels attained by average students; however, this can only come about if we manage to enroll these students in both effective preschool programs *and* in effective school programs.

To reach our most ambitious target (i.e., high-risk students achieving at the same level as low-risk students in third grade), our simulation suggests that we would need to increase high-risk students entry levels of achievement by about one half of a standard deviation and place them in schools that had a continuous positive effect on achievement of one third of a standard deviation. As we have seen, few, if any, current interventions manage to obtain or sustain these levels of effects on high-risk students' achievement; however, our simulations do not suggest that the problem is insurmountable, especially if the research and development community continues to work on more effective programming.

CONCLUSION

In summary, we used ECLS–K data to explore what it would take to get the most at-risk students to achieve the most ambitious expectations. Admittedly, the results of these simulations must be interpreted with care; although they are based on real data points for students within schools, we had to simulate what happens to children when they are put in more or less effective schools or if they enter schools with differing levels of achievement. Thus, our illustrations were not based on real interventions and, in some cases, were based on scenarios that are implausible given the current state of scalable interventions in the field. Ideally, we would have preferred to use data from randomized experiments to make our point, but, in fact, such comprehensive experimental data does not exist.

Despite these shortcomings, we find the simulations presented here somewhat encouraging. Although the simulations suggested that the U.S. education system currently lacks the capacity to raise high-risk students' reading achievement to the levels of reading achievement currently attained by America's most advantaged students, our simulations did suggest that it is possible to raise high-risk students' reading achievement to the level attained by the average student in the United States. As we saw, however, this result would occur only if high-risk children gained access to the highest quality early childhood programming that currently exists and attended elementary schools operating at the frontier of effectiveness for currently available, whole-school reform programs.

This is an important message, but it requires some elaboration. In our view, current debates about education reform are often too myopic and too optimistic. For example, in some policy settings, early childhood education is advanced as the sole panacea for raising the achievement of high-risk students, whereas in other policy settings, school reform is seen as the single panacea. Our simulations, however, suggest that both sorts of reforms are needed simultaneously—especially given the current state of the research in both prekindergarten and K–3 education programming. Our simulations also suggest that it is crucial to continue to improve on existing avenues of reform. A significant amount of work, for example, still must be done to improve even the best early education programs and even the best school reform programs if we are to produce the kinds of effects on student achievement that are large enough to reach our most ambitious learning goals for high-risk students. This process of improvement will undoubtedly take years.

Finally, although we strongly support efforts to improve educational programming, we also want to encourage policy makers to look beyond purely educational approaches to intervention to address the underlying risk factors that are creating the problem we seek to address in the first place. We have seen in all of our simulations, for example, that factors such as poverty, poor health, and lack of family support impede students' learning; therefore, a multipronged approach to social policy that includes not only educational intervention but also social policies that support family income and improve child health and mental health might be what is needed to provide the extra boost necessary to reach our most ambitious goals for high-risk students' educational achievement.

REFERENCES

Arnold, D.H. (1997). Co-occurrence of externalizing behavior problems and emergent academic difficulties in young high-risk boys: A preliminary evaluation of patterns and mechanisms. *Journal of Applied Developmental Psychology, 18*(3), 317–330.

Barnett, W.S. (1995). Long-term effects of early childhood programs on cognitive and school outcomes. *The Future of Children, 5*(3), 25–50.

Barnett, W.S. (2002). Early childhood education. In A. Molnar (Ed.), *School reform proposals: The research evidence* (pp. 1–26). Greenwich, CT: Information Age Publishing.

Berger, J.O. (1999). *Statistical decision theory and Bayesian analysis* (2nd ed.). New York: Springer Verlag.

Borman, G.D., Hewes, G.M., Overman, L.T., & Brown, S. (2002). *Comprehensive school reform and student achievement.* (Report No. 59). Baltimore: Center for Research on the Education of Students Placed At Risk. Retrieved May 9, 2007, from http://www.csos.jhu.edu

Brooks-Gunn, J., Duncan, G.J., & Aber, J.L. (1997). *Neighborhood poverty: Context and consequences for children* (Vol. 1.) New York: Russell Sage Foundation.

Brooks-Gunn, J., Klebanov, P.K., Smith, J., Duncan, G.J., & Lee, K. (2003). The black–white test score gap in young children: Contributions of test and family characteristics. *Applied Developmental Science, 7,* 239–252.

Brooks-Gunn, J., & Markman, L.B. (2005). The contribution of parenting to ethnic and racial gaps in school readiness. *The Future of Children, 1,* 139–168.

Burchinal, P., Roberts, J., Riggins, R., Jr., Zeisel, S., Neebe, E., & Bryant, D. (2000). Relating center-based child care to early cognitive and language development longitudinally. *Child Development, 71*(2), 339–357.

Coleman, J.S., Campbell, E., Hobson, C., McPartland, J., Mood, F., Weinfeld, F., et al. (1966). *Equality of educational opportunity.* Washington, DC: U.S. Government Printing Office.

Cook, M.D., & Evans, W.N. (2000). Families or schools? Explaining the convergence in white and black academic performance. *Journal of Labor Economics, 18,* 729–754.

Currie, J. (2005). Health disparities and gaps in school readiness. *The Future of Children, 15*(1),117–138.

Dauber, S.L., & Epstein, J.L. (1993). Parents' attitudes and practices of involvement in inner-city elementary and middle schools. In N.F. Chavkin (Ed.), *Families and schools in a pluralistic society* (pp. 53–72). Albany, NY: State University of New York Press.

Duncan, G.J., & Magnuson, K.A. (2005). Can family socioeconomic resources account for racial and ethnic test score gaps? *The Future of Children, 15*(1), 35–54.

Edmunds, R. (1979). Some schools work and more can. *Social Policy, 9,* 28–32.

Evans, G.W. (2004). The environment of childhood poverty. *American Psychologist, 59*(2), 77–92.

Feuerstein, A. (2000). School characteristics and parent involvement: Influences on participation in children's schools. *Journal of Educational Research, 92,* 29–38.

Foster, E.M. (2002). How economists think about family resources and child development. *Child Development, 73,* 1904–1914.

Garrett, P., Ng'andu, N., & Ferron, J. (1994). Poverty experiences of young children and the quality of their home environments. *Child Development, 64,* 331–345.

Goldstein, H. (1997). Methods in school effectiveness research. *School Effectiveness and School Improvement, 8*(4), 369–395.

Gutman, L.M., Sameroff, A.J., & Cole, R. (2003). Academic growth curve trajectories from 1st grade to 12th grade: Effects of multiple social risk factors and preschool child factors. *Developmental Psychology, 39*(4), 777–790.

Heck, R.H. (2006). Assessing school achievement progress: Comparing alternative approaches. *Educational Administration Quarterly, 42*(5), 667–699.

Hedges, L., & Nowell, A. (1998). The black–white test score convergence since 1965. In C. Jencks & M. Phillips (Eds.), *The black–white test score gap* (pp. 149–181). Washington, DC: Brookings Institution.

Hedges, L.V., Laine, R.D., & Greenwald, R. (1994a). Does money matter? A meta-analysis of studies of the effects of differential school inputs on student outcomes. *Educational Researcher, 23*(3), 5–14.

Hedges, L.V., Laine, R.D., & Greenwald, R. (1994b). Money does matter somewhere: A reply to Hanushek. *Educational Researcher, 23*(4), 9–10.

Henderson, A., & Berla, N. (1994). *A new generation of evidence: The family is critical to student achievement.* Washington, DC: Center for Law and Education.

Jackson, A. (2003). The effects of family and neighborhood characteristics on the behavioral and cognitive development of poor black children: A longitudinal study. *American Journal of Community Psychology, 32*(1/2), 175–186.

Jencks, C., & Phillips, M. (Eds.). (1998). *The black–white test score gap.* Washington, DC: Brookings Institution.

Kagan, S.L., Moore, E., & Bredekamp, S. (Eds.). (1995). *Reconsidering children's early learning and development: Toward shared beliefs and vocabulary.* Washington, DC: National Education Goals Panel.

Klebanov, P.K., Brooks-Gunn, J., McCarton, C., & McCormick, M.C. (1998). The contribution of neighborhood and family income to developmental test scores over the first three years of life. *Child Development, 69*(5), 1420–1436.

Lee, V.E., & Burkam, D.T. (2002). *Inequality at the starting gate: Social background differences in achievement as children begin school.* Washington, DC: Economic Policy Institute.

Lipsey, M., & Wilson, D. (1993). The efficacy of psychological, educational, and behavioral treatment: Confirmation from meta-analysis. *American Psychologist, 48,* 1181–1209.

Luyten H., Visscher, A., & Witziers, B. (2005). School effectiveness research: From a review of the criticism to recommendations for further development. *School Effectiveness and School Improvement, 16*(3), 249–279.

Magnuson, K.A., & Waldfogel, J. (2005). Early childhood care and education: Effects on ethnic and racial gaps in school readiness. *Future of Children, 15*(1), 169–196.

McCaffrey, D.F., Lockwood, J.R., Koretz, D.M., & Hamilton, L.S. (2003). *Evaluating value-added models for teacher accountability.* Santa Monica, CA: RAND.

McCaffrey, D.F., Lockwood, J.R., Koretz, D., Louis, T.A., & Hamilton, L. (2004). Models for value-added modeling of teacher effects. *Journal of Educational and Behavioral Statistics, 29*(1), 67–101.

McLeod, J.D., & Kaiser, K. (2004). Childhood emotional and behavioral problems and educational attainment. *American Sociological Review, 69*(5), 636–658.

McLoyd, V. (1998). Socioeconomic disadvantage and child development. *American Psychologist, 53,* 185–204.

National Assessment of Educational Progress. (2004). *Percentage of children by reading level, Grade 4.* Washington, DC: Author.

Neal, D. (2005). *Why has black–white skill convergence stopped?* (Working Paper No. 11090). Cambridge, MA: National Bureau of Economic Research.

Phillips, M., Crouse, J., & Ralph, J. (1998). Does the black–white test score gap widen after children enter school? In C. Jencks & M. Phillips (Eds.), *The black–white test score gap* (pp. 229–272). Washington, DC: Brookings Institution.

Pollack, J., Atkins-Burnett, S., Rock, D., & Weiss, M. (2005). *Early childhood longitudinal study, kindergarten class of 1998–99 (ECLS-K): Psychometric report for the third grade* (NCES 2005–062). Washington, DC: National Center for Education Statistics.

Purkey, W., & Smith, M. (1983). Effective schools: A review. *Elementary School Journal, 83*(4), 427–452.

Ramey, S.L., & Ramey, C.T. (1992). Early educational intervention with disadvantaged children—To what effect? *Applied and Preventive Psychology, 1,* 131–140.

Rathbun, A., & West, J. (2004). *From kindergarten through third grade: Children's beginning school experiences* (NCES 2004–007). Washington, DC: National Center for Education Statistics.

Raudenbush, S. (2004). What are value-added models estimating and what does this imply for statistical practice? *Journal of Educational and Behavioral Statistics, 29*(1), 121–129.

Raudenbush, S.W., & Bryk, A.S. (2002). *Hierarchical linear models: Applications and data analysis methods* (2nd ed.). Thousand Oaks, CA: Sage Publications.

Rothstein, R. (2004). The achievement gap: A broader picture. *Educational Leadership, 62*(3), 40–43.

Rowan, B., Bossert, S., & Dwyer, D. (1983). Research on effective schools: A cautionary note. *Educational Researcher, 12,* 24–31.

Rowan, B., Correnti, R., & Miller, R. (2002). What large-scale survey research tells us about teacher effects on student achievement: Insights from the Prospects study of elementary schools. *Teachers College Record, 104,* 1525–1567.

Scott-Jones, D. (1995). Parent–child interactions and school achievement. In B.A. Ryan, G.R. Adams, T.P. Gullotta, R.P. Weissberg, & R.L. Hampton (Eds.), *The family–school connection: Vol. 2. Theory, research, and practice* (pp. 75–109). Thousand Oaks, CA: Sage Publications.

Slavin, R.E., Karweit, N.L., & Madden, N.A. (1989). *Effective programs for students at-risk.* Boston: Allyn & Bacon.

Spira, E.G., & Fischel, J.E. (2005). The impact of preschool inattention, hyperactivity, and impulsivity on social and academic development: A review. *Journal of Child Psychology and Psychiatry, 46*(7), 755–773.

Stipek, D.J., & Ryan, R.H. (1997). Economically disadvantaged preschoolers: Ready to learn but further to go. *Developmental Psychology, 33,* 711–723.

Tate, R.L. (2000). Elaboration of HLM growth modeling results. *Florida Journal of Educational Research, 40*(2), 53–75.

Trzesniewski, K.H., Moffitt, T.E., Caspi, A., Taylor, A., & Maughan, B. (2006). Revisiting the association between reading achievement and antisocial behavior: New evidence of an environmental explanation from a twin study. *Child Development, 77*(1), 72–88.

West, J., Denton, K., & Reaney, L.M. (2001). *The kindergarten year: Findings from the Early Childhood Longitudinal Study, Kindergarten Class of 1998–99.* Washington, DC: National Center for Education Statistics. Available online at http://www.nces.ed.gov/pubs2001/2001023.pdf.

Zill, N. (1999). Promoting educational equity and excellence in kindergarten. In R.C. Pianta & M.J. Cox (Eds.), *The transition to kindergarten* (pp. 67–105). Baltimore: Paul H. Brookes Publishing Co.

5

Literacy Achievement in the Primary Grades in High-Poverty Schools

Louisa C. Moats and Barbara R. Foorman

Researchers have achieved consensus on several major questions pertaining to reading: How do typically progressing children learn to read? Why do some children have difficulty? What features of instruction are most likely to help the most children become good readers? This consensus, reflected in papers, books, and policy documents (e.g., Armbruster, Lehr, & Osborn, 2001; McCardle & Chhabra, 2004; National Institute of Child Health and Human Development, 2000; Neuman & Dickinson, 2001; Rayner, Foorman, Perfetti, Pesetsky, & Seidenberg, 2001; Snow, Burns, & Griffin, 1998; Stone, Silliman, Ehren, & Apel, 2004), is derived from decades of scientific work funded by the U.S. Department of Education, the National Institutes of Health, and many other institutions and agencies. Some schools serving high-poverty children can, and do, "beat the odds" (Denton, Foorman, & Mathes, 2003; Slavin, Madden, Dolan, & Wasik, 1996; Taylor, Pearson, Clark, & Walpole, 2000). Nevertheless, we have not yet succeeded in implementing research-based instruction on a widespread, consistent basis.

This chapter summarizes a body of work generated from a 5-year longitudinal program of reading research conducted in high-poverty, urban schools in Grades K–4, positioning major findings in relation to the context of current reading research. It highlights the importance of teachers and teaching in student progress and reports some detailed findings about teacher knowledge pertaining to reading and language. Professional development and school leadership are also noted to be critical influences on teachers' ability to raise the academic language proficiency and academic performance of students at risk.

COMPENSATORY AND SPECIAL EDUCATION PROGRAMS DO NOT ADEQUATELY SERVE THE NEEDS OF HIGH-POVERTY STUDENTS

Despite significant federal and state investments in compensatory education programs, persistent achievement gaps among students of various ethnic, socioeconomic, and linguistic backgrounds have been difficult to close. Many students who fall behind are assigned to remedial programs funded through Title I, but, on the whole, these entitlement programs have not been successful in narrowing the achievement gap. Within Title I, some programs have made a difference, such as *Success for All* (Borman et al., 2005). Successful programs often address much more than classroom or remedial reading instruction, embracing school scheduling and organization, leadership training, professional development, and small-group tutorial interventions. *Direct Instruction Reading* (Carnine, Silbert, & Kame'enui, 1997) is a proven and powerful reading intervention implemented in some high-poverty schools that has never enjoyed the widespread adoption or implementation it might deserve.

Special education services, although costly, have also not been the answer to the achievement gap. Half of the 6.2 million students served in special education programs are classified as having learning disabilities, and about 85% of those children have serious and intractable problems with reading and related language skills (President's Commission on Excellence in Special Education, 2002). Students with serious reading disabilities on average do not make any significant gains in relative standing if they are placed in special education between Grades 3 and 6 (Hanushek, Kain, & Rivkin, 1998; Torgesen et al., 2001). Special education placement usually offers too little, too late, when it comes to learning to read.

In spite of these chronic national trends, most serious reading problems appear to be preventable. Instruction, however, must begin early, aim to prevent the development of problems, keep close track of children's progress, and focus primarily on classroom instruction. The combination of strong classroom instruction with supplementary, focused interventions reduces the incidence of reading failure to about 5% of students or fewer at the first-grade level (Foorman, Brier, & Fletcher, 2003; Mathes et al., 2005; Torgesen, 2004, 2005). Supplementary instruction, however, need not involve one-to-one tutorials; results are usually as good with small-group instruction as with one-to-one instruction (Elbaum, Vaughn, Hughes, & Moody, 2000).

The major project with which we were involved for 5 years studied the conditions necessary for successful classroom reading instruction in high-poverty, urban schools serving predominantly African American students and students of mixed ethnicities. Funded by the National Institute of Child Health and Human Development (NICHD)[1] as part of its comprehensive program of research into

[1]Supported in part by grant HD30995, Early Interventions for Children with Reading Problems, from the National Institute of Child Health and Human Development (NICHD).

reading acquisition, the project was headed by Barbara R. Foorman and codirected by Jack Fletcher, David Francis, and Louisa C. Moats. In the course of this study, we learned much about the variables that predict reading outcomes, the school and classroom factors that improve reading and writing achievement, the language learning characteristics of the children, and the needs of teachers who work in such environments.

RESEARCH CONTEXT FOR THE EARLY INTERVENTIONS PROJECT

Prior to the initiation of our study in 1997, which was the second phase of a federally funded project already in progress between 1992 and 1997, the reading research community had demonstrated much about the nature of effective preventive and remedial reading instruction. As the National Reading Panel (NICHD, 2000) later asserted, classroom reading programs should teach the alphabetic code explicitly (Ehri et al., 2001; Foorman, Francis, Fletcher, Schatschneider, & Mehta, 1998; Foorman, Francis, Shaywitz, Shaywitz, & Fletcher, 1997). The goal of explicit code instruction is knowledge of the correspondences between phonemes (speech sounds) and graphemes (the letters and letter groups, such as *th*, that spell the phonemes) and application of that knowledge in word reading. Effective code-emphasis instruction in kindergarten and Grade 1 is explicit, systematic, and cumulative—not random or incidental. Automatic and fast word recognition is the goal so that students will become fluent readers of connected text. Fluency at both the word and text reading levels must be achieved so that children read with sufficient speed to support comprehension. Research-based instruction also includes robust vocabulary and comprehension components, no matter where the students are in word reading development, carried out through both oral and written language activities. All these principles were established prior to the publication of the National Reading Panel report.

Code-emphasis instruction in the early grades is advantageous because it prevents problems with the very beginning stages of literacy acquisition (Blachman, 2000; O'Connor & Jenkins, 1999; Schatschneider, Fletcher, Francis, Carlson, & Foorman, 2004). An important insight of modern reading research has been the recognition that phonics instruction may not "take" with young readers unless they are aware of the segments of speech represented by the graphemes used to spell words in an alphabetic writing system (Catts, Fey, Zhang, & Tomblin, 1999). Called *phoneme awareness* (PA), this foundational language skill requires conscious analysis of the internal details of speech, a linguistic achievement that is elusive for many students. Students who have difficulty acquiring PA may lack the experiences with language necessary to foster it or may not be "wired," or biologically predisposed, to figure out the structure of speech and connect that with print (Olson, 2004). Genetic predispositions for and against good reading skills operate through this underlying competence (Gilger & Wise, 2004). One of the most positive, recurring findings of research for the 20 years leading up to the mid-1990s was that children who lacked good phonological skills could be directly taught the identity of phonemes and how to mentally manipulate them. If this awareness was then linked with letters, then students were more likely to overcome early signs of risk for reading failure (Ehri et al., 2001; NICHD, 2000).

The report of the National Research Council (NRC; Snow et al. 1998), based on an expert panel's review of research in early reading instruction and intervention, identified the essential components of effective early literacy instruction that were later elaborated by the National Reading Panel (NICHD, 2000). These included 1) explicit instruction in the alphabetic principle, 2) teaching students to read for meaning, and 3) providing extended opportunities for practice reading connected text. In addition, oral language competency and writing skills were identified as necessary in a comprehensive lesson. The NRC was careful to point out that integration of these components of instruction was associated with the best results—that is, daily comprehensive lessons that included explicit teaching of the alphabetic code, development of reading fluency through a great deal of appropriate reading practice, and explicit teaching of comprehension skills and strategies.

Research on the timing, intensity, and composition of intensive intervention with students at risk also preceded our study (Torgesen, Wagner, Rashotte, Alexander, & Conway, 1997; Vellutino et al., 1996) and coincided with our study (Denton & Mathes, 2003). Using screening tests of phonological skills and letter knowledge, researchers identified children in kindergarten who showed significant signs of risk for reading failure. By second grade, in the study by Torgesen and colleagues, small group, daily intervention for ½ hour over the academic year brought 75% of the poor readers to grade-level reading. Vellutino and colleagues also identified middle-class children with very low word recognition skills at the beginning of Grade 1. After one semester of a comprehensive intervention that included decoding, fluency, and comprehension components, 70% of the poor readers were reading at grade level. After two semesters, more than 90% were at grade level. Early intervention—in Grades 1 and 2—was more effective than later intervention; intervention at Grades 3 and beyond required more hours, more expertise, and more concentrated practice than that which was carried out with the younger students. Even then, reading fluency rates were resistant to normalization when remediation was begun after second grade (Torgesen et al., 2001; Torgesen, 2005).

PURPOSE AND DESIGN OF THE EARLY INTERVENTIONS PROJECT

The Early Interventions Project was designed to begin classroom and remedial intervention in kindergarten and first grade and to follow children through the elementary grades to the end of Grade 4. The study had two overriding and complementary purposes: 1) to investigate the variables that contribute to reading success or failure in schools that are adopting research-based programs, and 2) to improve reading instruction in the participating schools. Although controlled studies had already shown the effectiveness of specific practices and the reasons why those were likely to work better than others, we gathered evidence pertaining to larger-scale implementations of research-based reading instruction in high-poverty environments.

The project provided instructional materials to all classrooms, with publishers' support, and required participants to implement those programs of instruction. Four core, comprehensive reading programs were used across the study, three of which had already been proven effective in reducing reading failure: *Collections for Young Scholars* (Open Court Reading, 1995); *Reading Mastery*, a direct instruction program of SRA (Carnine et al., 1997); *Success for All* (Slavin, Madden, Dolan, & Wasik, 1996); and one program that represented a literature-based approach (with a supplementary phonics kit added in the second year of the study), Houghton Mifflin's (1998) *Invitations to Literacy*. Funding was also provided to support tutorial interventions for 10% of the students.

The professional development provided to teachers was more extensive in the District of Columbia site than the Houston site, as described in a later section of this chapter. In Houston, only 3 days were available for teacher workshops; whereas in the District of Columbia, we provided not only an introductory summer workshop of 3–5 days, but 3 additional professional development days throughout the school year and ongoing courses that met weekly for teachers who voluntarily enrolled in them. A supplementary congressional grant was awarded to the project to support professional development stipends and consulting fees at the District of Columbia site.

SOCIAL, POLITICAL, AND EDUCATIONAL CONTEXT OF THE EARLY INTERVENTIONS PROJECT

According to our initial screening tests, between 70% and 80% of all students in the entering kindergarten classes were at risk for reading failure in the District of Columbia and in the Houston Independent School District. The schools themselves had resisted many reform efforts in the past. Teacher turnover was high, and the pool of certified, capable teachers was not sufficient to meet the demand. Expectations for staff and students were low, capable leadership was inconsistent or absent, and student transience was common. Aversive working environments in which resources were scarce and demands overwhelming often challenged the patience, skill, and persistence of staff and students. For example, school libraries sometimes had no books and classrooms were devoid of instructional materials and resources beyond what our project provided. Basic equipment such as copy machines, overhead projectors, or working tape recorders were frequently missing from the schools and classrooms. Schools opened late the first year because about one third of the buildings' roofs were not up to safety codes.

The context for change differed dramatically at each site, in spite of the positive and similar growth observed across the study schools in general. Houston

Independent School District enjoyed stable leadership for many years, a nationally acclaimed district reading initiative, and a long-term accountability system at the state level. Under such conditions, we expected that most schools would sustain positive growth in achievement; however, the subdistrict where this study was located had two area superintendents in 4 years. Likewise, the District of Columbia Public School system had three superintendents in the first 4 years of the study. The District of Columbia site had instituted accountability (in the form of the Stanford-9 Achievement Test) during the second year of our project, but prior to that adoption, no data were available on students' progress before third grade. There was no districtwide reading initiative during the 4 years we worked in the District of Columbia site, so our schools had only each other for support.

ACHIEVEMENT OF READING
IMPROVEMENT IN THE PRIMARY GRADES

Our study involved 1,400 children in 17 low-performing schools (8 in Houston and 9 in the District of Columbia). We followed the reading growth of children through fourth grade in two cohorts, one selected in kindergarten and the other in first grade. Children were assessed at the end of each year with an extensive, individually administered test battery and four other times during the year with brief measures of critical skills underlying reading acquisition, similar to those now included in the Dynamic Indicators of Basic Early Literacy Skills (Good & Kaminski, 2005) and the Texas Primary Reading Inventory (TPRI; Texas Education Agency, 2004–2006). At the end of Year 4 of the project, children who were finishing third and fourth grades were solidly at national average in both Houston and the District of Columbia. Students had achieved average standard scores on the Woodcock-Johnson Psychoeducational Battery–Revised (Woodcock & Johnson, 1989) Passage Comprehension subtest (97 and 98 in the District of Columbia and Houston, respectively) and Basic Reading Cluster (103 and 101 in the District of Columbia and Houston, respectively). There was considerable variability across individual teachers and schools, however (Foorman & Moats, 2004; Foorman et al., 2006; Mehta, Foorman, Branum-Martin, & Taylor, 2005).

FACTORS RELATED TO
LITERACY GROWTH AND OUTCOMES

The first phase of the study, conducted in Houston from 1992 to 1997, supported the advantage of explicit over implicit classroom instructional approaches in first and second grades (Foorman et al., 1997; Foorman et al., 1998). The continuation of the study, conducted between 1997 and 2002, showed the positive impact of phonological awareness instruction in kindergarten on Grade 1 reading outcomes (Foorman, Chen, et al., 2003); the importance of teacher content knowledge, teacher allocation of instructional time, and overall teacher quality on literacy development through Grade 4 (Foorman & Moats, 2004); and the complex interaction of instructional factors in Grades 1 and 2 in determining Grade 2 classroom results (Foorman et al., 2006).

Complex data analyses allowed researchers to understand the relationships among teacher, student, and classroom variables. Mehta and colleagues (2005) examined 1) the extent to which literacy is a unitary construct at the student and classroom levels, 2) the differences between language competence and literacy levels, and 3) the relative roles of teachers and students in predicting literacy outcomes. Utilizing data from 1,342 students in 127 classrooms in Grades 1–4, Mehta and colleagues found that language and literacy were separable at the student level but unified at the classroom level and that the roles of phonological awareness and writing in accounting for literacy development change as students progress. PA is a significant factor early in reading development but declines in importance as students progress. In contrast, the contribution of writing to the literacy construct becomes stronger after second grade.

Foorman and Schatschneider (2003) observed that teachers spent very little time on either writing instruction or meaningful spelling instruction and that spelling achievement lagged significantly behind reading at all levels. Even though reading scores were in the average range, spelling scores on the Kaufman Test of Educational Achievement (Kaufman & Kaufman, 1985) were significantly lower (89 and 87 in the District of Columbia and Houston, respectively; approximately the 24th and 20th percentiles). Learning to read was not enough to support learning to spell.

The No Child Left Behind Act of 2001 (PL 107-110) includes the Reading First program, which has awarded grants to states for schools willing to adopt research-based core, comprehensive reading programs. How important is the school's program in accounting for the progress made by classrooms? What accounts for successful implementation of a core program?

HOW MUCH DIFFERENCE DOES THE READING PROGRAM MAKE?

A consistent finding in our research was that reading achievement outcomes were determined more by school, teacher, and child factors than by the effect of a particular program of instruction. None of the four participating reading programs showed clear superiority in accounting for student reading achievement. In other words, the effect of any of the research-based, comprehensive programs was limited by 1) school effects and 2) lack of variability at the classroom level. A well-designed program in the hands of a low-performing teacher was of little effect, but a strong teacher could get results even with a program of weaker design.

Those schools whose overall achievement was higher than others were characterized by the same qualities that characterized the Flagship Schools identified in a Texas survey (Denton, Foorman et al., 2003; Foorman & Moats, 2004). Mutual respect, pride in academic achievement, and collegiality was evident in interactions among administrators, teachers, and students. Discipline was seldom an issue, and children were generally on task. Time spent on reading instruction was a priority in every classroom, in small-group intervention, in specialized tutorials, and in extended-day activities. Teachers bought into the instructional approach they had been given (Foorman & Moats, 2004), and they could explain the rationale for the approach and how it was used to prevent reading problems as well as to intervene with at-risk students.

The instructional programs, with the exception of the Houghton Mifflin program, focused on explicit, systematic instruction in phonological skills and phonics. Houghton Mifflin teachers used supplementary materials and activities to bolster that program's weaknesses, as modeled in their professional development workshops and courses. These elements were combined with vocabulary, oral language, and comprehension instruction and lots of reading practice. Teachers in higher performing schools communicated with parents about children's progress and provided ways for parents to extend reading opportunities.

SCREENING AND PREDICTION OF READING PROBLEMS

Evidence from other longitudinal studies, in addition to ours, converge on a restricted set of valid predictors for the identification of children at risk for reading difficulties: phonological awareness and identification of letter sounds; rapid naming of letters; vocabulary knowledge; and word reading, especially word reading fluency (Fletcher, Denton, Fuchs, & Vaughn, 2005; Good, Simmons, & Kame'enui, 2001; O'Connor & Jenkins, 1999; Vellutino, Scanlon, & Lyon, 2000; Wood, Hill, & Meyer, 2001). Taken together, these studies indicate that predictive validity of phonological awareness tasks depends on how and when these skills are assessed.

Schatschneider and colleagues (2004) found that phonological awareness and word reading tasks measure the same underlying constructs over time but that tasks vary in their predictive value at different points in development. For example, in kindergarten, initial sound comparisons and blending of onsets and rimes are predictive of first-grade reading, whereas in first grade it is blending and segmenting of multiple phonemes that predict end-of-year reading success. Moreover, assessments at the beginning of kindergarten are less reliable than those at the middle or the end, as children need time to acclimate to the school environment. Finally, letter–sound identification is more predictive than letter naming in the second half of kindergarten and the beginning of first grade. Identifying the sounds represented by letters is directly related to phonic decoding of words.

By third grade, oral reading fluency, indicated by words correct per minute on 1-minute timed passage readings, accounts for the most variance in sustained, silent reading comprehension (Torgesen, 2005). Vocabulary knowledge and verbal reasoning account for more and more of the variance in reading comprehension as children get older and have mastered basic decoding skills.

Such findings have collectively influenced the design and use of early screening instruments such as Dynamic Indicators of Basic Early Literacy Skills (DIBELS; Good & Kaminski, 2005) and the Texas Primary Reading Inventory (TPRI). The Early Interventions Project was a source of validation data for the construction of such screening instruments, but at the classroom level, teachers did not habitually use the screening data to inform their instruction. Without structured team meetings and opportunities to interpret student data, teachers did not use it purposefully. Current policies promoting "multi-tiered" instructional delivery systems (Fletcher et al., 2005) will require considerably more coaching for teachers in the use of screening data than we were able to provide.

WRITING: WHERE LANGUAGE PROBLEMS ARE EXPOSED

Each year during the Early Interventions Project, a structured writing sample was obtained from students in May. We undertook an intensive analysis of the writing skills of 40 fourth graders, randomly selected from classrooms where we had observed high- and low-quality writing instruction (Moats, Foorman, & Taylor, 2006). Although we were able to show the positive effects of stronger writing instruction on students' compositions, striking and unresolved problems of language formulation, transcription, and usage were ubiquitous across the writing samples. Although our students were scoring within the average range on standardized reading tests, spelling and writing were not developing at average levels. Spelling was highly correlated with reading, but spelling was developing at a comparatively slower rate, as previously noted.

Similar to students with language learning disabilities (LLD), our high-poverty students also appeared "overwhelmed by the multiple demands of . . . writing and appear[ed] to have difficulty allocating sufficient cognitive resources to meet various writing demands" (Singer & Bashir, 2004, p. 559). The 40 students in our study, however, were not designated as having LLD; they were average students in classrooms of struggling urban schools serving high-poverty, minority populations, many of whom were speakers of African American Vernacular English. The classroom language and writing instruction had not enabled these students to acquire the academic language proficiency necessary to support the planning, organization, text generation, and online revision skills of writing.

To deploy attention and working memory in the service of explicit planning, organization, text construction, and self-regulation strategies during the writing process, students must automatize many component skills of written language production (Berninger, 2000; Berninger, Cartwright, Yates, Swanson, & Abbott, 1994; Graham, 1997). These include handwriting fluency and legibility, knowledge of spelling, mastery of the words and language used in written

English, punctuation, and other conventions of written expression. Our students' use of language such as verb forms, subordinate clauses, grammatical word endings, punctuation, and spelling rules was very problematic.

The students' limited vocabularies, documented in the parent study as being significantly below average (seventh percentile in the study population when the study began), undoubtedly contributed to their dependence on repetitive uses of the same words and to under-elaboration of thoughts and ideas. The topic was provocative (i.e., "When I Was Frightened"), and compositions contained multiple references to violence, vulnerability, monsters, and various environmental threats. In this case, topic knowledge and engagement in the task may have been higher than would have been the case with a more banal assignment. The students had something to say but nevertheless struggled to write.

Part of our analysis probed in detail the specific difficulties the children experienced with the representation of words at the phonological, orthographic, and morphosyntactic levels. At the most basic level, students' fluency of output depends on their mastery of graphomotor skills of letter formation, alphabet production, word knowledge, grammar, and spelling. About one third of the fourth-grade students demonstrated very poor handwriting, which is known to interfere with compositional quality and fluency (Berninger et al., 1994). Handwriting problems were most likely attributable to lack of instruction, as so little direct teaching of writing skills was observed in earlier grades. The percent of time spent on writing instruction during reading/language arts instruction ranged from 3% to 11% in Houston from first to fourth grades and from 6% to 8% in the District of Columbia across those same grades (Foorman et al., 2006; Moats et al., 2006).

The ability to read Standard Academic English for comprehension does not appear to be sufficient to enable students with dialect differences or linguistic disparities to represent standard English forms in writing by the fourth-grade level. The awareness of and representation of speech sounds with graphemes, awareness and representation of morphosyntactic structures in spelling, and awareness and use of standard word and sentence forms each depend on the development of specific linguistic knowledge (Bryant, Nunes, & Bindman, 2000) as well as, perhaps, a nonspecific level of metalinguistic awareness that supports such skills as intrinsic and automatic comparison of dialects (Charity, Scarborough, & Griffin, 2004).

It is not possible to know, given our data, whether the children who struggled with the written representation of speech sounds, inflectional morphemes, and grammatical forms would have exhibited tacit awareness of these structures, for example on a recognition task, but were limited in their explicit and conscious expression in writing simply from lack of direct teaching and practice. Likewise, it is not possible to know how many children were lacking even tacit awareness of the Standard Academic English structures they were to use in written expression.

TEACHING—WHAT INFLUENCE DID PROFESSIONAL DEVELOPMENT HAVE?

Professional Development Program

In the District of Columbia site, professional development comprised an introductory summer workshop of 2–4 days that addressed both content knowledge of reading and language and instructional program implementation. These institutes were followed by two or three 3-credit courses each year, focused on foundation concepts in teaching reading with any comprehensive instructional program. The topics of those courses included Phonology and Reading Research (1 term, repeated yearly); Teaching Decoding (2 terms); Teaching Vocabulary and Comprehension (2 terms); and Teaching Writing.

Observers visited each classroom an average of five to six times during the year. Publishers' program consultants carried out monthly in-class visits and delivered demonstration lessons for the teachers. Principals and school-based change facilitators were included in all professional development. We thus maintained a continuous presence in the classes of all teachers, although only about half of the eligible teachers enrolled in formal courses that met after school or on weekends. During the fourth year of the project, reading coaches also worked intensively with individual teachers in their classrooms as the need arose.

After-school courses emphasized the conceptual underpinnings and research basis for effective classroom practice as well as the links between those concepts and the practices teachers used in their instructional programs. Teachers were asked to read, discuss, and summarize points from professional journal readings. Each topic was addressed in depth. In each class, we anchored practical teaching strategies to a larger theoretical framework, such as a model of reading processes, a model of reading instruction components, and a model of reading and spelling development. Throughout the courses, we emphasized the structure of English phonology and orthography. The interplay between theory and practice was continual, redundant, and consistent, just as Birman, Desimone, Porter, and Garet (2000) reported in their analysis of effective professional development projects that were part of the Eisenhower Professional Development Program.

Teachers' Views of Their Professional Development Experiences

We interviewed 50 K–4 teachers who had been with the project for 2 years or more to elicit teachers' impressions of the professional development program. Interviews were conducted, taped, and transcribed to preserve teacher anonymity. Forty-nine of the fifty teachers characterized their experience in the project as "positive" to "extremely positive." No teacher identified the payment of stipends as a primary motivator for their interest in taking courses. Rather, teachers linked their enthusiasm to improved student outcomes; the achievement of greater insight into the teaching of reading; the availability of material support; and enjoyment of a supportive, collaborative professional context in which learning was rewarding, reciprocal, useful, and exciting.

Teachers recognized immediate and long-term student gains on both classroom assessments and the district's Stanford-9 testing, attributing those gains to their own professional growth. Many stated specifically that they succeeded with at-risk, reluctant, and poor readers whom they had not been able to reach in previous years. Many stated that "all children can learn to read" if the programs are properly taught.

Teachers' Views of Conditions that Support Improvement

Many teachers commented that their own gains in phonological and phonic knowledge had a major positive impact on children's reading achievement. The information about language was new, even to those who had taught for many years. Knowledge of "sounds," when coupled with opportunities to learn and practice specific instructional techniques and strategies, was empowering.

Teachers expressed gratitude that, for the first time, they were working with comprehensive reading programs with all necessary support materials. Prior to the project's intervention, many had been working with few instructional materials, few books, and no working mechanical equipment such as tape recorders or overhead projectors. Teachers welcomed feedback, guidance, and encouragement given with the expectation of gradual, incremental improvement toward clearly defined teaching standards. They enjoyed watching model lessons, visiting peers' classrooms, role-playing during workshops, receiving tips from staff members, and team planning. Many valued the reciprocity embedded in the professional development learning experience. No teacher expressed a preference for being left alone or teaching without a core, comprehensive set of instructional materials. The importance of collegial networks for sustaining research-based practice has been noted as well by other researchers (e.g., Darling-Hammond & Post, 2000; Gersten, Chard, & Baker, 2000).

Teachers welcomed the structure imposed by project staff in the form of pacing guides, lesson scripts, and lesson plans. No teacher complained that structure and well-defined expectations for time management, pacing, or instructional priorities were either stifling or limiting. Rather, many protested that they had been overwhelmed by too many choices of activities in publishers' teaching manuals and too little assistance choosing essential lesson components. Several teachers mentioned that creativity was possible within the structure provided; only one requested less repetition in a program's format, although she acknowledged that repetition was effective for the children.

In summary, the model of professional development was enthusiastically endorsed by participating teachers. Sound, rigorous, consistent content; a constant interplay between knowledge, understanding, and improvement of classroom practices; permission to make gradual improvement over time; and the creation of a positive, rewarding professional and social context in which to learn and work were the factors most often praised by teachers.

RELATIONSHIP BETWEEN TEACHER KNOWLEDGE, TEACHER COMPETENCE, AND CLASSROOM OUTCOMES

Relationships among measures of teacher knowledge, teacher effectiveness, and student outcomes were studied at both sites (Moats & Foorman, 2003). Teacher knowledge was measured by an experimental 19-question multiple choice Teacher Knowledge Survey; teachers' general effectiveness in essential teaching routines and classroom management was measured with a structured observation instrument (Texas Teacher Appraisal System [TTAS]; Texas Education Agency, 1984). The Teacher Knowledge Survey included questions about orthographic, phonological, and morphological aspects of word structure; the components of reading instruction; and the significance of specific spelling, writing, and oral reading errors in student work samples. Eighty third- and fourth-grade teachers, during the fourth year of the study, took the Teacher Knowledge Survey at the beginning of the year and the end of the year. They were also rated during that year by observers who had achieved high interrater reliability with the TTAS (>.80; see Foorman & Schatschneider [2003] for further description of these instruments).

Teachers rated as more effective in their classroom teaching techniques had students with higher reading outcomes. The very modest relationships we were able to demonstrate between teacher knowledge, teaching effectiveness, and student outcomes support findings of other studies (Bos, Mather, Dickson, Podhajski, & Chard, 2001; Cunningham, Perry, Stanovich, Stanovich, 2004; McCutchen, Abbott et al., 2002; McCutchen & Berninger, 1999) that also document connections among these variables.

RESULTS OF TEACHER KNOWLEDGE SURVEYS

Knowledge surveys given to teachers of various levels of experience and education have consistently found major gaps in teachers' understandings about language structure, reading instruction, and the meaning of student assessments and work samples (Bos et al., 2001; Cunningham et al., 2004; McCutcheon, Abbott et al., 2002; McCutcheon, Harry, et al., 2002; Moats, 1995; Moats & Foorman, 2003; Spear-Swerling & Brucker, 2003, 2004). Knowledge surveys from our own and others' research consistently reveal that the most elusive concepts for teachers are

1. Differentiation of speech sounds from letters
2. Ability to detect the identity of phonemes in words, especially when the spelling of those sounds does not directly represent the sounds

3. Knowledge of the letter combinations (graphemes) that represent phonemes in familiar words and recognition of a word's regularity or irregularity

4. Identification of functional spelling units such as digraphs, blends, silent-letter spellings, and meaningful word parts (morphemes)

5. Conventions of syllable division and syllable spelling

6. Linguistic constituents of a sentence and the recognition of basic parts of speech

7. Recognition of children's difficulties with phonological, orthographic, morphologic, and syntactic learning from work samples and assessments

8. Understanding of the ways in which the components of reading instruction are causally related to one another

Findings from teacher knowledge studies converge in suggesting that teachers' knowledge of phonology and orthography is often underdeveloped for the purpose of explicit teaching of reading or writing. In addition, teacher content knowledge of language can be measured directly but is not closely associated with philosophical beliefs, teachers' self-assessments, or knowledge of children's literature. Finally, teachers' knowledge of and ability to apply concepts of phonology and orthography does correspond to primary grade children's reading and spelling achievement.

CORE ISSUE: WHO TEACHES THE CHILDREN?

Reading programs, state standards, and literacy curricula are only as good as those who are implementing them. A growing body of work suggests that most teachers are ill-prepared to implement core, classroom instruction and small-group intervention in accordance with research-based principles (Walsh, Glaser, & Dunne-Wilcox, 2006). If administrators and teachers are taught (as these authors once were) that students' reading depends more than anything else on gender, intelligence quotient score, family's education, socioeconomic status, handedness, or "learning style," they will have little reason to implement systematic, explicit instruction of essential language skills. If teachers believe, as many still do, that literature comprehension must be the primary focus of beginning reading instruction and that language learning and word recognition will fall into place naturally, through exposure to books and motivational experiences, then they are likely to perpetuate the cycle of failure.

Children's reading and writing success, especially in high-poverty schools, depends on teachers who will use every available minute to build language and academic skills. Ideally, teachers will be using the best-designed programs available to organize their instruction. In addition, they must be able to explain concepts, select examples, give corrective feedback, adjust the teaching cycle, and differentiate groups of children. Teachers who can model Standard American English usage, compare informal language with academic English, and explain the reasons why words are spelled the way they are can help students overcome initial language disadvantages. But how many teachers are able to do these things? Our teacher surveys, as well as those of other researchers, show repeatedly that practicing, licensed teachers in general know much too little about reading and language, including the identity of phonemes in words, the spelling rules and patterns of English, the conventions of academic English usage, and the organization of exposition. Such knowledge is necessary to implement a good program skillfully (Snow, Griffin, & Burns, 2005). Furthermore, teachers are not very good at estimating their own knowledge levels in any of these domains.

Some critics of these ideas argue that detailed and specific knowledge of language is unnecessary for teachers if they are given scripted programs to follow. Others emphasize that knowledge of *big ideas* or *essential components of instruction* (e.g., Coyne, Zipoli, & Ruby, 2006) is most important. In practice, however, detailed knowledge lies behind productive interactions between teachers and students. *High quality instruction*—defined as that which most efficiently enables children to achieve high levels of literacy—depends on the coherence of the content conveyed as well as the manner in which it is taught.

To illustrate, enumeration of concepts that underlie coherent instruction in just one domain of learning, word recognition, may be helpful. Coherent instruction, again, provides information about the language systems involved in the use of print and gives complete and accurate information to children, which they then internalize and generalize. The information provided enables children to integrate all aspects of word knowledge—sound, meaning, word origin, and usage conventions.

Phonological awareness instruction, to support phoneme blending and segmentation in beginning word recognition and spelling, necessitates differentiation of syllables (e.g., *ac-com-plish*) from onsets and rimes (e.g., *pl-ate*) and depends on a teacher's ability to count, pronounce, blend, segment, and manipulate the individual speech sounds in words (e.g., /p/-/l/-/ā/-/t/). If we want young children to distinguish the meanings of *cloud* and *clown,* for example, we should teach them first to recognize and pronounce ending consonants by highlighting the feature differences of those speech sounds. In this case, /n/ and /d/ are articulated similarly, with the tongue behind the teeth, and the critical distinguishing feature of the two phonemes is the nasality of /n/. Children who have been asked to attend to language at that level can more readily distinguish words that are similar in form but different in meaning.

As children progress, differentiation of syllables from morphemes is helpful because meaningful parts of words are reflected in the spelling system and provide a direct link to meaning. For example, *global* has two meaningful parts or morphemes: the base word *globe* and the adjective suffix *-al*. The silent *e* in the base word was dropped because the suffix begins with a vowel. A phrase such as *global warming* resonates more deeply with students who have thought about the structure of the words.

Informed word recognition instruction includes much more than letter–sound correspondence, but teachers are seldom trained in sufficient depth—or provided the instructional materials—to demystify language with such clarity. Some of the poorest results in our Teacher Knowledge Surveys occur on items having to do with knowledge of morphology and word structure. On one survey, given to 120 primary grade teachers in two states, an item asked teachers to identify which word has an adjective suffix: *natural, apartment, city, encircle,* or *emptiness.* Only 7 % of respondents correctly identified *natural.* If these results indicate what is typical, then it should not be surprising that the language learning needs of most children are not being met.

So far, we have no evidence that teachers are any better prepared to teach language form and use at the level of sentences, paragraphs, or lengthier discourse. Nevertheless, until we find ways to convey better command of language to students, they are unlikely to progress beyond current levels of literacy.

CONCLUSION

Multiple consensus reports link expectations for teacher knowledge and teaching skill to the scientific consensus on reading instruction. The fruits of scientific reading research, however, cannot be realized unless teachers understand and are prepared to implement those findings. Mandates for the practice of *scientifically based reading research,* such as those in the No Child Left Behind legislation, may have been premature before a concerted educational effort was undertaken to ensure that teachers and administrators understood what was intended.

Fundamental to differentiated instruction in language and literacy is the teacher's insight into the reasons why some children have difficulty and knowledge of research-based practices. Knowledge of language structure, language and reading development, and the dependence of literacy on oral language proficiency are prerequisite understandings for informed instruction of reading, along with extensive procedural knowledge of explicit teaching routines. We cannot blame teachers or hold them accountable for poor results if, as a profession, we have not defined the prerequisite levels of verbal proficiency necessary to teach literacy, are unwilling to invoke standards for entry into the profession, and have not offered teachers the kind of professional training that engages their interest, is respectful of their needs, and empowers them to be successful with children. Well-constructed and validated instructional materials are necessary and important tools for high-quality instruction, but merely disseminating these materials is unlikely to strongly affect teachers' behavior without attention to their attitudes, goals, and knowledge base.

A first course of action in addressing our need for a stronger teaching corps is to obtain more evidence that bears on these critical questions: What combination and sequence of experiences are most effective and rewarding for teachers who are learning to teach children how to read and use language? How much content knowledge and verbal skill should be expected before teachers are even admitted to a licensing program or admitted to a practicum in teaching? Within the confines of licensing programs, what concepts are priorities? What incentives will work best to attract and keep talented teachers? What is the difference between knowledge needed by specialists and knowledge needed by regular classroom teachers, and what is the difference in training time?

A second condition for successful and sustainable reduction of reading failure is to encourage school boards and administrators to adopt longer range implementation plans. These should include ample professional development time around a set of specific knowledge and practice standards (Moats, 1999). Several years are necessary to build a school culture that will support optimal achievement (Denton, Vaughn, & Fletcher, 2003; Fletcher et al., 2005; Gersten et al., 2000). Projects with a history of success include phases such as 1) planning and commitment to all aspects of change; 2) orientation, including baseline data collection, training of school personnel, and the establishment of teams; 3) initial implementation, in which the program is put into place according to plan and coaching is provided; 4) independent operation, characterized by increased self-sufficiency and evaluation of outcomes; and 5) institutionalization, in which all key aspects of a program—including use of regular classroom instructional materials, procedures for teaching intervention groups, a professional development curriculum, and use of student assessments—are integrated into the routine operation of the school. Sometimes up to 5 years are necessary before the maximum affect of a reading initiative is realized (King & Torgesen, 2006). This should seem realistic in light of the extensive knowledge required for skillful teaching of the essential components of instruction and the use of assessments that inform grouping. "Spray and pray" workshops will not be enough.

Third, teachers need multiple opportunities to view good models and to practice new procedures with helpful feedback that will lead to refinement of teaching skill. They cannot become experts at everything at once. Teaching high-poverty students is highly demanding. Teachers thrive on supportive interactions within collegial networks, as long as the shared learning activities pertain to a reasonable, specific, explicit set of professional learning objectives.

In summary, teaching and teachers hold the key to the literacy of high-poverty students. Educating the teachers, and building professional contexts in which they can do their valuable work, is as serious a business as educating the young students.

REFERENCES

Armbruster, B., Lehr, F., & Osborn, J. (2001). *Put reading first: The research building blocks for teaching children to read, K–3.* Washington, DC: National Institute for Literacy.

Berninger, V. (2000). Development of language by hand and its connections to language by ear, mouth, and eye. *Topics in Language Disorders, 20,* 65–84.

Berninger, V.W., Cartwright, A.C., Yates, C.M., Swanson, H.L., & Abbott, R.D. (1994). Developmental skills related to writing and reading acquisition in the intermediate grades: Shared and unique functional systems. *Reading and Writing, 6,* 161–196.

Birman, B.F., Desimone, L., Porter, A.C., & Garet, M.S. (2000). Designing professional development that works. *Educational Leadership, 57*(8), 28–33.

Blachman, B. (2000). Phonological awareness. In M.L. Kamil, P.B. Mosenthal, P.D. Pearson, & R. Barr (Eds.), *Handbook of reading research* (Vol. 3, pp. 483–502). Mahwah, NJ: Lawrence Erlbaum Associates.

Borman, G.D., Slavin, R.E., Cheung, A., Chamberlain, A., Madden, N., & Chambers, B. (2005). The national randomized field trial of Success for All: Second-year outcomes. *American Educational Research Journal, 42,* 673–696.

Bos, C., Mather, N., Dickson, S., Podhajski, B., & Chard, D. (2001). Educators' perceptions and knowledge of early reading. *Annals of Dyslexia, 51,* 97–120.

Bryant, P., Nunes, T., & Bindman, M. (2000). The relations between children's linguistic awareness and spelling: The case of the apostrophe. *Reading and Writing, 12,* 253–276.

Carnine, D.W., Silbert, J., & Kame'enui, E.J. (1997). *Direct instruction reading* (3rd ed.). Upper Saddle River, NJ: Prentice-Hall.

Catts, H.W., Fey, M., Zhang, X., & Tomblin, J.B. (1999). Language basis of reading and spelling disabilities: Evidence from a longitudinal study. *Scientific Studies of Reading, 3,* 331–361.

Charity, A.H., Scarborough, H.S., & Griffin, D.M. (2004). Familiarity with school English in African American children and its relation to early reading achievement. *Child Development, 75*(5), 1340–1356.

Coyne, M.D., Zipoli, R.P., & Ruby, M.F. (2006). Beginning reading instruction for students at risk for reading disabilities: What, when, and how. *Intervention in School and Clinic, 41*(3), 161–168.

Cunningham, A.E., Perry, K.E., Stanovich, K.E., & Stanovich, P.J. (2004). Disciplinary knowledge of K–3 teachers and their knowledge calibration in the domain of early literacy. *Annals of Dyslexia, 54,* 139–167.

Darling-Hammond, L., & Post, L. (2000). Inequality in teaching and schooling: Supporting high quality teaching and leadership in low income schools. In R.D. Kahlenberg (Ed.), *A nation at risk: Preserving public education as an engine for social mobility* (pp. 127–267). New York: Century Foundation Press.

Denton, C., Foorman, B.R., & Mathes, P.G. (2003). Schools that "beat the odds": Implications for reading instruction. *Remedial and Special Education, 24,* 258–261.

Denton, C., & Mathes, P.G. (2003). Intervention for struggling readers: Possibilities and challenges. In B.R. Forman (Ed.), *Preventing and remediating reading difficulties* (pp. 229–252). Baltimore: York Press.

Denton, C., Vaughn, S., & Fletcher, J. (2003). Bringing research-based practice to scale. *Learning Disability Research and Practice, 15,* 74–94.

Ehri, L.C., Nunes, S.R., Willows, D., Schuster, B., Yaghoub-Zadeh, Z., & Shanahan, T. (2001). Phonemic awareness instruction helps children to read: Evidence from the National Reading Panel's meta-analysis. *Reading Research Quarterly, 3,* 250–257.

Elbaum, B., Vaughn, S., Hughes, M.T., & Moody, S.W. (2000). How effective are one-to-one tutoring programs in reading for elementary students at risk for reading failure? A meta-analysis of the intervention research. *Journal of Educational Psychology, 92,* 605–619.

Fletcher, J.M., Denton, C.A., Fuchs, L., & Vaughn, S.R. (2005). Multi-tiered reading instruction: Linking general education and special education. In S.O. Richardson & J. Gilger (Eds.), *Research-based education and intervention: What we need to know.* (pp. 21–43). Baltimore: International Dyslexia Association.

Foorman, B.R., Breier, J.I., & Fletcher, J.M. (2003). Interventions aimed at improving reading success: An evidence-based approach. *Developmental Neuropsychology, 24*(2 & 3), 613–639.

Foorman, B.R., Chen, D.T., Carlson, C., Moats, L., Francis, D.J., & Fletcher, J. (2003). The necessity of the alphabetic principle to phonemic awareness instruction. *Reading and Writing, 16,* 289–324.

Foorman, B.R., Francis, D.J., Fletcher, J.M., Schatschneider, C., & Mehta, P. (1998). The role of instruction in learning to read: Preventing reading failure in at-risk children. *Journal of Educational Psychology, 90,* 37–55.

Foorman, B.R., Francis, D.J., Shaywitz, S.E., Shaywitz, B.A., & Fletcher, J.M. (1997). The case for early reading interventions. In B. Blachman (Ed.), *Foundations of reading acquisition and dyslexia: Implications for early intervention* (pp. 243–264). Mahwah, NJ: Lawrence Erlbaum Associates.

Foorman, B.R., & Moats, L.C. (2004). Conditions for sustaining research-based practices in early reading instruction. *Remedial and Special Education, 25*(1), 51–60.

Foorman, B.R., & Schatschneider, C. (2003). Measurement of teaching practices during reading/language arts instruction and its relationship to student achievement. In S. Vaughn & K.L. Briggs (Eds.), *Reading in the classroom: Systems for the observation of teaching and learning* (pp. 1–30). Baltimore: Paul H. Brookes Publishing Co.

Foorman, B.R., Schatschneider, C., Eakin, M.N., Fletcher, J.M., Moats, L.C., & Francis, D.J. (2006). The impact of instructional practices in grades 1 and 2 on reading and spelling achievement in high poverty schools. *Contemporary Educational Psychology, 31,* 1–29.

Gersten, R., Chard, D., & Baker, S. (2000). Factors enhancing sustained use of research-based instructional practices. *Journal of Learning Disabilities, 33*(5), 445–457.

Gilger, J.W., & Wise, S.E. (2004). Genetic correlates of language and literacy impairments. In C.A. Stone, E.R. Silliman, B.J. Ehren, & K. Apel (Eds.), *Handbook of language and literacy: Development and disorders* (pp. 25–48). New York: Guilford Press.

Good, R., & Kaminski, R. (2005). *Dynamic Indicators of Basic Early Literacy Skills* (6th ed.). Longmont, CO: Sopris West Educational Services.

Good, R., Simmons, D.C., & Kame'enui, E.J. (2001). The importance and decision-making utility of a continuum of fluency-based indicators of foundational reading skills for third-grade high-stakes outcomes. *Scientific Studies of Reading, 5,* 257–288.

Graham, S. (1997). Executive control in the revising of students with learning and writing difficulties. *Journal of Educational Psychology, 89,* 223–234.

Hanushek, E.A., Kain, J.F., & Rivkin, S.G. (1998). *Does special education raise academic achievement for students with disabilities?* (Working Paper No. 6690). Cambridge, MA: National Bureau of Economic Research.

Houghton Mifflin. (1996). *Invitations to literacy.* Boston: Author.

Kaufman, A.S., & Kaufman, N.L. (1985). *Kaufman Test of Educational Achievement.* Circle Pines, MN: American Guidance Service.

King, R., & Torgesen, J. (2006). Improving the effectiveness of reading instruction in one elementary school: A description of the process. In P. Blaunstein & R. Lyon (Eds.), *It doesn't have to be this way.* Lanham, MD: Scarecrow Press.

Mathes, P.G., Denton, C.A., Fletcher, J.M., Anthony, J.L., Francis, D.J., & Schatschneider, C. (2005). An evaluation of two reading interventions derived from diverse models. *Reading Research Quarterly, 40,* 148–182.

McCardle, P., & Chhabra, V. (Eds.). (2004). *The voice of evidence in reading research.* Baltimore: Paul H. Brookes Publishing Co.

McCutchen, D., Abbott, R.D., Green, L.B., Beretvas, S.N., Cox, S., Potter, N.S., et al. (2002). Beginning literacy: Links among teacher knowledge, teacher practice, and student learning. *Journal of Learning Disabilities, 35*(1), 69–86.

McCutchen, D., & Berninger, V. (1999). Those who know, teach well: Helping teachers master literacy-related subject matter knowledge. *Learning Disabilities Research and Practice, 14*(4), 215–226.

McCutchen, D., Harry, D.R., Cunningham, A.E., Cox, S., Sidman, S., & Covill, A.E. (2002). Reading teachers' content knowledge of children's literature and phonology. *Annals of Dyslexia, 52,* 207–228.

Mehta, P., Foorman, B.R., Branum-Martin, L., & Taylor, W.P. (2005). Literacy as a uni-dimensional multilevel construct: Validation, sources of influence, and implications in a longitudinal study in grades 1–4. *Scientific Studies of Reading, 9*(2), 85–116.

Moats, L.C. (1995). The missing foundation in teacher education. *American Educator, 19*(2), 9, 43–51.

Moats, L.C. (1999). *Teaching reading is rocket science.* Washington, DC: American Federation of Teachers.

Moats, L.C., & Foorman, B.R. (2003). Measuring teachers' content knowledge of language and reading. *Annals of Dyslexia, 53,* 23–45.

Moats, L.C., Foorman, B.R., & Taylor, W.P. (2006). How quality of writing instruction impacts high-risk fourth graders' writing. *Reading and Writing, 19,* 363–391.

National Institute of Child Health and Human Development. (2000). *Report of the National Reading Panel. Teaching children to read: An evidence-based assessment of the scientific research literature on reading and its implications for reading instruction: Reports of the subgroups* (NIH Publication No. 00-4754). Washington, DC: U.S. Government Printing Office.

Neuman, S.B., & Dickinson, D.K. (Eds.). (2001). *Handbook of early literacy research.* NY: Guilford Press.

No Child Left Behind Act of 2001, PL 107-110, 115 Stat. 1425, 20 U.S.C. §§ 6301 *et seq.*

O'Connor, R.E., & Jenkins, J.R. (1999). The prediction of reading disabilities in kindergarten and first grade. *Scientific Studies of Reading, 3,* 159–197.

Olson, R. (2004). SSSR, environment, and genes. *Scientific Studies of Reading, 8*(2), 111–124.

Open Court Reading. (1995). *Collections for young scholars.* Chicago: SRA/McGraw-Hill.

President's Commission on Excellence in Special Education. (2002). *President's Commission on Excellence in Special Education report: A new era: Revitalizing special education for children and their families.* Available online at http://www.ed.gov/inits/com missionsboards/whspecialeducation/reports/index.html

Rayner, K., Foorman, B., Perfetti, C.A., Pesetsky, D., & Seidenberg, M.S. (2001). How psychological science informs the teaching of reading. *Psychological Science in the Public Interest, 2,* 31–74.

Schatschneider, C., Fletcher, J., Francis, D., Carlson, C., & Foorman, B. (2004). Kindergarten prediction of reading skills: A longitudinal comparative study. *Journal of Educational Psychology, 96*(2), 265–282.

Singer, B.D., & Bashir, A.S. (2004). Developmental variations in writing composition skills. In C.A. Stone, E.R. Silliman, B.J. Ehren, & K. Apel (Eds.), *Handbook of language and literacy: Development and disorders* (pp. 559–582). New York: Guilford Press.

Slavin, R.E., Madden, N.A., Dolan, L., & Wasik, B.A. (1996). *Every child, every school, Success for All.* Thousand Oaks, CA: Corwin Press.

Snow, C.E., Burns, S.M., & Griffin, P. (1998). *Preventing reading difficulties in young children.* Washington, DC: National Academies Press.

Snow, C.E., Griffin, P., & Burns, S.M. (Eds.). (2005). *Knowledge to support the teaching of reading: Preparing teachers for a changing world.* San Francisco: Jossey-Bass.

Spear-Swerling, L., & Brucker, A.O. (2003). Teachers' acquisition of knowledge about English word structure. *Annals of Dyslexia, 53,* 72–103.

Spear-Swerling, L., & Brucker, A.O. (2004). Preparing novice teachers to develop basic reading and spelling skills in children. *Annals of Dyslexia, 54,* 332–364.

Stone, C.A., Silliman, E.R., Ehren, B.J., & Apel, K. (2004). *Handbook of language and literacy: Development and disorders.* New York: Guilford Press.

Taylor, B.M., Pearson, P.D., Clark, K., & Walpole, S. (2000). Effective schools and accomplished teachers: Lessons about primary-grade reading instruction in low-income schools. *The Elementary School Journal, 101,* 121–165.

Texas Education Agency. (1984). *Texas Teacher Appraisal System.* Austin, TX: Author.

Texas Education Agency. (2004–2006). *Texas Primary Reading Inventory (TPRI).* Austin: Texas Education Agency/University of Texas System. Available online at http:www.tpri.org

Torgesen, J.K. (2004). Avoiding the devastating downward spiral: The evidence that early intervention prevents reading failure. *American Educator, 28*(3), 6–19, 45–47.

Torgesen, J.K. (2005). Remedial interventions for students with dyslexia: National goals and current accomplishments. In S.O. Richardson & J. Gilger (Eds.), *Research-based education and intervention: What we need to know.* Baltimore: International Dyslexia Association.

Torgesen, J.K., Alexander, A.W., Wagner, R.K., Rashotte, C.A., Voeller, K., Conway, T., et al. (2001). Intensive remedial instruction for children with severe reading disabilities: Immediate and long-term outcomes from two instructional approaches. *Journal of Learning Disabilities, 34,* 33–58.

Torgesen, J.K., Wagner, R.K., Rashotte, C.A., Alexander, A.W., & Conway, T. (1997). Preventive and remedial interventions for children with severe disabilities. *Learning Disabilities, 8,* 51–61.

Vellutino, F.R., Scanlon, D.M., & Lyon, G.R. (2000). Differentiating between difficult-to-remediate and readily remediated poor readers: More evidence against the IQ-achievement discrepancy definition for reading disability. *Journal of Learning Disabilities, 33,* 223–238.

Vellutino, F.R., Scanlon, D.M., Sipay, E.R., Small, S.G., Pratt, A., Chen, R., et al. (1996). Cognitive profiles of difficult-to-remediate and readily remediated poor readers: Early intervention as a vehicle for distinguishing between cognitive and experiential deficits as basic causes of specific reading disability. *Journal of Educational Psychology, 88,* 601–638.

Walsh, K., Glaser, D., & Dunne-Wilcox, D. (2006). *What education schools aren't teaching about reading—and what elementary teachers aren't learning.* Washington, DC: National Council for Teacher Quality.

Wood, F., Hill, D., & Meyer, M. (2001). *Predictive Assessment of Reading.* Winston-Salem, NC: Author.

Woodcock, R.W., & Johnson, M.B. (1989). *Woodcock-Johnson Psychoeducational Battery–Revised.* Allen, TX: DLM.

6

Social and Academic Achievement of Children and Youth in Urban, High-Poverty Neighborhoods

Charles R. Greenwood

The purpose of this chapter is to provide a brief synthesis of my research, which has been primarily problem driven by a strong focus on improving the social and academic achievements of children and youth in an urban, high-poverty community in Kansas City, Kansas. This work has been guided by the mission of the Juniper Gardens Children's Project (JGCP), a 43-year collaboration between faculty of the University of Kansas and residents of the northeast Kansas City, Kansas, neighborhoods (see http://www.jgcp.ku.edu). The JGCP is 1 of 12 centers in the Kansas University Schiefelbusch Institute for Life Span Studies. The project has operated uninterrupted since 1964, and my work there began in the winter of 1978 when I accepted a position as a young research associate. I am currently the director of the JGCP and, with my 13 faculty colleagues, operate collaborative research projects funded by the U.S. Department of Education, the National Institute of Child Health and Human Development, the Centers for Disease Control and Prevention, and the Administration on Children, Youth and Families that seek to intervene to promote the language, literacy, and social-emotional proficiency of area children and youth. This focus is broad, ranging

This work is dedicated to the generations of children and families living in the northeast neighborhoods of Kansas City, Kansas. Preparation of this manuscript was supported by grants from the U.S. Office of Education, Office of Special Education Programs (Grant Nos. H024S60010, H324D990048, H324D990051, and H324D980066) and by the Kansas Intellectual and Developmental Disabilities Research Center (Grant No. HD002528). This work represents the perspective of the author and no endorsement by supporting agencies should be inferred.

from early childhood, to middle childhood, to adolescence and young adulthood. The work has been interdisciplinary, targeting the risks and effects of poverty in combination with disability, including learning disabilities, intellectual disabilities, and social-emotional behavior disorders as well as other disability conditions embraced by the fields of early intervention, special education, general education, human development, and child psychology (Greenwood, 1999).

Since the beginning, the work has taken an empirical, experimental approach to testing potential solutions to the social-behavioral and academic achievement problems of area youth in local child care, preschools, and public schools. The JGCP effort has always been about development and evaluation of the efficacy and effectiveness of interventions intended for implementation by teachers, parents, and peers in classrooms and homes—in the natural conditions of the community. Thus, the interventions that are designed are intended to be mediated by local teachers, peers, and parents with support from manuals and training and, over time, by addition of computer technology and media including software, multimedia, web sites, and educational media or television.

Complementary goals at JGCP have been 1) to develop practical but rigorous forms of measurement for examining environmental risk conditions, fidelity of intervention implementation, and monitoring of individual child progress over time; 2) to disseminate and scale up the use of effective intervention practices; and 3) to provide a context for the mentoring doctoral and postdoctoral researchers and their research agendas. In pursuit of these goals, JGCP researchers have developed and validated new measurement approaches, used them to examine the effects of problem conditions (i.e., risk), and developed and refined evidence-based intervention practices (see Figure 6.1) (Greenwood, 2003). (See http://www.jgcp.ku.edu/About _JG/Mission.htm for a description of the mission of JGCP.)

The common thread running through this work has been the integration of descriptive and experimental research at the level of concept and empirical data such that the focus of intervention development has been on changing alterable variables as potential solutions with clinical and social significance (Greenwood, Hart, Walker, & Risley, 1994). The theoretical perspective reflected in this work has been *ecological, interactional, and developmental,* wherein one's proficiency in reading, for example, is shaped by one's personal contexts of family, school, and friends and one's learning contexts are mutually influenced by one's increasingly proficient or deficient reading skills (i.e., social-behavioral or academic) in school over time. In this framework, interventions are contextual factors designed to influence skill development in socially desired ways.

When synthesizing my work for this chapter, I clearly saw that my research spanning the domains in Figure 6.1 has been integrative, hypothesis generating, hypothesis testing, and programmatic in nature. To be empirical required that measurement instruments be developed that were sensitive to ecological-interactional-developmental constructs and variables associated with risks and problem conditions (i.e., poverty) and that these measures also be shown to be sensitive to

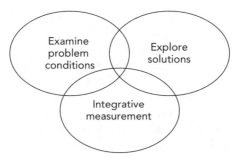

Figure 6.1.   Integration of key research areas. (*Source:* Greenwood, 2003.)

intervention effects. An additional requirement of the validity of instruments was that the constructs and variables be measured reliably, reflecting what children, students, teachers, and parents actually did in natural settings and not what they reported they did. Thus, instrument development focused on quantifying what participants were doing through direct observation, testing, and the analysis of products of their behavior. To be ecological-interactional-developmental, these instruments needed to include objective indices of the actual features of children's environments (e.g., ecological contexts) to address research questions about the structure of real situations as well as their function (i.e., the child/student response in these situations). Examples of research validating such measures are briefly presented in this chapter, followed next by findings from key studies using these measures to examine problem conditions and their effects both with and without interventions. In the final section, findings from these areas are pulled together, and implications are discussed.

ECOLOGICAL-INTERACTIONAL-DEVELOPMENTAL MEASUREMENT RESEARCH

In this section, two specific examples of a range of measures developed and validated for use in my program of research and that of close colleagues are presented. One reflects research on language learning in the homes of very young children birth to 36 months of age; the other reflects research on instruction and student learning in early elementary school classrooms. Although these measures clearly differ in the content they assess, both measures are similar in ecological-interactional-developmental theory and method (i.e., objective, direct observation).

Measuring the Home Language Learning Environment (Hart and Risley Code)

The Hart and Risley code was designed to measure individual children's growth in learning to talk as well as the child's language environment, consisting of parents', siblings', and friends' talk heard by the child in the home and addressed directly to the child (Hart & Risley, 1989). Using 1980s state-of-the-art technology, monthly 1-hour long audiotape recordings were made of each language learner and the talk addressed to him or her in the home (Hart & Risley, 1995). In addition to the audio recording, an observation coding scheme was implemented during the hour in which the audio recording was made. The audio recordings were transcribed, entered for computer analysis, and coded linguistically. In addition, the coded ecological variable information was entered in temporal relationship with the home language data so that descriptive information about the child's language environment, parent language, and child talk were available as well as conditional analyses of the data (e.g., number of initiations, turns, and contingencies between child and parent talk). Because the data were collected by trained observers and transcribers, measures of interobserver agreement and score reliability were conducted and reported (see Hart & Risley, 1995).

The number of indicators available from this instrument were extensive (Hart & Risley, 1999, Appendix B, p. 269). A selected few included the following:

- *For the child:* words, babble, nonverbal behaviors
- *For the parent:* words, picking up or putting down the child
- *For the parent and the child:* linguistic codes for what they said (e.g., noun, verb, clauses, tenses, functions)
- *For the home language environment:* the speaker (e.g., parent, child, sibling), routine care, games and books, unstructured activities

The technical validity features of the code included indices of interobserver agreement, construct validity, and predictive validity (Hart & Risley, 1992, 1995; Walker, Greenwood, Hart, & Carta, 1994). The Hart and Risley Code was subsequently adapted for use on notebook computers using digital recorders (see Table 6.1) and most recently speech recognition software (Infoture, 2007).

Measuring the Classroom Instructional Environment (Code for Instructional Structure and Student Academic Response and Variations)

A similar direct observation measure was developed for study of students' response to instruction in elementary school classrooms (Greenwood & Delquadri, 1988; Greenwood, Schulte, Dinwiddie, Kohler, & Carta, 1986).[1] The Code for Instructional Structure and Student Academic Response (CISSAR) was designed to measure theoretical features of the classroom environment (e.g., subject matter, task, grouping); teacher behavior relative to the child being observed (e.g., teaching, no response); and student behavior, including active academic responding (e.g., read-

---

[1]An online description of the EBASS software for implementing CISSAR, MS-CISSAR, and ESCAPE observation instruments can be found at http://www.jgcp.ku.edu/EBASS/ebass_descrp.htm

Table 6.1.   Measurement instruments and tools

Hart and Risley Language-Interaction Code—Enables computerized analyses of the development of spoken language in terms of interaction and ecological contexts within the home (Hart & Risley, 1989, 1995).

Parent–Infant Computerized Code for the Observation of Language Interactions (PIC-COLI)—A computerized version of the earlier Hart and Risley code that uses a note-book computer with digital audio recording capabilities. This upgrade made data recording more accurate and efficient to transcribe and prepare for statistical analysis (Walker, Hart, & Greenwood, 1994).

Code for Instructional Structure and Student Academic Response (CISSAR)—Provides observational measurement of student and teacher behavior in classroom settings. Its purpose is to quantify students' academic behavior within the context of specific instructional variables, practices, and teacher behavior (Greenwood, Delquadri, Stanley, Terry, & Hall, 1985).

Code for Instructional Structure and Student Academic Response–MainStream Version (MS-CISSAR)—Performs measurements similar to the CISSAR but is designed for use in general and special education classrooms and is adaptable to environments and behaviors of students with intellectual disabilities and special needs (Carta, Greenwood, Schulte, Arreaga-Mayer, & Terry, 1988).

Ecobehavioral System for the Complex Assessment of Preschool Environments (ES-CAPE)—An observation system for evaluating the instructional effectiveness of preschool programs and interventions. Like the CISSAR and MS-CISSAR, it measures ecological, teacher, and student variables in close temporal relation and provides indices of student engagement, talk, and inappropriate behavior overall or conditionally by specific ecological dimensions (Carta, Greenwood, & Atwater, 1985).

Ecobehavioral Assessment Systems Software (EBASS)—A software system that integrates with the CISSAR, MS-CISSAR, and ESCAPE for use on notebook computers (Greenwood, Carta, Kamps, Terry, & Delquadri, 1994; Greenwood & Hou, 1995).

Ecobehavioral System for the Contextual Recording of Interactional Bilingual Environments (ESCRIBE)—Supports direct observational measurement of ecological, teacher, and student behaviors in culturally and linguistically diverse classrooms (e.g., English as a Second Language) (Arreaga-Mayer, Carta, & Tapia, 1992).

Code for Interactive Recording of Caregiving and Learning Environments (CIRCLE 1–2)—A hand-held computer observation system used with children 4–36 months old and their caregivers in the home and child care center. CIRCLE 1 is designed for use with infants (Atwater, Montagna, Creighton, Williams, & Hou, 1993).

Individual Growth and Development Indicators for Infants and Toddlers—Designed for early interventionists interested in tracking the monthly or quarterly growth and development of young children (Greenwood, Carta, & Walker, 2005). Data are collected using paper and pencil recording sheets and processed using a web site (http://www.igdi.ku.edu).

- *Early Communication Indicator (ECI)* (Greenwood et al., 2006; Luze, Greenwood, Carta, Cline, & Kuntz, 2002)
- *Early Problem Solving Indicator (EPSI)* (Greenwood, Walker, Carta, & Higgins, 2006)
- *Early Social Indicator (ESI)* (Carta, Greenwood, Luze, Cline, & Kuntz, 2004)
- *Early Movement Indicator (EMI)* (Greenwood, Luze, Cline, Kuntz, & Leitschuh, 2002)

ing aloud, silent reading, writing), passive attending (e.g., looking at the teacher, raising hand), and problem behavior (e.g., inappropriate locale, disrupting). The CISSAR was subsequently adapted specifically for the quantification of instruction in special education settings (MS-CISSAR; Kamps, Greenwood, & Leonard, 1991), in preschool settings (ESCAPE; Carta, Greenwood, & Robinson, 1987), and in program settings serving English Language Learners (ELLs) (ESCRIBE; Arreaga-Mayer, Carta, & Tapia, 1994).

With all of these instruments, observers collected data relative to a single focal student using sequential momentary sampling paced by brief time intervals (Greenwood, Carta, & Dawson, 2000). Single students rather than groups of students were observed to generate hypotheses regarding the experiences provided to them and their response. At the end of the first 10-second interval, classroom ecology was recorded; at the end of the second 10-second interval, teacher behavior was recorded; and at the end of the third 10-second interval, the students' behavior was recorded. This sequence was repeated over the entire period of observation, which varied in duration based on the study design and purpose of the research (e.g., Greenwood, 1991b; Greenwood, Abbott, & Tapia, 2003) (see Table 6.1). The technical adequacy of the CISSAR (and its variations) includes controlling software—Ecobehavioral Assessment Software System (EBASS)—for notebook computers (Greenwood, Carta, Kamps, Terry, & Delquadri, 1994; Greenwood & Hou, 1995); paced observations as well as computed interobserver agreement and score reliability; and supported studies of the construct, criterion, and predictive validity of the instruments (Greenwood, Horton, & Utley, 2002).

RISK AND PROBLEM CONDITIONS

The way poverty affects the personal environments in which children grow in their learning of language and early literacy skills is of keen interest to researchers interested in improving the social and academic outcomes of young children (e.g., Whitehurst, 1996). Two areas of investigation are of particular interest: the school readiness of poor children and the instructional effectiveness in elementary school for poor children.

Effect of Home Poverty on Children's Early Language Learning and Subsequent School Readiness

Hart and Risley's (1995) longitudinal investigation of 42 young children, learning to talk at home beginning at 9 months of age, produced ground-breaking results:

> A University of Kansas study in the early 1980s reached the breathtaking conclusion that 3-year-olds with professional parents had developed more advanced vocabularies compared to children of mothers on welfare—to say nothing of the 3-year-olds of those mothers. "These children lack the kind of environment we just presume most kids will be exposed to," says Isabel V. Sawhill, Senior Fellow at the Brookings Institution. (Starr, 2002)

Children and families in three different family socioeconomic status (SES) groups (i.e., welfare [low SES], blue collar [mid-level SES], professional [high SES]) were studied longitudinally over a period of 2½ years. The Hart and Risley code was used to record interactions during monthly, 1-hour observations in the home. Based on these observations, Hart and Risley (1995) reported that low-SES parents talked to their child less than did blue-collar parents, who in turn talked less to their child than did professional parents. These differences included talk heard by the child as well as talk addressed directly to the child by the parents. In the case of language addressed to the children, low-SES parents talked to their child 2.5 times less per hour, per day than children in high-SES families (197 [low SES] versus 482 words per hour [high SES]). In cumulative terms, over a 2½ year time span, low-SES parents addressed approximately 9 million words to their children compared with 35 million words by high-SES parents. Many more meaningful differences favoring the children in professional families were documented, including increased number of interactions, increased number of questions asked, more instances of direct teaching, child's familiarity with unusual words, parents' use of standard pronunciation, parents' use of complex syntax, and fewer prohibitions.

The large differences in the cumulative amount of talk parents addressed to their child were stunning. Equally stunning were the large differences in the children's spoken vocabulary development. Children whose parents addressed more language to them by 36 months of age had acquired and used significantly more vocabulary in their talk by 36 months of age. And, their monthly vocabulary growth trajectories accelerated faster and steeper. Follow-along investigation of these children as they experienced the first few grades of elementary school produced direct implications of spoken vocabulary proficiency, intelligence quotient (IQ) score, school readiness, and achievement in basic academic skills in kindergarten and the early elementary grades (Greenwood, Hart et al., 1994). Children from low-SES families at 36 months scored lower in receptive vocabulary on the Peabody Picture Vocabulary test and were not ready for school by kindergarten; in addition, they performed significantly lower in basic academic skills than their high-SES peers by the end of first grade.

In summary, this work identified potentially alterable problem conditions in the earliest learning environments of children from low-SES families with respect to spoken vocabulary growth and language development. Spoken vocabulary is a precursor to early literacy and school readiness at kindergarten as well as a proxy for verbal IQ score (Whitehurst & Lonigan, 2001). The work suggests potentially alterable mechanisms by which parental interventions focused on talking more frequently and differently may lead to accelerated outcomes for children reared in low-SES and undereducated families.

Effects of Poverty-Related Differences in Classroom Instruction on Students' Engagement in Active, Academic Responding and Achievement

Results of similar longitudinal descriptive research on the instruction received by low- versus high-SES students in the elementary grades also produced intriguing, large differences in how students were taught basic academic skills in reading, language, and arithmetic and in the amount of time students spent engaged in active academic responding. As with Hart and Risley's work, differences also suggested alterable variables that might lead to more accelerated growth in achievement for low-SES students. Our initial search for meaningful differences in how low-SES students were taught in school and responded to instruction was based on informal observations in inner-city elementary classrooms. For example, we reported that reading instruction was often not held for the entire time it was scheduled, that teachers lectured predominately with students expected to sit and listen, that the lowest group in reading often met for less rather than more time in supervised instruction, and that students' typical response to teacher-led instruction was passive attention with infrequent examples of academic responding (Greenwood, Carta, Hart, Thurston, & Hall, 1989; Greenwood, Delquadri, & Hall, 1984).

Subsequent research using the CISSAR observation system (Stanley & Greenwood, 1981), which sought to compare classroom instruction and student response in low- versus high-SES schools, tended to confirm these anecdotal observations. From an initial study comparing schools divergent in SES (Title I versus non–Title I schools) at the fourth grade, we reported finding statistically significant differences in students' performance in standardized tests of basic skills. Although this difference in mean achievement was expected, more intriguing were similar differences in how students were taught and students' engagement in academic responding. Fourth-grade students in low-SES schools were more frequently taught by teachers who lectured using the chalkboard or overhead projector; whereas teachers in high-SES schools combined lectures with more small-group and independent seatwork activities, with students assigned to complete work (Stanley & Greenwood, 1983). Students in low-SES classrooms responded to instruction with significantly less engagement in active academic responding— 12 minutes less per day—than did their counterparts in higher-SES (non–Title I) schools. These findings were based on CISSAR observations that spanned all subject matter instruction over an entire school day (Greenwood et al., 1984).

These findings of both instructional and student response differences were replicated in a second study of students in low- versus high-SES schools. By October of first grade, students in low-SES schools were 0.3 grade levels behind their high-SES peers. This gap grew to 3.5 grade levels by the end of sixth grade. In addition, as in the earlier fourth-grade study, a gap also existed in students' engagement in active academic responding. Low-SES students engaged in academic responding an average of 6 minutes per day less than their high-SES peers. Cumulatively, over all of elementary school (Grades K–5), this gap grows to 364 hours, reflecting substantially different functional histories of using and displaying academic behavior in response to instruction in elementary school (Greenwood, Hart, et al., 1994).

Like the Hart and Risley work in the home, this work on classroom instruction and students' response to it in low-SES schools revealed meaningful differences in both instruction and students' responses relative to high-SES schools

(Greenwood, Hart, et al., 1994). These differences included an ever-widening gap in achievement by the end of sixth grade. Collectively, these findings seemed to reveal poverty-induced mechanisms in terms of what parents and teachers know (vocabulary and instructional practice) and how they interacted with children and students in ways different from those in nonpoverty home and school environments. These parenting and teaching differences put children from low-SES families on a trajectory of lower language proficiency from birth to 3 years of age, which is associated with lower IQ scores and lower receptive language skill. Children from low-SES families also experience lower achievement than their middle- to high-SES peers from first through sixth grade, with the achievement gap widening to more than 3 grade levels by the end of sixth grade and 364 hours less cumulative engagement in academic responding.

These findings have been at the forefront of this nation's efforts to improve the home language and early literacy environments of young children to in turn alter the rates of language growth and proficiency prior to entry into kindergarten and early preschool and elementary school environments (Shonkoff & Phillips, 2000; Shore, 1997; Thompson, 1995). In particular, initiatives to increase the amount of time parents spend reading to their young children at home (e.g., Parents as Teachers), to employ educational television to teach the precursors of reading (e.g., *Between the Lions*), and to conduct innovative research efforts to employ television to boost home literacy in at-risk, low-SES families have been framed around this earlier work. This work also has led to personal efforts to convey to parents the primary messages from the Hart and Risley (1995) work: You need to talk more and longer to your language-learning child (Raspberry, 2003a, 2003b). To date, replications of Hart and Risley's work have been hampered because of tremendous costs associated with transcription and coding of language samples. Future innovations—for example, using advanced speech-recognition software tools for this purpose—are in progress (Infoture, 2007). These findings also lead to the hypothesis that elementary school instruction that systematically improves daily engagement in active academic responding of low-SES schools, while at the same time being acceptable and sustainable by teachers, might accelerate students' subject matter learning.

RESEARCH ON INSTRUCTIONAL INTERVENTION AND PREVENTION TECHNIQUES

Together We Can!: ClassWide Peer Tutoring (CWPT) for Basic Academic Skills (Greenwood, Delquadri, & Carta, 1997) was developed to test the aforementioned hypothesis (Greenwood, Delquadri, & Hall, 1989; Greenwood, Terry, Utley, Montagna, & Walker, 1993). A peer tutoring instructional strategy for testing this hypothesis experimentally was first suggested by informal observations that even first- to third-grade students who had failed to respond to teacher-led classroom instruction were able to make rapid and sustained progress learning to read when taught one-to-one by a highly qualified tutor outside of the classroom (Delquadri, 1978). It also was obvious that students who were tutored responded favorably to one-to-one teaching by interacting and responding to the tutor's prompts and corrections. The development of CWPT became a search for a cheap but effective, sustainable, and acceptable approach to providing such instruction for students in low-SES schools (Greenwood, Maheady, & Delquadri, 2002).

Research focused on how peer tutoring might be used classwide for a daily portion of subject matter instruction in reading, spelling, and math. These key principles guided its design: 1) application in the general education classroom with all students participating (classwide); 2) explicit strategies for including ELLs and students with disabilities (instructional strategies); 3) maximum adaptability to local curricula to promote acceptability (integration with existing curricula and policies) and, therefore, scalability and sustainability; and 4) eventual use of computer software to support continuous progress monitoring and teacher implementation.

CWPT has subsequently become known as a peer-assisted learning strategy (PALS). The core reading process involved in CWPT involves daily 35- to 45-minute sessions during which half the students in a classroom tutor and supervise the reading of the other half. Once the first 15 minutes of tutoring have passed, the teacher signals the tutor and tutee dyads (one triad if an unequal number of students) to stop and trade roles. For the next 15 minutes, the tutors become tutees and vice versa for a second tutoring round on the same material. In the last 15 minutes, students report individual points earned and a winning team for the day is determined based on the highest point total. Because the primary goal of CWPT is to accelerate intensity (i.e., engagement and volume of response for all students engaged in the material), its immediate effects on reading are in terms of accuracy, fluency, and comprehension of the material.

In reading CWPT, daily sessions typically occur three or more times per week in coordination with teacher-led instruction in which background knowledge is activated, new material is introduced, and students read to the teacher as determined by the adopted curriculum, with formative evaluation of progress. Teacher planning and design decisions—flexible methods of peer pairing, choice of curriculum, peer-teaching strategies—shape the core process. Tutor and tutee pairs change weekly or with every new unit of reading material to avoid negative effects such as boredom or the stigma of always being the tutee and never the tutor. Partners are assigned by the teacher, typically paired from among members of the same or adjacent reading groups; however, to include the lowest-performing students, teachers may pair higher-functioning students with lower-functioning students. Some additional strategies include having the high-performing student read first as a model for the lower-performing student. These and other decisions are all made privately by the teacher as part of his or her weekly planning.

CWPT is adaptable with respect to integration with local curricula, making it readily scalable. At the elementary level, CWPT is integrated to create a comprehensive reading program for Grades 1–5, focused on evidence-based beginning reading skills, fluency, and reading comprehension (see review by the *What Works Clearinghouse* peer review and posted report identifying CWPT developed by Greenwood and colleagues as a promising practice in the teaching of beginning reading at http://ies.ed.gov/ncee/wwc/reports/beginning_reading/cwpt/). Combined with teacher-led instruction and aligned peer-teaching materials, CWPT may be used to scaffold phonemic activities, word reading fluency, vocabulary and spelling mastery, passage oral reading fluency, and retell reading comprehension as appropriate before and after third grade. CWPT also is used for literature-based activities when peer tutors are guided by teacher-developed study guides (Greenwood & Hou, 2001; Greenwood, Hou-Reynolds, Abbott, & Tapia, 2004). For example, when using CWPT to teach and learn phonemes or letter names, tutees may say the sound or sounds associated with a particular letter on a flashcard or simply say what letter they see.

The Beginning Reading–CWPT curricula and teacher support software (Terry, Abbott, Delquadri, & Reynolds, 2005) is composed of 16 evidence-based skill modules, listed in Table 6.2, that can be selected and flexibly used by teachers for initial instruction and reused for review and refresher sessions. Each of the modules is supported by computer software for creating picture flashcards specific to each module for use in the peer tutoring sessions. The flashcards, provided in the Beginning Reading–CWPT software, are planned by the teacher (Terry & Greenwood, 2004). The tutor provides correction and tallies the tutee's responses using points. When using CWPT with word and passage reading, tutees read brief passages from the curriculum to their tutor. The tutor provides points for correctly read sentences and error correction. Teachers assess the fluency of the students' reading using oral reading rate measures. When using CWPT for reading comprehension, the tutee responds to who, what, when, where, and why questions (and other comprehension promoting tasks) concerning the passage provided by the tutor. The tutee may also respond to prediction questions and other questions. The tutor corrects responses and provides feedback using materials and his or her own knowledge. When using CWPT with advanced subject matter (e.g., literature, science), peer teaching is guided by study guides (Greenwood & Hou, 2001).

Adaptations of the curricula—variations in content, tasks, and materials; behavioral supports; inclusion of paraprofessionals as translators or for assistance—can be made to include individual students with disabilities or ELLs. For example, in CWPT programs in inclusive classrooms, students with autism and behavioral disabilities also earned points for appropriate social interactions such as offering help and sharing information (Kamps, Leonard, Potucek, & Garrison-Harrell, 1995). As another example, a child with a hearing impairment and his or her paraprofessional may participate in CWPT with a peer tutor without disabilities by having the paraprofessional provide sign language translation. A somewhat similar translation strategy may apply with ELLs. For example, the teacher of an ELL may use another student in the classroom to help introduce the spelling or vocabulary

Table 6.2.   Beginning Reading–CWPT modules and skills taught

 1. *Word Discrimination*—Hear a sentence, identify the beginning, middle, and end words; then hear a series of words, repeat the words to make a sentence.
 2. *Letter–Sound Association*—Hear a sound, repeat it, say its letter name; hear a sound, write its letter.
 3. *Letter–Symbol Identification*—See a letter, say its name; hear a letter, write it.
 4. *Beginning Sounds*—Hear a word, say the beginning sound.
 5. *Ending Sounds*—Hear a word, say the ending sound.
 6. *Two-Letter Sound Blends*—Hear a word, say the 2-letter sound blend.
 7. *Sound Identification*—Hear a word, say all sounds in the word.
 8. *Sound Blending*—Hear a sequence of sounds, say the word.
 9. *Matching Sounds*—Hear a word and a sound, say if the sound is present in the word.
10. *Common Sounds*—Hear two words, say the sound that is common in both words.
11. *Subtracting Sounds*—Hear a word, take out a sound, say the word/sound(s) that are left.
12. *Switching Sounds*—Hear a word, switch one sound for another, say the new word.
13. *Working with Syllables*—Hear a series of syllable sounds, say them fast to say the word; hear a word and say the syllable sounds.
14. *Sight Word Vocabulary*—Using the Dolch sight words, see a word and say it; hear the word and write it.
15. *CWPT Oral Reading*—See grade-level sentences, paragraphs, and passages; read orally at an 85% accuracy level.
16. *CWPT Comprehension*—Read grade-level material; answer related comprehension questions orally and written, including vocabulary, factual, recall, sequential, and inferential information.

to the entire class in the second language in addition to having the items presented in writing or in combination with pictures. For passage reading, a non-English or limited English speaker can be paired with a more fluent bilingual speaker to assist with pronunciation and comprehension of text (Arreaga-Mayer, 1998).

EFFECTIVENESS OF CLASSWIDE PEER TUTORING

Initial work developing CWPT used single-subject research designs to demonstrate efficacy and to examine some essential components (see Greenwood, 1996, for a review). The effectiveness of CWPT was established in a randomized trial and follow-along study of 12 years duration. In this experimental study, teachers implemented CWPT beginning in first grade. Teachers in subsequent grades then also implemented CWPT so that students received a prospective exposure beginning in first grade and continuing through fourth grade. Follow-along measures were obtained for students in middle and high school (Greenwood, Maheady, & Delquadri, 2002). Contrasted in the design were instruction (CWPT integrated into the teacher-led curriculum versus teacher-led instruction without CWPT) and school SES (low-SES [Title I] versus upper-SES [non–Title I schools]). Low-SES, Title I schools were randomly assigned to 1) use CWPT in daily reading, spelling, and math instruction for 90 minutes per day (30 minutes for each subject daily, 4 days per week) or to 2) continue conventional instruction without peer-tutoring components. Upper-SES (non–Title I) schools in the same inner-city school district served as another nontreatment comparison group by using the same curricula and conventional teacher-led instruction according to district policies.

Results indicated that CWPT used progressively over Grades 1–4 in low-SES schools 1) significantly improved students' classroom engagement during instruction and reduced socially inappropriate classroom behavior and 2) accelerated reading, language, and mathematics performance on standardized tests compared with both the low- and upper-SES comparison groups (Greenwood, 1991a, 1991b; Greenwood, Delquadri, et al., 1989). We also reported that, when adjusted for initial ability (first-grade pretest and IQ scores), low-SES CWPT students in fourth grade were not significantly different in achievement from the upper-SES comparison group students. It appeared that the CWPT group had closed the achievement gap that existed between the groups in first grade by the end of fourth grade.

These accelerated effects in elementary school for low-SES CWPT group students compared with upper-SES controls were associated with 1) higher achievement outcomes in reading, language, math, social studies, and science and 2) lower use of special services in middle school (Greenwood et al., 1993). In high school, the low-SES CWPT group was significantly less likely than the low-SES control group to drop out of school (Greenwood, 1996; Greenwood & Delquadri, 1995).

Effect sizes between low-SES CWPT versus the low–SES control group in the original elementary school study averaged .72, ranging from .37 (math), to .57 (reading), to −.83 (a reduction in inappropriate behavior), to 1.41 (academic engagement). Using Cohen's (1988) criteria, these effects are moderate to large in educational significance. At the middle school follow-up, the average effect size was .44 (a moderate effect), ranging from .35 (language), to .39 (reading), to .57 (math) on achievement test measures (Greenwood, Kamps, Terry, & Linebarger, 2006).

The effect size for reduction in special education services between groups was .54; the proportion of students served in less restrictive services compared with controls was .73. The effect size for reduction in the number of students who were high school dropouts was .66. To my knowledge, these studies are the only ones in the literature reporting later life outcomes of PALS interventions.

To date, PALS interventions based largely on CWPT procedures have been evaluated across a range of subject matter (e.g., reading, language arts, mathematics, science, social studies) and across a range of students (e.g., general education versus special needs) and elementary classroom settings (e.g., including instruction for ELLs). In a synthesis ($N = 90$ group comparative studies in elementary school), Rohrbeck, Ginsberg-Block, Fantuzzo, and Miller

(2003) reported that the average effect size for PALS was .59 (59% of PALS group students exceeded the achievement of non-PAL group students), a moderate effect size overall. Students in urban settings, from low-income backgrounds, and of minority status experienced larger gains than students from suburban middle- to high-income backgrounds. Younger students experienced larger gains in achievement than older students. Greater academic effects were produced by programs in which students controlled more of the PALS procedures, including goal setting, using guiding tutoring roles, monitoring progress, evaluating performance, selecting rewards, and administering rewards. PALS programs that included individualized compared with group evaluation procedures were associated with larger outcomes. PALS programs in which interdependent reward contingencies rather than individualized or group contingencies existed produced greater achievement.

Thus, strong evidence exists that it is possible to accelerate students' learning in low-SES schools and prevent the number of children needing special education services for reading problems when students are taught to play the roles of both teacher and learner, progress is monitored frequently, and contingencies of reinforcement for performance are used. This knowledge of the risk mechanisms and interventions capable of accelerating the language and literacy of children in poverty has taken a number of other directions since this early work, including educational television, evidence-based reading curricula, and schoolwide 3-tiered models of reading and behavior prevention.

EDUCATIONAL TELEVISION AND EARLY LITERACY

Television offers a powerful way to serve the literacy needs of children in poverty whose personal educational resources are limited in terms of parent education and books and literature in the home. Television holds promise because of the quality of instruction that can be produced. In addition, despite the lack of literacy resources in the homes of children who are poor, 99% of all U.S. homes have a television set (Mielke, 1994; Statistical Abstracts, 2000), making it possible to deliver instruction to children through this medium.

Building on their success in teaching preschoolers school readiness through television (i.e., Sesame Street), producers in collaboration with leading reading experts created a new television program for young children, *Between the Lions (BTL)*. *BTL* incorporates evidence-based early literacy skills (Strickland & Rath, 2000) and presents children with an environment and experiences known to foster emergent literacy. These experiences focus on both holistic processes (e.g., understanding different reading or writing contexts, prior knowledge, motivation) as well as direct instruction composed of visual and auditory stimuli (e.g., print on screen with changing initial or final consonants) that have been specifically designed to teach concepts of print, the alphabetic principle, phonemic awareness, and letter–sound correspondences.

In a test of the effectiveness of *BTL* in a randomized trial, 17 one-half hour episodes from the first season of the new series were used (Linebarger, 2000; Linebarger, Kosanic, Greenwood, & Doku, 2003).[2] Participants in this first randomized trial were 164 kindergarten and first-grade students. These children were recruited from classrooms in three elementary schools in the greater Kansas City metropolitan area. Eighty-one percent of the children were European American, seven percent were Hispanic, six percent were African American, and six percent were from other backgrounds. Thirty-six percent of the families reported incomes below $30,000; twenty-eight percent reported incomes between $30,000 and $45,000; and thirty-six percent reported incomes above $45,000. Eight percent of the children had an identified disability.

Randomized experimental viewing groups of kindergarten and first-grade children watched one *BTL* episode each day. The viewing group watched the program in their classrooms in the afternoon during their computer free time from the end of February through the beginning of April, with days off for spring break and district-scheduled vacation days. Children in the control group continued their usual instruction and schedule during the viewing phase.

Analyses controlled for the effects of initial differences at pretest, family SES, and home literacy experiences. The most prominent finding was improvement in the emergent literacy skills for kindergarten children who watched *BTL*. These improvements were moderated by the child's reading risk status. Significantly higher word recognition and Test of Early Reading Ability (Hresko, Reid, & Hammill, 2001) scores were achieved for *BTL* viewers compared with nonviewers (Cohen's *d* effect sizes ranged from 0.46 to 0.91, averaging 0.70).

In addition, higher means and accelerated slopes for *BTL* viewers were noted for phonemic awareness and letter–sound tasks (accounting for 58% and 47% of the variance in the intercept and 36% and 0% of the variance in the slope, respectively). Children who were most at risk for reading failure improved on concepts of print tasks (first graders) and word recognition tasks (both kindergartners and first graders). Given that television represents universally available technology for reaching all children, having children view a program such as *BTL* should help a significant number of students by extending early literacy instruction and reinforcing and motivating children within the home and in the classroom.

With confirmation of the ability of the program by itself to support children's acquisition of early literacy skills, the creators of the program decided to develop instructional materials to accompany the program's curriculum and to involve educators in the learning process. A demonstration project was funded to evaluate whether these instructional materials, in combination with viewing *BTL*,

---

[2]An online report on the efficacy of *Between the Lions* can be found at http://www.pbs.org/readytolearn/research/btlkansassum.pdf

could further support children's literacy skill development. The Mississippi Literacy Initiative was created and delivered in preschool, kindergarten, and first-grade classrooms in two different locations: the Choctaw Indian Reservation and the Delta region of the state. Teachers showed the students two half-hour *BTL* episodes each week and received training in how to use a set of related children's books and resources along with the series to help teach reading. In a school-year–long evaluation, researchers reported improvements in basic early literacy skills for both populations (Prince, Grace, Linebarger Atkinson, & Huffman, 2002). *BTL* replication and effectiveness trials are in progress (Annenberg School for Communication of the University of Pennsylvania, 2001), most notably one involving an American Indian Head Start Initiative involving 12 different tribes in the southwest United States with both home and Head Start components.

EVIDENCE-BASED READING CURRICULA AND SCHOOLWIDE 3-TIER PREVENTION MODELS

Continuing to examine problem conditions in high-poverty schools, a line of work examined features of the reading curriculum associated with students' progress in learning to read. Evidence-based reading curricula offer advantages in the early reading instruction of students in high-poverty schools because what, when, and how material is taught is based on study designs capable of generating causal results that are rigorous and believable. Whether students in real high-poverty schools actually make differential progress learning to read with evidence-based curricula is not clear, however. To investigate this issue locally in Kansas City Metro schools, we were able to examine and compare students' growth in early literacy skills in five high-poverty elementary schools serving similar student populations using curricula that varied in scientific basis (Kamps et al., 2003). Beginning in kindergarten and Grades 1 and 2, students with parental permission in these five schools were tracked fall, winter, and spring for the next 3 years using the Dynamic Indicators of Basic Early Literacy Skills (DIBELS). The curricula used in these schools were literature-based programs (Schools 1, 2, and 5), the Success for All program (School 4), and the Reading Mastery program (School 3). Compared with the literature-based curricula, both the Success for All and Reading Mastery programs included a greater number of evidence-based components; in addition, the skills (e.g., phonemic awareness) in these programs were taught with explicit rather than implicit instruction strategies. Teaching evidence-based reading skills ensures students are proficient with the precursors needed to be successful readers. When all steps are taught directly, instruction becomes intensive and explicit (Mathes, Torgesen, Allen, & Howard Allor, 2002), as compared with implicit instruction, in which many students simply don't learn the skills that teachers do not teach.

Results indicated that students' growth in DIBELS (i.e., letter-naming fluency, nonsense word fluency, and oral reading fluency) was differentially influenced by the school's reading curriculum. In fact, when comparing students in the same grade, students in the Reading Mastery and Success for All programs made significantly greater progress learning to read (i.e., rate of growth over time and endpoint scores) as indicated by all three measures (i.e., letter-naming fluency, nonsense word fluency, oral reading fluency) than students using the literature-based curricula. The Reading Mastery curriculum outperformed the Success for All curriculum (Kamps et al., 2003). These findings for Reading Mastery were consistent with findings previously reported (Foorman, Francis, Fletcher, & Schatschneider, 1998). We also reported that students in the study with one or more risk factors (academic or behavioral) at the start also made greater progress over time using the Reading Mastery curriculum compared with the Success for All and literature-based curricula.

These findings led to work testing the effectiveness of a schoolwide, 3-tiered model of reading and behavior prevention as an effective and sustainable means of improving the environment and outcomes of students attending high-poverty schools (Kamps & Greenwood, 2006).[3] Based on universal and frequent screening and progress monitoring, the 3 tiers—primary, secondary, and tertiary—are used to individualize and intensify instructional interventions in support of key skills. All students receive the primary level of instruction. In this case, an evidence-based reading curriculum is used for all students including struggling readers and students with disabilities. These procedures were supported by experimental studies of effective reading instruction (e.g., Foorman et al., 1998) as well as our own work. Those students who do not respond to the primary level of instruction, measured again with the DIBELS, receive secondary-level interventions in the form of small-group instruction and peer-tutoring experiences. The Tier 2 experiences are in addition to primary-level instruction using the evidence-based curriculum. Students who do not respond to secondary-level instruction receive tertiary-level interventions—one-to-one, highly explicit instruction combined with more frequently progress monitoring. Although this work is in progress (Kamps & Greenwood, 2005b), initial results appear favorable.

Compared with schools that use evidence-based curricula, schools that do not use evidence-based programs will be faced with increasing numbers of students who are struggling to read and, consequently, are recommended for special education services. Without appropriate change in reading instruction, students who struggle to learn to read do not make progress on their own (Chard & Kame'enui, 2000; Juel, 1988; Kamps et al., 1989). From a prevention perspective, the use of an evidence-based reading curriculum as a primary or universal intervention is a good first step in improving the instructional environment, improving student

---

[3]An online description of the schoolwide 3-tier reading and behavior prevention/intervention model can be found at http://www.lsi.ku.edu/jgprojects/r&b/Index.htm or http://www.wcer.wisc.edu/cce/kansas.html

outcomes, and reducing the subpopulation of struggling readers and students with reading disabilities in high-poverty schools (Kamps & Greenwood, 2005a).

CONCLUSION

The purpose of this chapter was to provide a brief synthesis of my program of research and that of colleagues concerning lessons learned about the poverty mechanisms affecting children's social and academic achievement, including evidence-based intervention practices that have emerged. Findings from multiple descriptive and experimental studies—some longitudinal, spanning 10 or more years—were reviewed. Embracing an empirical approach from the beginning, our research validated direct observation measures based on an ecological-interactional-developmental framework for use in the homes and classrooms of children in a high-poverty community. The measures were then used to provide descriptive data on these environmental contexts, the behaviors of parents and teachers in these settings, and students' responses to these behaviors. By describing and comparing these parameters in both low- and high-SES settings, it proved possible to identify meaningful differences in the situations and in the parenting and teaching interactions, revealing ways that reduced, limited, slowed, failed to expand, and at times prohibited desired child response (e.g., talk to parent, engagement in active academic responding).

Overall, children and students' opportunities to respond and their actual production of desired behavior were reduced in high-poverty environments in terms of both daily and cumulative estimates. On average, these limitations in experiences in early life led to lower developmental trajectories. This slowed development continued over time in terms of lower vocabulary, lower IQ scores, lack of school readiness, and delayed basic skills achievement in early elementary school years. In the absence of effective early interventions to change their learning environments and to increase child response in language development and academic behavior, the intellectual and academic achievement gaps for these children did not close; in fact, they grew larger. This view of early learning mechanisms proved extendable to educational television, evidence-based reading curricula, and schoolwide models of prevention in impoverished homes and schools by examining students' trajectories of growth in key skills monitored frequently over time in the presence of these environmental interventions.

This research contributed uniquely to theories of developmental retardation (Baumeister, Kupstas, & Klindworth, 1990; McDermott & Altekruse, 1994; Shonkoff & Phillips, 2000), the most prevalent form of retardation linked to environmental causes such as deprivation and nonstimulating environments. This research also expanded knowledge of how decreased interactions with parents and teachers over time actually functioned to produce lower levels of responding and learning over time. Although it was no news that impoverished environments are underresourced physically and intellectually, including undereducated parents or overextended and often underqualified teachers (Guin, 2004), how it is that these environments functioned to produce poor child outcomes and what might be done about it was of critical importance.

These findings pointed to alterable variables with potential for change using interventions to change the details of these interactions in meaningful ways at earlier ages. The findings also supported the ecological-interactional-developmental framework and the integration of descriptive and experimental data in early intervention and educational research.

These descriptive data informed new interventions and related concepts such as the opportunity to respond, fidelity of implementation, treatment failure, and response to intervention, which could be assessed and altered in experimental studies by changing the way parents and teachers interacted with the children. Results of these studies in schools resulted in a number of important new interventions (e.g., CWPT, PALS) and provided additional evidence in support of the causal interaction mechanisms that are either risk or protective factors in the development of language and early literacy of children living in poverty.

There are several themes in our most current work and future plans. One is developing measures and research seeking to identify the language and early literacy precursors in preschool and earlier in the lives of infants and toddlers (Greenwood, Carta, Walker, Hughes, & Weathers, 2006; Greenwood, Walker, Carta, & Higgins, 2006; McConnell, McEvoy, & Priest, 2002). We seek the means of intervening earlier in homes and in child care to remove risk by improving learning environments and, thus, the developmental and academic outcomes of children in poverty. Another theme is improving early language and literacy intervention in the local community via supports for Early Head Start programs and an Early Reading First Project using evidence-based practices and intensive progress monitoring techniques to inform decisions about individualizing instruction. In the context of growth in the number of new measures capable of monitoring progress in children birth to age 5, we are seeking to examine the extent to which 3-tier prevention model components can be conceptualized and applied to early childhood in preschool, child care, and home-based services for young children with developmental delays (see http://www.critec.org for a description of this newest work).

REFERENCES

Annenberg School for Communication of the University of Pennsylvania. (2001). *News: Deborah Linebarger to assess effectiveness of American Indian Literacy Initiative in New Mexico.* Retrieved from http://www.asc.upenn.edu/asc/Application/NewsDetails. asp? ID=111

Arreaga-Mayer, C. (1998). Language sensitive peer-mediated instruction for culturally and linguistically diverse learners in the intermediate elementary grades. In R.M. Gersten & R.T. Jimenez (Eds.), *Promoting learning for culturally and linguistically diverse students* (pp. 73–90). Belmont, CA: Wadsworth.

Arreaga-Mayer, C., Carta, J.J., & Tapia, Y. (1992). *ESCRIBE: Ecobehavioral system for the contextual recording of interactional bilingual environments.* Kansas City: University of Kansas, Juniper Gardens Children's Project.

Arreaga-Mayer, C., Carta, J.J., & Tapia, Y. (1994). Ecobehavioral assessment of bilingual special education settings: The opportunity to respond revisited. In R. Gardner, D. Sainato, J. Cooper, T. Heron, W. Heward, J. Eskleman, et al. (Eds.), *Behavior analysis in education: Focus on measurably superior instruction* (pp. 225–240): Pacific Groves, CA: Brooks/Cole.

Atwater, J.B., Montagna, D., Creighton, M., Williams, R., & Hou, L.S. (1993). *Code for interactive recording of caregiving and learning environments (CIRCLE).* Kansas City: University of Kansas, Juniper Gardens Children's Project.

Baumeister, A.A., Kupstas, F., & Klindworth, L.M. (1990). New morbidity: Implications for prevention and children's disabilities. *Exceptionality, 1,* 1–16.

Carta, J.J., Greenwood, C.R., & Atwater, J.B. (1985). *Ecobehavioral system for complex assessments of preschool environments: ESCAPE.* Kansas City: University of Kansas, Juniper Gardens Children's Project.

Carta, J.J., Greenwood, C.R., Luze, G.J., Cline, G., & Kuntz, S. (2004). Developing a general outcome measure of growth in social skills for infants and toddlers. *Journal of Early Intervention, 26*(2), 91–114.

Carta, J.J., Greenwood, C.R., & Robinson, S. (1987). Application of an eco-behavioral approach to the evaluation of early intervention programs. In R. Prinz (Ed.), *Advances in the behavioral assessment of children and families* (Vol. 3, pp. 123–155). Greenwich, CT: JAI Press.

Carta, J.J., Greenwood, C.R., Schulte, D., Arreaga-Mayer, C., & Terry, B. (1988). *Code for instructional structure and student academic response: Mainstream version (MS-CISSAR).* Kansas City: University of Kansas, Bureau of Child Research, Juniper Gardens Children's Project.

Chard, D.J., & Kame'enui, E.J. (2000). Struggling first-grade readers: The frequency and progress of their reading. *Journal of Special Education, 34*(1), 28–38.

Cohen, J. (1988). *Statistical power analysis for the behavioral sciences* (2nd ed.). Mahwah, NJ: Lawrence Erlbaum Associates.

Delquadri, J.C. (1978). *An analysis of the generalization effects of four tutoring procedures on oral reading responses of eight learning disability children.* Unpublished doctoral dissertation, University of Kansas, Lawrence.

Foorman, B.R., Francis, D.J., Fletcher, J.M., & Schatschneider, C. (1998). The role of instruction in learning to read: Preventing reading failure in at-risk children. *Journal of Educational Psychology, 90*(1), 37–55.

Greenwood, C.R. (1991a). Classwide peer tutoring: Longitudinal effects on the reading language and mathematics achievement of at-risk students. *Journal of Reading, Writing, and Learning Disabilities International, 7,* 105–124.

Greenwood, C.R. (1991b). Longitudinal analysis of time engagement and academic achievement in at-risk and non-risk students. *Exceptional Children, 57,* 521–535.

Greenwood, C.R. (1996). Research on the practices and behavior of effective teachers at the Juniper Gardens Children's Project: Implications for the education of diverse learners. In D. Speece & B.K. Keogh (Eds.), *Research on classroom ecologies: Implications for inclusion of children with learning disabilities.* (pp. 39–67). Hillsdale, NJ: Lawrence Erlbaum Associates.

Greenwood, C.R. (1999). Reflections on a research career: Perspective on 35 years of research at the Juniper Gardens Children's Project. *Exceptional Children, 66*(1), 7–21.

Greenwood, C.R. (2003). Commentary: Building community laboratories for experimental studies. *School Psychology Review, 32*(4), 515–519.

Greenwood, C.R., Abbott, M., & Tapia, Y. (2003). Ecobehavioral strategies: Observing, measuring, and analyzing behavior and reading interventions. In S. Vaughn & K.L. Briggs (Eds.), *Reading in the classroom: Systems for the observation of teaching and learning* (pp. 53–82). Baltimore: Paul H. Brookes Publishing Co.

Greenwood, C.R., Carta, J.J., & Dawson, H. (2000). Observational methods for educational settings. In T. Thompson, D. Felce & F.J. Symons (Eds.), *Behavior observation: Technology and applications in developmental disabilities* (pp. 229–252). Baltimore: Paul H. Brookes Publishing Co.

Greenwood, C.R., Carta, J.J., Hart, B., Thurston, L., & Hall, R.V. (1989). A behavioral approach to research on psychosocial retardation. *Education and Treatment of Children, 12*, 330–346.

Greenwood, C.R., Carta, J.J., Kamps, D., Terry, B., & Delquadri, J. (1994). Development and validation of standard classroom observation systems for school practitioners: Ecobehavioral assessment systems software EBASS. *Exceptional Children, 61*, 197–210.

Greenwood, C.R., Carta, J.J., & Walker, D. (2005). Individual growth and development indicators (IGDIs): Tools for assessing intervention results for infants and toddlers. In B. Heward et al. (Eds.), *Focus on behavior analysis in education: Achievements, challenges, and opportunities* (pp. 103–124). Columbus, OH: Pearson/Prentice-Hall.

Greenwood, C.R., Carta, J.J., Walker, D., Hughes, K., & Weathers, M. (2006). Preliminary investigations of the application of the Early Communication Indicator (ECI) for infants and toddlers. *Journal of Early Intervention, 28*(3), 178–196.

Greenwood, C.R., & Delquadri, J. (1988). Code for instructional structure and student academic response: CISSAR. In M. Hersen & A.S. Bellack (Eds.), *Dictionary of behavioral assessment techniques* (pp. 120–122). New York: Pergamon.

Greenwood, C.R., & Delquadri, J. (1995). ClassWide Peer Tutoring and the prevention of school failure. *Preventing School Failure, 39*(4), 21–25.

Greenwood, C.R., Delquadri, J., & Carta, J.J. (1997). *Together we can!: ClassWide Peer Tutoring for basic academic skills.* Longmont, CO: Sopris West.

Greenwood, C.R., Delquadri, J., & Hall, R.V. (1984). Opportunity to respond and student academic performance. In W. Heward, T. Heron, D. Hill, & J. Trap-Porter (Eds.), *Behavior analysis in education* (pp. 58–88). Columbus, OH: Merrill.

Greenwood, C.R., Delquadri, J., & Hall, R.V. (1989). Longitudinal effects of ClassWide Peer Tutoring. *Journal of Educational Psychology, 81*, 371–383.

Greenwood, C.R., Delquadri, J., Stanley, S.O., Terry, B., & Hall, R.V. (1985). Assessment of eco-behavioral interaction in school settings. *Behavioral Assessment, 7*, 331–347.

Greenwood, C.R., Hart, B., Walker, D., & Risley, T.R. (1994). The opportunity to respond revisited: A behavioral theory of developmental retardation and its prevention. In R. Gardner, D.M. Sainato, J.O. Cooper, T.E. Heron, W.L. Heward, J.W. Eshleman, et al. (Eds.), *Behavior analysis in education: Focus on measurably superior instruction* (pp. 213–223). Pacific Grove, CA: Brooks/Cole.

Greenwood, C.R., Horton, B.T., & Utley, C.A. (2002). Academic engagement: Current perspectives on research and practice. *School Psychology Review, 31*(3), 328–349.

Greenwood, C.R., & Hou, L.S. (1995). *Ecobehavioral Assessment Systems Software (EBASS)—Version 3.0: Technical manual.* Kansas City: University of Kansas, Juniper Gardens Children's Project.

Greenwood, C.R., & Hou, S. (2001). *The ClassWide Peer Tutoring Learning Management System (CWPT-LMS): Manual for Teachers.* Kansas City: University of Kansas, Juniper Gardens Children's Project.

Greenwood, C.R., Hou-Reynolds, S., Abbott, M., & Tapia, Y. (2004). *Together we can: ClassWide Peer Tutoring Learning Management System (CWPT-LMS).* Kansas City: University of Kansas, Juniper Gardens Children's Project.

Greenwood, C.R., Kamps, D., Terry, B., & Linebarger, D. (2006). Primary intervention: A means of preventing special education (pp. 73–103). In D. Haager, J. Klingner, & S. Vaughn (Eds.), *Evidence-based reading practices for response to intervention.* Baltimore: Paul H. Brookes Publishing Co.

Greenwood, C.R., Luze, G.J., Cline, G., Kuntz, S., & Leitschuh, C. (2002). Developing a general outcome measure of growth in movement for infants and toddlers. *Topics in Early Childhood Special Education, 22*(3), 143–157.

Greenwood, C.R., Maheady, L., & Delquadri, J. (2002). ClassWide Peer Tutoring. In G. Stoner (Ed.), *Interventions for achievement and behavior problems* (2nd ed., pp. 611–649). Washington, DC: National Association for School Psychologists.

Greenwood, C.R., Schulte, D., Dinwiddie, G., Kohler, F., & Carta, J.J. (1986). Assessment and analysis of eco-behavioral interaction. In R. Prinz (Ed.), *Advances in behavioral assessment of children and families.* (Vol. 2, pp. 69–98). Greenwich, CT: JAI Press.

Greenwood, C.R., Terry, B., Utley, C.A., Montagna, D., & Walker, D. (1993). Achievement placement and services: Middle school benefits of ClassWide Peer Tutoring used at the elementary school. *School Psychology Review, 22*(3), 497–516.

Greenwood, C.R., Walker, D., Carta, J.J., & Higgins, S. (2006). Developing a general outcome measure of growth in the cognitive abilities of children 1 to 4 years old: The Early Problem-Solving Indicator. *School Psychology Review, 35*(4), 535–551.

Guin, K. (2004, August 16). Chronic teacher turnover in urban elementary schools. *Education Policy Analysis Archives, 12*(42). Retrieved August 24, 2006, from http://epaa.asu.edu/epaa/v12n42

Hart, B., & Risley, T.R. (1989). The longitudinal study of interaction systems. *Education and Treatment of Children, 12,* 347–358.

Hart, B., & Risley, T.R. (1992). American parenting of language-learning children: Persisting differences in family–child interactions observed in natural home environments. *Developmental Psychology, 28,* 1096–1105.

Hart, B., & Risley, T.R. (1995). *Meaningful differences in the everyday experience of young American children.* Baltimore: Paul H. Brookes Publishing Co.

Hart, B., & Risley, T.R. (1999). *The social world of children learning to talk.* Baltimore: Paul H. Brookes Publishing Co.

Hresko, W.P., Reid, D.K., & Hammill, D.D. (2001). *TERA-3: Test of Early Reading Ability* (3rd ed.). Austin, TX: PRO-ED.

Infoture. (2007). *The LENA System.* Boulder, CO: Author. Retrieved online March 2, 2008, at http://www.lenababy.com/LenaSystem/AboutLena.aspx

Juel, C. (1988). Learning to read and write: A longitudinal study of 54 children from first through fourth grades. *Journal of Educational Psychology, 80,* 437–447.

Kamps, D., Carta, J., Delquadri, J., Arreaga-Mayer, C., Terry, B., & Greenwood, C.R. (1989). School-based research and intervention. *Education and Treatment of Children, 12,* 359–390.

Kamps, D., & Greenwood, C.R. (2005a). Formulating secondary-level reading interventions. *Journal of Learning Disabilities, 38*(6), 500–509.

Kamps, D., & Greenwood, C.R. (2005b, September 29 & 30). *Session III: Database presentation III and Q & A.* Paper presented at the Topical Forum I: Applying RTI to SLD Determination Decisions, Kansas City, MO.

Kamps, D., & Greenwood, C.R. (2006, February). *Strength of treatment as a mediator of three tiered reading intervention effects.* Washington, DC: U.S. Department of Education, Office of Special Education Programs.

Kamps, D., Greenwood, C.R., & Leonard, B. (1991). Ecobehavioral assessment in classrooms serving children with autism and developmental disabilities. In R.J. Prinz (Ed.), *Advances in behavioral assessment of children and families* (pp. 203–237). New York: Jessica Kingsley.

Kamps, D., Leonard, B., Potucek, J., & Garrison-Harrell. (1995). Cooperative learning groups in reading: An integration strategy for students with autism and general classroom peers. *Behavior Disorders, 21*(1), 89–109.

Kamps, D., Wills, H.P., Greenwood, C.R., Thorne, S., Lazo, J.F., Crockett, J.L., et al. (2003). A descriptive study of curriculum influences on the early reading fluency of students with academic and behavioral risks. *Journal of Emotional and Behavioral Disorders, 11*(4), 211–224.

Linebarger, D. (2000, June). *Summative evaluation of Between the Lions.* Unpublished report prepared for the WGBH Educational Foundation, University of Kansas, Kansas City.

Linebarger, D., Kosanic, A.Z., Greenwood, C.R., & Doku, N.S. (2003). Effects of viewing the television program "Between the Lions" on the emergent literacy skills of young children. *Journal of Educational Psychology, 96*(2), 297–308.

Luze, G.J., Greenwood, C.R., Carta, J.J., Cline, G., & Kuntz, S. (2002). *Developing a general outcome measure of growth in social skills for infants and toddlers.* Kansas City: University of Kansas, Juniper Gardens Children's Project, Early Childhood Research Institute for Measuring Growth and Development.

Mathes, P.G., Torgesen, J.K., Allen, S.H., & Howard Allor, J.K. (2002). *First grade PALS (Peer-Assisted Literacy Strategies).* Longmont, CO: Sopris West.

McConnell, S.R., McEvoy, M.A., & Priest, J.S. (2002). Growing measures for monitoring progress in early childhood education: A research and development process for Individual Growth and Development Indicators. *Assessment for Effective Intervention, 27*(4), 3–14.

McDermott, S.W., & Altekruse, J.M. (1994). Dynamic model for preventing mental retardation in the population: The importance of poverty and deprivation. *Research in Developmental Disabilities, 15*(1), 49–65.

Mielke, K. (1994). Sesame Street and children in poverty. *Media Studies Journal, 8,* 125–134.

Prince, D.L., Grace, C., Linebarger, D.L., Atkinson, R., & Huffman, J.D. (2002). *Between the Lions Mississippi literacy initiative: A final report to Mississippi Educational Television and WGBH Educational Foundation.* Starkville: Mississippi State University, The Early Childhood Institute.

Raspberry, W. (2003a, August 25). Reaching parents early. *Washington Post,* p. A17.

Raspberry, W. (2003b, November). *Baby Steps—William Raspberry Column.* Washington, DC: Home and School Institute, Mega Skills Education Center.

Rohrbeck, C.A., Ginsberg-Block, M.D., Fantuzzo, J.W., & Miller, T.R. (2003). Peer-assisted learning interventions with elementary school students: A meta-analytic review. *Journal of Educational Psychology, 95*(2), 240–257.

Shonkoff, J.P., & Phillips, D.A. (2000). *From neurons to neighborhoods: The science of early childhood development.* Washington, DC: National Academies Press.

Shore, R. (1997). *Rethinking the brain: New insights into early development.* New York: Families and Work Institute.

Stanley, S.O., & Greenwood, C.R. (1981). *Code for instructional structure and student academic response (CISSAR): Observers' manual.* Kansas City: University of Kansas, Juniper Gardens Children's Project, Bureau of Child Research.

Stanley, S.O., & Greenwood, C.R. (1983). Assessing opportunity to respond in classroom environments through direct observation: How much opportunity to respond does the minority disadvantaged student receive in school? *Exceptional Children, 49,* 370–373.

Starr, A. (2002, August 26). The importance of teaching tots. *Business Week.* Retrieved March 2, 2008, from http://www.businessweek.com/magazine/content/02_34/ b3796661.htm

Statistical Abstracts. (2000). Washington, DC: Government Printing Office.

Strickland, D.S., & Rath, L.K. (2000, August). Between the Lions: Public television promotes early literacy. *Reading Online, 4.* Available online at http://www.readingonline.org/articles/art_index.asp?HREF=/articles/strickland/index.html

Terry, B., Abbott, M., Delquadri, J., & Reynolds, S. (2005). *The Beginning Reading ClassWide Peer Tutoring (BR-CWPT): Teacher Support Software.* Kansas City: University of Kansas, Juniper Gardens Children's Project.

Terry, B., & Greenwood, C.R. (2004). *ClassWide Peer Tutoring infused into the beginning reading curriculum of young children.* Kansas City: University of Kansas, Juniper Gardens Children's Project.

Thompson, T. (1995). Children have more need of models than critics: Early language experience and brain development. *Journal of Early Intervention, 19*(3), 264–272.

Walker, D., Greenwood, C.R., Hart, B., & Carta, J.J. (1994). Improving the prediction of early school academic outcomes using socioeconomic status and early language production. *Child Development, 65*, 606–621.

Walker, D., Hart, B., & Greenwood, C.R. (1994). *Parent–Infant Computerized Code for the Observation of Language Interactions: PICCOLI.* Kansas City: University of Kansas, Juniper Gardens Children's Project.

Whitehurst, G.J. (1996). Language processes context: Language learning of children reared in poverty. In L.B. Adamson & M.A. Romski (Eds.), *Research on communication and language disorders: Contribution to theories of language development.* Baltimore: Paul H. Brookes Publishing Co.

Whitehurst, G.J., & Lonigan, C.J. (2001). Emergent literacy: Development from prereaders to readers. In S.B. Neuman & D.K. Dickinson (Eds.), *Handbook of early literacy research* (pp. 11–29). New York: Guilford Press.

II

How Instruction Can Make a Difference

Susan B. Neuman

Recognizing the tremendous constraints that poor children face, Section II addresses how instruction can make a difference. It begins with the language of instruction and examines how other instructional supports may improve children's literacy growth and achievement. Central to these issues are the principles of universal design, recognizing that a one-size-fits-all approach to instruction will never be sufficient if we are to accommodate the range of learner needs and necessary scaffolding supports.

Chapters 7 and 8 address the important issues of language differences and dialects. In Chapter 7, Claude Goldenberg tackles the complex debate over the language of instruction—the bilingual education question that has historically dominated the field. He examines two major reviews of research (the National Literacy Panel and the Center for Research on Education, Diversity & Excellence) and summarizes the results in terms of key instructional features that benefit second language learners. In Chapter 8, Holly K. Craig examines the language-reading linkages for African American students. Examining trends in national data sets, she reports that although poverty has a role in the underachievement of African American students, oral language is a much stronger influence on reading outcomes. What this means is that interventions that support students' ability to develop linguistic flexibility and adaptation skills have the potential to dramatically improve reading outcomes.

Deborah C. Simmons and her colleagues at Texas A&M University in Chapter 9 explore the significant role that principles of instructional design play in optimizing learning rates and development for children who live in high-poverty circumstances. They argue convincingly that improvements in language are not enough; rather, acceleration is essential to broaden and deepen children's knowledge of vocabulary, concepts, and text genres, which they examine through efficacy trials of a book reading intervention designed to optimize these skills.

137

Chapter 10 offers a cautionary note to instructional strategists working on designs for learning. In this chapter, David H. Rose and Gabrielle Rappolt-Schlichtmann make the important case that there are multiple pathways to learning and that it is essential to create curricula that are flexible enough to support the diversity of students in our classrooms and beyond. The authors suggest three central principles that serve as a foundation for the development of materials in and out of school settings.

Allan Paivio in Chapter 11 further emphasizes these points through his analysis of dual coding theory. He argues through years of systematic research that cognition involves two distinct subsystems—a verbal system that specializes in language and a nonverbal imagery system that deals with nonlinguistic objects and events. Functionally independent, the nonverbal and verbal codes can have important additive effects on recall and cognition. Paivio's theory essentially lays the groundwork for bootstrapping instruction with technological supports—video, television, and moving images—for building synergy and redundancy in learning to read.

The final chapter by Robert E. Slavin and his colleagues, Nancy A. Madden and Bette Chambers of Success for All, uses Paivio's theory to examine the benefits of embedded multimedia as an example of educational reform in practice. Given the extraordinary amount of evidence that these colleagues have amassed over a decades-long research enterprise, it is most fitting to end this section on the promise that evidence may hold for significant and lasting changes in literacy achievement for high-poverty children.

7

Improving Achievement
for English Language Learners

Claude Goldenberg

Imagine you are a second-grade student. During reading and language arts, you will be faced with an ambitious learning agenda. It will likely include irregular spelling patterns, diphthongs, syllabication rules, regular and irregular plurals, and common prefixes and suffixes—what has traditionally been called *structural analysis*. The agenda also will include lessons about following written instructions, interpreting words with multiple meanings, locating information in expository texts, using comprehension strategies and background knowledge to understand what you read, cause and effect, and features of texts such as theme, plot, and setting. You will be expected to read fluently and correctly at least 80 words per minute, adding approximately 3,000 words to your vocabulary over the year from different types of texts. In addition, you'll be expected to write narratives and friendly letters using appropriate forms, organization, critical elements, capitalization, and punctuation, revising your writing as needed.

You will have a similar agenda in math. If you are fortunate enough to attend a school in which all instruction has not been completely eclipsed by reading and math, you will also be tackling topics such as motion, magnetism, life cycles, environments, weather, and fuel; the physical attributes of objects; family histories and timelines; labeling continents and major landmarks on maps; and learning how important historical figures made a difference in the lives of others.

My thanks to Patricia Gándara, Fred Genesee, Bill Saunders, Michael Graves, Timothy Shanahan, Michael Kamil, Ronald Gallimore, Jessie Sullivan, and Robert Rueda for their helpful comments on previous versions of this chapter.

The expectations created by state and district academic standards can be a bit overwhelming both for students and for teachers.[1]

If you do not speak English very well, your job will be to learn what everyone else is learning—and learn English as well. And not just the kind of English you will need to talk with your friends and teacher about classroom routines, what you like to eat, what you are having for lunch, where you went over the weekend, or who was mean to whom on the playground. You will need what is called *academic English,* a term that refers to more abstract, complex, and challenging language that eventually will permit you to participate successfully in general classroom instruction. Academic English involves things such as relating an event or a series of events to someone who was not present; being able to make comparisons between alternatives and justify a choice; knowing different forms and inflections of words and their appropriate use; and possessing and using content-specific vocabulary and modes of expression in different academic disciplines such as mathematics and social studies. As if this were not enough, you eventually will need to be able to understand and produce academic English both orally and in writing (Scarcella, 2003). If you do not, you likely will fall behind your classmates, make poorer grades, get discouraged, fall further behind, and have fewer educational and occupational choices.

This is the situation faced by millions of students in U.S. schools who do not speak English fluently. Their number has grown dramatically since the early 1990s. In 1990, 1 of every 20 public school students in Grades K–12 was an English language learner (ELL)—a student who speaks English either not at all or with enough limitations that he or she cannot fully participate in mainstream English instruction. Today, the figure is 1 in 9. By the mid-2020s, demographers estimate it might be 1 in 4. The ELL population has grown from 2 million to 5 million since 1990, a period when the overall school population increased relatively little. States not typically associated with non-English speakers—South Carolina, North Carolina, Tennessee, Georgia, and Indiana—each saw an increase in the ELL population of at least 400% between 1993–1994 and 2003–2004.

ELLs in the United States come from more than 400 different language backgrounds; however, by far the largest proportion—80%—are Spanish speakers. This is an important fact to bear in mind because Spanish speakers in the United States tend to come from lower economic and educational backgrounds than either the general population or other immigrants and language minority populations. Consequently, most ELLs are at risk for poor school outcomes not only because of language but also because of socioeconomic factors. Speakers of

---

[1]Most of the preceding list was derived from content standards for second grade adopted by the California State Board of Education, available online at http://www.cde.ca.gov. Reading fluency figures are from Behavioral Research & Teaching (2005); vocabulary is from Lehr, Osborn, and Hieberg (n.d.). Additional resources include Nagy and Herman (1987) and Stahl and Nagy (2006).

Asian languages (e.g., Vietnamese, Hmong, Chinese, Korean), who generally, although certainly not uniformly (Hmong students are among the exceptions), tend to be of higher socioeconomic status, comprise the next largest groups—about 8% of the ELL population.

What sort of instructional environments are these students in? The question is difficult to answer, partly because of definitional and reporting inconsistencies from state to state (U.S. Department of Education, 2005; Zehler et al., 2003). National data from a 2001–2002 school year survey (Zehler et al., 2003) reflect that a majority of ELLs—approximately 60%—are in essentially all-English instruction. Beyond this, it is impossible to say what is typical. If anything, the picture has become even more complex over the past decade. California, Arizona, and Massachusetts have enacted laws that curtail bilingual education; the number of students receiving bilingual education has declined in those states. However, even in states that require bilingual education—New Jersey, Texas, Illinois, New York, and New Mexico—the trends vary. In Texas, the number of students in bilingual education has gone up a bit. In Illinois, it has stayed about the same. In New York and New Jersey, it has gone down (Zehr, 2007a).

The shifting landscape is partly due to the accountability requirements of the No Child Left Behind Act of 2001 (PL 107-110), particularly in basic skills such as reading and math, and how individual states interpret them. No Child Left Behind permits assessing ELLs in their primary language for up to 3 years, and in some cases for an additional 2 years; however, most states do not take advantage of this flexibility. The pressures on educators to immerse students in English are thus nearly overwhelming (Zehr, 2007a). This is ironic because the best evidence available shows that instruction in the primary language makes a positive contribution to academic achievement (particularly in reading) *in the second language*. This point will be discussed at length in the following section.

About 12% of ELLs apparently receive no services or support at all related to their limited English proficiency. This might be a violation of the 1974 Supreme Court decision in *Lau v. Nichols,* which requires schools to teach ELLs so that they have "a meaningful opportunity to participate in the public educational program" (p. 563). Somewhat fewer than half of ELLs receive all-English instruction with some amount of *LEP services.* (ELLs were formerly called *LEP,* or *limited English proficient;* the term is sometimes still used.) *LEP services* can include aides or resource teachers specifically for ELLs, instruction in English as a second language (ESL), and/or content instruction designed specifically for students with limited English proficiency. The remaining ELLs—about 40%—are in programs that make some use of their primary language. Here again there is a wide range, with nothing being typical. In some cases, the native language is used extensively and students are taught academic skills in that language (e.g., how to read and write in Spanish). In other cases, students are taught academic skills in English and their primary language is used only for "support" (e.g., translations, explanations, or previews of material in Spanish prior to an all-English lesson)

(Zehler et al., 2003). There is no way to know the amount of support students receive or, most critically, the quality of the instruction and whether it is helpful for student achievement.

There are numerous program models that states report using with ELLs (U.S. Department of Education, 2005; see Genesee, 1999, for a description of the different program alternatives for ELLs, ranging from all-English instruction to different forms of bilingual education). Variability is again the rule. All 50 states, as well as Washington, D.C., and Puerto Rico, report some type of ESL instruction, but no state uses only one program model. Some states have as many as eight or nine different programs. New Mexico reports using 10 different programs (U.S. Department of Education, 2005). Clearly, it is difficult to generalize about the varied and complex instructional landscape for ELLs.

Regardless of the type of instruction ELLs receive, schools in the United States have not done a particularly good job of promoting high levels of achievement among this fast-growing segment of the K–12 population. On state and national tests, students who are learning English consistently underperform in comparison to their English-speaking peers. In California, for example, approximately 50% of students who are fluent in English receive scores of "proficient" or "advanced" on the California Standards Test in English Language Arts (the actual percent proficient or advanced ranges from a high of 68% in Grade 4 to a low of 46% in Grade 11). In contrast, among ELLs who have already been enrolled in school for 12 months or more, the percent who score "proficient" or "advanced" in English language arts ranges from a high of 28% in 2nd grade to a dreadfully low 4% in 10th and 11th grades (data are from the California Department of Education web site, http://cde.ca.gov). The national picture shows the same discrepancies. On the 2005 National Assessment of Educational Progress (NAEP; see http://nces.ed.gov/nationsreportcard/), 4th-grade ELLs scored 35 points below non-ELLs in reading, 24 points below non-ELLs in math, and 32 points below non-ELLs in science. Those are very large gaps—on the 4th-grade NAEP, 10 points is roughly equivalent to a grade level. Similar gaps also have been found in reading, math, and science among 8th graders.

These discrepancies should be no surprise, of course. Even if they have been in the United States for a year, ELLs are limited in their English proficiency, and the tests cited here are *in English*. This points, again, to the important and very complex question of how and particularly in what language ELLs should be assessed. If ELLs are assessed in English, we are almost certain to underestimate what they know and put them at even greater risk of poor achievement. This is problematic both from a policy perspective and instructionally. How can we design effective policies and practices if we systematically misjudge the knowledge and skills of a large number of students? There is no way to know whether ELLs tested in English receive low scores because of lagging content knowledge and skills or because of limited English proficiency or both. Unfortunately, many states do not take advantage of even the modest provisions in the No Child Left Behind Act that permit assessing ELLs in their primary language for up to 3, possibly 5, years. In 2005, a group of school districts sued the state of California to force it to allow Spanish-speaking ELLs to take state-mandated tests in Spanish. Plaintiffs in *Coachella Valley Unified School District v. California* argued that the state "violated its duty to provide valid and reliable academic testing" (King, 2007). In a preliminary ruling, however, the judge indicated that the court lacked the jurisdiction to decide the case (Zehr, 2007b).

Whatever the explanation for these achievement gaps, they bode ill for ELLs' future educational and vocational options. They also bode ill for the society as a whole because the costs of large-scale underachievement are very high (Natriello, McDill, & Pallas, 1990). Passage of the No Child Left Behind Act raised the stakes for educators higher than ever. Schools cannot meet their annual yearly progress goals unless all major subgroups at the school—including ELLs—meet achievement targets. Teachers of ELLs, as well as site and district administrators, are thus under tremendous pressure. It is imperative that teachers, administrators, other school staff, and policy makers understand the state of their knowledge regarding how to improve the achievement of these students.

Unfortunately, the state of their knowledge is very modest. This is true for several reasons, among them that debates over language of instruction—the so-called "bilingual education" question—have historically dominated this field, and as a result, there has been relatively little solid research on many other important topics. (*Bilingual education* is a term used to describe any instructional approach that teaches academic skills, such as reading, in the native language in addition to teaching students academic skills in English, or whatever the societal language is. For descriptions of the various approaches that fall under the bilingual umbrella, see Genesee, 1999.) Research and policy affecting ELLs have historically been fueled by ideological and political considerations (Crawford, 1999), often with less attention paid to coherent programs of research that could shed light on ways to improve these students' educational outcomes. The net result has been a research base that is inadequate for informing comprehensive policies and practices—including, very critically, guidelines for determining the skills and knowledge teachers need to be effective with ELLs. As if this were not enough, the research is practically nonexistent for secondary-level students. With the exception of a handful of studies about middle-school ELLs, almost all the research we have is at the elementary level. Because the issues change as children go through school, findings from elementary school might not be particularly useful in high school. In higher grades, the learning is more complex and the achievement gaps are wider than in early grades. Adolescence ushers in questions of identity, motivation, and peer groups as well as a wide range of other factors that change in fundamental ways what teachers and parents must address. Although the picture is slowly changing, the available research offers precious little guidance.

STUDIES AGREE ON KEY FINDINGS

Two major reviews of the research on educating ELLs were completed in 2006—
one by the National Literacy Panel (NLP; August & Shanahan, 2006) and the other
by researchers associated with the Center for Research on Education, Diversity &
Excellence (CREDE; Genesee, Lindholm-Leary, Saunders, & Christian, 2006).
The NLP comprised 18 researchers with expertise in literacy, language development, the education of language minority students, assessment, and quantitative
and qualitative research methods. These researchers, whose work took nearly 3
years, identified more than 3,000 reports, documents, dissertations, and publications produced from approximately 1980 to 2002 that were candidates for inclusion in their review. Fewer than 300 of these documents met the criteria for inclusion: They had to be empirical (i.e., they collected, analyzed, and reported data
rather than stated opinions, advocated positions, or reviewed research), deal with
clearly identified language-minority populations, and study children and youth ages
3–18. The CREDE report was produced over 2 years by a core group of four researchers (and three coauthors), all of whom had been engaged in language minority and language research for many years. Like the NLP, the CREDE panel conducted literature searches to identify candidate empirical research reports on
language minority students from preschool to high school, but their searches were
not as extensive as those of the NLP. Approximately 200 articles and reports comprised the final group of studies the CREDE panel reviewed and on which they
based their conclusions. The studies the CREDE panel reviewed were published
during approximately the same period as the studies the NLP reviewed.

Although they covered a lot of the same terrain, the CREDE and NLP reports differed in some ways. For example, the CREDE report only examined research conducted in the United States and only took into consideration outcomes
in English; the NLP included studies conducted anywhere in the world (as long
as they were published in English) and took into consideration outcomes in children's first or second language. The CREDE panelists included quantitative studies (experiments or correlational research) almost exclusively, whereas the NLP
also included qualitative studies.[2] The CREDE panel reviewed research that addressed children's English language development, literacy development, and
achievement in the content areas (science, social studies, mathematics). In con-

---

[2]Experimental studies are considered the gold standard if one wants to determine the effect of a
particular program or type of instruction. Experiments include treatment and comparison groups as
well as other controls designed to ensure that any impacts found can be attributed to the treatment
(as opposed to differences, for example, between two groups of students). Correlational studies can
establish that there is a relationship between two things (e.g., an instructional method and student
achievement), but they cannot indicate that one thing caused another. Qualitative studies generally
attempt to describe and analyze rather than measure and count. Precise and highly detailed qualitative studies can establish causation (e.g., a part of a lesson that led to student learning), but because
the number of participants in a qualitative study is typically low, they are not good for establishing
generalizability.

trast, the NLP only looked at influences on literacy development (and aspects of oral language that are closely related to literacy, such as phonological awareness and vocabulary). A final and very important difference between the two reports was the criteria used to determine whether to include studies of bilingual education. The NLP used more stringent criteria, resulting in a difference in the two reports' findings regarding how long ELLs should receive bilingual instruction. This difference is described in the section that follows.

These two reviews used various methods to synthesize the research and draw conclusions that would be helpful to educators and that would also identify areas for additional future study.[3] In doing their reviews, both sets of panelists paid particular attention to the quality of the studies and the degree to which reported findings were adequately supported by the research undertaken. The reports warrant our attention because they represent the most concerted effort to date to identify the best knowledge available and set the stage for renewed efforts to find effective approaches to help ELLs succeed in school. It would be impossible to summarize fully the reports here, though educators are encouraged to obtain and study them, but their key conclusions can help us forge a new foundation for improving the education of children from non–English-speaking homes. The findings can be summarized in three major points:

1. Teaching students to read in their first language promotes higher levels of reading achievement *in English.*

2. What we know about good instruction and curriculum in general holds true for ELLs as well.

3. ELLs require instructional accommodations when instructed in English.

Teaching Students to Read in Their First Language Promotes Higher Levels of Reading Achievement in English

To date, five meta-analyses[4] have concluded that bilingual education promotes academic achievement in students' *second* language (Francis, Lesaux, & August, 2006; Greene, 1997; Rolstad, Mahoney, & Glass, 2005; Slavin & Cheung, 2005;

---

[3]Readers should be aware of the dramatic discrepancy between the research base for English speakers and English language learners. For example, the National Reading Panel (NICHD, 2000) synthesized findings from more than 400 experimental studies of instruction in phonological awareness, phonics, vocabulary, reading fluency, and reading comprehension. In contrast, the National Literacy Panel (August & Shanahan, 2006) could identify only 17 experimental studies of instructional procedures despite the fact that they considered more topics and used looser inclusion criteria.

[4]A *meta-analysis* is a statistical technique that allows researchers to combine data from many studies and calculate the average effect of an instructional procedure. It is useful because studies often come to conflicting conclusions. Some find positive effects of a program, others find negative effects of the same type of program, and yet others find no effects. Even among studies that report positive findings, the effects can be small or large. The questions a meta-analysis addresses are these: Taking into account all the relevant studies on a topic, *overall,* is the effect positive, negative, or zero? And if it is overall positive or negative, what is the magnitude of the effect—large, and therefore meaningful; small, and therefore of little consequence; or something in between? Are there additional factors (e.g., student characteristics) that influence whether effects are large or small?

Willig, 1985). This finding most clearly applies to learning to read. Findings for other curricular areas are much more equivocal. Nonetheless, this is an extraordinary convergence. To appreciate the strength of the finding, readers should understand how unusual it is even to have five independent meta-analyses on the same issue conducted by five independent researchers from diverse perspectives. The fact that they all reached essentially the same conclusion is noteworthy. With the exception of Willig (1985), none of the meta-analysts have or had any particular investment, professionally or otherwise, in bilingual education. They were completely nonpartisan, methodologically rigorous, and independent researchers. (Willig was also rigorous but had worked in the field of bilingual education; therefore, skeptics might suspect a probilingual education agenda.) I know of no other finding in the entire educational research literature that can claim to be supported unanimously by five independent meta-analyses conducted over a 20-year span. In fact, this might be one of the strongest findings in the entire field of educational research. Period. Although many questions remain about the role of the primary language in educating ELLs, the consistent findings from these meta-analyses should put to rest the idea that English-only instruction is preferable.

Approximately two dozen experiments have been conducted and reported over the past 35 years comparing reading instruction that uses students' primary and secondary languages with second language immersion (which in the United States would, of course, be English). The NLP conducted a meta-analysis using 17 of these studies (the others did not meet their stringent methodological criteria). The analysis concluded that teaching ELLs to read in their primary language, compared with teaching them to read in their second language only, boosts their reading achievement *in the second language.* In other words, a child's second language reading achievement will be higher if he or she is first taught to read in his or her home language compared with being taught to read in the second language right off the bat. The higher-quality, more rigorous studies in this analysis showed the strongest effects of all.

Although there are other possible explanations, the key to explaining how primary language instruction results in higher achievement in English is probably what educational psychologists call *transfer. Transfer* is one of the most venerable and important concepts in education. With respect to ELLs, a substantial body of research reviewed by both the CREDE and NLP researchers suggests that literacy and other skills and knowledge transfer across languages. That is, if you learn something in one language—such as decoding, comprehension skills, or a concept such as *democracy*—you either already know it in (i.e., transfer it to) another language or can more easily learn it in another language. Transfer also explains another important finding first pointed out in the meta-analysis by Slavin and Cheung (2005), published a year before the NLP report appeared[5]: ELLs can

---

[5]Robert Slavin was a member of the National Literacy Panel working on the meta-analysis of instructional language. He resigned in order to publish his review before the panel's work was completed.

be taught to read in their primary language and in English simultaneously (at different times in the school day) with mutual benefit to literacy development in both languages. Teachers cannot assume that transfer is automatic, however. Students sometimes do not realize that what they know in their first language (e.g., cognates such as *elefante* and *elephant*; or *ejemplo* and *example*). Jiménez puts it this way: "Less successful bilingual readers view their two languages as separate and unrelated, and they often see their non-English language backgrounds as detrimental" (1997, p. 227). It is necessary that teachers be aware of what students know and can do in their primary language so they can help them apply their knowledge and skills to tasks in English.

Transfer of reading skills across languages appears to occur even if languages use different alphabetic systems, although the different alphabets probably diminish the degree of transfer. For example, studies of transfer between English and Spanish find relatively high correlations on measures of word reading and spelling. Some studies of English and non-Roman alphabets (e.g., Arabic or Persian), in contrast, find much lower correlations. Comprehension skills, however, appear to transfer readily between languages with different alphabets, such as English and Korean.

Transfer is a critical point because opponents of primary language instruction often argue that time spent in the first language is wasted from the standpoint of promoting progress in the second. The opposite is actually true: Productive learning in one language makes a positive contribution to learning in the second language. Because academic learning—which is what schools and teachers must be most concerned with—is most efficient and productive in the language one knows best, the clear conclusion from this research (keeping in mind that research is strongest with respect to teaching reading) is that teaching academic skills in the learner's stronger language is the most efficient approach to take.

The effects of primary language instruction are modest, but they are real. Researchers gauge the effect of a program or an instructional practice in terms of an *effect size,* which tells how much improvement can be expected from using the program or practice. The average effect size of primary language reading instruction over 2–3 years (the typical length of time children in the studies were followed) is around 0.35–0.40; estimates range from about 0.2 to about 0.6, depending on how the calculation is done. What this means is that teaching students to read in their primary language can boost achievement in their second language by a total of approximately 12–15 percentile points (in comparison to students who do not receive primary language instruction) over 2–3 years. Although this is not a huge difference, neither is it trivial. These effects are reliable, and they apply to elementary as well as secondary students. (Although only 2 of the 17 studies the NLP included in the meta-analysis were with secondary students, both produced positive effects.)

To provide some perspective, the National Reading Panel (National Institute of Child Health and Human Development [NICHD], 2000), which reviewed experimental research on English speakers only, found that the average effect size of phonics instruction is 0.44, a bit larger than the likely average effect size of primary language reading instruction. Primary language reading instruction is clearly no panacea, just as phonics instruction is no panacea, but relatively speaking, it makes a meaningful contribution to reading achievement *in English*.

There is yet another reason to consider bilingual instruction for ELLs, and that is the inherent advantage of knowing and being literate in two languages. It should come as no surprise that the meta-analyses found that in addition to promoting achievement in the second language, bilingual instruction also promotes achievement in the primary language. In other words, it helps students become bilingual. Knowing two languages confers numerous obvious advantages—cultural, intellectual, cognitive (e.g., Bialystock, 2001), vocational, and economic (Saiz & Zoido, 2005). Many would argue that bilingualism and biliteracy ought to be our educational goal for ELLs (see, for example, Gándara & Rumberger, 2006). I would agree but take it a step further: It should be a goal for all students.

Of course, in many schools, the questions of how long and to what extent bilingual instruction should be used do not even arise. Instruction in the primary language is sometimes not feasible, either because there are no qualified staff or because students come from numerous language backgrounds or, sadly, because of uninformed policy choices or political decisions, such as California's Proposition 227. ELLs can still be helped to achieve at higher levels. Although the research here is not as solid as the research on primary language instruction—which itself is incomplete in many respects—educators have two other important principles, supported by research to varying degrees, on which to base their practice. We turn to them now.

What We Know About Good Instruction and Curriculum in General Holds True for English Language Learners

Both the CREDE and NLP reports conclude that ELLs learn in much the same way as non-ELLs (although accommodations are almost certainly necessary, as discussed in the next section). Good instruction for students in general tends to be good instruction for ELLs in particular. If instructed in the primary language, the application of effective instructional models to ELLs is transparent; all that differs is the language of instruction. But even when instructed in English, effective instruction is similar in important respects to effective instruction for non-ELLs.

As a general rule, all students tend to benefit from clear goals and learning objectives; meaningful, challenging, and motivating contexts; a curriculum rich with content; well-designed, clearly structured, and appropriately paced instruction; active engagement and participation; opportunities to practice, apply, and transfer new learning; feedback on correct and incorrect responses; periodic review and practice; frequent assessments to gauge progress, with reteaching as needed; and opportunities to interact with other students in motivating contexts and appropriately structured contexts. Although these instructional variables have not been studied with ELLs to the degree they have been with English speakers, existing studies suggest that what is known about effective instruction in general ought to be the foundation of effective teaching for ELLs. There are, of course, individual or group differences: Students might require or benefit from more or less structure, practice, review, autonomy, challenge, or any other dimension of teaching and learning. This is as likely to be true for ELLs as it is for English speakers.

The NLP found that ELLs learning to read in English, just like English speakers learning to read in English, benefit from explicit teaching of components of literacy (e.g., phonemic awareness, phonics, vocabulary, comprehension, writing). A study in England, for example, found that Jolly Phonics had a stronger effect on ELLs' phonological awareness, alphabet knowledge, and application to reading and writing than did a Big Books approach (Stuart, 1999). Other studies reviewed by the NLP also showed similar effects of directly teaching the sounds that make up words, how letters represent those sounds, and how letters combine to form words.

In fact, studies published since the NLP and CREDE reports completed their reviews continue to show the positive impact of structured, explicit instruction on beginning reading skills. Vaughn and colleagues (2006) have shown the benefits of small-group explicit instruction for at-risk first-grade readers. The intervention was conducted in either English or Spanish, depending on each child's instructional language. In both languages, the intervention consisted of explicit phonological and phonics (decoding) instruction as well as instruction in fluency, oral language, vocabulary, and comprehension. Compared with children who received their school's existing intervention, children in Vaughn and colleagues' program scored higher on multiple measures of reading and academic achievement. In a study conducted solely in English, Roberts and Neal (2004) also showed that ELLs were more likely to learn what they were explicitly taught: Preschool children in a comprehension-oriented group learned more vocabulary and print concepts than children in a letter-rhyme–focused group. In contrast, children in the letter-rhyme group learned more letter names and how to write letters.

Studies of vocabulary instruction for ELLs also show that students are more likely to learn words when they are directly taught. Just as with English speakers, ELLs learn more words when the words are embedded in meaningful contexts and students are provided with ample opportunities for their repetition and use, in contrast to looking up dictionary definitions or presenting words in single sentences. In a preschool study, Collins (2005) showed that explaining new vocabulary helped Portuguese-speaking children acquire vocabulary from storybook reading. Although children with higher initial English scores learned more words, explaining new words was helpful for all children, regardless of how little English they knew. Similarly, a study reviewed by the NLP involving fifth graders showed that explicit vocabulary instruction, using words from texts appropriate for and likely to interest the students, combined with exposure to and use of the words in numerous contexts (e.g., reading and hearing stories, discussions, posting target words, writing words and definitions for homework) led to improvements in word learning and reading comprehension (Carlo et al., 2004). These are principles of effective vocabulary instruction that have been found to be effective for English speakers (e.g., Beck, McKeown, & Kucan, 2002).

Other types of instruction that the NLP review found to be promising with ELLs include cooperative learning (i.e., students working interdependently on group instructional tasks and learning goals), encouraging reading in English, discussions to promote comprehension (i.e., instructional conversations), and mastery learning. A mastery learning study reviewed by the NLP was particularly informative because the researchers found this approach (which involves precise behavioral objectives permitting students to reach a *mastery* criterion before moving to new learning) more effective in promoting Mexican American students' reading comprehension than an approach that involved teaching to the students' supposed cultural learning style.

The CREDE report concluded that "the best recommendation to emerge from our review favors instruction that combines interactive and direct approaches" (Genesee et al., 2006, p. 140). *Interactive* refers to instruction with give and take between learner and teacher, in which the teacher is actively promoting students' progress by encouraging higher levels of thinking, speaking, and reading at their instructional levels. Examples of interactive teaching include structured discussions (i.e., instructional conversations), brainstorming, and editing and/or discussing student or teacher writing. *Direct* approaches emphasize explicit and direct teaching of skills or knowledge, such as letter–sound associations, spelling patterns, vocabulary words, and mathematical algorithms. Typically, direct instruction uses techniques such as modeling, instructional input, corrective feedback, and guided practice to help students acquire knowledge and skills as efficiently as possible. The CREDE report noted that "Direct instruction of specific skills [is important to help students gain] mastery of literacy-related skills that are often embedded in complex literacy or academic tasks" (Genesee et al., 2006, p. 140).

In contrast to interactive and direct teaching, the report found, at best, mixed evidence supporting what it termed *process approaches*. These are approaches in which students are exposed to rich literacy experiences and literacy materials but receive little direct teaching or structuring of learning. In one study, for example, students were exposed to alternative reading and writing strategies on wall charts, but this was insufficient to ensure the strategies would be employed. In another study, Spanish-speaking ELLs who received structured writing lessons outperformed students who received extended opportunities to do "free writing." The CREDE report concluded that process strategies are "not sufficient to promote acquisition of the specific skills that comprise reading and writing . . . . [F]ocused and explicit instruction in particular skills and subskills is called for if ELLs are to become efficient and effective readers and writers" (Genesee et al., 2006, pp. 139–140).

A question that has been receiving increased attention is whether ELLs can make progress that is comparable to non-ELLs (August & Shanahan, 2006; Gersten et al., 2007). There is some evidence that they can, despite their limited English. Particularly with respect to phonological, decoding, and word recognition skills—early reading skills that require relatively little language proficiency—ELLs appear to be capable of learning at levels similar to that of English speakers if they are provided with good, structured, explicit teaching. Many of the studies supporting this conclusion, however, were conducted in Canada, where the ELL population is far different from the ELL population in the United States. Because of highly restrictive immigration laws and distance from Mexico and Central America, the Canadian ELL population comes from families with higher incomes and education levels. A longitudinal study of Latino students in an early transition bilingual education program (students receive Spanish and English literacy instruction in kindergarten and first grades) has reported early English literacy achievement close to national norms (Lindsey, Manis, & Bailey, 2003; Manis, Lindsey, & Bailey, 2004); however, whether typical ELLs in the United States can achieve on levels comparable to non-ELLs, and if so under what conditions, remains an open question (Leafstedt, Richards, & Gerber, 2004).

English Language Learners Require Instructional Accommodations When Instructed in English

The NLP review concluded that in the earliest stages of learning to read, when the focus is on sounds, letters, and how they combine to form words that can be read, ELLs are more likely to make progress that is comparable to that of English speakers provided the instruction is clear, focused, and systematic. In other words, when the language requirements are relatively low—as they are for learning phonological skills (the sounds of the language and how words are made up of smaller constituent sounds), letter–sound combinations, decoding, and word recognition—it is possible for ELLs to make the sort of progress expected of native English speakers, although they still may require some additional support as a result of language limitations. However, as content gets more challenging and language demands increase, more and more complex vocabulary and syntax are required, and the need for accommodations to make the content more accessible and comprehensible will increase accordingly.

ELLs' language limitations begin to slow their progress as vocabulary and content knowledge become more relevant for continued reading (and general academic) success, typically around third grade. Learners who know the language can concentrate on the academic skills they need to learn; however, learners who do not know the language or do not know it well enough must devote part of their attention to learning the skills and part of their attention to learning and understanding the language in which those skills are taught. This is why it is critical that teachers work to develop ELLs' English oral language skills, particularly vocabulary, and their content knowledge from the time they start school, even before they have learned the reading basics. Vocabulary development is, of course, important for all students, but it is particularly critical for ELLs. There can be little doubt that explicit attention to vocabulary development—everyday words as well as more specialized academic words—needs to be part of ELLs' school programs.

What constitutes effective vocabulary instruction for ELLs, and how does it differ from effective instruction for English speakers? As I have already discussed, there are probably many similarities. Collins (2005), cited previously, found that preschool ELLs acquired more vocabulary when the teacher explained words contained in a storybook read to the children. ELLs benefit from clear explanations, just as native English speakers do; however, Collins also found that children who began with lower English scores learned less than children with higher English scores. That is, knowing less English made it harder to learn additional English. What might have helped the children with lower initial English proficiency gain more English vocabulary? Another preschool study (Roberts & Neal, 2004) found that pictures helped children with low levels of oral English learn story vocabulary (e.g., dentist, mouse, cap). The *visual representation* of concepts, not just a language-based *explanation*, provided children with additional support in learning the vocabulary words. There is scant research on this topic, but we would also expect that songs, rhymes, chants, and additional opportunities to use and repeat words would help build vocabulary among young ELLs.

It is a good bet that effective strategies for English speakers will involve some sort of accommodations or adjustments to make them as effective with ELLs. Roberts and Neal (2004) provided an example that is related to the critical issue of assessment, which I mentioned previously in the chapter. Roberts and Neal attempted to teach preschool ELLs rhyming skills, an important aspect of phonological awareness. The way they assessed rhyming skill was by prompting the children with a word and asking them to provide a word that rhymed. If the tester said *lake,* the child would be expected to produce, for example, *cake.* As it turned out, regardless of instructional group, *all* of the children did very poorly on the assessment. The average score on the rhyming test was less than 1, meaning that a lot of children simply did not respond. Why? Probably because the task demand was simply beyond the children; they were unable to *produce* a rhyming word because their vocabularies were so limited. The children were, in essence, given a test that measured their productive vocabularies as much as it measured their rhyming skills. The study would probably have obtained different results if the researchers had presented pairs of words and asked the children to distinguish between rhyming and nonrhyming pairs or had children select the rhyming word from several possible choices.

This example suggests two things: First, it is essential that ELLs be assessed in a way that uncouples language proficiency from content knowledge; language limitations can obscure an accurate picture of what children actually know and can do. Second, and directly following from Robert and Neal's (2004) study, an important instructional accommodation for ELLs might be to tailor task demands to children's English language proficiency. Teachers should not expect children to produce language beyond their level of English proficiency; conversely, they should provide children with language-learning and language-use tasks that challenge them and stretch their language development.

What about for older children? Some clues for vocabulary instruction are offered in the study by Carlo and colleagues (2004), also cited previously, who examined the effects of a vocabulary instruction program on fifth-grade Spanish-speaking ELLs and native English speakers. The approach Carlo and colleagues took was based on principles of vocabulary instruction found to be valid for children who already speak English (e.g., explicit teaching of words, using words from texts likely to interest students, multiple exposures to and uses of the words in numerous contexts). The researchers included additional elements: activities such as charades that actively involved learners in manipulating and analyzing word meanings; writing and spelling the words numerous times; strategic uses of Spanish (e.g., previewing lessons using Spanish texts, providing teachers with translation equivalents of the target words, using English–Spanish cognates, such as *supermarket* and *supermercado*); and selection of texts and topics on immigration that were expected to resonate with the Mexican and Dominican immigrant students. Overall, the experimental program produced relatively strong effects in terms of students' learning the target vocabulary. It produced much smaller, but still significant, effects on reading comprehension. Particularly noteworthy is that the effects of the program were equivalent for ELLs and English-speaking students. Thus, although the researchers acknowledge that they cannot determine which of the extra ELL supports explain the program's impact on these students, their demonstration that, with additional support, a program can have a similar impact on both ELLs and English speakers is very important.

The following paragraphs provide a possible list of supports or accommodations for ELLs who receive English-only instruction. Some of these are only now starting to be investigated empirically; others have data from studies that fail to control for important variables, therefore limiting our conclusions. Still others have no supporting data.

Accommodations Using Students' Primary Language as a Scaffold

The first group of accommodations involves use of the primary language. Readers should note the contrast between the use of the native language in bilingual instruction and use of the native language in an English immersion context. In bilingual education, students are taught language arts and sometimes math and other subjects such as social studies in their primary language. In contrast, when the primary language is used as an accommodation in an English immersion context, instruction is basically in English, but the primary language is used to make the instruction more meaningful or comprehensible. This does not involve teaching children academic skills in their primary language nor attempting to promote primary language development per se. Instead, the primary language is used as a bridge, or *scaffold,* to learning the content in English. There are several possible examples of using the primary language as a support for ELLs, including using primary language for clarification and explanation, using primary language to introduce new concepts, and miscellaneous other uses.

Use of the Primary Language for Clarification and Explanation
Primary language can be used by the teacher, a classroom aide, a peer, or a volunteer in the classroom to clarify or explain concepts presented in English. Although this approach makes intuitive sense, I know of no research that actually gauges its effectiveness. It is easy to see how explaining or clarifying concepts in students' primary language can help provide ELLs with access to what is going on in the classroom; however, it is also not difficult to imagine downsides. For example, if someone other than the teacher (e.g., a peer) provides the explanations, he or she might not be accurate; ELL students may come to depend on a translator as a crutch and not exert themselves to learn English; or ELL students may tune out teaching in English if translations or periodic explanations in the primary language are offered throughout lessons.

Use of Primary Language to Introduce New Concepts
Introducing new concepts in the primary language prior to the lesson in English, then reviewing the new content, again in the primary language (sometimes called *preview–review;* see Ovando, Collier, & Combs, 2003), also may be beneficial to ELLs. This is different from clarification and explanation because this "frontloads" the new learning in the student's primary language and then reviews it after the lesson as opposed to providing ongoing explanation or translation. When the real lesson is delivered in English, the student already is somewhat familiar with the content, but he or she has to concentrate to get the message as it is delivered in English. Because of the previewing, the language used in the lesson should be more comprehensible and, in principle at least, the student should walk away knowing more content *and* more language (e.g., vocabulary, key phrases). By reviewing lesson content after the lesson, the teacher checks to see whether students accomplished the lesson objective. The NLP reviewed a study by Ulanoff and Pucci (1999) that provided some support for the effectiveness of this approach. Prior to reading a book in English, teachers previewed difficult vocabulary in the primary language (Spanish) then afterward reviewed the material in Spanish. This produced better comprehension and recall than the control conditions—reading the book in English and doing a simultaneous Spanish translation while reading.

Other Primary Language Supports
One can imagine numerous variations on the primary language support theme. A study not included in the NLP provides a creative example. Fung, Wilkinson, and Moore (2003) found that introducing reciprocal teaching strategies in students' primary language improved reading comprehension in the second language. Reciprocal teaching is a tech-

nique for promoting reading comprehension. Students are taught four strategies—asking questions about the text, summarizing what they have read, clarifying the text's meaning, and predicting what will come next. This set of strategies
has been found to promote reading comprehension among students who are adequate decoders but poor comprehenders. Fung and colleagues taught middle
school ELLs reciprocal teaching strategies in their primary language and in
English. They then found that students used more reading comprehension and
monitoring strategies *and* their reading comprehension improved when they read
in English. Although the authors suggested that teaching reading strategies in students' home language can be an effective form of primary language support, the
study did not compare home-language–assisted reciprocal teaching with English-
only reciprocal teaching; therefore, we do not really know the role primary language support itself played in improving student comprehension.

Another type of primary language support consists of focusing on the similarities and/or difference between English and the students' native language (e.g.,
if using the Roman alphabet, some letters represent the same sounds in English
and other languages whereas others do not). In addition, languages have cognates;
that is, words with shared meanings from common etymological roots (e.g., *geography* and *geografía*). Calling students' attention to these cognates could help extend their vocabularies and improve their comprehension; however, we do not
know the effect of cognate instruction per se. The Carlo and colleagues (2004)
vocabulary program described previously used cognates as one strategy to help
ELLs develop their vocabularies and improve comprehension, but as previously
discussed, the intervention comprised many elements, and it is impossible to
know the effect of any one. Nonetheless, there are a number of useful sources of
Spanish–English cognates that teachers of ELLs can consult (e.g., Calderón et al.,
2003). Nash (1999) offers an exhaustive, book-length list, but see also Prado
(1996), for false cognates that can cause problems, such as (my personal favorite)
embarrassed and *embarazada*. The latter, in Spanish, means *pregnant.* When put
in the masculine form—*embarazado*—it can really light up a classroom of
Spanish-speaking adolescents.

Accommodations Using Only English In addition to accommodations that make use of students' primary language, a number of accommodations have been suggested that make use only of English. All of these accommodations appear to be "generic" scaffolds and supports; that is, there is little
obviously tailored to ELLs. They might, in fact, be effective strategies for many
students, particularly those who need more learning support than is typically provided in teaching and learning situations in which verbal exchanges of information predominate. These English-only accommodations include the following:

• Providing predictable and consistent classroom management routines, aided
  by diagrams, lists, and easy-to-read schedules on the board or on charts, to
  which the teacher refers frequently

- Using graphic organizers that make content and the relationships among concepts and different lesson elements visually explicit
- Providing additional opportunities for practice, either during the school day, after school, or for homework
- Providing redundant key information (e.g., visual cues, pictures, and physical gestures about lesson content and classroom procedures)
- Identifying, highlighting, and clarifying difficult words and passages within texts to facilitate comprehension and, more generally, greatly emphasizing vocabulary development
- Helping students consolidate text knowledge by having the teacher, other students, and ELLs themselves summarize and paraphrase
- Giving students extra practice in reading words, sentences, and stories to build automaticity and fluency
- Providing opportunities for extended interactions with teacher and peers
- Adjusting instruction (e.g., teacher vocabulary, rate of speech, sentence complexity, expectations for student language production) according to students' oral English proficiency
- Targeting both content and English language objectives in every lesson
- Using reading materials that take into account students' personal experiences, including relevant aspects of their cultural background, which aids their reading comprehension (although proficiency in the language of the text has a stronger influence on comprehension than familiarity with passage content)

The accommodations students need probably will change as they develop increased English proficiency. Students who are beginning English speakers will need a great deal of support, sometimes known as *instructional scaffolding*. For example, at the very beginning levels, teachers will have to speak slowly and somewhat deliberately, with clear vocabulary and diction; use pictures or other objects to illustrate the content being taught; and ask students to respond either nonverbally (e.g., pointing or signaling) or in one- or two-word utterances. As they gain in proficiency, students will need less accommodation; for example, teachers can use more complex vocabulary and sentence structures and expect students to respond with longer utterances, and visual information can be presented in written form as well as in pictures. Conversely, more accommodation may be needed when completely new or particularly difficult topics are taught. It might also be that some students in some contexts will require more accommodations than others. We are utterly lacking the data necessary to offer such guidelines. In any case, proficiency in academic English (as distinct from conversational English, which can be acquired to a reasonably high level in approximately 2–3 years) can require 6 or more years (Genesee et al., 2006), so some degree of support will probably be required for a substantial portion of ELLs' schooling.

Why does proficiency in academic English take 4 or 5 more years than proficiency in conversational English? There are several possible reasons. Conversational English probably is used more often than academic English and is fairly limited in the vocabulary and forms of expression it requires. It is also almost always contextualized by gestures, intonation, and references to familiar and concrete situations. In contrast, academic English is generally not used outside of school and tends to present new vocabulary, more complex sentence structures, and rhetorical forms not typically encountered in nonacademic settings. Academic forms of the language also are used to refer to abstract and complex concepts in subject matter disciplines (e.g., science, literature, mathematics, social studies, the arts), particularly as students progress through the grades. Knowing conversational English obviously helps in learning academic English, but the latter is clearly a more challenging task.

ENGLISH LANGUAGE DEVELOPMENT AND OTHER CONSIDERATIONS

It should be apparent that providing English language development (ELD) instruction to ELLs is critically important. Unfortunately—and surprisingly—the CREDE report (Genesee et al., 2006) reveals that research can tell us very little about how or even whether we can accelerate progress in oral ELD. Studies have shown that specific aspects of language can be taught at least in terms of short-term learning effects (e.g., vocabulary, listening comprehension, grammatical elements; see meta-analysis on second language teaching in Norris & Ortega, 2000), but we do not really know how to accelerate the overall process of language learning.

Based on descriptive studies of ELLs in the United States, the CREDE report (Genesee et al., 2006) concluded that it takes at least 6 years (e.g., from kindergarten to Grade 5 or later) for most students to go from being a nonspeaker of a language to having nativelike proficiency. Even students who are in all-English instruction do not begin to show advanced intermediate levels—which are still short of nativelike proficiency—for at least 4 years (i.e., Grade 3 or later). The idea that children will quickly become fluent in English if immersed in all-English instruction is contradicted by the research literature. Certainly exceptions can be found, but fluency within a year of English immersion in school is not the norm among the ELL population in the United States. Can the process be meaningfully sped up so that ELLs can benefit from mainstream English instruction earlier in their educational careers? The answer to this question is unknown. The absence of such research, combined with the obvious need to develop English proficiency as students acquire knowledge and skills across the curriculum, places a huge burden on both students and teachers.

One question that frequently arises is whether ELD should be taught separately or integrated with the rest of the curriculum. A 2006 study suggests that

English language achievement is somewhat enhanced by a separate ELD period. Saunders, Foorman, and Carlson (2006) found that when a separate ELD block was used, teachers spent more time on oral English and were more efficient and focused in their use of time. The ELD block was, by design, targeted at language development, and students who received a separate ELD block scored somewhat higher than students who did not. When there was no ELD block, less time was spent focusing on English per se, and more time was spent on other language arts activities such as reading. It is important to bear in mind that this study was limited to kindergarten, and the effect was small. If the findings are accurate, however, the cumulative effect of a separate block of ELD instruction over many years could be substantial. At the moment, however, this is speculation.

Some educators also have suggested that instruction for ELLs must be tailored to students' culture. This suggestion is based on the observation that individual cultural groups speak, behave, and interact differently; therefore, educators should use instructional approaches that are *culturally compatible* (i.e., that build on or complement students' behavior and interactional patterns). Many readers will be surprised to learn that the NLP (August & Shanahan, 2006) concluded there is little evidence to support the proposition that culturally compatible instruction enhances the actual achievement of ELLs. In fact, as mentioned previously, a study reviewed by the NLP found that a mastery learning/direct-instruction approach produced better effects on Mexican American students' reading comprehension than did an approach tailored to their cultural characteristics. Some studies, most of which are methodologically very weak, have indicated that culturally accommodated instruction can promote engagement and higher-level participation during lessons. This is a meaningful finding, but it is not the same as establishing a connection between culturally accommodated instruction and measured achievement. The hypothesis is certainly plausible, and future research might establish such a connection; however, for now, it appears that developing lessons with solid content and clearly structured instruction would be a better use of teachers' time.

Another proposition with dubious research backing is that grouping ELLs and English speakers during instruction will, in itself, promote ELLs' oral English proficiency. (Simply grouping or pairing students together should not be confused with well-implemented cooperative learning, for which we have evidence of effects on ELLs' student learning; see previous discussion.) Teachers sometimes assume that pairing ELLs and English speakers will provide ELLs with productive language-learning opportunities, but the CREDE synthesis casts doubt on this. One study described the case of an ELL whose teacher relied almost exclusively on classmates to support the student's classroom participation. Because the assignments were far beyond this child's language and academic skills, her peers "were at a loss as to how to assist her" (Platt & Troudi, 1997, cited in Genesee et al., 2006, p. 28). Another study, an examination of cooperative learning in a sixth-grade classroom, found that English speaking students and ELLs rarely engaged in interactions that might promote learning. More typically, English speakers cut the interactions short to finish the assignment, as did the student in the first study: "Just write that down. Who cares? Let's finish up." (p. 28). If teachers use cooperative or peer-learning activities, they must make sure that English speakers are grouped with ELLs who are not so lacking in English skills that meaningful communication and task engagement becomes problematic. In addition, tasks that students engage in must be carefully designed to be instructionally meaningful and provide suitable opportunities for students to participate at their functional levels. Simply pairing or grouping students together and encouraging them to interact or help each other is not sufficient.

IMPLICATIONS FOR IMPROVING INSTRUCTION

Practically, what do these findings and conclusions mean? The following is the sort of instructional framework to which our current state of knowledge points:

- If feasible, children should be taught reading and possibly other basic skills in their primary language. Primary language instruction 1) develops first language skills, thereby promoting bilingualism and biliteracy, 2) promotes learning (particularly learning to read) in English, and 3) can be carried out as children also learn to read (and learn other academic skills) in English. We lack definitive studies regarding whether there are optimal lengths of time for ELLs to receive primary language instruction; however, the answer to this question will partly depend on what our goals are for the education of ELLs.

- As needed, students should be helped to transfer what they know in their first language to learning tasks presented in English; teachers should not assume that transfer is automatic.

- Teaching in the first and second languages can be approached similarly; in fact, what we know about effective instruction in general should be the foundation for how we approach instruction of ELLs. Direct and explicit instruction is probably especially helpful.

- Adjustments or accommodations will be necessary, probably for several years and, at least for some students, until students reach sufficient familiarity with academic English to permit them to be successful in mainstream instruction; more complex learning might require more accommodations.

- ELLs need intensive ELD instruction (especially targeting academic English), but we have little data on how or even whether the process of English language acquisition can be accelerated.

- ELLs also need academic content instruction, just as all students do; although ELD is crucial, it should not completely supplant instruction designed to promote academic content knowledge.[6]

---

[6]Starting in Fall 2007, English language learners in Arizona spend 4 hours per day learning exclusively English (Kossan, 2007). This virtually guarantees they will not receive instruction to promote academic content knowledge, which is no less necessary than English proficiency for school success.

CONCLUSION

Local or state policies, such as California's, that block the use of the primary language and limit instructional accommodations for ELLs are simply not based on the best scientific evidence available. Moreover, these policies make educators' jobs more difficult, which is unconscionable under any circumstance but especially egregious in light of increased accountability pressures they and their students face. Despite many remaining questions, we have useful starting points for renewed efforts to improve the achievement of this fastest growing segment of the school-age population. If educators and their students are to be held accountable, practice and policy must be based on the best evidence we have. Otherwise, claims of *scientifically based practice* are simply hollow slogans.

REFERENCES

August, D., & Shanahan, T. (Eds.). (2006). *Developing literacy in second-language learners: Report of the National Literacy Panel on language-minority children and youth.* Mahwah, NJ: Lawrence Erlbaum Associates.

Beck, I., McKeown, M., & Kucan, L. (2002). *Bringing words to life: Robust vocabulary instruction.* New York: Guilford Press.

Behavioral Research & Teaching. (2005, January). *Oral reading fluency: 90 years of assessment* (BRT Technical Report No. 33). Eugene, OR: Author. Available online at http://www.jhasbrouck.com

Bialystock, E. (2001). *Bilingualism in development: Language, literacy, & cognition.* New York: Cambridge University Press.

Calderón, M., August, D., Durán, D., Madden, N., Slavin, R., & Gil, M. (2003). *Spanish to English transitional reading: Teacher's manual.* Baltimore: Success for All Foundation. Adapted version available online at http://www.ColorinColorado.org

Carlo, M.S., August, D., McLaughlin, B., Snow, C.E., Dressler, C., Lippman, D., et al. (2004). Closing the gap: Addressing the vocabulary needs of English language learners in bilingual and mainstream classrooms. *Reading Research Quarterly, 39,* 188–215.

Collins, M. (2005). ESL preschoolers' English vocabulary acquisition from storybook reading. *Reading Research Quarterly, 40,* 406–408.

Crawford, J. (1999). *Bilingual education: History, politics, theory, and practice* (4th ed.). Los Angeles: Bilingual Education Services.

Francis, D., Lesaux, N., & August, D. (2006). Language of instruction. In D. August & T. Shanahan (Eds.), *Developing literacy in second-language learners: Report of the National Literacy Panel on language-minority children and youth* (pp. 365–413). Mahwah, NJ: Lawrence Erlbaum Associates.

Fung, I., Wilkinson, I., & Moore, D. (2003). L1-assisted reciprocal teaching to improve ESL students' comprehension of English expository text. *Learning and Instruction, 13,* 1–31.

Gándara, P., & Rumberger, R. (2006). *Resource needs for California's English learners.* Santa Barbara, CA: University of California Linguistic Minority Research Institute. Available online at http://www.lmri.ucsb.edu/publications/jointpubs.php

Genesee, F. (Ed.). (1999). *Program alternatives for linguistically diverse students* (Educational Practice Report 1). Santa Cruz, CA: Center for Research on Education, Diversity & Excellence.

Genesee, F., Lindholm-Leary, K., Saunders, W., & Christian, D. (2006). *Educating English language learners.* New York: Cambridge University Press.

Gersten, R., Baker, S.K., Shanahan, T., Linan-Thompson, S., Collins, P., & Scarcella, R. (2007). *Effective literacy and English language instruction for English Learners in the elementary grades: A practice guide* (NCEE 2007-4011). Washington, DC: U.S. Department of Education, Institute of Education Sciences, National Center for Education Evaluation and Regional Assistance. Retrieved from http://ies.ed.gov/ncee.

Greene, J. (1997). A meta-analysis of the Rossell and Baker review of bilingual education research. *Bilingual Research Journal, 21,* 103–122.

Jiménez, R. (1997). The strategic reading abilities and potential of five low-literacy Latina/o readers in middle school. *Reading Research Quarterly, 32,* 224–243.

King, M. (2007, May 22). English-only tests, judge rules. *Santa Cruz Sentinel.* Available online at http://www.santacruzsentinel.com/archive/2007/May/22/local/stories/04local.htm

Kossan, P. (2007, July 14). New learners must spend 4 hours a day on English. *The Arizona Republic.* Available online at http://www.azcentral.com/arizonarepublic/news/articles/0714english0714.html

Lau v. Nichols, 414 U.S. No. 72-6520, pp. 563–572.

Leafstedt, J.M., Richards, C.R., & Gerber, M.M. (2004). Effectiveness of explicit phonological-awareness instruction for at-risk English learners. *Learning Disabilities Research & Practice, 19,* 252–261.

Lehr, F., Osborn, J., & Hiebert, E. (n.d.). *A focus on vocabulary.* Honolulu, HI: Pacific Resources for Education and Learning.

Lindsey, K., Manis, F., & Bailey, C. (2003). Prediction of first-grade reading in Spanish-speaking English-language learners. *Journal of Educational Psychology, 3,* 482–494.

Manis, F.R., Lindsey, K.A., & Bailey, C.E. (2004). Development of reading in Grades K–2 in Spanish-speaking English-language learners. *Learning Disabilities Research & Practice, 19*(4), 214–224.

Nagy, W.E., & Herman, P.A. (1987). Breadth and depth of vocabulary knowledge: Implications for acquisition and instruction. In M.C. McKeown & M.E. Curtis (Eds.), *The nature of vocabulary acquisition* (pp. 19–35). Hillsdale, NJ: Lawrence Erlbaum Associates.

Nash, R. (1999). *Dictionary of Spanish cognates thematically organized.* Sylmar, CA: NTC.

National Institute of Child Health and Human Development. (2000). *Report of the National Reading Panel. Teaching children to read: An evidence-based assessment of the scientific research literature on reading and its implications for reading instruction: Reports of the subgroups* (NIH Publication No. 00-4754). Washington, DC: U.S. Government Printing Office.

Natriello, G., McDill, E., & Pallas, A. (1990). *Schooling disadvantaged students: Racing against catastrophe.* New York: Teachers College Press.

No Child Left Behind Act of 2001, PL 107-110, 115 Stat. 1425, 20 U.S.C. §§ 6301 *et seq.*

Norris, J., & Ortega, L. (2000). Effectiveness of L2 instruction: A research synthesis and quantitative meta-analysis. *Language and Learning, 50,* 417–528.

Ovando, C., Collier, V., & Combs, M.C. (2003). *Bilingual and ESL classrooms: Teaching in multicultural contexts* (3rd ed.). Boston: McGraw Hill.

Prado, M. (1996). *Dictionary of Spanish false cognates.* Sylmar, CA: NTC.

Roberts, T., & Neal, H. (2004). Relationships among preschool English language learners' oral proficiency in English, instructional experience and literacy development. *Contemporary Educational Psychology, 29,* 283–311.

Rolstad, K., Mahoney, K., & Glass, G. (2005). The big picture: A meta-analysis of program effectiveness research on English language learners. *Educational Policy, 19,* 572–594.

Saiz, A., & Zoido, E. (2005). Listening to what the world says: Bilingualism and earnings in the United States. *Review of Economics and Statistics, 87,* 523–538.

Saunders, W., Foorman, B., &. Carlson, C. (2006). Do we need a separate block of time for oral English language development in programs for English learners? *Elementary School Journal, 107,* 181–198.

Scarcella, R. (2003). *Academic English: A conceptual framework* (Technical report 2003-1). Santa Barbara, CA: Linguistic Minority Research Institute. Available online at http:// lmri.ucsb.edu

Slavin, R., & Cheung, A. (2005). A synthesis of research on language of reading instruction for English language learners. *Review of Educational Research, 75*, 247–281.

Stahl, S.A., & Nagy, W. (2006). *Teaching word meanings.* Mahway, NJ: Erlbaum

Stuart, M. (1999). Getting ready for reading: Early phoneme awareness and phonics teaching improves reading and spelling in inner-city second language learners. *British Journal of Educational Psychology, 69*, 587–605.

Ulanoff, S.H., & Pucci, S.L. (1999). Learning words from books: The effects of read-aloud on second language vocabulary acquisition. *Bilingual Research Journal, 23*, 409–422.

U.S. Department of Education. (2005). *Biennial evaluation report to Congress on the implementation of the State Formula Grant Program, 2002–2004: English Language Acquisition, Language Enhancement and Academic Achievement Act* (ESEA, Title III, Part A). Washington, DC: Author.

Vaughn, S., Mathes, P., Linan-Thompson, S., Cirino, P., Carlson, C., Pollard-Durdola, S., et al. (2006). Effectiveness of an English intervention for first-grade English language learners at risk for reading problems. *The Elementary School Journal, 107*, 154–180.

Willig, A. (1985). A meta-analysis of selected studies on the effectiveness of bilingual education. *Review of Educational Research, 55*, 269–317.

Zehr, M. (2007a, May 8). *NCLB seen as damper on bilingual programs.* Retrieved April 30, 2007, from http://www.edweek.org.

Zehr, M. (2007b, May 23). Another take on Coachella Valley Unified School District v. California. *Learning the language.* Available online at http://blogs.edweek.org/edweek/ learning-the-language

Zehler, A.M., Fleischman, H.L., Hopstock, P.J., Stephenson, T.G., Pendzick, M.L., & Sapru, S. (2003). *Descriptive study of services to LEP students and LEP students with disabilities. Volume I: Research report.* Arlington, VA: Development Associates.

8

Effective Language Instruction for African American Children

Holly K. Craig

A black–white achievement gap characterizes the performances of African American students and their non-Hispanic white peers. Is the black–white achievement gap simply a poverty gap? The development of effective instructional strategies designed to eliminate the black–white achievement gap depends on the answer to this question. If the achievement gap is due to and synonymous with a racial poverty gap, then there is no imperative to develop instructional strategies specific to African Americans. Any instructional strategy designed to overcome the profoundly harmful effects of poverty on learning also should succeed in reducing the black–white achievement gap. If, however, poverty does not explain the achievement gap and unique factors are contributing to poorer academic outcomes for African American students, then the nature of these distinctive barriers must be understood and addressed.

This chapter discusses the role of poverty in underachievement by African American students. The thesis of this chapter is twofold. First, poverty has the potential to affect the academic achievement of any student in profoundly negative ways. Thus, poverty matters to the academic achievement of the nation's African American students because disproportionately high numbers of African American students live in low socioeconomic status (LSES) homes. Second, poverty alone

This work was supported by the Center for Improvement of Early Reading Achievement (CIERA) at the University of Michigan through the U.S. Department of Education, Office of Educational Research and Improvement, Grant R305R70004; the U.S. Department of Education, Office of Educational Research and Improvement, Grant R305T990368; and the National Institutes of Health, National Institute of Deafness and Other Communication Disorders, Grant 1 RO1 DC 02313-01A1. Stephanie Hensel, Erin Quinn, and Lingling Zhang are all actively involved in the program of research on which this chapter is based. Their contributions to the ideas represented here are gratefully acknowledged.

is not a sufficient explanation for the black–white achievement gap. A number of other potential influences must be considered. As discussed later in this chapter, oral language skills are an important new direction in this line of research, with critical implications for strategic instruction with many African American students.

WHAT IS THE BLACK–WHITE ACHIEVEMENT GAP?

The black–white achievement gap is a term used to refer to the performance disparities between African American and non-Hispanic white students. The gap is long-standing. It was initially recorded in the early 1900s at a time when performance comparisons were first beginning to be made (Fishback & Baskin, 1991). The gap has spanned the many subsequent generations and continues essentially unabated today.

The black–white achievement gap includes a black–white test score gap (Jencks & Phillips, 1998), such that African American students are much less likely than their non-Hispanic white peers to perform at basic competency levels on major tests. For example, the prevalence of reading below basic levels in fourth grade is much greater for African American students than their non-Hispanic white peers—58% compared with 24% on the 2005 administration of the National Assessment of Educational Progress (NAEP; Perie, Grigg, & Donahue, 2005). The black–white test score gap is observable at school entry, continues through high school, and characterizes performances across all major content areas. To illustrate, Figure 8.1 displays performance disparities in three major academic content areas, for elementary grades through high school, on administrations of the NAEP (Braswell et al., 2001; Grigg, Daane, Jin, & Campbell, 2003; O'Sullivan, Lauko, Grigg, Qian, & Zhang, 2003). Regardless of grade or academic content area African Americans score lower than their non-Hispanic white peers.

The achievement gap is not limited to test score differences. Disparities are observable on almost any measure of achievement used to compare African American and non-Hispanic white students. Further, the achievement gap continues into adulthood. On many major benchmarks of adult success, African Americans attain lower levels than non-Hispanic whites. Table 8.1 provides some critical examples for children and adults.

WHAT IS THE BLACK–WHITE POVERTY GAP?

A black–white poverty gap also exists. Poverty is often defined operationally in terms of family income. Family income determines access to a variety of important fundamentals such as food, shelter, clothing, and medical care. When these necessities are inadequate, a child's health can be compromised with deleterious effects on a wide-ranging array of learning factors, including school attendance (Rooney et al., 2006) and cognitive development (Bradley & Corwyn, 2002). Homes where parents cannot provide financially for their children are characterized by high levels of stress and can create a context ripe for the emergence of be-

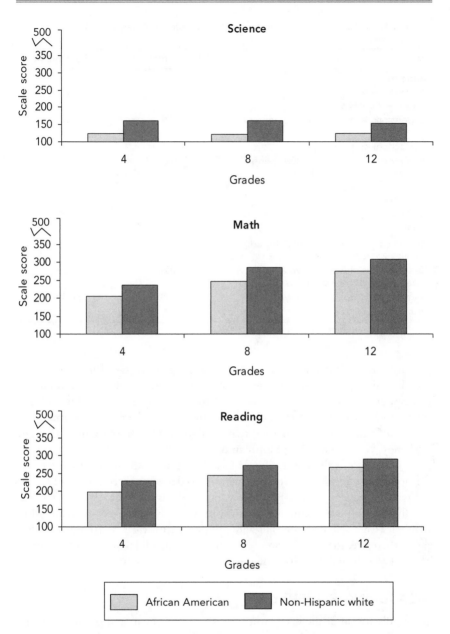

Figure 8.1.   Average scale scores on the National Assessment of Educational Progress across three subjects. (*Sources:* Braswell et al., 2001; Grigg, Daane, Jin, & Campbell, 2003; O'Sullivan, Lauko, Grigg, Qian, & Zhang, 2003.)

havior and socioemotional difficulties (McLoyd, 1990), which impede learning. Students from low-income homes often attend lower-quality schools and are taught by poorer-quality teachers with lower expectations for achievement,

Table 8.1.   Important achievement indicators for African Americans and non-Hispanic whites

Indicator	African American	Non-Hispanic white
Students		
Grade retention for elementary and secondary students	18%	9%
Suspensions/expulsions for elementary and secondary students	35%	15%
High school drop-outs	13%	7%
Number of students per 1,000 taking Advanced Placement exams	53	185
18- to 24-year-olds in college or universities	31%	39%
Children living in poverty	31%	9%
Adults		
Median earnings (in year 2000) for adult males 25 years and over	$28,167	$36,668
25- to 29-year-olds who have a bachelor's degree or higher	18%	34%
Unemployment for 16- to 24-year-olds	18.5%	7.4%
Births per 1,000 15- to 19-year-old females	82	33

Note: Data taken from Hoffman & Llagas (2003).

thereby perpetuating inequalities at the "starting gate" (Lee & Burkham, 2002). Children living in low-income homes also have access to fewer community resources, and those that are available tend to be of poorer quality. Further, students from low-income families live in communities where libraries, museums, and other educationally enriching resources are scarce (Brooks-Gunn, Duncan, Klebanov, & Sealand, 1993; Hoffman & Llagas, 2003).

The rates of child poverty for African American children are far greater than for non-Hispanic whites. African American students are three times as likely to be living in poverty as non-Hispanic white students; 31% of African American children live in poverty compared with approximately 9% of non-Hispanic white children (see Table 8.1). Overall and compared with their non-Hispanic white peers, therefore, the population of African American children is at risk for being affected acutely and negatively by poverty and its covariates.

MEASURING POVERTY

In any discussion of the black–white gaps in achievement and poverty, it is important to acknowledge the many measurement issues that complicate poverty research and exercise appropriate caution when interpreting results. (See, for example, Duncan & Magnuson (2005) for a fuller discussion of measurement issues.) There is no single, best measure of socioeconomic status (SES; Liberatos, Link, & Kelsey, 1988). Poverty is a complex and multidimensional concept, often resulting in combined effects across a number of more discrete variables. Many scholars adopt the term *SES* to represent social stratification. In their research they compare low- and middle socioeconomic status (LSES [as stated previously] and MSES, respectively) homes, in part as a better way to capture the multiplicity of variables and covariates affecting a child living in impoverished circumstances.

For more than a decade at the University of Michigan, we have been examining language and literacy relationships for African American students. Our approach to measuring poverty and its covariates has been to create a binary variable and designate families as either LSES or MSES. Some students qualified for the free or reduced-price lunch program, meeting the federal qualifications for the program, and therefore, were designated LSES. Most students were classified as LSES or MSES based on the Hollingshead Four Factor Index of Social Status (HI; Hollingshead, 1975) using self-reported family data. Rather than determining poverty status based on income, the HI considers four types of information: caregiver education, caregiver occupation, gender, and marital status. The HI uses weighted scores from these factors to identify five social strata, the lowest level being unskilled labor and menial service work and the highest level being major business and professional-level work. This scale has the advantage, therefore, of not depending on a single measure but of being the composite of a set of potentially influential variables, including the maternal/caregiver education variable. Maternal education is known to be an important predictor of reading achievement (Chall, Jacobs, & Baldwin, 1990; Entwisle, Alexander, & Olson, 1997) and of foundational reading skills, such as vocabulary breadth (Washington & Craig, 1999). Further, the scale is scored from information provided fairly readily by families, avoiding more sensitive reporting about household income, which may yield high no-response rates (Entwisle & Astone, 1994). In addition, the occupation factor is tied to the titles and codes in the U.S. Census; therefore, new employment categories (e.g., software programmer) can be fit fairly readily into the 9-point occupation scale, thereby maintaining its currency.

Unfortunately, there is little guidance in the extant literature about how to apply the specifics of the HI to African American families, and it may be appropriate to develop more precise guidelines. Assignment of the same social strata score to African Americans and non-Hispanic whites may not capture real differences that exist between the two groups. For example, African American male adults earn about 25% less than their non-Hispanic white peers (see Table 8.1). Earning differentials persist even when controlling for years of education (Hoffman & Llagas, 2003). Accumulated assets and overall wealth are other significant financial differences that distinguish the two populations. African Americans are less likely than their non-Hispanic white peers to inherit money from the prior generation, and when inheritances are received, they are smaller. African Americans are less likely than non-Hispanic whites to be gifted sizeable amounts of money at times representing significant life events, for example, receiving family financial assistance toward the purchase of a first home (Darity & Nicholson, 2005).

In this context of unknown measurement guidelines, we adopted a fairly prag-
matic approach to the problem of defining SES within our sample. We designated
families as LSES when their scores fell within the two lowest levels of the HI strata
and as MSES when their scores fell within the two highest strata. The middle stra-
tum was less clear, and designations were made on a case-by-case basis that considered occupation and gender. In particular, if the HI for a female head of household
in one family and a male head of household in another both fell in the middle stra-
tum, the female was considered LSES and the male MSES because of differential
wages for males and females performing the same jobs (Spraggins, 2000). This binary SES variable has been informative in a number of studies (Craig &
Washington, 1994; Craig, Washington, & Thompson, 2005; Washington & Craig,
1998).

IS THE BLACK–WHITE ACHIEVEMENT GAP JUST ANOTHER MANIFESTATION OF THE BLACK–WHITE POVERTY GAP?

Are the poverty and achievement gaps between African American and non-
Hispanic white Americans simply the same thing? This question has merit because
so many African American children are impoverished, and poverty disadvantages
children for learning. The historical literature on achievement shows that the
knowledge base on this topic was built in part on the faulty practice of comparing
LSES African Americans to MSES non-Hispanic whites so that past research designs often confounded race and socioeconomic status (Graham, 1992; Hill,
Murry, & Anderson, 2005; McLoyd & Randolph, 1985). It would be unfortunate
if improving our understanding of the methodological flaws of past research results
in a dismissive assumption that the achievement gap has no validity apart from the
poverty gap. As Meier (2002) observed, the assumption that the black–white
achievement gap is really a poverty gap is more comfortable for many Americans.
Poverty is a broad societal problem rather than a specific educational one; therefore, if we believe that underachievement by African Americans is a result of
poverty, as educators we may feel little specific responsibility to address the problem. If, however, poverty is only part of the cause and other factors are involved,
then we must rally our resources and find any education-based solutions with potential to ameliorate the full set of problems causing underachievement.

The limited research on the language and literacy development of African
American children provides remarkably little focused inquiry on the impact of
SES. Socioeconomic status may be included as a sample descriptor for the African
American participants, but it is not often included as a control variable nor is it
examined for its potential as a predictor or covariate. This is unfortunate because,
when considered as part of the research design, SES has been quite revealing. To
illustrate, Craig, Connor, and Washington (2003) followed two cohorts of young
African American students across the early elementary grades and found that their
performance trajectories differed by SES. At the time of project entry, Cohort 1

was comprised of preschoolers from LSES homes enrolled in a state-funded program for children at risk, which emphasized early language and literacy learning. Cohort 2 was comprised of kindergartners from MSES homes. All resided in the same community and attended the same schools. Despite differences in SES at the outset, by first grade, the LSES cohort was performing as well as the MSES cohort, and by second and third grades, the LSES cohort was outperforming the MSES cohort on standardized tests of reading. It appeared that the high-quality early childhood program experienced by the LSES preschoolers yielded measurable and durable benefits, which mitigated at least in part the effects of their economic disadvantage.

In addressing this question of explanatory overlap between the achievement and poverty gaps, I draw from two data sources and focus specifically on achievement in reading. First, insights can be gleaned from published reports of national databases. Second, I discuss trends apparent in data gathered during the last decade as a part of my own research program at the University of Michigan. I draw on these sources to lay out the case that poverty alone is an insufficient explanation for the black–white achievement gap.

National Trends Based on Family Income

Figure 8.2 displays data gathered from national sources on the percentage of children younger than 18 years living in poverty (U.S. Census Bureau, n.d.) and on reading achievement (Perie et al., 2005) for approximately the same time frame, disaggregated by race. In 1992, 46% of African American children lived in poverty compared with 13% of non-Hispanic whites, a gap of 33%. In 2000, the childhood poverty gap narrowed from 33% to 22% (the difference between 31% for African American children and 9% for non-Hispanic whites). It is noteworthy that although 4% fewer non-Hispanic whites were living in poverty, a remarkable *15% fewer* African American children were living in poverty during this time frame. Most of this narrowing in the gap occurred between 1992 and 2000, during a period of strong economic growth in the United States. Since then, there has been a leveling off of the poverty differences between black and non-Hispanic white Americans, corresponding to a time of slower economic growth. Whereas African American families have less accumulated wealth to buffer them in times of financial need (Darity & Nicholson, 2005), they are particularly dependent on the health of the U.S. economy for their own financial well-being (Lamb, Land, Meadows, & Traylor, 2005). By implication, when the U.S. economy rebounds, progress in closing the black–white poverty gap should resume. If the economy then remains healthy, even though poverty per se will not be eliminated, we might hope to see an end to the childhood poverty gap between the races within our lifetimes.

Did this considerable improvement in childhood well-being for African American students correspond to an appreciable narrowing of the black–white

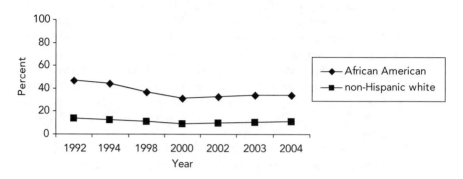

Children living below the poverty level

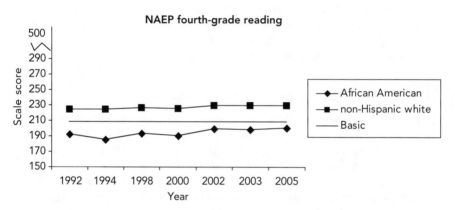

Figure 8.2. The percentages of African American and non-Hispanic white children younger than 18 years living in poverty in the United States (U.S. Census, n.d.) from 1992 to 2004 and National Assessment of Educational Progress (NAEP; Perie, Grigg, & Donahue, 2005) scale scores for fourth-grade reading from 1992 to 2005.

test score gap for reading? Examination of NAEP 4th-, 8th-, and 12th-grade data indicates that this was not the case. By way of example, during approximately the same time span, from 1992 to 2005, an examination of 4th-grade reading scores from the NAEP for African American students revealed a gain of 8 scale score points. As a group, therefore, African American students were performing closer to the basic level (score of 208 out of 500), one of three achievement levels on the NAEP indicating partial mastery of prerequisite knowledge and skills for reading. Non-Hispanic whites, however, improved as well, up 5 scale score points. These improvements for both populations, therefore, netted only a very small narrowing of the reading gap, by 3 points. Overall, as the poverty gap decreased, the reading test score gap also decreased, but negligibly. See Figure 8.2 for the 4th-grade data. By implication, if this rate of progress were to continue in the forthcoming decades, it could take approximately 150 years to close the black–white test score gap in reading! Overall, there is regrettably little evidence from these national trends that a significant decrease in poverty levels will yield a measurable improvement in reading levels. Based on these national data, it seems unlikely that eliminating the black–white poverty gap will eliminate the black–white achievement gap for reading.

The University of Michigan Data

Approximately 270 of the African American students enrolled in the elementary grades in public schools in southeast lower Michigan who have participated in studies within our research program have scores available from standardized reading tests. The performances of these students constituted the basis for these analyses. Communities within southeast lower Michigan varied in the sample, although most of the students ($n = 155$, 76%) were residents of an urban-fringe community of Detroit. Approximately half of the students were male, and half were female. Forty-six percent of the children were from LSES homes, and fifty-four percent were from MSES homes. When interpreting their reading performances, it is noteworthy that students in the LSES and MSES groups showed no significant performance differences on a nondiscriminatory measure of general cognitive skill, the Triangles subtest of the Kaufman Assessment Battery for Children (K-ABC, Kaufman & Kaufman, 1983). Therefore, any achievement differences observed between the two groups were not due to significant differences in cognitive skill. Reading tests were administered by the schools and included the Metropolitan Achievement Test (MAT; 1993) for second and third graders and the Michigan Educational Assessment Program (MEAP; 1999–2001) for fourth graders. Test scores were converted to z-scores for analysis purposes.

When the data were collected, the research questions focused specifically on the language and literacy development of typically developing African American students. Although the focus of this research was not on the role of poverty, information about SES has been collected consistently. Therefore, this data set situates us very well to ask how African American students from LSES homes are faring academically compared with other members of the same population, particularly African American students living in the same communities and attending the same schools but from MSES homes.

Oral language comprehension and production and standardized scores of reading achievement were available for all students. See Table 8.2 for the oral language measures. Examination of the data using factor analysis revealed a fairly clear pattern in which there were two oral language skill components (see Table 8.3). Component I was labeled a Comprehension Factor (COMP) representing the common unobserved variable that was strongly related to standard scores on the Peabody Picture Vocabulary Test–Third Edition (PPVT-III; Dunn & Dunn, 1997) and the number of correct responses on a *wh-* question (Wh-q; Craig &

Table 8.2.   The oral language comprehension and production measures

Domain	Skill	Performance measure
Oral language comprehension (COMP)	Vocabulary size and diversity	Standard scores, Peabody Picture Vocabulary Test–Third Edition (PPVT-III; Dunn & Dunn, 1997)[a]
	Understanding requests	Number of targeted responses on a *wh-* questions task (Wh-q; Craig & Washington, 2000)
Oral language production (PROD)	Narrative sentence production (Craig et al., 2005)	Complex syntax rates (Csyn)
		Mean length of communication units, in words (MLCU)
		Number of different words in sample (NDW)

[a]PPVT-III, a nondiscriminatory revision of the earlier versions of the Peabody Picture Vocabulary Test, Third Edition (Dunn & Dunn, 1997).

Washington, 2000) task. Component II was labeled a Production Factor (PROD), representing the common latent variable that was strongly related to complex syntax rates (Csyn); mean lengths, in words, of communication units (MLCU); and the number of different words (NDW) in the sample. Component I explained 29%; Component II, 44%; and the two components together explained 73% of the total variation among the five performance measures.

Direct Effects of Socioeconomic Status on Reading Achievement

For the purposes of the present discussion, structural equation modeling (SEM) was adopted because of its utility in examining the relative strengths of potential interrelationships among variables, especially when latent factors are involved (Kline, 2005). The SEM was tested with the covariance matrix of 269 partici-

Table 8.3.   Varimax-Rotation Principal components analysis

Performance measure	Component I	Component II	Communalities
PPVT-III	.834	.105	.707
Wh-q	.828	.119	.700
Csyn	.066	.858	.740
MLCU	.056	.939	.884
NDW	.245	.739	.606
Percent total variance	28.99%	43.76%	72.75%

Key: Csyn, percentage frequencies of complex syntactic forms; MCLU, mean length of communication units in words; NDW, numbers of different words; PPVT-III, Peabody Picture Vocabulary Test–Third Edition (Dunn & Dunn, 1997); Wh-q, frequency of correct responses on *wh-* questions task.

pants, using Amos 6.0 statistical software (Arbuckle, 2005). Using SEM, relation-ships among our binary LSES and MSES groupings, oral language skills (COMP and PROD), and reading (READ) were examined. See Table 8.4 for results. The model was a good fit to the data: $\chi^2(9) = 14.949$, $p = .092$, RMSEA = 0.050, 90% CI = (0, 0.093).[1]

The SES model showed a statistically significant direct effect of SES group on READ after controlling for COMP and PROD (see Figure 8.3). Although the direct pathway was statistically significant, the effect was not a strong one (un-standardized coefficient = .247; $p = .044$). The finding that SES exerted a direct effect on reading achievement for African American students is consistent with a study by Nievar and Luster (2006), which examined the reading recognition skills of African American students in one of the very few studies of SES and reading with this population. Their measurement of SES was an income-to-poverty ratio, and when a variety of other variables were controlled that related to family processes, family income in early childhood was found to exert a significant di-rect effect on later reading recognition scores.

Comparison of Reading Outcomes by Socioeconomic Status Group

Whereas SES exerted a direct, although not strong, influence on reading, differ-ences in reading performances between the two groups were probed further. Within our larger data set, we have standardized reading achievement scores for 155 first- through fourth-grade boys and girls from LSES and MSES homes, all residing in the same urban-fringe community. I draw from this subset in the dis-cussion that follows.

Regardless of SES, second, third, and fourth graders all performed below the expected standard z-score mean ($M = 0$) (see Table 8.5). The reading tests were

Table 8.4. Regression weights estimates for the model

	Estimate	Standard error	Standardized estimate	Critical ratio	p
SES → COMP	4.034	1.728	0.178	2.335	.020
SES → PROD	0.023	0.021	0.078	1.098	.272
COMP → READ	0.051	0.012	0.535	4.414	***
PROD → READ	1.177	0.552	0.161	2.131	.033
SES → READ	0.247	0.123	0.114	2.017	.044

*Note:*** $p < .001$; COMP, Comprehension Factor; PROD, Production Factor; READ, Reading Standard Scores; SES, socioeconomic status.

---

[1]For RMSEA (root mean square error of approximation): ≤ 0.05, close approximate fit; > 0.05 and < 0.08, reasonable error of approximation, good fit (McDonald & Ho, 2002).

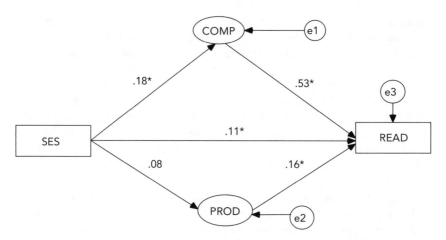

Figure 8.3. The relationships among socioeconomic status (SES) based on the low SES (LSES) and middle SES (MSES) groupings; the oral language factors (Comprehension Factor [COMP], Production Factor [PROD]); and reading outcomes (READ). (*Statistically significant, see Table 8.4 for p values.)

normed on the general population, and as such the test means (*M*) and standard deviations (*SD*) provide an estimate of the performance of the Michigan urban-fringe sample of African American students compared with state and national samples of students. Accordingly, the Michigan African American students were not performing at test levels expected for the general population. Their performance was within normal expectations but fell in the lower half of the expected performance distribution, consistent with national trends for African American students.

We expected SES to contribute to the reading outcomes of African American students, and this was observed. In our Michigan data set, however, the effects were grade-sensitive (see Table 8.5). In first grade, significant differences were observed between groups, with the MSES students performing close (*M* = .02) to the expected z-score mean (*M* = 0), whereas the LSES students performed considerably lower (*M* = −.69). After first grade, performance differences by SES group largely disappeared. For students in Grades 2–4, most students performed below the standard z-score mean, regardless of SES group membership (73% of LSES and 69% of MSES). The mean z-scores were not significantly different by SES [*t*(99) = .810, *p* = .420], and the amount of score dispersion was comparable by group as well. Figure 8.4 displays these relationships as box plots.

It is not surprising that children are most similar to their families early in the school years, when the potential influences of schooling have not yet had an opportunity to take effect. These trends are consistent with the observations of Lee and Burkham (2002) that poverty exerts its greatest impact at the time of school entry. For African American children, schooling seems to level the effects of

Table 8.5.   Mean (*M*) and standard deviation (*SD*) reading achievement *z*-scores for African Americans in Grades 1–4 by socioeconomic status

	Grade 1	Grade 2	Grade 3	Grade 4
LSES *M*	−0.69	−0.62	−0.74	−0.65
SD	0.90	1.00	0.88	1.04
n	15	13	16	4
MSES *M*	0.02	−0.46	−0.49	−0.66
SD	0.99	0.90	0.86	1.01
n	39	28	21	19
Difference	0.71	0.16	0.25	0.01
p	.019*	.608	.397	.993

*Key: *p* < .05; LSES, low socioeconomic status; M, mean; MSES, middle socioeconomic status; n, number in subsample; p, probability; SD, standard deviation.*

poverty and close the performance gap between LSES and MSES African American students. It appears that this is accomplished by having the MSES students lose ground the longer they attend school, in terms of their relative position to the expected test score means. Unfortunately, the leveling effect is not accomplished by having the LSES students make substantial gains.

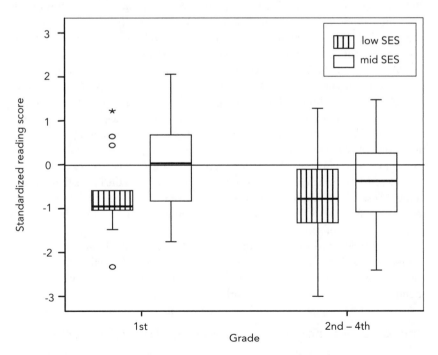

Figure 8.4.   Box plot of reading achievement *z*-scores for first graders and for second to fourth graders by socioeconomic status (SES).

Role of Oral Language in Early Literacy Experiences

When searching for potential factors contributing to the black–white achievement gap, linguistic differences between African American and non-Hispanic white children are important considerations because early oral language skills lay the foundation for literacy growth (Snow, Burns, & Griffin, 1998). Although often framed in educational contexts as an emergent reading skill, for African American students it is also important to consider the oral language processes that underlie introductions to literacy.

Prior to school entry, many African American students have early language–literacy experiences that differ from those of their non-Hispanic white peers. Early exposure to stories in African American homes often takes the form of oral, collaborative, fictionalized narratives (Heath, 1983; Vernon-Feagans, 1996). This oral tradition differs from the storybook reading that characterizes early language–literacy linkages for non-Hispanic whites, which is so predictive of later reading skills in the general population (Bus, van IJzendoorn, & Pelligrini, 1995; Scarborough & Dobrich, 1994). Furthermore, compared with their non-Hispanic white peers, African American preschoolers own fewer books and may not be read to on a daily basis (Federal Interagency Forum on Child and Family Statistics [FIFCFS], 2003; Nettles & Perna, 1997). First experiences with print may arise from environmental exposures, for example, learning to recognize trademarks or signage (Craig & Washington, 2004b; Purcell-Gates, 1996), and these environmental forms may not present conventional sound–symbol correspondences.

Although all children experience environmental print at an early age, the primacy of this exposure for urban African American children is noteworthy because of the lack of balance with storybook reading. Early grade teachers, therefore, may play a particularly critical role for African American students by helping these children disentangle the variations adopted for public and commercial purposes (e.g., the pronunciation of *Nike* versus *came*) and the rules underlying conventional sound–letter associations found in books. Parents can become important allies in this process. For example, African American parents can read to their children the books that are sent home by teachers (Connor, 2002; Robinson, Larsen, & Haupt, 1996). In the context of increasing adult literacy levels among African American adults, home book programs may be of special importance for African American families. Home book programs are designed to increase the number of books in the home, thereby supporting increased frequencies of daily book-reading activities (Robinson et al., 1996) and the forging of stronger associations between conventional sound–symbol correspondences that are so important to early reading acquisition.

Role of Oral Language for Elementary-Grade Students

Since the 1990s, the oral language skills of African American elementary-grade students have been the focus of intensive inquiry, motivated in part by the recognition that oral language skills play an important role in reading acquisition; yet, tools for examining the oral language skills of African American students were biased (Arnold & Reed, 1976; Taylor & Payne, 1983; Wiener, Lewnau, & Erway, 1983). For example, an early and widely used version of the Peabody Picture Vocabulary Test–Revised (PPVT-R, Dunn & Dunn, 1981) has consistently been shown to discriminate against African American students (Adler & Birdsong, 1983; Kresheck & Nicolosi, 1973; Washington & Craig, 1992) but continues to be used as a major measure of their oral language skill (National Institute of Child Health and Human Development Early Child Care Research Network, 2005).

Oral language reference profiles for syntax and semantics in the form of both expressive and receptive skills, as well as culture-fair tools for their assessment, are now available for African American preschoolers through fifth graders (Craig & Washington, 2006; Craig et al., 2005; Jackson & Roberts, 2001; Seymour, Bland-Stewart, & Green, 1998; Seymour, Roeper, & de Villiers, 2003; Thomas-Tate, Washington, Craig, & Packard, 2006). Although studies of the interrelationships among specific oral language skills and reading in this population are scarce, those available are promising. They show that early preschool syntax and phonological knowledge predict second- and third-grade reading skills of African American students (Craig, Connor, et al., 2003; Poe, Burchinal, & Roberts, 2004), and it is well-established that both of these aspects of language are amenable to change (Castles & Coltheart, 2004; Fey, Cleave, Long, & Hughes, 1993).

Our Michigan data set reveals some important relationships between SES, oral language skills, and reading achievement. Although in the Michigan data set SES made a statistically significant contribution to reading achievement scores, oral language skills contributed more (see Figure 8.3). Both of the language factors were significantly related to READ (COMP: $p < .001$; PROD: $p = .033$).

Socioeconomic status was significantly related to one of the language factors, COMP ($p = .020$), but not to PROD ($p = .272$). COMP had a higher prediction power (.53) on reading than SES (.11). For every one standard deviation increase in COMP, READ increased by approximately one half of a standard deviation. The predictive power of PROD was much lower (.16). There was a statistically significant indirect effect of SES on READ through COMP (Sobel test, $z = 2.046$, $p = .041$), but there was no indirect effect through PROD (Sobel test, $z = 0.974$, $p = .330$). This indirect effect of SES on READ through COMP appeared to be of approximately the same magnitude (.18) as the direct effect of SES on READ (.11). Furthermore, the total effect of SES on READ (sum of direct and indirect effects $= .29$) was less than the effect of the oral language factor COMP (.53) on READ.

The model outcomes underscore the importance of oral language skills for reading achievement and further indicate that SES exerted both direct and indirect effects on these reading outcomes of African American students. The indirect effects of SES exerted their influence through oral language comprehension, and overall, oral language comprehension skills were the strongest predictor of reading achievement in the model.

Contribution of Dialect to Reading Outcomes

Not considered in this model is the potential impact of another important language characteristic: the student's status as a dialect speaker. The heritage language of many African American students is African American English (AAE), a rule-governed variety of English associated with African American culture. AAE is not an inferior form of Standard American English (SAE), and the legitimacy of this language variation is no longer debatable (Green, 2002). Despite its validity as a linguistic form, however, many educators have not, and do not, value AAE. Uninformed prejudices against the legitimacy of AAE perpetuate negative stereotypes. Negative stereotypes can undercut more constructive attempts to improve understanding of this heritage language form and to build literacy skills in students who are AAE speakers. This is no longer a question of linguistic validity; it is a question of values. Educational leaders should find ways to eliminate linguistic prejudice. Teachers must value the cultural backgrounds of all of their students and equip African American students for the language demands of the classroom and curriculum.

In our northern U.S. sample of African American students living in Michigan, we observed approximately 40 different AAE features characterizing the spontaneous discourse of school-age children (Craig, Thompson, Washington, & Potter, 2003; Washington & Craig, 1994). These features evidenced systematic morphological and phonological variations from other varieties of English. For children from LSES homes, greater AAE feature production rates were positively correlated with more sophisticated syntactic and semantic skills at the time of school entry (Craig & Washington, 1994, 1995). In other words, for young, urban LSES African American students, being a heavy dialect user was not a deficiency; it was a sign of greater linguistic skill.

A number of scholars have proposed that African American students shift away from AAE toward SAE with increased exposure to the mainstream dialect, particularly during schooling (Adler, 1992; Battle, 1996; Fishman, 1991; Ratusnik & Koenigsknecht, 1975). Several studies (Charity, Scarborough, & Griffin, 2004; Connor & Craig, 2006; Craig & Washington, 2004a) have demonstrated that AAE feature production rates bear an important relationship to reading achievement. In these studies, African American students who shifted away from their heritage dialect forms in school contexts and adopted the SAE forms of classrooms and the curriculum scored better on standardized tests of reading achievement.

Specifically, Charity et al. (2004) observed that greater linguistic familiarity with SAE as measured by exact repetition of SAE sentences correlated with higher scores on the Woodcock Reading Mastery Tests–Revised (WRMT-R; Woodcock, 1987) for kindergarten- to second-grade African American students. In the Michigan data, we observed that AAE feature production rates underwent two shifts and have proposed that the significance of the shifting process is not circumscribed to the spoken linguistic domain but has an important impact on reading success. We found that students who were speakers of AAE demonstrated a significant downward rate of AAE feature production during oral discourse between the middle to end of kindergarten and the middle to end of first grade (Craig & Washington, 2004a). We observed a second shift, in third grade, during oral reading (Craig, Thompson, Washington, & Potter, 2004). The first shift substantially reduced the rate of morphological types of AAE features, and the second shift substantially reduced the rate of phonological features. It is noteworthy that the first shift corresponded to the transition to full-day instruction and the second to the curricular transition away from emphasizing the decoding of text to a focus on comprehension.

This pattern of linguistic adaptation characterized the discourse of approximately two thirds of the African American first to fifth graders in our sample of African American students; however, approximately one third of the students showed no evidence of dialect shifting (Craig & Washington, 2004a). Students who shifted away from their heritage language forms toward the SAE of classrooms and text did so in the absence of direct instruction in SAE. Of particular importance for the present discussion, the shifters scored better on standardized tests of reading achievement than those who did not make this shift (Craig & Washington, 2004a). As can be seen in Figure 8.5, most of the dialect shifters scored within one standard deviation of the expected reading z-score mean, and their average group score was considerably better than that of the students who did not shift: independent $t(197) = 3.21, p = .002$, effect size $d = 0.72$.

A major limitation in much of this research is the cross-sectional nature of the research designs. Lower dialect production levels across grades and differences in dialect production rates with language and literacy contexts have been interpreted as evidence that individual students are shifting their morphological and phonological forms away from AAE toward SAE. In the Michigan data, we do have repeated measures on 22 typically developing African American students assessed first as preschoolers or kindergartners and a second time between first and fifth grades. Dialect production rates decreased over time again for most students (approximately two thirds), confirming the relationship observed in our cross-sectional data between grade and dialect shifting (Craig, Hensel, & Quinn, 2005).

African American elementary-grade students also showed differences in their feature production rates by context, providing further support for the view that many African American students undergo a process of linguistic adaptation as part of early schooling. Thompson, Craig, and Washington (2004) compared the feature production of third-grade students in three different language–literacy contexts, using repeated measures analyses. Every student produced AAE features during oral narratives, most did so when reading aloud text written in SAE (92%), but only 62% produced AAE features during a spontaneous writing task involving the generation of a brief story. In other work, Connor and Craig (2006) observed that more linguistically skilled preschoolers showed evidence of dialect shifting between production contexts even at this early grade. Preschoolers who

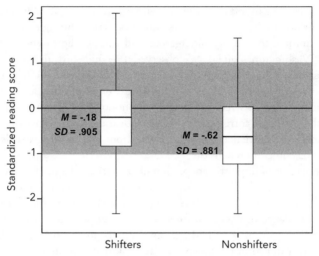

Figure 8.5. Box plots of z-scores for first through fifth graders who shifted toward Standard American English in their discourse and those who did not (the shaded areas correspond to ± 1 standard deviation, the expected performance range).

used AAE features with greater frequencies during oral narrative production generally demonstrated better knowledge of SAE compared with students who were lower feature producers, as evidenced by better imitation of SAE sentences. For many of these children, we found that heavy AAE use in preschool was related to greater linguistic flexibility and metalinguistic awareness, placing these children at lower risk for later reading difficulties.

Together, these language studies indicate that African American students who beat the odds, regardless of early economic disadvantage, are children with strong oral language skills. Better oral language skills at school entry include being strong dialect speakers. AAE is not a problem; it is lack of additional skill in SAE and in oral language comprehension that is problematic. Across the elementary grades, African American children with strong language skills are dialect speakers who have the linguistic flexibility to learn to adapt to the discourse practices of the curriculum and text, which is advantageous in their performance on standardized tests of reading achievement. Language sophistication is a key variable to the school success of African American students. African American students who speak AAE and also learn to speak SAE have the potential to do well in school. Instructional strategies for AAE-speaking students should embrace their skill in their heritage language and find ways to build connections to text through SAE.

CONCLUSION

The black–white achievement gap is not well explained by poverty. It is the case that a black–white poverty gap also exists, but as discussed in this chapter, poverty and, more generally, SES do not account for the magnitude or the durability across grades of the disparities between African American and non-Hispanic white students.

With a focus on reading achievement, this chapter examined published research reports on language–reading linkages for African American students, trends in national data sets, and multiple subsets of data within the Michigan project on African American language and literacy development. Together, these research sources demonstrated that although SES exerted statistically significant direct and indirect effects on reading, oral language skills—especially oral language comprehension skills—were a much stronger influence on reading achievement outcomes. A student's status as a dialect speaker appears to be an important piece to this puzzle.

African American students with broad linguistic repertoires that include both AAE and SAE are more linguistically skilled and more academically successful. By implication, early strategic instruction in oral language skills designed to develop linguistic flexibility and adaptation abilities has particular potential to improve the reading outcomes of African American students. The extant literature already provides teachers with important foundational principles for designing effective reading instruction for African American students (Rickford, 2005). If the theses proposed in this chapter are valid, however, then additional new information is needed to design constructive approaches specific to the teaching of SAE for curricular purposes, particularly the reading of conventional texts, when the students are AAE speakers. Contrastive analysis, in which teachers make explicit comparisons between SAE and AAE forms and help African American students learn to dialect shift (Sweetland, 2006; Wheeler & Swords, 2006), represents an intuitively sound but as yet largely untested instructional approach. Resolution of the black–white achievement gap needs education-based solutions, and research about how to provide early language instruction with this population should be a priority.

REFERENCES

Adler, S. (1992). *Multicultural communication skills in the classroom*. Boston: Allyn & Bacon.

Adler, S., & Birdsong, S. (1983). Reliability and validity of standardized testing tools used with poor children. *Topics in Language Disorders, 3*(3), 76–87.

Arbuckle, J.L. (2005). *Amos 6.0* [Computer software]. Spring House, PA: Amos Development Corporation.

Arnold, K.S., & Reed L. (1976). The Grammatic Closure subtest of the ITPA: A comparative study of black and white children. *Journal of Speech and Hearing Disorders, 41,* 477–485.

Battle, D.E. (1996). Language learning and use by African American children. *Topics in Language Disorders, 16,* 22–37.

Bradley, R.H., & Corwyn, R.F. (2002). Socioeconomic status and child development. *Annual Review of Psychology, 53,* 371–399.

Braswell, J.S., Lutkus, A.D., Grigg, W.S., Santapau, S.L., Tay-Lim, B.S.-H., & Johnson, M.S. (2001). *The nation's report card: Mathematics 2000* (NCES 2001-517).

Washington, DC: U.S. Department of Education, Office of Educational Research and Improvement, National Center for Education Statistics.

Brooks-Gunn, J., Duncan, G.J., Klebanov, P.K., & Sealand, N. (1993). Do neighborhoods influence child and adolescent development? *American Journal of Sociology, 99*, 353–395.

Bus, A.G., van IJzendoorn, M.H., & Pelligrini, A.D. (1995). Joint book reading makes for success in learning to read: A meta-analysis on intergenerational transmission of literacy. *Review of Educational Research, 65*, 1–21.

Castles, A., & Coltheart, M. (2004). Is there a causal link from phonological awareness to success in learning to read? *Cognition, 91*, 77–111.

Chall, J.S., Jacobs, V.A., & Baldwin, L.E. (1990). *The reading crisis: Why poor children fall behind.* Cambridge, MA: Harvard University Press.

Charity, A.H., Scarborough, H.S., & Griffin, D.M. (2004). Familiarity with School English in African American children and its relation to early reading achievement. *Child Development, 75*, 1340–1356.

Connor, C.M. (2002). Preschool children and teachers talking together: The influence of child, family, teacher, and classroom characteristics on children's developing literacy. *Dissertation Abstracts International, 63*(07), 2452 (UMI No. 3057929).

Connor, C.M., & Craig, H.K. (2006). African American preschoolers' language, emergent literacy skills, and use of African American English: A complex relation. *Journal of Speech, Language, and Hearing Research, 49*, 771–792.

Craig, H.K., Connor, C.M., & Washington, J.A. (2003). Early positive predictors of later reading comprehension for African American students: A preliminary investigation. *Language, Speech, and Hearing Services in Schools, 34*, 31–43.

Craig, H.K., Hensel, S.L., & Quinn, E.J. (2005). *Dialect shifting by African American students in the elementary grades: Evidence from longitudinal data.* Unpublished manuscript.

Craig, H.K., Thompson, C.A., Washington, J.A., & Potter, S.L. (2003). Phonological features of child African American English. *Journal of Speech, Language, and Hearing Research, 46*, 623–635.

Craig, H.K., Thompson, C.A., Washington, J.A., & Potter, S.L. (2004). Performance of elementary grade African American students on the Gray Oral Reading Tests. *Language, Speech, and Hearing Services in Schools, 35*, 141–154.

Craig, H.K., & Washington, J.A. (1994). The complex syntax skills of poor, urban, African American preschoolers at school entry. *Language, Speech, and Hearing Services in Schools, 25*, 181–190.

Craig, H.K., & Washington, J.A. (1995). African American English and linguistic complexity in preschool discourse: A second look. *Language, Speech, and Hearing Services in Schools, 26*, 87–93.

Craig, H.K., & Washington, J.A. (2000). An assessment battery for identifying language impairments in African American children. *Journal of Speech, Language, and Hearing Research, 43*, 366–379.

Craig, H.K., & Washington, J.A. (2004a). Grade-related changes in the production of African American English. *Journal of Speech, Language, and Hearing Research, 47*, 450–463.

Craig, H.K., & Washington, J.A. (2004b). Language variation and literacy learning. In C.A. Stone, E.R. Silliman, B.J. Ehren, & K. Apel (Eds.), *Handbook of language and literacy: Development and disorders* (pp. 228–247). New York: Guilford Press.

Craig, H.K., & Washington, J.A. (2006). *Malik goes to school: Examining the language skills of African American students from preschool to 5th grade.* Mahwah, NJ: Lawrence Erlbaum Associates.

Craig, H.K., Washington, J.A., & Thompson, C.A. (2005). Oral language expectations for African American children in grades 1 through 5. *American Journal of Speech–Language Pathology, 14*, 119–130.

Darity, W.A., Jr., & Nicholson, M.J. (2005). Racial wealth inequality and the black family. In V.C. McLoyd, N.E. Hill, & K.A. Dodge (Eds.), *African American family life: Ecological and cultural diversity* (pp. 78–85). New York: Guilford Press.

Duncan, G.J., & Magnuson, K.A. (2005). Can family socioeconomic resources account for racial and ethnic test score gaps? *Future of Children, 15,* 35–54.

Dunn, L., & Dunn, L. (1981). *Peabody Picture Vocabulary Test–Revised.* Circle Pines, MN: American Guidance Service.

Dunn, L., & Dunn, L. (1997). *Peabody Picture Vocabulary Test–Third Edition.* Circle Pines, MN: American Guidance Service.

Entwisle, D.R., Alexander, K.L., & Olson, L.S. (1997). *Children, schools, and inequality.* Boulder, CO: Westview Press.

Entwisle, D.R., & Astone, N.M. (1994). Some practical guidelines for measuring youth's race–ethnicity and socioeconomic status. *Child Development, 65,* 1521–1540.

Federal Interagency Forum on Child and Family Statistics. (2003). *America's children: Key national indicators of well-being.* Washington, DC: U.S. Government Printing Office.

Fey, M.E., Cleave, P.L., Long, S.H., & Hughes, D.L. (1993). Two approaches to the facilitation of grammar in children with language impairment: An experimental evaluation. *Journal of Speech and Hearing Research, 36,* 141–157.

Fishback, P.V., & Baskin, J.H. (1991). Narrowing the black–white gap in child literacy in 1910: The roles of school inputs and family inputs. *Review of Economics and Statistics, 73,* 725–728.

Fishman, J.A. (1991). *Reversing language shift: Theoretical and empirical foundations of assistance to threatened languages.* New York: Multilingual Matters.

Graham, S. (1992). Most of the subjects were white and middle class. *American Psychologist, 47*(5), 629–639.

Green, L.J. (2002). *African American English: A linguistic introduction.* Cambridge, UK: Cambridge University Press.

Grigg, W.S., Daane, M.C., Jin, Y., & Campbell, J.R. (2003). *The nation's report card: Reading 2002* (NCES 2003-521). Washington, DC: U.S. Department of Education, Institute of Education Sciences, National Center for Education Statistics.

Heath, S.B. (1983). *Ways with words.* Cambridge, UK: Cambridge University Press.

Hill, N.E., Murry, V.M., & Anderson, V.D. (2005). Sociocultural contexts of African American families. In V.C. McLoyd, N.E. Hill, & K.A. Dodge (Eds.), *African American family life: Ecological and cultural diversity* (pp. 21–44). New York: Guilford Press.

Hoffman, K., & Llagas, C. (2003). *Status and trends in the education of blacks* (NCES 2003-034). Washington, DC: U.S. Department of Education, National Center for Education Statistics.

Hollingshead, A.B. (1975). *Four factor index of social status.* New Haven, CT: Yale University, Department of Sociology.

Jackson, S.C., & Roberts, J.E. (2001). Complex syntax production of African American preschoolers. *Journal of Speech, Language, and Hearing Research, 44,* 1083–1096.

Jencks, C., & Phillips, M. (Eds.). (1998). *The black–white test score gap.* Washington, DC: Brookings Institution Press.

Kaufman, A., & Kaufman, N. (1983). *Kaufman Assessment Battery for Children.* Circle Pines, MN: American Guidance Service.

Kline, R.B. (2005). *Principles and practice of structural equation modeling.* New York: Guilford Press.

Kresheck, J.D., & Nicolosi, L. (1973). A comparison of black and white children's scores on the Peabody Picture Vocabulary Test. *Language, Speech, and Hearing Services in Schools, 4,* 37–40.

Lamb, V.L., Land, K.C., Meadows, S.O., & Traylor, F. (2005). Trends in African American child well-being, 1985–2001. In V.C. McLoyd, N.E. Hill, & K.A. Dodge (Eds.), *African American family life: Ecological and cultural diversity* (pp. 45–77). New York: Guilford Press.

Lee, V.E., & Burkham, D.T. (2002). *Inequality at the starting gate: Social background differences in achievement as children begin school.* Washington, DC: Economic Policy Institute.

Liberatos, P., Link, B.G., & Kelsey, J.L. (1988). The measurement of social class in epidemiology. *Epidemiologic Reviews, 10,* 87–121.

McDonald, R.P., & Ho, M.H. (2002). Principles and practice in reporting structural equation analyses. *Psychological Methods, 7,* 64–82.

McLoyd, V.C. (1990). The impact of economic hardship on black families and children: Psychological distress, parenting, and socioemotional development. *Child Development, 61,* 311–346.

McLoyd, V.C., & Randolph, S.M. (1985). Secular trends in the study of Afro-American children: A review of child development, 1936–1980. In A.B. Smuts & J.W. Hagen (Eds.), *Monographs of the Society for Research in Child Development, 50*(Serial No. 211), 4–5.

Meier, D. (2002). *In schools we trust: Creating communities of learning in an era of testing and standardization.* Boston: Beacon Press.

Metropolitan Achievement Tests. (7th ed.). (1993). San Antonio, TX: Harcourt Brace.

Michigan Educational Assessment Program, State Summary Essential Skills Reading Grade 4. (1999–2001). Lansing: State of Michigan.

National Institute of Child Health and Human Development Early Child Care Research Network. (2005). Pathways to reading: The role of oral language in the transition to reading. *Developmental Psychology, 41,* 428–442.

Nettles, M.T., & Perna, L.W. (1997). *The African American education data book: Volume II. Preschool through high school.* Ann Arbor, MI: Frederick D. Patterson Research Institute of College Fund/UNCF.

Nievar, M.A., & Luster, T. (2006). Developmental processes in African American families: An application of McLoyd's theoretical model. *Journal of Marriage and Family, 68,* 320–331.

O'Sullivan, C.Y., Lauko, M.A., Grigg, W.S., Qian, J., & Zhang, J. (2003). *The nation's report card: Science 2000* (NCES 2003-453). Washington, DC: U.S. Department of Education, Institute of Education Sciences, National Center for Education Statistics.

Perie, M., Grigg, W.S., & Donahue, P.L. (2005). *The nation's report card: Reading 2005* (NCES 2006-451). Washington, DC: U.S. Department of Education, National Center for Education Statistics.

Poe, M.D., Burchinal, M.R., & Roberts, J.E. (2004). Early language and the development of children's reading skills. *Journal of School Psychology, 42,* 315–332.

Purcell-Gates, V. (1996). Stories, coupons, and the TV Guide: Relationships between home literacy experiences and emergent literacy knowledge. *Reading Research Quarterly, 31,* 406–428.

Ratusnik, D.L., & Koenigsknecht, R.A. (1975). Influence of certain clinical variables on black preschoolers' nonstandard phonological and grammatical performance. *Journal of Communication Disorders, 8,* 281–297.

Rickford, A.E. (2005). Everything I needed to know about teaching I learned from my children: Six deep teaching principles for today's reading teachers. *Reading Improvement, 42,* 112–128.

Robinson, C.C., Larsen, J.M., & Haupt, J.H. (1996). The influence of selecting and taking picture books home on the at-home reading behaviors of kindergarten children. *Reading Research and Instruction, 35,* 249–259.

Rooney, P., Hussar, W., Planty, M., Choy, S., Hampden-Thompson, G., Provasnik, S., et al. (Eds.). (2006). *The condition of education 2006* (NCES 2006-071). Washington, DC: U.S. Department of Education, National Center for Education Statistics.

Scarborough, H.S., & Dobrich, W. (1994). On the efficacy of reading to preschoolers. *Developmental Review, 14*, 245–302.

Seymour, H.N., Bland-Stewart, L., & Green, L.J. (1998). Difference versus deficit in child African American English. *Language, Speech and Hearing Services in Schools, 29*, 96–108.

Seymour, H.N., Roeper, T.W., & de Villiers, J. (2003). *Diagnostic Evaluation of Language Variation–Criterion-Referenced edition.* San Antonio, TX: Psychological Corporation.

Snow, C., Burns, S., & Griffin, P. (1998). *Preventing reading difficulties in young children.* Washington, DC: National Academies Press.

Spraggins, R.E. (2000). *Census brief: Women in the United States: A profile.* Washington, DC: U.S. Census Bureau.

Sweetland, J. (2006, November). *A sociolinguistic approach to teaching Standard English.* Paper presented at NWAV 35, The Ohio State University, Columbus.

Taylor, O.L., & Payne, K.T. (1983). Culturally valid testing: A proactive approach. *Topics in Language Disorders, 3*, 8–20.

Thomas-Tate, S.R., Washington, J.A., Craig, H.K., & Packard, M.E.W. (2006). Performance of African American preschool and kindergarten students on the Expressive Vocabulary Test. *Language, Speech, and Hearing Services in Schools, 37*, 143–149.

Thompson, C.A., Craig, H.K., & Washington, J.A. (2004). Variable production of African American English across oracy and literacy contexts. *Language, Speech, and Hearing Services in Schools, 35*, 269–282.

U.S. Census Bureau. (n.d.). *Historical poverty tables.* Retrieved June 30, 2006, from http://www.census.gov/hhes/www/poverty/histpov/hstpov3.html

Vernon-Feagans, L. (1996). *Children's talk in communities and classrooms.* Cambridge, MA: Blackwell.

Washington, J.A., & Craig, H.K. (1992). Performances of low-income, African American preschool and kindergarten children on the Peabody Picture Vocabulary Test–Revised. *Language, Speech, and Hearing Services in Schools, 23*, 329–333.

Washington, J.A., & Craig, H.K. (1994). Dialectal forms during discourse of urban, African American preschoolers living in poverty. *Journal of Speech and Hearing Research, 37*, 816–823.

Washington, J.A., & Craig, H.K. (1998). Socioeconomic status and gender influences on children's dialectal variations. *Journal of Speech, Language, and Hearing Research, 41*, 618–626.

Washington, J.A., & Craig, H.K. (1999). Performances of at-risk, African American preschoolers on the Peabody Picture Vocabulary Test–III. *Language, Speech, and Hearing Services in Schools, 30*, 75–82.

Wheeler, R.S., & Swords, R. (2006). *Code-switching: Teaching Standard English in urban classrooms.* Urbana, IL: National Council of Teachers of English.

Wiener, F.D., Lewnau, L.E., & Erway, E. (1983). Measuring language competency in speakers of black American English. *Journal of Speech and Hearing Disorders, 48*, 76–84.

Woodcock, R.W. (1987). *Woodcock Reading Mastery Tests, Revised.* Circle Pines, MN: American Guidance Service.

9

Shared Book Reading Interventions

Deborah C. Simmons, Sharolyn D. Pollard-Durodola,
Jorge E. Gonzalez, Matthew J. Davis, and Leslie E. Simmons

It has been more than 40 years since President Lyndon Johnson declared a national War on Poverty. From 1964 to 1968, the United States launched national education programs, such as Head Start, that continue today and have improved the preparedness of many preschool children from economically disadvantaged families. The results of these programs have been mixed but promising (Chambers, Cheung, & Slavin, 2006; Shonkoff & Phillips 2000): Long-term outcomes of participating in Head Start and other preschool programs include fewer grade repetitions, greater probability of high school graduation, higher lifetime earnings, and reduced incidence of criminal behavior (Garces, Duncan, & Currie, 2002). These hard-fought battles and improved outcomes notwithstanding, the war on poverty has not been won.

The costs of poverty are manifold. Childhoods lived in poverty can have pernicious effects, placing children at high risk for many problems as a result of economic stress that negatively affects relationships and interactions and economic deprivation that limits resources available for goods, services, and time that facilitate children's development (Ryan, Fauth, & Brooks-Gunn, 2006). Among the most insidious costs of a childhood lived in poverty are unrealized and underrealized academic and educational outcomes. Although the reduction of poverty is generally not the direct province of educators, intercepting and altering the potential negative outcomes associated with poverty are. Thus, enhancing academic achievement through quality instruction and attenuating the impact of growing up in low-income homes and neighborhoods should be the explicit mission of educators. A plausible solution to changing the low poverty–low academic achievement odds is early intervention, specifically high-quality instruction during critical windows of opportunity. Following, we summarize the impact of poverty on language development, then turn our focus to early intervention design to address the challenges of limited literacy and language opportunities.

IMPACT OF POVERTY ON LANGUAGE DEVELOPMENT

Since the 1980s, research has replicated findings that have advanced our understanding of the relationship between poverty and language development. Although a comprehensive review of the literature is beyond the scope of this chapter, in the following section, we summarize selected environmental and experiential risk factors associated with poverty and profile language disparities found to exist between children of low-income and higher-income households.

Environmental and Experiential Risks of Low-Income Households

Compared with wealthier children, children from low-income households often experience the following:

- Substantially less cognitive stimulation and enrichment (Evans, 2004)
- Limited opportunities to engage in literary activities with parents (Evans, 2004; Hart & Risley, 1995)
- Poorer quality and quantity of parental verbalizations (Hart & Risley, 1995)
- Impoverished home learning environments (e.g., literacy materials, library use, reading to children) (Duncan & Brooks-Gunn, 2000)
- Shorter parental speech utterances (Hart & Risley, 2003; Hoff, 2003)
- Less exposure to print media (Neuman & Roskos, 1993)
- Less-qualified teachers and poorer quality instruction (Cirino, Pollard-Durodola, Foorman, Carlson, & Francis, 2007).

Language and Literacy Disparities of Children from Low-Income Households

Often associated with these environmental and experiential risks for children from low-income families are disparities in language development between children from low-income families and children from higher-income households that include the following:

- Significant receptive and expressive vocabulary and language disparities (Hart & Risley, 1995) that, without intervention, remain stable over time
- Limited and less coherent background knowledge of concepts necessary to "connect" with text (Hirsch, 2006; Justice & Ezell, 2001; Neuman, 2006; Willingham, 2006)
- Lack of well-developed oral language skills that lay a foundation for literacy skills (Catts, Hogan, & Fey, 2003; Chaney, 1998; Metsala, 1999).

This summary of environmental and experiential risk factors related to language and literacy disparities, although not exhaustive, nevertheless makes clear the challenges facing concerned educators. A common denominator is the reality of "less"—less opportunity, less experience, less interaction, less coherence in the curriculum, and less knowledge of content and concepts, which limits the acquisition of more content and concept knowledge. A primary challenge for educators, therefore, is how to address the reality of "less" and accelerate learning rates for poor children who enter school with literacy and language levels significantly below those of their more advantaged peers. Simply stated, how do we design learning experiences that will close the experiential/opportunity gap that children from low-income households bring to school?

In this chapter, we address the economics of instruction, the premise of acceleration, and the significant role that principles of instructional design play in optimizing learning rates and development for children from high-poverty backgrounds. We then describe the application of these principles in the design and development of a new preschool book-based intervention that illustrates how design principles can be used to broaden and deepen children's knowledge of vocabulary, concepts, and text genres. The intervention is part of Project Words of Oral Reading and Language Development (WORLD; Gonzalez, Simmons, & Pollard-Durodola, 2004), a 3-year development grant from the Institute of Education Sciences (IES) Reading Comprehension and Reading Scale-up Research (NCER-05-01). The purpose of the grant is to develop interventions that address specific sources of reading comprehension difficulties, especially among at-risk populations from low-income backgrounds and/or racial, ethnic, and linguistic minority groups that have underachieved academically. We are evaluating the efficacy of this intervention and in this chapter describe the principles that guided our intervention development and design.

Instructional Design Principles to Accelerate Language and Literacy Learning and Reduce Disparities

The theoretical framework that guides our efforts to accelerate learning and reduce language and literacy disparities is grounded in the intersection of Carroll's (1963) model of school learning and Engelmann and Carnine's (1991) theory of instructional design. More than 4 decades ago, Carroll proposed a model of school learning to address the problem of achievement disparities that was grounded in the economics of instruction. Identifying time as the most important variable to school learning, Carroll's simple equation indicated that school learning was a function of time spent over time needed.

School Learning = f(time spent/time needed)

Carroll explained that time spent is the result of opportunity and perseverance. Opportunity is a function of time allocated, and learner perseverance is a function of involvement with the academic content or engagement rate. Furthermore, time needed is moderated by the quality of instruction and learner aptitude and ability. His premise was that the variables of opportunity to learn and quality of instruction are the direct province of educators and, if properly managed, can mediate the effects of learner variables (e.g., limited vocabulary, suppressed cognitive development).

The instructional implication of Carroll's model for closing the language/literacy gap is that if instructional opportunities are maximized and students are highly engaged in high-quality instruction, more can be taught in less time (Becker, 1992). The amount of time needed for learning can be moderated by the quality of instruction. The interaction of opportunity to learn and quality of instruction have direct relevance for efforts to optimize learning among children with identified risks related to poverty.

Quality of instruction has many dimensions, but at the core are the teacher's experience and expertise and the design of instructional materials. Some evidence suggests that access to high-quality teachers who can provide effective instruction may be limited by geography and the poverty level of the school's population (Cirino et al., 2007). Therefore, quality of instructional design has been the centerpiece of our work and used to actually improve the quality of instruction.

A theory of instruction begins with the assumption that the environment is the primary variable in accounting for what the learner learns (Engelmann & Carnine, 1991). A theory of instructional design, in turn, assumes that a primary variable in the environment is the instructional curriculum and materials that largely influence what is taught and learned. Specifically, the clearer and more robust the communication of information, the greater the likelihood a child will acquire that information. Engelmann and Carnine (1991) proposed that the greater the needs of the learner, the greater the responsibility of instruction. Consequently, for children who enter school with "less," the quality of instructional design holds promise for acceleration of learning rates whereby children can actually learn "more." High-quality instructional materials that focus on priority skills, scaffold task difficulty, and communicate information clearly and efficiently are, therefore, indispensable for children who have so much to learn.

To accelerate learning, we propose that we must attend to the architecture of instruction and the opportunities for learning inherent in those materials. Instruction that accelerates learning: 1) begins during a critical window of preschool years, 2) maximizes learning time through high levels of relevant learner engagement, and 3) increases instructional quality through tested principles of instructional design. Following, we describe the foundational design of instruction principles engineered and researched over the past 4 decades by Engelmann, Carnine, Kame'enui, and colleagues. We then illustrate how these principles are applied within the context of Project WORLD.

ACCELERATING LEARNING THROUGH QUALITY OF INSTRUCTIONAL DESIGN AND LANGUAGE INTERACTION OPPORTUNITY

Instructional design refers to the way information in a particular domain (e.g., social studies, science, reading, mathematics) is selected, prioritized, sequenced, organized, and scheduled within a highly orchestrated series of lessons and materials that make up a course of study (Simmons & Kame'enui, 1998). According to Smith and Ragan (1993), instructional design refers to the "systematic process of translating principles of learning and instruction into plans for instructional materials and activities" (p. 2). As Smith and Ragan pointed out, "An instructional designer is somewhat like an engineer—both plan their works based on principles that have been successful in the past—the engineer on the laws of physics, and the designer on basic principles of instruction and learning" (p. 2).

The instructional designer is concerned with developing the architectural pedagogy for communicating symbolic information that has a high probability of preventing learner errors, misconceptions, and misrules (Tennyson & Christensen, 1986). Instructional design is concerned with the intricacies of analyzing, selecting, prioritizing, sequencing, and scheduling the communication of information before it is packaged for delivery or implemented. In other words, it is the behind-the-scenes activity that appears as the sequence of objectives, schedule of tasks, components of instructional strategies, amount and kind of review, number of examples, extent of teacher direction, and support explicated in teachers' guides and instructional materials. Instructional design, then, is the blueprint for instruction that carries significant potential support for students who may be at risk for learning difficulties. Some blueprints are skeletal, providing little instructional specification; others have fundamental flaws that fail to provide an adequate foundation on which to build skills and support future learning success. To accelerate learning in the Project WORLD intervention, we began with the premise that carefully articulated and specified instructional design serves as the framework for increasing learning.

Instructional Design Framework

Our framework for designing the preschool WORLD intervention was determined a priori and is based on a set of principles consolidated by researchers at the National Center to Improve the Tools of Educators at the University of Oregon (NCITE; Dixon, Carnine, & Kame'enui, 1992). The principles have served as a blueprint for strategies across content areas (Kame'enui, Carnine, Dixon, Simmons, & Coyne, 2002). The curriculum design principles were derived from "numerous studies and investigations [that] have identified features of high quality educational tools for diverse learners" (Carnine, 1994, p. 345).

These principles are central to designing language and early reading instruction that responds to the acute instructional needs of children of poverty—those who are vulnerable and need intensive and systematic methods to achieve the complex rules and strategies required of reading and language. The framework and curricular implications are essential for children "for whom simply keeping pace with their peers amounts to losing more and more ground" (Kame'enui, 1993, p. 379). NCITE associates (Dixon et al., 1992) identified the following six principles that traverse a range of academic contents and are sufficiently encompassing, sensitive, and flexible to capture the distinct and critical features of varying academic domains and cognitive constructs (e.g., phonological awareness, metacognition): *big ideas, conspicuous strategies, mediated scaffolding, strategic integration, judicious review,* and *primed background knowledge.*

For the WORLD intervention, we also drew on research in shared book and dialogic reading intervention models designed to enhance children's oral language and listening comprehension abilities (Whitehurst & Lonigan, 1998). According to Chambers and colleagues (2006), early childhood curriculum models have been categorized along a continuum with direct instruction (Bereiter & Engelmann, 1966) as one anchor on the continuum and child-centered, developmental, maturational models as the opposite anchor. Our conceptual model sought to integrate the seemingly disparate approaches to developing children's language and listening comprehension through use of 1) an intentional design that specified the content and concepts to be taught, with 2) explicit and plentiful opportunities for children to discuss, elaborate, and relate vocabulary, concepts, and content. To address the latter goal of the intervention, we added a seventh principle: *intentional opportunities for language interaction.* A brief description follows each design principle with illustrative examples from our WORLD preschool vocabulary and comprehension intervention.

Empirical Basis and Instructional Design Framework of the WORLD

To construct the WORLD intervention, we first reviewed extant research on shared book reading to establish an empirical foundation for our methods. Research conducted over the last 15 years verifies that researcher-developed shared book reading interventions facilitate language and literacy development (De Temple & Snow, 2003; Ezell & Justice, 2005; Wasik & Bond, 2001). Specifically, we learned that reading and discussing books with children provides a powerful instructional context for facilitating and accelerating linguistic growth (McKeown & Beck, 2003; Teale, 2003; Whitehurst & Lonigan, 1998) and can have a significant impact on the school readiness of children from low-income families (Zevenbergen, Whitehurst, & Zevenbergen, 2003). Moreover, there is emerging evidence that specific methods used in shared book reading (e.g., repeated readings, explicit vocabulary instruction) advance vocabulary development of children who enter with limited knowledge of word meanings (Coyne, Simmons, Kame'enui, & Stoolmiller, 2004; Dickinson & Smith, 1994; Hargrave & Senechal, 2000). Storybook reading that engages students in discussions about words and concepts across multiple text genres (e.g., narrative, informational) can positively influence comprehension (Duke, Bennett-Armistead, & Roberts, 2003; Morrow & Brittain, 2003). Studies validate that dialogic interactions before and after shared reading are more beneficial than passive listening for children (Reese, Cox, Harte, & McAnally, 2003). Justice, Meier, and Walpole's (2005) review of research identified repeated readings and brief in-context definitions as effective components of shared book reading. Moreover, guidance in how to select vocabulary focuses attention on the concreteness and importance of words (Beck, McKeown, & Kucan, 2002; Biemiller, 2003; De Temple & Snow, 2003; Stahl, 2003). This growing body of research on shared book reading substantiates that "how" we read books to children matters considerably to children's language learning (Justice et al., 2005; Kaderavek & Justice, 2002).

Despite convergence in the findings, surprisingly little attention has been directed to the influence of other important pedagogical and procedural issues related to how to read books (van Kleeck, 2003). The WORLD intervention specifically sought to integrate validated recommended practices from shared book reading with a recognized set of instructional design principles. The instructional design or building blocks for the WORLD intervention are based on the seven-principle framework outlined below.

Principle 1: Big Ideas   *Big ideas* are concepts and principles that facilitate the most efficient and broadest acquisition of knowledge across a range of examples in a domain (Carnine, 1994). Big ideas serve as anchoring concepts by which "small" ideas can often be understood. In instructional curricula, big ideas serve to emphasize what is important. The principal assumptions supporting big idea instruction are that not all curriculum objectives and related activities contribute equally to academic development and that more essential information should be taught more thoroughly than less important information (Brophy, 1992; Carnine, 1994). Specifically, some concepts are fundamental, whereas others are simply *not* essential. For children of poverty who enter with less knowledge than their more advantaged peers, it is important that big ideas become prominent features of instruction.

In early vocabulary and language development, the environmental and experiential conditions that coexist in low-income homes often result in significant disparities in children's breadth and depth of knowledge. To close these gaps, we must identify the domains of knowledge, vocabulary, and comprehension strategies preschoolers need to possess and teach them deeply. The content, or big ideas, for the WORLD intervention were built on three interdependent domains designed to strengthen children's 1) knowledge of world concepts, 2) word or vocabulary knowledge, and 3) text structure for comprehension. Through the strategic integration of these domains, the intervention addresses multiple underlying causes of comprehension difficulties. In contrast to the majority of existing book-reading approaches, our book selections were linked to themes focused on broadening and deepening the knowledge base of a few select concepts or big ideas.

For our shared book reading intervention, big idea vocabulary and world concepts were linked to recommended guidelines for what preschool children should be capable of with regard to use of vocabulary knowledge and application of listening comprehension strategies. Therefore, big ideas included both the content or vocabulary and concepts we wanted children to learn as well as outcomes for what children should be able to do.

Big Idea 1: World Knowledge   To acquire the very basic foundations for later learning, children must develop a coherent understanding of knowledge and concepts (Neuman, 2006). Further, to comprehend new content, children need a threshold level of knowledge about the topic of discussion. When children experience difficulties in comprehending, it is often due to lack of knowledge of the subject matter and related concepts (Walsh, 2003). For many children, comprehension difficulties exist because their prior experiences did not provide the conceptual background on which to build new knowledge. Project WORLD aims to develop world knowledge through focused themes that build and activate background knowledge that is both appropriate for preschool and important for later learning. Examples of world knowledge developed in the WORLD intervention include concepts related to nature and living things. Activities taught children to differentiate and discuss things in nature (e.g., things not made by people such as water, air, and sunlight) and to identify and discriminate living from nonliving things (e.g., living things eat, grow, and use air).

Big Idea 2: Word Knowledge   Children who enter school with less depth and breadth of vocabulary knowledge need multiple exposures to certain words that carry meaning and to many words, in general, to develop associative level knowledge (Baker, Simmons, & Kame'enui, 1998). Books serve as lexical reservoirs that can be drawn on to build vocabulary (De Temple & Snow, 2003). Nevertheless, there has been relatively little work in adult–child shared reading on the effects of building vocabulary networks with thematically and conceptually related books.

Vocabulary must be fostered intensively in the earliest grades and largely built through broad exposure to content-rich knowledge (Hirsch, 2006) using different text genres. Words are learned incrementally and cumulatively after multiple exposures (Stahl, 1991). As a child encounters a word repeatedly, more and more information accumulates; however, some words need to be explicitly taught and reviewed to develop fully and flexibly (Stahl, 1991). In WORLD, words were selected to develop lexical sets (e.g., *water, liquid, frozen*) to enable students to develop associative knowledge. Words were selected based on their importance utility (Beck et al., 2002). Somewhat different from existing research-based shared reading practices, we continued our focus on big ideas and identified important, depictable words that were thematically related and could be applied to the higher-order concepts. For instance, children learned to classify vocabulary pictures by categories (e.g., this is a living thing; this is not a living thing) and to describe how words "go together." For instance, snow and ice are both kinds of water.

Big Idea 3: Knowledge of Text Structure Research suggests that providing children with informational texts early in their schooling may help mitigate the uneven distribution of out-of-school experiential learning opportunities among children from various backgrounds (Duke, 1999; Hirsch, 2006). Though multiple structures exist, reading comprehension researchers are keenly aware of the traditional overreliance on narrative forms in the early grades. It has been stressed that reading stories is insufficient to familiarize children with the numerous nonnarrative forms of language (Smolkin & Donovan, 2000). Evidence shows that sharing expository texts promotes more child interactions around concept building and vocabulary dialogue with adults (van Kleeck, 2003). In fact, informational book read-alouds can foster a context for engaging in direct instruction of comprehension (Smolkin & Donovan, 2000). Young children can learn content, as well as language, from informational as well as narrative text (Duke et al., 2003). Smolkin and Donovan (2000) proposed that both teachers and parents attend more to vocabulary and comprehension when interacting with children around informational texts, thus reinforcing the notion that informational texts have vocabulary-building potential. WORLD integrates narrative and informational texts (i.e., both genres each week) and teaches critical features of stories and informational texts.

In summary, instruction on "big ideas" allows concepts, vocabulary, and text structures to be studied deeply, over extended periods of time, and with multiple exposures. This may seem counterintuitive to the prevailing practice to expose children to a range of important topics and vocabulary; however, acceleration begins with the assumption that not all knowledge and content is equally important and that unless high-priority content is learned and mastered, acceleration cannot occur.

Building Blocks of Intervention

Figure 9.1 depicts the content, concepts, vocabulary, and comprehension that served as building blocks for the WORLD intervention. We began with science content derived from examining the prekindergarten guidelines for the state of Texas and mapped that content against the science content of the Core Knowledge preschool guidelines (Core Knowledge Foundation, 2000). Two themes were identified, *nature* and *living things,* that served as conceptual foci for the intervention. By organizing instruction around nature and living things, we were able to provide students with multiple exposures to vocabulary and recur-

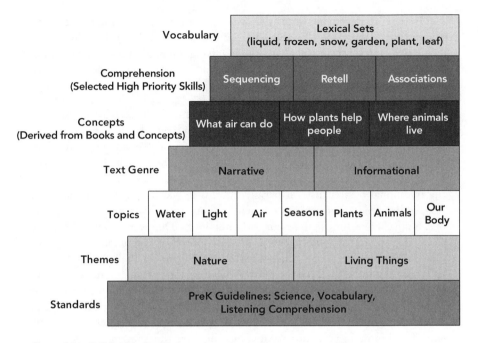

Figure 9.1. Building blocks of intervention.

ring concepts so that knowledge was integrated and studied with increasing depth and dimension across the theme. Theoretically, organizing big ideas by themes allows students to gain greater depth in content knowledge and facilitates comprehension and retention of vocabulary knowledge (Barrera, 1992; De Leon & Medina, 1998; Guthrie & Wigfield, 2000).

Within each theme, lessons were organized into related topics (e.g., within the nature theme were the topics *water, light, air,* and *seasons*) to prime background knowledge in high-utility content and strategically integrate concepts with previously learned material. Each topic included narrative and informational texts. Each week focused on a concept that was developed through book reading. For instance, during the first theme on nature and the topic of water, the teacher read two books, *Rain Talk* (Serfozo, 1990) and *Amazing Water* (Berger, 1996) and taught the concepts of how water moves and what water can do. The same book was read on two successive days. The first day introduced the book, concept, the new vocabulary, and comprehension questions. The second day reviewed vocabulary and extended comprehension of text structure.

Comprehension activities were designed to develop knowledge of text structure and high-priority comprehension outcomes. Comprehension outcomes emphasize learning information and facts from books, predicting events in a story, sequencing events, retelling three- to five-sequence stories, and answering literal and inferential questions. Storybooks facilitated the study of story characters, the main idea ("the big thing that happened"), setting, and story problem; and informational texts provided opportunities to learn more about concepts.

Vocabulary outcomes focused on developing a steady increase in receptive and expressive vocabulary and using these terms in contextualized and decontextualized settings. Regarding vocabulary, we strategically developed lexically related sets of words selecting Tier II words with high utility and importance for later learning. Tier II words are defined as "high frequency words for mature language users… that allow students to describe with greater specificity people and situations with which they already have some familiarity" (Beck, McKeown & Kucan, 2002, pp. 16–17). To scaffold difficulty, early lessons introduced two vocabulary words per book and progressed to three words per text for a total of six words explicitly taught each week. We used explicit teaching to preteach vocabulary word meanings and model correct syntactic use of words while also discussing what was learned or making real-life connections. Because books were chosen based on the appropriateness of their themes, target words were selected to deepen understanding of critical science topics. For example, in the storybook *Gilberto and the Wind* (Ets, 1963), the overarching theme is nature, the topic is air, and the concept is what air can do. Three words, *wind* (air that moves), *float* (when something stays up in the air or water), and *scatter* (to throw things all around), were taught to assist students in learning more about the role of air within the natural world.

In addition to the strategic selection of target words, children received multiple exposures to words before, while, and after reading the text. Prior to reading the text, the teacher primed the children's background knowledge by talking about the theme and the topic and previewing the vocabulary with engaging picture concept cards. For example, students talked about pictures that show 1) how wind can move pieces of paper, 2) how something can float by staying up in the air or water, and 3) how air can scatter or move things around. Furthermore, while reading the book, the teacher stopped to discuss the three target words when they first appeared on the page and showed illustrations of *wind, float,* and *scatter.* After reading, target words were reviewed, employing the picture concept cards used before reading so that students could "be the teacher" and help the group recall what the words mean. Comprehension questions provided an additional exposure to the target words as children discussed how kites *float* in the air and how the wind and air *scattered* the leaves. Lastly, scientific and word knowledge were integrated with life experiences when children described things they do outside when it is windy.

In addition to the big ideas that framed the content and outcomes of the intervention, we employed six additional design principles. Following, we describe the remaining principles and illustrate their application in the WORLD intervention.

Principle 2: Conspicuous Strategies   To accelerate learning, preschool children must learn vocabulary both incidentally and intentionally. Conspicuous strategies are those intentional steps teachers use to explicitly teach word meanings or to teach students how to derive meanings through context or word analysis. Vocabulary acquisition is not an either/or situation; however, because children of poverty often enter preschool with far less knowledge than their more advantaged peers and have not acquired vocabulary through incidental exposure, vocabulary instruction of high-priority words must be conspicuous or explicit (Baker et al., 1998).

Use of numerous instructional methods has led to increased student knowledge of individual words that could be expected from incidental learning opportunities; however, converging evidence of curriculum design in vocabulary acquisition demonstrates that vocabulary development for diverse learners must be explicit and unambiguous and consist of carefully designed and delivered teacher actions (Baker et al., 1998). In vocabulary instruction, this translates into direct presentation of word meanings using clear definitions or explanations across multiple examples and contexts (Coyne et al., 2004). Research in vocabulary instruction shows that by employing conspicuous strategies, teachers can make better sense of where, why, and how strategy use results in success or failure (Baker et al., 1998). In the WORLD intervention, conspicuous or explicit strategies are used in initial sequences of instruction and then faded as learners become more independent and knowledgeable. To explicitly teach word meanings, we use simple, child-friendly definitions or definitions supported by pictures (Beck et al., 2002). For example, *liquid* is taught as *something wet* such as water or juice. Illustrations are also used to convey as concrete and generalizable a meaning as possible. For vocabulary instruction within the WORLD intervention, conspicuous instruction is used in a range of activities that teach initial definitions and examples within the book to outside-the-book comparisons of vocabulary. The following lesson excerpt illustrates an instructional strategy that teaches children to identify the similarities in two illustrations.

> Look at this picture. What does this picture show? Everyone . . .
> —*(children respond) Raindrop*
> It's my turn to be the teacher and tell us about a raindrop. A raindrop is a tiny bit of water that falls from the sky. Now it's (student's name) turn to be the teacher and tell us what a raindrop is.
> —*responses will vary*
> Yes, a raindrop is a tiny bit of water that falls from the sky. Now, look at my new picture of a raindrop. These pictures both show raindrops. Now, I'll tell you what is the same about the raindrops. They are both drops of water, and they both make things wet. Now, you tell me what is the same about the raindrops in these pictures. They are both drops of water, what else? They both . . .

—*come from rain*
—*make things wet (and so forth)*
Yes, they are both rain and make things wet.

In addition to vocabulary, the WORLD intervention teaches other skills and strategies explicitly using an instructional model followed by multiple examples. Conspicuous strategies are used to teach story sequencing and retells. In the initial 2 weeks of the intervention, conspicuous strategies are employed to prompt dialogic discussions of what happened in the storybook or to recall new facts learned from informational books. After rereading *Rain Talk* (Serfozo, 1990) on the second day of the first intervention week, for example, students are asked to sequence important story events by retelling what happened first, next, and last. An instructional step in conspicuous strategies consists of a teacher modeling how to identify what happened first, next, and last using pictures from the story. The teacher might say, "Now I'll find the picture of what happened first." After selecting the appropriate event, she would continue, "It's my turn to tell what happened first: First the girl saw raindrops falling from the sky. Now it's (student's name) turn to tell us what happened first. Start by saying *first*." Last, the teacher would retell the entire story and prompt a group retelling of events by a verbal prompting of *first, next,* and *last.* The intervention progressed from having children retell three-part story sequences to retelling five-part story sequences on their own. As the number of sequences retold increased (e.g., from three to four), we reintroduced a conspicuous teacher model.

These vocabulary and sequencing examples illustrate the importance of carefully designed and delivered teacher actions that facilitate dialogic discussions about "big ideas" within the context of shared book reading. In summary, the conspicuous strategy principle is used to accelerate initial learning; however, these instructional strategies once taught are then transferred to allow students to demonstrate independence.

Principle 3: Mediated Scaffolding   *Mediated scaffolding* refers to the personal guidance, assistance, and support that teachers, peers, materials, or tasks provide a learner. Rosenshine (1995) classified versions of scaffolds as "procedural prompts" that range from key words that help children generate questions as they read (e.g., who, what, when) to frameworks for concept maps. Scaffolds can be seen as temporary supports to assist the learner during initial learning and have a history of empirical support for this purpose (Vygotsky, 1978). On new or difficult tasks, scaffolding may be substantial and then systematically and gradually faded as learners acquire knowledge and skills. Scaffolding can be achieved through careful selection of examples that progress from less difficult to more challenging, the use of illustrations and concrete examples to teach concepts, or scaffolded progression of instructional tasks from simpler to more complex (e.g., from three-sequence to four- and then five-sequence retells).

Mediated scaffolding refers to external supports that provide students with sufficient help during initial learning to foster independence but not so much assistance that they become overreliant on it (Baker et al., 1998). Supports may come in the amount of teacher guidance provided, the language supports available, or the complexity of the task. The supports are systematically faded as teacher instruction is minimized, tasks are generalized to a range of new examples, and task difficulty increases.

An example of mediated scaffolding in our intervention extends Dickinson's descriptive research on book reading documenting the importance of dialogic reading and discussion (Dickinson & Smith, 1994). Our scaffolds progress from low-cognitive tasks (e.g., labeling, identifying) to those requiring high-cognitive abilities (e.g., associating, relating). Early in our lessons, students are asked to merely identify or label specific vocabulary or concepts. Next, they define and describe target words and progress to activities that require them to associate and relate words to one another and to personal experiences. A second type of vocabulary scaffold within our intervention relies on brief elaborations of vocabulary words while reading a book (Hargrave & Senechal, 2000; Justice et al., 2005; Wasik & Bond, 2001; Wasik, Bond, & Hindman, 2006). In our interventions, teachers also scaffold vocabulary learning by providing brief, point-of-use elaborations in child-friendly definitions (Beck et al., 2002).

Principle 4: Strategic Integration   *Strategic integration* involves carefully combining new information with what the learner already knows to produce more generalizable, higher-order skills. Integrating new information with existing knowledge increases the likelihood that new information will be understood at a deeper level. The integration must be strategic so that new information does not become confused with what the learner already knows. Likewise, it must be parsimonious, emphasizing critical connections. In our lessons, we purposefully designed "lesson units" around themes such as nature and topics such as water, air, and light and systematically taught the "sameness" features of nature. Nature consists of things that are not made by people, such as water, air, and sunlight. We then added examples each week to build a body of integrated knowledge.

Strategic integration within vocabulary instruction refers to the thoughtful planning, consideration, and sequencing of vocabulary activities to promote and accelerate vocabulary development (Baker et al., 1998). We know that making target vocabulary salient and meaningful helps children benefit from instruction (Justice, 2002; Wasik & Bond, 2001). Critical research findings show that word learning is maximized when words are taught in meaningful contexts (Hirsch, 2006). In fact, the most critical factor in learning from context is the degree to which children can integrate information presented in texts with prior knowledge (Senechal, Thomas, & Monker, 1995). To integrate new words into their lexicons, children need multiple exposures and opportunities with words. New information that is thoughtfully and strategically integrated with previously acquired knowledge across multiple contexts has the highest probability of being retained over time (Baker et al., 1998).

Within the WORLD intervention, strategic integration of new information with what the learner already knows is primarily accomplished through weekly organization of "twin texts"—one storybook and one informational text—which are associated by theme and topic. When learning that nature is "all the things that are not made by people," children learn that water, air, and sunlight play crucial roles in the natural world. Weekly texts address and develop one of these topics (e.g., water, air) deeply so that children integrate vocabulary and world concepts learned from the storybook with concepts presented in the informational text. In this process, vocabulary is integrated within the broader context of structured thematic knowledge and children are cumulatively exposed to relationships between thematic vocabulary and concepts. Children understand new information by relating it to what they already know, as narrative and informational text and vocabulary words within and among books are connected by a big idea theme and smaller topic. For example, within the thematic unit of *nature,* children learn concepts about light as they listen to the storybook *Moonbear's Shadow* (Asch, 1985), which facilitates a discussion of the target words *shadow, noon,* and *sky.* Within the same week, these concepts are further developed and integrated with knowledge about target words *light, bright,* and *dark,* which are introduced in the informational text *Light* (Parker, 2006). During the last lesson on light, a cumulative review of word and world concepts takes place with activities that enable children to make associations and connections among concepts learned during the entire week. These vocabulary and world concepts are then integrated within subsequent lessons. Table 9.1 illustrates an example of the thematic arrangement of books and words to facilitate conceptual integration.

Principle 5: Judicious Review   Successful learning also depends on a review process to reinforce the essential building blocks of information within a content domain. According to Dempster (1991), the pedagogical jingle of "practice makes perfect" is simply not a reliable standard to ensure successful learning. Simple repetition of information does not ensure efficient learning. Kame'enui and Carnine (1998) identified four critical dimensions of judicious review: 1) sufficient to enable a student to perform the task without hesitation, 2) distributed over time, 3) cumulative with less complex information integrated into more complex tasks, and 4) varied to illustrate the wide application of a student's understanding of the information.

Vocabulary learning formats that occur in the context of shared book reading constitute a platform that is especially suited for "review" of previously learned vocabulary. Research documents that effective vocabulary instruction employs thoughtfully scheduled review and practice with multiple opportunities to use new words to help children strengthen associations and relations of newly acquired knowledge (Coyne et al., 2004). Judicious review places a high premium on the

Table 9.1. Sample thematic arrangement of books and words to facilitate conceptual integration for the theme of nature and the topic of water

	Book and concept	Vocabulary	Word meaning
Week 1	*Rain Talk* by Mary Serfozo (How rain moves)	1. *Raindrop*	A tiny bit of water that falls from the sky
		2. *Drain*	Something that moves water out
	Amazing Water by Melvin Berger	1. *Liquid*	Something wet like water or juice
	(What water can do)	2. *Frozen*	Something that gets cold and hard
Week 2	*A Snowy Day* by Ezra Jack Keats	1. *Snow*	Frozen water that falls from the sky
	(What happens when water freezes)	2. *Melt*	When something gets warm and turns into liquid
	Snow by Marion Dane Bauer	1. *Cloud*	The white thing in the sky that rain and snow come from
	(What happens when water freezes)	2. *Snowflake*	One little piece of snow

value of review and application of previously learned information that is carefully distributed, cumulative, and varied. Evidence shows that after repeated review and careful exposure to books, children's questions are centered less on the book's pictures and begin to reflect questions about the word meanings (Kaderavek & Justice, 2005).

So how does a teacher select information for review, schedule review to ensure retention, and design activities to extend the learner's understanding of the skills, concepts, or strategies? Within WORLD lessons, preschool students experience multiple exposures to individual vocabulary (e.g., *liquid, plants, seasons*) in a variety of tasks and contexts. We also promote information retention by providing weekly practice on all vocabulary taught within a theme. At the end of 6 weeks of instruction, students will have learned 32 words related to nature, organized in lexically related sets. The four critical dimensions of judicious review are accomplished in our shared book reading intervention through repeated readings of storybooks and informational texts and cumulative activities that retain new words in the lessons as children learn vocabulary and world knowledge connected by theme and topic.

The scope and sequence of our intervention consists of 5-day lessons in which new information is introduced on Days 1 and 3 and reviewed on Days 2 and 4. Day 5 is a cumulative review. For example, when children learn about the topic *our body* within the theme of *living things,* the teacher constructs a discussion on different ways we can help our bodies when we are sick. Three related target words are taught within the context of the story while reading the storybook *Arthur's Chicken Pox* (Brown, 1994) on the first day. On the second day of instruction, the storybook is read again without stopping, followed by activities that require children to 1) review the book within the context of the theme and topic and 2) apply concept knowledge using the target words. The same process occurs when reading the related informational text, *Eating Right* (Salzman, 2004), which reinforces knowledge about keeping our bodies healthy. Repeated reading of the text on the second day of instruction helps children to remember vocabulary knowledge and concepts (Biemiller & Boote, 2006; Kaderavek & Justice, 2005). The provision of extended opportunities and exposures to critical concepts and vocabulary strengthens associations and retention of previously learned material.

Day 5 of each week serves as a cumulative review of both word and world concepts with opportunities for students to apply and integrate knowledge learned from the present week and from previous lessons. Activities progress from simple tasks to those requiring more complex knowledge and higher-order thinking. In this judicious review, simpler tasks require students to label pictures of vocabulary words learned across several weeks in addition to retelling a story sequentially or recalling knowledge learned from an informational text as it relates to the topic and theme. More complex tasks require students to use their knowledge to discuss the big thing (i.e., main idea) that happened in a story and to make associations between target words and concepts outside the familiar context of the storybook and informational text.

In the activity Things That Go Together, for example, the teacher uses different picture concept cards to compare critical attributes of vocabulary and concepts. Students see a new picture of melting ice cubes and label the picture as *melt*. They are then presented with a picture of frozen vines, which they label as *frozen*. Students subsequently finish the following sentence: "*Melt* (point to the ice cubes) and *frozen* (point to the frozen vines) are both things that happen to _____ (water)." This type of activity requires students to apply information they have learned about water while constructing meaningful associations between the vocabulary words *melt* and *frozen*.

Principle 6: Primed Background Knowledge   *Priming* is a brief reminder or exercise requiring the learner to retrieve known information. Successful acquisition of new information depends largely on the knowledge the learner brings to a task, the accuracy of that information, and the degree to which the learner gains access to it and uses it. For students who enter with limited knowledge of language and literacy, priming background knowledge is critical to success.

Students with diverse learning needs, however, may not gain access to information in memory efficiently and effectively or may not consistently rely on effective strategies to identify unknown words. In such cases, a teacher primes the critical background knowledge for understanding new vocabulary and related concepts within the context of a big idea (theme) that facilitates connecting new knowledge with what the student already knows. Vygotsky (1978) described the importance of drawing parallels between book concepts and knowledge gained via one's cultural or familiar home connections because such experiences assist students in connecting the realm of the familiar to the unfamiliar and facilitate deep understanding of topics. For example, it is much more effective to learn about how water freezes in a discussion on nature and the familiar uses of water (e.g., drinking, swimming) than to read a book about water freezing without such a discussion. In short, by priming critical background knowledge, students are more able to talk deeply about and remember concepts and vocabulary related to a big idea.

Verbal display of background knowledge is rarely addressed in book-sharing research (van Kleeck, 2003). This is a glaring omission as priming or activating background knowledge greatly helps students draw on their personal experiences as a way to make sense of newly encountered information (Baker et al., 1998). Children need to acquire the language and background knowledge required of their lessons and texts. Teachers can play a prominent role in helping students acquire the background knowledge necessary to incorporate critical information and skills. Without these building blocks, children have great difficulty developing into strong comprehenders (Hirsch, 2006). Too often, research shows a concern with ensuring that lessons and texts do not exceed the language and knowledge children already possess (Neuman, 2006). However, having children in our intervention discuss what happens when water freezes prior to learning new words such as *snow* (frozen water that falls from the sky), *snowflake* (one little piece of frozen water that falls from the sky), and *melt* (when something gets warm and turns into a liquid) enhances their ability to see knowledge as structured relationships and better relate new information to what is already known (Nagy, 1988). Within the WORLD intervention, background building and activating activities occur daily in an activity labeled Talk About Theme and Topic. The following example illustrates how the kinds of water and attributes of nature are integrated to strengthen conceptual networks.

> Yesterday, we read an information book about water. What are some different kinds of water we learned?
> —*snow, cloud, water to play in, ice*
> Yes, these are all types of water. Remember, water is something in nature. Nature is all the things that are not made by people such as water, air, and sunlight. What are some things in nature? Everyone...
> —*water, air, and sunlight*

Principle 7: Intentional Opportunities for Language Interaction   This principle was added to the original six-principle framework to address intentionally designed opportunities for children to respond, discuss, and relate to high-priority content. In our intervention, we use a range of language opportunities in which students' responses vary according to the language task. In Carroll's (1963) model, student involvement with academic content during time allocated for instruction was central to maximizing learning opportunities. In essence, engagement rate was the percentage of time students were involved in the learning process. Dialogic reading practices (Whitehurst & Lonigan, 1998) involve opportunities for children to use language to identify, define, describe, discuss, relate, sequence, retell, and associate content from books. Our intervention sought to balance the need to 1) increase the rate at which information can be presented and practiced and 2) actively engage students in tasks that are highly relevant to the content of instruction.

The WORLD intervention was designed to maximize opportunities for student engagement via scripted lessons, small-group instruction, group and individual turns, and intentionally specified opportunities to discuss and respond. We elaborate on each of these as follows.

Scripted Lessons   Scripted approaches or specified curricular programs have been successfully utilized in school reforms (Borman, Hewes, Overman, & Brown, 2003; Mac Iver & Kemper, 2002). They rely on lessons that are highly specified for the teacher with expected student responses. Encouraging brisk pacing, the lessons include techniques for introducing new skills, correcting student errors, and monitoring of student behaviors (Carlson & Francis, 2002; Carnine, Silbert, & Kame'enui, 1997). In the WORLD intervention, scripted lessons were provided to preschool teachers to ensure consistency in the teaching of vocabulary and conceptual knowledge, to assist in managing instructional time, and to provide scheduled opportunities for student engagement and dialogic discussions. The lessons were designed to ensure that all preschool interventionists, from varied educational and professional backgrounds, were able to manage instructional time utilized before, during, and after reading books and provide opportunities for extending children's oral responses. Teaching from a scripted lesson, however, does not result in a robotlike delivery of instruction in which teachers simply "read the script" (Grossen, 2002). Effective teachers using scripted approaches constantly respond to the nuances in students' performance by providing mediated scaffolding and ongoing monitoring of student responses. In summary, our scripted lessons provide instructional clarity of critical content so that students are able to learn through explicit, scaffolded instruction.

Small-Group Format   The preschool teachers in our study taught small groups of 6–10 students, a format that facilitated high student engagement and allowed teachers to provide feedback at both the individual and the group level. Although the typical practice of book reading involves reading to the entire class, some evidence suggests that small-group instruction may provide greater instructional intensity (Vaughn & Linan-Thompson, 2003; Vaughn, Linan-Thompson, & Hickman, 2003) and facilitate the dialogic nature of teacher–student interactions. For children living in poverty, small-group instruction may be especially crucial in the acceleration of vocabulary development and comprehension abilities, as it affords opportunities to respond, discuss, and use language.

Group and Individual Turns   Opportunities for group and individual turns allow preschool teachers to informally assess student mastery of vocabulary knowledge, text structures, and comprehension of book content as well as facilitate opportunities to engage in dialogic discussions. In the WORLD intervention, opportunities for group responses are scheduled before, during, and after reading the book. For example, prior to reading any book, all students in the group must demonstrate the ability to connect the theme and topic to life experiences and to develop appropriate concept knowledge necessary for comprehending book content. Group responses are also used while reading text to ensure that all students can label vocabulary concepts depicted in text illustrations. Individual turns are strategically scheduled after reading the book to provide an opportunity to "be the teacher" within the context of reviewing vocabulary concepts. During individual turns, preschool teachers extend oral language responses so that students receive individual feedback or modeling of appropriate syntax and word usage.

Intentionally Designed Opportunities to Discuss and Respond Because our shared book reading intervention was piloted with preschool teachers, we were able to observe whether the instructional activities promoted responses and discussion. Over time, some activities were modified or new ones created to increase the amount of instructional time spent in dialogic discussions. Specifically, a range of opportunities were strategically scheduled within the scripted lessons to facilitate talk about words, critical story grammar elements (e.g., character, main idea, setting), and book content within the context of a theme and topic and to assist students in applying new concepts in lively discussions about life. The progression of these activities ranged from simple to more complex. For example, talking about how animals, plants, and human bodies need water, air, and sunlight to live was less cognitively demanding than discussing the critical attributes of pictures that show what air can or cannot do. Opportunities to discuss and respond were usually followed by suggestions in the lesson for teacher scaffolding of oral student responses.

CONCLUSION

In this chapter, we maintained that language development is an economic matter. Specifically, it is a matter of investment, resource management, and quality instruction. For many children in low-income households, the stresses and realities of poverty result in meager experiential investments and yield less knowledge of concepts and vocabulary that enable later learning. Children who enter school with "less" as defined within this context require skillfully engineered instruction that accelerates learning and maximizes the resource of time. To maximize time and positively alter learning trajectories, we build interventions based on principles that teach high-priority concepts, integrate knowledge, and engage students in relevant opportunities to discuss, describe, and associate new knowledge with familiar concepts. We contend that acceleration requires the most careful selection, arrangement, and management of information to maximize learning rates. We are in the midst of evaluating the effects of a book reading intervention designed to optimize preschool children's world and vocabulary knowledge through the application of instructional design principles outlined in this chapter. Through these efforts, we seek to build and bolster the conceptual knowledge base that will serve them in subsequent grades and content areas.

REFERENCES

Asch, F. (1985). *Moonbear's shadow*. New York: Aladdin Paperbacks.

Baker, S.K., Simmons, D.C., & Kame'enui, E.J. (1998). Vocabulary acquisition: Research bases. In D.C. Simmons & E.J. Kame'enui (Eds.), *What reading research tells us about children with diverse learning needs* (pp. 183–218). Mahwah, NJ: Lawrence Erlbaum Associates.

Barrera, R.B. (1992). The cultural gap in literature-based literacy instruction. *Education and Urban Society, 24,* 227–243.

Beck, I.L., McKeown, M.G., & Kucan, L. (2002). *Bringing words to life: Robust vocabulary instruction*. New York: The Guilford Press.

Becker, W.C. (1992). Direct instruction: A twenty year review. In R.P. West & L.A. Hamerlynck (Eds.), *Designs for excellence in education: The legacy of B.F. Skinner* (pp. 71–112). Longmont, CO: Sopris West.

Bereiter, C., & Engelmann, S. (1966). *Effectiveness of direct verbal instruction on IQ performance and achievement in reading and arithmetic.* New York: Brunner/Mazel.

Berger, M. (1996). *Amazing water.* New York: Newbridge Educational.

Biemiller, A. (2003). Oral comprehension sets the ceiling on reading comprehension. *American Educator, 27,* 23–24.

Biemiller, A., & Boote, C. (2006). An effective model for building meaning vocabulary in primary grades. *Journal of Educational Psychology, 98,* 44–62.

Borman, G.D., Hewes, G.M., Overman, L.T., & Brown, S. (2003). Comprehensive school reform and achievement: A meta-analysis. *Archives of Educational Research, 73*(2), 125–230.

Brophy, J. (1992). Probing the subtleties of subject-matter teaching. *Educational Leadership, 49*(7), 4–8.

Brown, M. (1994). *Arthur's Chicken Pox.* Boston: Little, Brown & Co.

Carlson, C.D., & Francis, D.J. (2002). Increasing the reading achievement of at-risk children through direct instruction: Evaluation of the Rodeo Institute for Teacher Excellence (RITE). *Journal of Education for Students Placed at Risk. Special Issue: Research on Direct Instruction in Reading, 72*(2), 141–166.

Carnine, D.W. (1994). Introduction to the mini-series: Diverse learners and prevailing, emerging, and research-based educational approaches and their tools. *School Psychology Review, 23,* 341–350.

Carnine, D., Silbert, J., & Kame'enui, E. (1997). *Direct instruction* (3rd ed.). Upper Saddle River, NJ: Prentice Hall.

Carroll, J. (1963). A model for school learning. *Teacher College Record, 64,* 723–733.

Catts, H.W., Hogan, T., & Fey, M.E. (2003). Subgrouping poor readers on the basis of individual differences in reading-related abilities. *Journal of Learning Disabilities, 36,* 151–164.

Chambers, B., Cheung, A., & Slavin, R. (2006). Effective preschool programs for children at risk for school failure. In B. Spodek & O. Saracho (Eds.), *Handbook of research on the education of young children* (pp. 323–347). Mahwah, NJ: Lawrence Erlbaum Associates.

Chaney, C. (1998). Preschool language and metalinguistic skills are links to reading success. *Applied Psycholinguistics, 19,* 433–446.

Cirino, P.T., Pollard-Durodola, S.D., Foorman, B.R., Carlson, C., & Francis, D.J. (2007). Teacher characteristics, classroom instruction, and student literacy and language outcomes in bilingual kindergartners. *Elementary School Journal, 107,* 341–364.

Core Knowledge Foundation. (2000). *Core knowledge preschool.* Charlottesville, VA: Core Knowledge Foundation.

Coyne, M.D., Simmons, D.C., Kame'enui, E.J., & Stoolmiller, M. (2004). Teaching vocabulary during shared storybook readings: An examination of differential effects. *Exceptionality, 12,* 145–162.

De León, J., & Medina, C. (1998). Language and preliteracy development of English as a second language learners in early childhood special education. In R.M. Gersten & R.T. Jiménez (Eds.), *Promoting learning for culturally and linguistically diverse students* (pp. 26–41). New York: Wadsworth.

De Temple, J., & Snow, C.E. (2003). Learning words from books. In A. van Kleek, S.A. Stahl, & E.B. Bauer (Eds.), *On reading books to children* (pp. 16–36). Mahwah, NJ: Lawrence Erlbaum Associates.

Dempster, F.N. (1991). Synthesis of research on reviews and tests. *Educational Leadership, 4,* 71–76.

Dickinson, D.K., & Smith, M.W. (1994). Long-term effects of preschool teachers' book readings on low income children's vocabulary and story comprehension. *Reading Research Quarterly, 29,* 105–122.

Dixon, R., Carnine, D.W., & Kame'enui, E.J. (1992). *Research synthesis in mathematics: Curriculum guidelines for diverse learners. Monograph for National Center to Improve the Tools of Educators.* Eugene: University of Oregon.

Duke, N.K. (1999). *Using nonfiction to increase reading achievement and word knowledge.* Occasional paper of the Scholastic Center for Literacy and Learning, New York.

Duke, N.K., Bennett-Armistead, V.S., & Roberts, E.M. (2003, Spring). Filling the nonfiction void: Why we should bring nonfiction into the early-grade classroom. *American Educator,* 30–35.

Duncan, G.J., & Brooks-Gunn, J. (2000). Family poverty, welfare reform, and child development. *Child Development, 71,* 188–196.

Engelmann, S., & Carnine, D. (1991). *Theory of instruction: Principles and applications.* Eugene, OR: ADI Press.

Ets, M.H. (1978). *Gilberto and the wind.* New York: Penguin Books.

Evans, G.W. (2004). The environment of childhood poverty. *American Psychologist, 59,* 77–92.

Ezell, H.K., & Justice, L.M. (2005). *Shared storybook reading: Building young children's language and emergent literacy skills.* Baltimore: Paul H. Brookes Publishing Co.

Garces, E., Duncan, T., & Currie, J. (2002). Longer-term effects of head start. *American Economic Review, 92,* 999–1012.

Gonzalez, J.E., Simmons, D.C., & Pollard-Durodola, S. (2004). *Project Words of Oral Reading and language development.* College Station: Texas A&M University.

Grossen, B. (2002). The BIG accommodation model: The direct instruction model for secondary schools. *Journal of Education for Students Placed at Risk. Special Issue: Research on Direct Instruction in Reading, 72*(2), 241–263.

Guthrie, J., & Wigfield, A. (2000). Engagement and motivation in reading. In M.L. Kamil, P.B. Mosenthal, P.D. Pearson, & R. Barr (Eds.), *Handbook of reading research* (Vol. 3, p. 403–422). Mahwah, NJ: Lawrence Erlbaum Associates.

Hargrave, A.C., & Senechal, M. (2000). A book reading intervention with preschool children who have limited vocabularies: The benefits of regular reading and dialogic reading. *Early Childhood Research Quarterly, 15,* 75–90.

Hart, B., & Risley, T.R. (1995). *Meaningful differences in the everyday experiences of young American children.* Baltimore: Paul H. Brookes Publishing Co.

Hart, B., & Risley, T.R. (2003). The early catastrophe: The 30 million word gap. *American Educator, 27*(1), 4–9.

Hirsch, E.D. (2006). The case for bringing content into the language arts book and for knowledge-rich curriculum core for all children. *American Educator, 30,* 8–18.

Hoff, E. (2003). The specificity of environmental influence: Socioeconomic status affects early vocabulary development via maternal speech. *Child Development, 74,* 1368–1378.

Justice, L., & Ezell, H.K. (2001). Written language awareness in preschool children from low-income households: A descriptive analysis. *Communication Disorders Quarterly, 22,* 123–134.

Justice, L.M. (2002). Word exposure conditions and preschoolers' novel word learning during shared storybook reading. *Reading Psychology, 23,* 87–106.

Justice, L.M., Meier, J., & Walpole, S. (2005). Learning new words from storybooks: An efficacy study with at-risk kindergartners. *Language, Speech, and Hearing Services in the Schools, 36,* 17–32.

Kaderavek, J., & Justice, L.M. (2002). Shared storybook reading as an intervention context: Practices and potential pitfalls. *American Journal of Speech-Language Pathology, 11,* 395–406.

Kaderavek, J.N., & Justice, L.M. (2005). The effect of book genre in the repeated readings of mothers and their children with language impairment: A pilot investigation. *Child Language Teaching and Therapy, 21*(1), 75–92.

Kame'enui, E.J. (1993). Diverse learners and the tyranny of time: Don't fix blame; fix the leaky roof. *Reading Teacher, 46*(5), 376–383.

Kame'enui, E.J., & Carnine, D.W. (Eds.). (1998). *Effective teaching strategies that accommodate diverse learners.* Columbus, OH: Merrill-Prentice Hall.

Kame'enui, E.J., Carnine, D.W., Dixon, R.C., Simmons, D.C., & Coyne, M.D. (2002). *Effective teaching strategies that accommodate diverse learners.* Columbus, OH: Merrill-Prentice Hall.

Mac Iver, M.A., & Kemper, E. (2002). The impact of direct instruction on elementary students' reading achievement in an urban school district. *Journal of Education for Students Placed at Risk. Special Issue: Research on Direct Reading Instruction, 72*(2), 197–220.

McKeown, M., & Beck, I.L. (2003). Taking advantage of read-alouds to help children make sense of decontextualized language. In A. van Kleeck, S. Stahl, & E. Bauer (Eds.), *On reading books to children: Parents and teachers* (pp. 159–176). Mahwah, NJ: Lawrence Erlbaum Associates.

Meacham, S.J. (2001). Vygotsky and the blues: Re-reading cultural connections and conceptual development. *Theory Into Practice, 40,* 190–197.

Metsala, J.L. (1999). Young children's phonological awareness and nonword repetition as a function of vocabulary development. *Journal of Educational Psychology, 91,* 3–19.

Morrow, L.M., & Brittain, R. (2003). The nature of storybook reading in the elementary school: Current practices. In A. van Kleeck, S.A. Stahl, & E.B. Bauer (Eds.), *On reading books to children* (pp. 140–158). Mahwah, NJ: Lawrence Erlbaum Associates.

Nagy, W.E. (1988). *Teaching vocabulary to improve reading comprehension.* Newark, DE: International Reading Association.

Neuman, S.B. (2006). How we neglect knowledge and why. *American Educator, 30,* 24–27.

Neuman, S.B., & Roskos, K. (1993). Access to print for children of poverty: Differential effects of adult mediation and literacy-enriched play settings on environmental and functional print tasks. *American Educational Research Journal, 30*(1), 95–122.

Parker, V. (2006). *Light.* Chicago, IL: Heinemann Library.

Reese, E., Cox, A., Harte, D., & McAnally, H. (2003). Diversity in adults' styles of reading books to children. In A. van Kleek, S.A. Stahl, & E.B. Bauer (Eds.), *On reading books to children* (pp. 27–57). Mahwah, NJ: Lawrence Erlbaum Associates.

Rosenshine, B. (1995). Advances in research on instruction. *Journal of Educational Research, 88*(5), 262–268.

Ryan, R., Fauth, R., & Brooks-Gunn, J. (2006). Childhood poverty: Implications for school readiness and early childhood education. In B. Spodek & O. Saracho (Eds.), *Handbook of research on the education of young children* (pp. 323–347). Mahwah, NJ: Lawrence Erlbaum Associates.

Salzman, M.E. (2004). *Eating right.* Edina, MN: ABDO Publishing.

Senechal, M., Thomas, E., & Monker, J. (1995). Individual differences in 4-year-old children's acquisition of vocabulary during storybook reading. *Journal of Educational Psychology, 87,* 218–229.

Serfozo, M. (1990). *Rain talk.* New York: MacMillan Publishing.

Shonkoff, J.P., & Phillips, D.A. (2000). *From neurons to neighborhoods: The science of early childhood development.* Washington, DC: National Academies Press.

Simmons, D.C., & Kame'enui, E.J. (1998). *What reading research tells us about children with diverse learning needs: Bases and basics.* Mahwah, NJ: Lawrence Erlbaum Associates.

Smith, P.L., & Ragan, T.J. (1993). *Instructional design.* New York: Macmillan.

Smolkin, L.B., & Donovan, C.A. (2000). *The contexts of comprehension: Information book read alouds and comprehension acquisition.* Report for the Center for the Improvement of Early Reading Achievement, Ann Arbor, MI.

Stahl, S.A. (1991). Beyond the instrumentalist hypothesis: Some relationships between word meanings and comprehension. In P.J. Schwanenflugel (Ed.), *The psychology of word meanings* (pp. 157–186). Hillsdale, NJ: Lawrence Erlbaum Associates.

Stahl, S.A. (2003). Words are learned incrementally over multiple exposures. *American Educator, 27,*18–23.

Teale, W.H. (2003). Reading aloud to young children as a classroom instructional activity: Insights from research and practice. In A. van Kleek, S.A. Stahl, & E.B. Bauer (Eds.), *On reading books to children* (pp. 114–139). Mahwah, NJ: Lawrence Erlbaum Associates.

Tennyson, R., & Christensen, D.L. (1986). *Memory theory and design of intelligent learning systems.* Paper presented at the meeting of the American Educational Research Association, San Francisco.

van Kleeck, A. (2003). Research on book sharing: Another critical look. In A. van Kleek, S.A. Stahl, & E.B. Bauer (Eds.), *On reading books to children* (pp. 272–320). Mahwah, NJ: Lawrence Erlbaum Associates.

Vaughn, S., & Linan-Thompson, S. (2003). What is special about special education for students with learning disabilities? *Journal of Special Education. Special Issue: What is Special About Special Education, 37*(3), 140–147.

Vaughn, S., Linan-Thompson, S., & Hickman, P. (2003). Response to instruction as a means of identifying students with reading/learning disabilities. *Exceptional Children, 69,* 391–409.

Vygotsky, L.S. (1978). *Mind in society.* Cambridge, MA: Harvard University Press.

Walsh, K. (2003). Basal readers: The lost opportunity to build background knowledge that propels comprehension. *American Educator, 31,* 25–27.

Wasik, B.A., & Bond, M.A. (2001). Beyond the pages of a book: Interactive book reading and language development in a preschool classroom. *Journal of Educational Psychology, 93,* 243–250.

Wasik, B.A., Bond, M.A., & Hindman, A. (2006). The effects of language and literacy intervention on head start children and teachers. *Journal of Educational Psychology, 98,* 63–74.

Whitehurst, G.J., & Lonigan, C.J. (1998). Child development and emergent literacy. *Child Development, 69*(3), 848–72.

Willingham, D.T. (2006). How knowledge helps. *American Educator, 30,* 30–38.

Zevenbergen, A.A., Whitehurst, G.J., & Zevenbergen, J.A. (2003). Effects of shared-reading intervention on the inclusion of evaluative devices in narratives of children from low-income families. *Applied Developmental Psychology, 24,* 1–15.

10

Applying Universal Design for Learning with Children Living in Poverty

David H. Rose and Gabrielle Rappolt-Schlichtmann

The relationship between achievement in school and social status in childhood is well documented. Research demonstrates that, as a group, children living in poverty exhibit test scores that are significantly lower than national norms by the preschool years (Bradley & Corwyn, 2002; Brooks-Gunn & Duncan, 1997; Evans, 2004). This association exists across cultures and persists throughout childhood. Termed the *achievement gap,* children living in poverty tend to underperform in comparison to their more affluent counterparts on tests of cognitive performance even when school resources are increased (Bempechat, 1992; Jencks & Phillips, 1998; Lubienski, 2001; Lubienski & Shelley, 2003; Moses & Cobb, 2001). Though research attempting to explain this gap in performance is still in its infancy, there is much that teachers and school administrators can now do to bring underperforming students up to speed.

In truth, every classroom can be characterized by its great diversity of learners, including students who are learning English as their second language, students reading below grade level, students with behavior problems, students from varied cultural backgrounds, and students who have learning disabilities. The challenge is in meeting the needs of a diverse student body who have widely divergent skills. From our standpoint, this challenge is better conceived of as being met not by developing a new pathway but by developing multiple pathways. It is essential to create curricula that are flexible enough to support multiple pathways to literacy, paths that are diverse enough to match the diversity of students in our classrooms. Only by providing multiple paths can we hope to reach the same high standards with students who start from very different places (Fullan, Hill, & Crevola, 2006).

How can educators and education change to efficiently and effectively support all students in meeting the high standards we have set for them? Exercise provides a useful metaphor. The equipment in physical fitness gyms are set up to maximize gains while minimizing the time spent working out. Nautilus machines exquisitely adjust to each individual, positioning the exerciser perfectly so that his or her time is efficiently used to get the maximum benefit from the time spent. These machines individualize the supports provided (the chair, pulleys, and so forth are all adjustable) so that each individual is optimally positioned for successful exercise, and they individualize the resistance or weight so that each person is challenged appropriately.

As with the fitness gym, educators and education need to better position students to learn, providing appropriate support and just the right level of challenge to successfully meet the needs of a diverse student body. We need to create flexible curricula that have the same individualizing capacity as the physical fitness equipment, positioning students to effectively and efficiently learn. Within the field of special education there are examples of such curricula and a framework called Universal Design for Learning (UDL) that guides their development. The UDL movement is expanding rapidly as a new approach to providing the right level of support and challenge for each student, even those with disabilities. We would like to introduce the ideas and practices of UDL in this chapter because we believe it has important application to students whose disadvantages are more economic and cultural than physical or cognitive.

WHAT IS UNIVERSAL DESIGN FOR LEARNING?

Universal design originated in the field of architecture, where structures are created to accommodate the full range of users, including those with disabilities, with resulting benefits for everyone (e.g., consider the multiple uses of curb cuts and captioned video). UDL extends this concept to the educational domain by applying advances in the understanding of how the brain processes information to the design of curricula that can accommodate broad student needs at the outset.

The *universal* in UDL does not mean "one size fits all" but rather that learning designs accommodate the widest possible range of learner needs and preferences. To that end, three central principles serve as the foundation for UDL and for the development of curricula and curriculum materials:

- Provide multiple means of *representation* to give learners various ways of acquiring information and knowledge
- Provide multiple means of *expression* to give learners alternatives for demonstrating what they know
- Provide multiple means of *engagement* to tap into learners' interests, offer appropriate challenges, and increase motivation

By making instructional goals, strategies, and materials highly flexible along these three parameters, potential barriers to learning are lowered and opportunities to learn are increased.

Since 1990, research on UDL has focused on the role of technology in instructional interventions embedded with research-based instructional practices and instructional design based on UDL theory (Rose & Meyer, 2002). Reliance on print materials, with their lack of flexibility for access, raises many barriers to achievement for many students. Information delivered in a printed book is uniform and provides little support for individualization; as a result, each student faces exactly the same information in exactly the same way. The flexibility of digital media makes it easier to customize the learning experience to meet individual needs through universally designed learning tools, curricula, and strategy-based interventions. The flexibility afforded by digital educational materials include the ability to modify the perceptual characteristics of text, to modify text content, to transform text into speech, and to embed relevant prompts and scaffolds directly in text where they can be individually presented to provide individualized support for developing strategies and skills (e.g., Farmer, Klein, & Bryson, 1992; Matthew, 1997). For example, Dalton, Pisha, Eagleton, Coyne, and Deysher (2002a) developed a universally designed reading environment (digital-Universal Learning Editions; d-ULEs) offering digital texts with embedded reading strategy instruction based on reciprocal teaching (Palincsar & Brown, 1984; Palincsar & Dalton, 2005).

In these d-ULEs, students with decoding and fluency problems can use text-to-speech (TTS) technology to have individual words or passages read aloud with synchronized highlighting. To develop comprehension, strategy instruction prompts, hints, think-alouds, and model responses are embedded in the digital text. Strategy support is leveled so that students move from high to low support, with the goal of independent application of strategies. For example, at Level 1, students select a good summary from three multiple-choice options. At Level 2, they review a list of points from the passage and identify the important points. At Level 3, students construct a summary using highlighted text in the passage and complete a self-check rubric. At Level 4, students create a summary and complete the self-check rubric. At Level 5, students choose a strategy that they feel would be most helpful. Students' online responses are collected in a computer worklog for review and evaluation by the student and the teacher.

Until recently, it would not have been practical to develop the kind of flexible and educative curricula and tools described here and envisioned by UDL for underresourced schools because of technological limitations. Similarly, it would not have been practical at these schools to develop highly interactive strategic instruction using the UDL approach. Fortunately, advances in digital technologies now make the development of interwoven UDL tools, texts, content curricula, and strategy-based interventions possible. Furthermore, advances in the National Instructional Materials Accessibility Standards (NIMAS; http://nimas.cast.org) open the door for UDL curricular design.

In the section that follows, we will illustrate through one extended example the ways in which modern digital media, delivering individualized and evidence-based practices, can provide a proper platform for the kinds of individualized and targeted instruction that will be required to raise achievement levels for all students.

PRACTICAL EXAMPLE: THINKING READER

Researchers at the Center for Applied Special Technology (CAST; http://www.cast.org) have developed and evaluated an example of UDL as it is applied to the teaching of reading comprehension strategies. After formative evaluation, revision, and summative research studies, these prototypes have been commercialized and published by Tom Snyder Productions as *Thinking Reader* (*TR*; 2004).

At the core of the *TR* are nine digitally based narrative texts that can provide highly individualized supports for a wide variety of learners. Central to the pedagogy of *TR* is the evidence-based practices developed by Palincsar and Brown (1984) that comprise the reciprocal teaching approach to improving reading comprehension. Studies of reciprocal teaching conducted by its designers (Palincsar & Brown, 1984, 1989) and meta-analyses of their and others' replications (Rosenshine & Meister, 1994) indicate that reciprocal teaching is a robust intervention leading to positive gains in students' comprehension of instructed text, as well as transfer text, and modest gains on standardized measures of reading comprehension. In particular, research indicates that reciprocal teaching improves students' comprehension and self-monitoring skills through an apprenticeship model of learning.

In the traditional format of reciprocal teaching, teacher and students engage in an instructional dialogue about the text, co-constructing their understanding of the text as they apply several strategies: predicting, questioning, summarizing, and clarifying. The goal of reciprocal teaching is not to teach strategies per se but rather to teach students how to apply strategies in the service of developing deep understanding. Core to reciprocal teaching is the notion of *scaffolding*, in which supports are dynamically adjusted to meet the needs of the learner in relation to the demands of the task (Vygotsky, 1978; Wood, Bruner, & Ross, 1976).

In collaboration with Anne-Marie Palincsar, Bridget Dalton and her colleagues at CAST incorporated supports for reciprocal teaching directly into *TR*, a digital reading environment that was designed in accordance with UDL principles (Palincsar & Dalton, 2005). Within that UDL environment, graduated strategy supports could be customized and individualized to individual readers. The primary goal of *TR* is to develop engaged, active, and strategic readers who are able to comprehend academically rigorous literature. It is aligned with state standards and curriculum frameworks for comprehension and literature. The following sections describe the prototype for *TR* as well as the research that guided and evaluated it. Providing multiple means of recognition, expression, and engagement are the major tenants of a UDL design, each is discussed in turn with regard to *TR*'s design in the following sections.

Providing Multiple Means of Recognition

Students differ in the ways that they perceive and comprehend information that is presented to them. At the extreme are students who have sensory disabilities for whom some forms of representation are completely inaccessible. More prevalent are students who, because of their particular profile of perceptual or cognitive strengths and weaknesses, find information presented in some formats much more accessible than others (e.g., students with dyslexia, aphasia, or intellectual disabilities). In reality, there is no one way of presenting information that will be optimal for all students; alternative means of representation are key to providing access to instructional materials *and* to learning.

Sensory and Perceptual Options   Reading comprehension is impossible when the letters and words that comprise the written text are inaccessible to the reader. Within *TR*, the digital text is highly flexible and can be presented in many formats, allowing for customization in size, color, or font to reduce the barriers to some students that would be imposed by any one particular format. This variation is important for students with low vision or color blindness, for example. For students who are completely blind, the full text can be automatically read aloud or produced in refreshable Braille.

Linguistic Options   Reading comprehension is also difficult or impossible when a student cannot accurately and fluently recognize the individual words and their meanings. Three examples of optional "linguistic" supports follow.

Word Recognition Support   *TR* provides optional supports for word recognition and decoding. Specifically, *TR* provides a TTS capability that allows students to click on any word, phrase, or passage and have it read aloud. The text is read with synthetic voice accompanied by synchronized highlighting. Although the research is not completely consistent, studies of TTS with adolescent learners have produced generally positive results, improving comprehension of supported text, and, in some cases, transferring to reading of print text (Elkind, Cohen, & Murray, 1993; Lundberg & Oloffson, 1993; Strangman & Dalton, 2005).

In *TR*, TTS is essential as an access tool for struggling readers who might not be able to read the text otherwise. Although it is not possible to separate the effect of TTS from the effects of other *TR* supports, Dalton and colleagues have found in several studies of *TR* and similar digital strategic reading environments that students reading with *TR* improve their performance on print-based measures, suggesting that the TTS is not impeding skill development (Dalton et al., 2002a; Dalton, Schleper, Kennedy, & Lutz, 2005). Furthermore, adolescents consistently rate the TTS feature as "very useful" (Dalton, unpublished data). Because TTS is no substitute for a human voice as a model of expressive reading, the TSP version of *TR* also offers reading of the full text (in phrases, sentences, or paragraphs) in human recorded speech to provide a strong model of reading expression and fluency.

Vocabulary Support   Reading comprehension is a function of readers' depth and breadth of vocabulary knowledge. Good readers know many more words than struggling readers and are better able to use contextual cues and morphological knowledge to determine word meaning (Nagy & Scott, 2004). Vocabulary support via hyperlinks to a glossary or annotation is commonplace in hypertext environments with the assumption that readers will benefit from just-in-time support.

Research on K–12 hypertexts typically combine glossary hyperlinks with other supports with generally positive results (Higgins, Boone, & Lovitt, 1996; Horney & Anderson-Inman, 1999; Proctor, Dalton, & Grisham, 2007; Reinking & Schreiner, 1985). In *TR*, students have access to embedded vocabulary hyperlinks, some of which include an illustrative graphic. The definitions are consistent with the meaning of the word as used in the text, and a Spanish translation is provided.

English Language Support   The primary text of *TR* is English. As a support for English language learners, however, the commercially released version of *TR* provides vocabulary support in Spanish as well as English. Research prototypes at CAST have increased the support for English language learners considerably, including wider use of Spanish and Spanish-speaking mentors, with promising results overall.

Prompts   As students individually read the text, they are periodically prompted to stop and apply a strategy. In addition to the four reciprocal teaching strategies of predict, question, clarify, and summarize (Palincsar & Brown, 1984), TR includes *visualization* as a fifth strategy (Pressley, 2006) as well as a *feeling response* option to encourage students to make a personal connection to the text.

Cognitive Scaffolds   The scaffolding of the text centers on students' strategy use. For example, *TR* offers five levels of support for each comprehension strategy listed previously. These graduated levels of support allow students to move at their own pace from high support to low support to independent application of each of the strategies, ending with an open response option that allows students to make independent choices about which strategies to employ. The scaffolding system includes a number of options: the way the strategy task is represented, the response options for students, and the availability of three pedagogical agents who function as peer coaches, providing models, think-alouds, and hints. Level of scaffolding is also varied so that strategies that are more difficult, such as summarization, offer more support than strategies that are easier, such as prediction. Finally, students and teachers may access the "Strategy Help" section, which provides basic information about each strategy (e.g., What is it? Why should I use it? How do I use it?).

Feedback and Assessment Options   Self-monitoring and self-regulation are essential to successful reading (Englert, Raphael, Anderson, & Stevens, 1991; Paris, Cross, & Lipson, 1984). In addition, embedded assessment and frequent monitoring of students' progress contributes to student learning (Campione & Brown, 1987; Cioffi & Carney, 1997; Feuerstein et al., 1986). *TR* is designed to support students' self-evaluation and teachers' assessment of students. All of students' responses to the *TR* strategy prompts are collected in an electronic worklog that may be viewed by the student or teacher at any time, and students may revise responses. Corrective and instructive feedback is provided, automatically and immediately, for closed items.

Approximately three times per novel, students are prompted to self-evaluate and describe their progress using their worklog responses as supporting evidence. Again, there are pedagogical agents to provide models and think-alouds. Students meet with their teacher in a worklog conference to discuss their evaluation and to set goals for further progress.

The TSP version of *TR* adds some additional features that strengthen the assessment component. First, teachers may select responses in the worklog to draw students' attention to a particular entry, and they may generate teacher messages to individuals or groups of students to give them feedback. Second, the qualitative worklog entries are complemented by several embedded "Comprehension Quick Checks" that include literal and inferential questions and provide a quantitative measure of students' understanding of the novel. The latter results are provided in graphical form and show cumulative progress. Teachers may also view assessment results and worklogs at the individual student level or at the class level.

Providing Multiple Means of Expression

Students differ in the ways that they can navigate a learning environment and express what they know. That is, any group of students will not share the same capacities for action within or across domains of knowledge. Some students have specific motor disabilities that limit the kinds of physical action they can take and the kinds of tools that they can use to respond or construct knowledge. Other students have adequate motor control but lack the integration of action into skills that is demanded to be successful in one domain or another. Still others are skillful within a domain but lack the strategic and organizational abilities that would be required to manage those skills effectively to achieve goals. Within the learning environment, some students are able to express themselves well in text but not in oral speech, and vice versa. Some can express themselves well in drawing but not in words. In reality, there is no one means of expression that will be optimal for all students; alternative means of expression are essential.

The *TR* is focused on developing reading strategies rather than on teaching students to express themselves. Because of that, there are much fewer options or supports for expression. There are, however, opportunities for students to respond, and it is essential that all students have an opportunity to develop their ability to respond effectively.

Motor and Physical Options   Students may respond to prompts and queries either by keyboarding or by voice. Accessible options for keyboarding are also built in so that the program can be used by students who use a variety of assistive technologies.

Media and Communication Options   Students may respond to queries or prompts either by writing or by speaking into a microphone.

Planning and Organizational Options   Among the strategy scaffolds offered for students, there are many that have options to help students plan and organize their responses. These take the form of prompts or sentence fragments that guide students in preparing to write or speak.

Providing Multiple Means of Engagement

Students also differ markedly in the ways in which they can be engaged or motivated to learn. Some students are highly engaged by spontaneity and novelty; others are disengaged, even frightened, by those aspects in a learning environment. Similarly, some students are engaged by risk and challenge in a learning environment; others seek safety and support. Some students are attracted to dynamic social types of learning; others shy away and recede from social forms. There is not one means of engaging students that will be optimal; alternative means of engagement are critical.

Strategic readers are engaged readers. Students' perceptions about themselves as readers and learners, their ability to persist in the face of challenge, their interest in a particular topic or author, their anxiety about personal issues at home or school, and so forth are all key factors that influence the outcomes of any particular reading experience (Guthrie, 2001; Guthrie & Cox, 2001; Pressley, 2006). No two students, or even the same student under different circumstances, are motivated and engaged in the same way. Good designs provide options.

Recruiting Interest   The key to recruiting interest and engagement in *TR* is that it is comprised of a collection of award-winning authentic books that are motivationally age-appropriate (i.e., with themes and narratives appeal to the interests of adolescent readers rather than to their decoding level). The literature in *TR* is not supplemental or remedial but is the same literature that is typically assigned to, or read recreationally by, high-achieving students, thus reducing the stigma of lowered expectations and elevating the opportunities for intrinsically motivated peer-to-peer interaction and discussion around shared experiences and interests.

Sustaining Motivation and Effort   Although interest in the narratives and characters of the quality literature is a primary means for sustaining motivation and effort, the addition of the wide variety of scaffolds provides options that will help students experience the right level of challenge to sustain engagement in learning over a long period and even allows learners to vary the challenge and support as social or emotional conditions change. Providing choice for the student—in scaffolds, methods of responding, look, and feel—is itself a key to engagement, especially for adolescents.

Building Intrinsic Motivation and Self-Regulation   Strategic reading ultimately requires that learners set their own goals and a purpose for reading, monitor their progress, and adapt processes and strategies in response to difficulties and task requirements. *TR* provides graduated experiences in self-reflection and scaffolds for helping students monitor their own progress, building their capacity for independence as self-motivated, intentional readers.

EXPERIMENTAL RESEARCH ON THE EFFECTIVENESS OF THE UNIVERSAL DESIGN FOR LEARNING APPROACH

It is not enough to show that the core practices and instructional elements of UDL, or even a specific application of UDL (as described previously), are evidence based. It is essential also to show that the UDL approach can be applied effectively, and at scale, in full districtwide implementations. This is challenging (and necessary) because adequate implementation of UDL will require more than adoption of new technologies or techniques; it will require comprehensive reform throughout a whole school system—from the process of setting standards and objectives, to choosing curricular materials and methods, to training teachers and administrators, to the delivery of support services, to educating and engaging parents, and finally to the ways in which individual and districtwide progress is measured.

There are no schools or districts where UDL is thus fully realized, and there are not even any full-scale curricula or professional development programs with which to systemically actualize the principles of UDL. Although a number of schools, districts, and even states are now initiating the UDL approach, those reforms are only partial implementations and are far from ready for rigorous outcome research.

In the meantime, however, there are research studies that have examined the results of UDL applications in real classroom settings. Although none of these will substitute for large studies at the systemic level, they provide the basis on which such larger studies will depend. In what follows, we will illustrate an example of a line of UDL research that is now available, recognizing the need for a great deal more across many content domains, in many different settings, and over many different time and population scales.

There is a growing body of research that highlights the positive impact of hypertext, hypermedia, and computer-mediated instruction on diverse learners' reading development above and beyond comparable print-text approaches (Cognition and Technology Group and Vanderbilt Learning Technology Center, 1993; Dalton & Strangman, 2006; Kamil, Intrator, & Kim, 2000; Leu, 2000;

Reinking & Schreiner, 1985; Reinking, McKenna, Labbo, & Kieffer, 1998; Strangman & Dalton, 2005). The most frequently described and researched forms of digital support provide access to the content. For example, a struggling reader might use TTS technology to have the text read aloud or view a multimedia definition of a vocabulary word that is new to him or her. Work by Dalton and colleagues (2002a) indicates that such access technology used in combination with hypertexts designed to support students' strategic processing of text (e.g., a student might be prompted to make a prediction about what will happen next in the story) shows particular promise.

For example, Dalton and colleagues (2002a) investigated the impact of traditional versus computer-supported strategy instruction as embodied in *TR* with 102 middle school struggling readers. Students in both conditions used the reciprocal teaching strategies of predict, question, clarify, and summarize (Palincsar & Brown, 1984), as well as visualization (Pressley, 1997), to read and respond to three age-appropriate novels. Students in the control condition engaged in reciprocal teaching discussions as they read the novels in print, whereas students in the experimental group read the novels in *TR*, d-ULE. Students in the computer condition engaged with the same literature but in *TR* digitized versions. To develop comprehension, pedagogical agents offered strategy instruction prompts, hints, and models. Strategy support was leveled so that students could move from high to low support, with the goal of independent application of strategies. Students' online responses were then collected in a computer worklog for review and evaluation by both the student and teacher.

After controlling for gender and pretest scores on comprehension and vocabulary, students in the computer condition demonstrated significantly greater gains in comprehension on the *Gates MacGinitie Reading Achievement Test* than did their peers in the traditional print-based reciprocal teaching condition. It is important to note that reciprocal teaching itself is considered a robust intervention; the effect of the d-ULE represents impacts above and beyond the reciprocal teaching approach in print-based material.

The effect size was moderate, equating to approximately half a grade level of reading achievement gain. For these struggling readers who read at or below the 25th percentile prior to intervention, this was a meaningful increase. A comparison of the two groups' on-task behavior revealed that students reading the digital novels spent significantly more time on instructional tasks and had significantly more opportunities to respond to strategies than did their peers using traditional strategy instruction. Qualitative analyses of student and teacher interviews and questionnaires indicated that students viewed the *TR* digital text as extremely helpful. Teachers' responses focused on the positive impact on students' engagement and self-efficacy and the relative ease of integrating *TR* into their curriculum and teaching.

Dalton and colleagues at CAST have continued to develop d-ULEs and study their use with struggling and typically achieving readers in elementary and middle school classrooms (Dalton & Gordon, 2007; Dalton & Proctor, 2007; Dalton & Strangman, 2006; Palincsar & Dalton, 2005; Proctor et al., 2007). Although most of that work focuses on students with learning disabilities or students who are deaf, Proctor and colleagues (2007) examined the effects of a d-ULE on English language learner vocabulary knowledge and reading comprehension skill. An English language learner d-ULE was developed from a prototype previously created for struggling readers (Dalton & Pisha, 2001; Dalton, Pisha, Eagleton, Coyne, & Deysher, 2002b). This Spanish–English d-ULE was adapted using the principles of UDL (Rose & Meyer, 2002) and derived from classic research on reading comprehension including reciprocal teaching (Guthrie & Cox, 2001; Palincsar & Brown, 1984, 1989; Palincsar & Dalton, 2005; Wigfield, Eccles, & Rodriguez, 1998).

Sixteen Spanish-speaking English language learners and 14 native English-speaking monolinguals were enrolled in the study and followed for 4 weeks while they and their classmates used the d-ULE as a part of their curriculum. Change in standardized reading vocabulary scores was associated with frequency of access to hyperlinked glossary items, such that greater access to the glossary was correlated with vocabulary gain between the pre- and posttest. Lower pretest vocabulary scores were associated with greater gains between the pre- and posttests.

A similar pattern was detected between student access to coaching avatars and reading comprehension outcomes. Avatars provided support to students about the productive use of reading comprehension strategies. Greater access to coaching avatars was associated with larger gains in standardized reading comprehension scores between the pre- and posttest. As with vocabulary, lower pretest reading comprehension scores were associated with greater gains in reading comprehension between the pre- and posttest. These results indicate that English language learners benefited from the d-ULE as they made use of the digitally embedded features in such a way as to promote the learning of new vocabulary and effective use of reading comprehension strategies. (For more on this work, see Proctor et al., 2007.)

CONCLUSION

The achievement gap is both pernicious and persistent. Reducing that gap will require instructional approaches that are much more effective than our present methods. The effectiveness of instructional methods and materials, very much like exercise equipment, depends on their ability to be individualized. Instruction will not succeed in raising achievement levels for struggling students unless it is much more targeted and focused and much more adaptable to individual learners. Instruction requires customizability to provide the *precision* that is needed for substantial progress (Fullan et al., 2006)

In this chapter, we have focused on one digital instructional environment, *TR*, that is an example of UDL. Our intent is not to dwell on this specific application but to demonstrate that there are already commercially available examples of curricula that apply the principles of UDL to achieve the individualization and

precision needed to close achievement gaps. What makes this precision and targeting possible in these new kinds of applications is their successful capitalization
on the flexibility of digital technology. What makes effective use of that technology's flexibility is the embedding of evidence-based practices, such as reciprocal
teaching, directly within core instructional programs. What makes those practices
effective is that they are embedded within an overall curriculum that is universally designed.

For students who live in poverty, like students who have disabilities and other
students "in the margins," providing precise adjustments in the available supports
and challenge is critical to effective instruction, equally as important in education
as it is in effective exercise. To close achievement gaps, teachers will need literacy
tools that are as diverse and differentiated as the students themselves. With modern
technology and practices such as UDL, we can now provide those tools. We must.

REFERENCES

Bempechat, J. (1992). Fostering high achievement in African American children: Home,
school, and public policy influences. *Trends and Issues, 16.* (ERIC Document Reproduction Service No. ED348464)

Bradley, R.H., & Corwyn, R.F. (2002). Socioeconomic status and child development.
Annual Reviews of Psychology, 53, 371–399.

Brooks-Gunn, J., & Duncan, G.J. (1997). The effects of poverty on children. *The Future
of Children: Children and Poverty, 7*(2), 55–71.

Campione, J.C., & Brown, A.L. (1987). Linking dynamic assessment with school achievement. In C.S. Lidz (Ed.), *Dynamic assessment: An international approach to evaluating
learning potential* (pp. 82–115). New York: Guilford Press.

Cioffi, G., & Carney, J.J. (1997). Dynamic assessment of composing abilities in children
with learning disabilities. *Educational Assessment, 4*(3), 175–202.

Cognition and Technology Group and Vanderbilt Learning Technology Center. (1993).
Examining the cognitive challenges and pedagogical opportunities of integrated media systems: Toward a research agenda. *Journal of Special Education Technology, 12*(2), 118–124.

Dalton, B., & Gordon, D. (2007). Universal design for learning. In M.F. Giangreco &
M.B. Doyle (Eds.), *Quick-guides to inclusion: Ideas for educating students with disabilities*
(2nd ed., pp. 123–136). Baltimore: Paul H. Brookes Publishing Co.

Dalton, B., & Pisha, B. (2001, December). *Developing strategic readers: A comparison of
computer-supported versus traditional strategy instruction on struggling readers' comprehension of quality children's literature.* Paper presented at the 51st Annual National Reading
Conference, San Antonio, TX.

Dalton, B., Pisha, B., Eagleton, M., Coyne, P., & Deysher, S. (2002a). *Engaging the text:
Final report to the U.S. Department of Education.* Peabody, MA: CAST.

Dalton, B., Pisha, B., Eagleton, M., Coyne, P., & Deysher, S. (2002b). *A universally designed digital strategic reading environment to enhance reciprocal teaching and improve middle-school struggling readers' comprehension.* Manuscript submitted for publication.

Dalton, B., & Proctor, C.P. (2007). Reading as thinking: Integrating strategy instruction in
a universally designed digital literacy environment. In D.S. McNamara (Ed.), *Reading
comprehension strategies: Theories, interventions, and technologies* (pp. 423–442). Mahwah,
NJ: Lawrence Erlbaum Associates.

Dalton, B., Schleper, D., Kennedy, M., & Lutz, L. (2005). *Shared reading project: Chapter
by chapter—Thinking Reader: Final report.* Wakefield, MA: CAST.

Dalton, B., & Strangman, N. (2006). Improving struggling readers' comprehension through scaffolded hypertexts and other computer-based literacy programs. In M.C. McKenna, L.D. Labbo, R.D. Kieffer, & D. Reinking (Eds.), *International handbook of literacy and technology* (Vol. II, pp. 75–92). Mahwah, NJ: Lawrence Erlbaum Associates.

Elkind, J., Cohen, K., & Murray, C. (1993). Using computer based readers to improve reading comprehension of students with dyslexia. *Annals of Dyslexia, 43*, 238–259.

Englert, C., Raphael, L., Anderson, H., & Stevens, D. (1991). Making strategies and self talk visible: Writing instruction in regular and special education classrooms. *American Educational Research Journal, 28*, 337–372.

Evans, G. (2004). The environment of childhood poverty. *American Psychologist, 59*(2), 77–92.

Farmer, M., Klein, R., & Bryson, S. (1992). Computer assisted reading: Effects of whole-word feedback on fluency and comprehension in readers with severe disabilities. *Remedial Special Education, 13*(2), 50–60.

Feuerstein, R., Rand, Y., Jensen, M., Kaniel, S., Tzuriel, D., Ben-Shachar, N., et al. (1986). Learning potential assessment. *Special Services in the Schools, 2*(2–3), 85–106.

Fullan, M., Hill, P., & Crevola, C. (2006). *Breakthrough.* Thousand Oaks, CA: Corwin Press.

Guthrie, J.T. (2001, March). Contexts for engagement and motivation in reading. *Reading Online, 4*(8). (ERIC Document Reproduction Service No. EJ662484)

Guthrie, J.T., & Cox, K. (2001). Classroom conditions for motivation and engagement in reading. *Education Psychology Review, 13*(3), 283–302.

Higgins, K., Boone, R., & Lovitt, T. (1996). Hypertext support for remedial students and students with disabilities. *Journal of Learning Disabilities, 29*(4), 402–412.

Horney, M., & Anderson-Inman, L. (1999). Supported text in electronic reading environments. *Reading & Writing Quarterly: Overcoming Learning Difficulties, 15*, 127–168.

Jencks, C., & Phillips, M. (Eds.). (1998). *The black–white test score gap.* Washington, DC: Brookings Institute.

Kamil, M., Intrator, S., & Kim, H. (2000). The effects of other technologies on literacy and literacy learning. In M. Kamil, P. Mosenthal, P. Pearson, & R. Barr (Eds.), *Handbook of reading research* (pp. 771–788). Mahwah, NJ: Lawrence Erlbaum Associates.

Leu, D. (2000). Our children's future: Changing the focus of literacy and literacy instruction. *The Reading Teacher, 53*, 424–431.

Lubienski, S.T. (2001, April). *A second look at mathematics achievement gaps: Intersections of race, class, and gender in NAEP data.* Paper presented at the annual meeting of the American Educational Research Association, Seattle.

Lubienski, S.T., & Shelley, M.C., II. (2003, April). *A closer look at U.S. mathematics instruction and achievement: Examinations of race and SES in a decade of NAEP data.* Paper presented at the annual meeting of the American Educational Research Association, Chicago.

Lundberg, I., & Oloffson, A. (1993). Can computer speech support reading comprehension. *Computers in Human Behavior, 9*, 283–293.

Matthew, K. (1997). A comparison of influence of interactive CD-ROM storybooks. *Journal of Research on Computing in Education, 29*(3), 263.

Moses, R.P., & Cobb, C.E. (2001). *Radical equations: Math literacy and civil rights.* Boston: Beacon Press.

Nagy, W., & Scott, J. (2004). Vocabulary processes. In R.R. Ruddell & N. Unrau (Eds.), *Theoretical models and processes of reading* (5th ed., pp. 574–593). Newark, DE: International Reading Association.

Palincsar, A.S., & Brown, A.L. (1984). Reciprocal teaching of comprehension-fostering and comprehension-monitoring activities. *Cognition & Instruction, 1*(1), 117–175.

Palincsar, A.S., & Brown, A.L. (1989). Classroom dialogues to promote self-regulated comprehension. In J. Brophy (Ed.), *Teaching for meaningful understanding and self-regulated learning* (pp. 35–71). Greenwich, CT: JAI.

Palincsar, A.S., & Dalton, B. (2005). Speaking literacy and learning to technology: Speaking technology to literacy and learning. In B. Maloch, J. Hoffman, D. Schallert, C. Fairbanks, & J. Worthy (Eds.), *54th yearbook of the national reading conference* (pp. 83–102). Oak Creek, WI: National Reading Conference.

Paris, S., Cross, D., & Lipson, M. (1984). Informed strategies for learning: A program to improve children's reading awareness and comprehension. *Journal of Educational Psychology, 76*(6), 1239–1252.

Pressley, M. (1997). The cognitive science of reading. *Contemporary Educational Psychology, 22*, 247–259.

Pressley, M. (2006). *Reading instruction that works: The case for balanced teaching.* New York: Guilford Press.

Proctor, C.P., Dalton, B., & Grisham, D.L. (2007). Scaffolding English language learners and struggling readers in a universal literacy environment with embedded strategy instruction and vocabulary support. *Journal of Literacy Research, 39*(1), 71.

Reinking, D., & Schreiner, R. (1985). The effects of computer mediated text on measures of reading comprehension and reading behavior. *Reading Research Quarterly, 20*(5), 536–552.

Reinking, D., McKenna, L., Labbo, L., & Kieffer, R. (Eds.). (1998). *Handbook of literacy and technology: Transformations in a post-typographic world.* Mahwah, NJ: Lawrence Erlbaum Associates.

Rose, D.H., & Meyer, A. (2002). *Teaching every student in the digital age: Universal design for learning.* Alexandria, VA: Association for Supervision and Curriculum Development.

Rosenshine, B., & Meister, C. (1994). Reciprocal teaching: A review of the research. *Review of Educational Research, 64*(4), 479–530.

Strangman, N., & Dalton, B. (2005). Using technology to support struggling readers: A review of the research. In D. Edyburn, K. Higgins, & R. Boone (Eds.), *The handbook of special education technology research and practice* (pp. 545–569). Whitefish Bay, WI: Knowledge by Design.

Thinking Reader [Computer software]. (2004). Watertown, MA: Tom Snyder Productions/Scholastic.

Vygotsky, L.S. (1978). *Mind in society: The development of higher psychological processes.* Cambridge, MA: Harvard University Press.

Wigfield, A., Eccles, J.S., & Rodriguez, D. (1998). The development of children's motivation in school contexts. *Review of Research in Education, 23*, 73–118.

Wood, D., Bruner, J.S., & Ross, G. (1976). The role of tutoring in problem solving. *Journal of Child Psychology and Psychiatry, 17*(2), 89–100.

11

The Dual Coding Theory

Allan Paivio

This chapter presents a dual coding theoretical and prescriptive analysis of early education in nonimpoverished and impoverished environments. The first of two parts begins with the historical background of two intellectual solitudes that eventually came together in dual coding theory (DCT) followed by a summary of the theory and supporting evidence. The second part focuses on a developmental DCT hypothesis that bears most directly on educational applications relevant to the theme of this book. I draw especially on a 2006 update and extension of DCT (Paivio, 2007) as well as earlier publications (Clark & Paivio, 1991; Sadoski & Paivio, 2007) relevant to education.

HISTORICAL BACKGROUND

DCT has its roots in the practical use of imagery as a memory aid 2,500 years ago (Yates, 1966). The memory emphasis evolved into broader applications of imagery aimed at accelerating the acquisition of knowledge. Language was always implicated but became explicitly involved as an educational partner when imagery began to be systematically externalized as pictures. The language emphasis increased during the Renaissance when influences from imagery mnemonics systems and formal logic brought words and things together in a "new logic" in which language was intended to mirror the structure of the world (Rossi, 2000). Religious iconoclasm and other influences raised doubts about the efficacy and morality of imagery and elevated language to the dominant position that it still occupies in education. Modern empirical evidence led to a revival of imagery and the beginnings of an educationally relevant DCT. The following summarizes some of the main events and players in this long drama.

The apex of the imagery mnemonic tradition was Giordano Bruno's 16th-century occult memory system (Yates, 1966), which sought to unify earthly knowledge and the supercelestial world of ideas using variants of the ancient method of loci linked to magical star images organized according to the associative structure of astrology. For example, one Brunian method combined 1) a square architectural system of rooms subdivided into places for storing images of everything in the physical world with 2) a round "Lullian" memory device (Yates, 1966), in which moveable concentric wheels were used like a slide ruler to combine different subjects and predicates to generate new propositions. Bruno's version of the round system contained the celestial figures and images that were to animate, organize, and unify the earthly images contained in the memory rooms.

Bruno's writings directly inspired Tommaso Campanella's (1602) philosophical utopia, *The City of the Sun,* in which images externalized as pictures were used entirely for educational purposes. In the story, the city itself serves as the basis for the classical mnemonic system. Earthly knowledge is represented in innumerable pictures and explanations that adorn outer walls, temples, and galleries of the city. There are mathematical figures; pictures of the seas and rivers; specimens of minerals, trees, herbs, wines, and animals of all kinds; representations of weather phenomena; depictions of mechanical arts; and historically important people. Teachers provide verbal instruction by reading aloud explanatory verses that accompany the pictures and by reading from one great book. We see later that it is not much of a conceptual stretch to interpret Campanella's pictorial–verbal educational system in dual coding theoretical terms.

The great educational pioneer Jan Amos Comenius took the further step of concretizing Campanella's instructional system in actual pictures and descriptions. His book *Orbis Sensualium Pictus* ("The World Explained in Pictures") was the mother of all children's picture textbooks. First published in Nuremburg in 1658, it has been used over the past three centuries as the model for more than 200 editions in 26 languages. The *Orbis* was intended as a visual textbook for learning Latin and other languages. It contains none of the occult elements of its imagery ancestors but is instead a straightforward summary of the world in 150 pictures with titles. The objects in the pictures are numbered and accompanied by parallel columns of labels and short sentences describing the numbered objects, thus explaining about 2,000 words from different domains (e.g., astronomical, animal, plant, occupations, abstract notions).

The *Orbis* reflected Comenius's commitment to concretization as an educational method. He argued that teachers must enable children to have direct experience with things, for

> Things are essential, words only accidental; things are the body, words but the garment; things are the kernel, words the shell and husk. Both should be presented to the intellect at the same time, but particularly the things, since they are as much objects of understanding as is language. (Comenius, 1896 translation, p. 267; cited in Piaget, 1993)

DCT and its educational implications parallel the historical emphasis on concretization of knowledge through imagery and pictures; however, the mnemonists who inspired Campanella and Comenius learned about the effectiveness of imagery from their own experiences and historical anecdotes. They did not know whether it worked better than verbal methods advocated over the centuries. Moreover, although Comenius envisaged a full-scale science of education, he did not develop that science even as applied to the concretization principle he espoused. Today, we have ample scientific evidence and a more explicit theoretical framework in which to embed the facts.

WHAT IS DUAL CODING THEORY?

Cognition, according to DCT, involves the activity of two distinct subsystems, shown in Figure 11.1—a verbal system specialized for dealing directly with language and a nonverbal (imagery) system specialized for dealing with nonlinguistic objects and events. The systems are assumed to be composed of internal representational units, called *logogens* and *imagens,* that correspond to verbal and nonverbal perceptual-motor units and are activated when one recognizes, manipulates, or just thinks about words or things. The representations are modality spe-

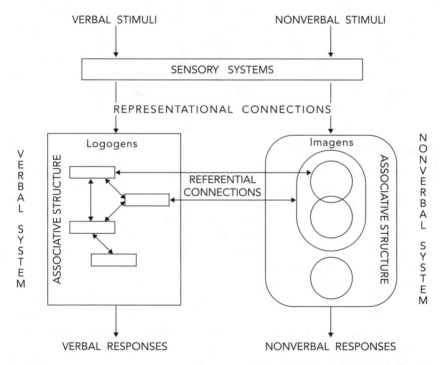

Figure 11.1. Structural model of dual coding theory showing the representational units and their referential and associative interconnections. The referentially unconnected units correspond to abstract-word *logogens* and "nameless" *imagens,* respectively. (From Paivio, A. [1986/1990]. *Mental representations: A dual coding approach* [p. 67]. New York: Oxford University Press; reprinted by permission of Oxford University Press, Inc.)

cific so that we have different logogens and imagens corresponding to the visual, auditory, haptic (tactile), and motor properties of language and objects. The representations are connected to sensory input and response output systems as well as to each other so that they can function independently or cooperatively to mediate nonverbal and verbal behavior. The representational activity may or may not be experienced consciously as imagery and inner speech.

The theory means that both systems are generally involved in language phenomena. The verbal system is a necessary player in all language games, but it is sufficient in only a few. In the most interesting and meaningful language games, the verbal system draws on the rich knowledge base and gamesmanship of the nonverbal system. Conversely, the nonverbal system cannot play language games on its own, but it can play complex nonverbal "solitaire." The verbal system dominates in some tasks (e.g., crosswords) and the nonverbal imagery system in others (e.g., jigsaw puzzles). *Cognition* is this variable pattern of the interplay of the two systems according to the degree to which they have developed.

The modality-specific nature of DCT distinguishes it from more abstract, common coding theories of cognition. Theories that emphasize the dominance of language arose from religious and educational opposition to imagery during the Renaissance. Such theories peaked in modern behaviorist interpretations of thought as inner speech. Another class of common coding theories postulate abstract mental entities and processes, usually called *propositions* or *schemata*. More complex hybrid theories are essentially augmented forms of dual coding in which verbal and nonverbal representations are connected to an abstract conceptual system of some kind. Much research has been directed at testing DCT against the alternatives.

EMPIRICAL EVIDENCE

DCT research focused initially on memory and soon expanded to other cognitive phenomena. Memory remains crucial, however, because it is the basis of all knowledge and thought. The memory emphasis is further justified here because learning and memory are at the heart of educational goals.

Especially important for DCT and its applications are the beneficial effects of concreteness and imagery on memory. In regard to concreteness, memory performance generally increases uniformly from abstract words (e.g., *truth, justice*) to concrete words (e.g., *chair, lobster*) to objects (or their pictures). In the case of language, the concreteness effect occurs with materials ranging in length from words to sentences to long passages, with concrete memory exceeding abstract memory performance by a 2:1 ratio on average. The concreteness advantage is even more striking in associative memory tasks in which recall of response items is cued by concrete stimulus words or by pictures.

The effects can be explained by two DCT hypotheses. One hypothesis is that nonverbal and verbal codes, being functionally independent, can have additive effects on recall. For example, participants in free recall experiments are likely to name presented objects covertly and thus create a nonverbal (pictorial) and a verbal memory trace. They can also set up a dual verbal–nonverbal memory trace by imaging to concrete words, but this is somewhat less likely than naming pictures, hence the lower memory for concrete words than pictures. Abstract words are difficult to image and therefore are least likely to be dually coded. The expected additive memory benefit of dual coding has been confirmed in numerous experiments (e.g., Paivio, 1975; Paivio & Lambert, 1981), which also suggested that the nonverbal code is mnemonically stronger (contributes more to the additive effect) than the verbal code.

The further benefit of cuing recall by concrete stimuli was predicted from the DCT *conceptual peg hypothesis*, which states that compound images that link pairs (e.g., *monkey–bicycle* imaged as a monkey riding a bicycle) are formed during presentation and are reinstated during recall by a concrete stimulus (e.g., *monkey*), thereby increasing the probability of recalling the response (e.g., *bicycle*). The prediction was first confirmed strongly (Paivio, 1965) using concrete (C) and abstract (A) nouns paired in every stimulus–response combination (CC, CA, AC, AA). The results showed that stimulus concreteness had a much stronger beneficial effect (accounting for 8 times more recall variance) than concreteness of the to-be-recalled responses. The general pattern was replicated with additional controls and other materials, including variously paired pictures and words.

Begg (1972) simultaneously supported both the additivity and conceptual peg hypotheses using adjective–noun phrases that were either concrete and high in imagery value (e.g., *white horse*) or abstract and low in imagery value (e.g., *basic truth*). Participants were asked to recall individual words from the phrases, entire phrases, or one word from each phrase given the other as a cue. Begg reasoned that concrete phrases would be integrated in memory by images (e.g., of a white horse) whereas abstract phrases would be recalled as separate words so that twice as many concrete words as abstract words would be remembered in free recall, with a further increment for concrete words in cued recall because the entire mediating image would be reintegrated by the cues. Begg's free recall results actually exceeded prediction in that recall of concrete phrases was more than double that of abstract phrases, consistent with the image superiority addendum to the code-additivity hypothesis. Moreover, in agreement with the conceptual peg hypothesis, recall was 6 times higher when cued by a concrete word than by an abstract word.

It is important in the present context that the concreteness effects have been obtained with different age groups, with qualifications that are especially notable in the case of picture–word comparisons. For example, language-competent young children do not recall pictures better than words in a free verbal recall task unless they are required to name the pictures during presentation. Presumably they do not spontaneously name pictures as readily as do older individuals. This finding is consistent with a developmental interpretation of DCT, to be explained later.

Even more relevant are the qualifications in associative learning tasks in which pictures can serve as stimulus or response items. The effects for children were systematically studied (Dilley & Paivio, 1968) with preschool, kindergarten, and first-grade children. Five paired associates (e.g., *bird–shoe, hat–star*) were presented in all four stimulus–response combinations of pictures and auditorily presented words (necessary because the sample included children below reading age). Verbal recall was tested by presenting the first item of each pair and requiring the child to recall its partner verbally. Ten alternating study–test trials were given. The most striking result was that recall was much higher for picture–word pairs than for all other combinations and lowest for word–picture pairs, even for the preschool children. The positive effect of pictures as stimuli was consistent with conceptual peg hypothesis. The negative effect of pictures as responses, not obtained with adults, was predicted from the hypothesis that children would experience difficulty in decoding the memory image of an object into the appropriate verbal response.

The role of imagery and dual coding on memory have been directly studied using participants' reports of their imagery and verbal thought processes during a memory task and by instructing them to use different strategies. Sadoski (1985) had third and fourth graders read an unillustrated basal reader story aloud and then answer a series of comprehension questions, retell the story, and report any images recalled from the story either before or after the retelling. The story included a particularly dramatic climax. Children who were questioned prior to story recall and reported a climax image recalled more of the story than those who did not report a climax image. There was no such effect for children who recalled their imagery after recalling the story. Sadoski suggested that the climax image functioned as a conceptual peg for subsequent story recall.

In other studies, dual coding interpretations of concreteness effects have been supported by participants' reports of selective use of imagery strategies to learn concrete material and verbal strategies to learn abstract material. Moreover, instructions to use imagery augment recall, especially for concrete language but even for abstract language if conditions encourage participants to concretize abstract words (e.g., imagine *justice* as a frocked judge).

DCT competitors explain the relevant findings in terms of abstract representations (e.g., propositions, schemata) or general structural and processing correlates of dual coding variables (e.g., concrete materials are processed more deeply, encoded more distinctively, or have more contextual support than abstract material). Evidence (e.g., Paivio, 2007; Richardson, 2003) continues to favor DCT over these other explanations of the critical effects. At the same time, variables emphasized in other theories have long been accepted and investigated from the DCT perspective. For example, contextual variables and distinctiveness of images have been shown to affect performance in different memory tasks in ways that were predicted from DCT. All remain relevant in educational applications of the theory.

Other behavior and neuropsychological studies provide further relevant support for the theory. For example, Thompson and Paivio (1994) showed that object pictures and sounds had additive effects on memory, thereby supporting the DCT assumption that sensory components of multimodal objects are functionally independent. Similar effects have been demonstrated for combinations of other modalities. Brain scan studies have shown that different brain areas are activated by concrete and abstract words as well as by pictures as compared with words in comprehension and memory tasks. Brain scan and lesion studies have uncovered distinct representational substrates for almost every conceivable sensorimotor modality of objects and their attributes, whether accessed directly by perceptual stimuli or indirectly (cross-modally) by words. For example, words that name colors or actions activate the same brain areas as perceived colors and action patterns. Such results strongly support the functional and structural reality of multimodal imagens and logogens as described previously—our brains apparently "contain" auditory, haptic, and motor imagens and logogens, which are housed in different locations and accessed by different neural pathways.

DUAL CODING THEORY
COGNITIVE DEVELOPMENTAL HYPOTHESIS

Cognitive growth according to DCT is based on multiple learning processes of observation, classical conditioning, operant learning, and imitation. It involves progressive elaboration of cognitive representations and processes from a nonverbal base to dual coding systems that include language as well. The salient stages are identified in the following hypothesis: Dual coding development begins with the formation of a substrate of nonverbal representations and imagery derived from the child's observations and behaviors related to concrete objects and events and relations among them. Language builds on this foundation and remains functionally connected to it as referential connections are being formed so that the child responds to object names in the presence or absence of the objects and begins to name and describe them (even in their absence). The events, relations, and behaviors are dynamically organized (repeated with variations) and thereby display natural syntax that gets incorporated into the imagery as well. The natural syntax is enriched by motor components derived from the child's actions, which have their own patterning. This basic stage becomes elaborated as function words are acquired and intraverbal networks expand through usage. Abstract verbal skills are eventually attained so that language becomes relatively autonomous, free of dependence on situational contexts and imagery.

The growth can be described more generally as a bootstrapping process in which dual coding systems pull themselves upward using their own resources, thus constituting an increasingly complex and powerful feed-forward system. The idea is compatible with the Herbartian concept of apperceptive mass, a knowledge structure that grows with experience. The concept greatly influenced education and was reflected as well in the Piagetian concepts of assimilation and accom-modation of new information with schemata. The difference here is that DCT emphasizes the functional importance of the nonverbal and verbal components of the growing apperceptive mass (Paivio, 2007). Moreover, unlike the schema-based Piagetian concepts, the DCT sensorimotor systems are modality specific rather than amodal and abstract.

All developmental stages are empirically supported. Nonverbal cognitive representations manifest themselves early in recognition responses (e.g., habitua-tion) to people and objects before there is any hint of language. Language shows up later in name-related behaviors such as looking at or searching for named ob-jects—proof of referential connections between logogens and imagens. A glim-mer of autonomous verbal behavior shows up early in vocal mimicry of speech sounds, including one's own (i.e., *echolalia*), but it appears more clearly later in the verbal associative skills involved in comprehension and production of se-quences of two or more words, some of which can be classified as grammatical.

The grammatical phase was supported most directly by Moeser and Bregman (1973) in an experiment in which participants learned a miniature arti-ficial grammar with or without syntax-correlated referents. Participants who re-ceived different sentence exemplars presented only as strings of nonsense words showed no learning after 3,200 trials. Those who saw the sentences along with syntax-correlated referent pictures showed rapid learning and could subsequently learn new instances from verbal contexts alone. The authors noted that their re-sults were consistent with predictions from the dual coding analysis of syntax learning just described, particularly the conclusion that "the grammars first learned by children will be 'tied to' the syntax of concrete objects and events . . . via the medium of imagery . . . and only later will more abstract grammars emerge" (Paivio, 1971, pp. 437–438). Moeser and Bregman's data have been carefully reexamined from a mental-models perspective on language that is com-patible with DCT (Strømnes, 2006).

EDUCATIONAL APPLICATIONS OF DUAL CODING THEORY

The developmental hypothesis is a natural bridge to the educational applications of DCT because the hypothesis contrasts with developmental assumptions that apparently underlie mainstream approaches to education in western countries. The following section 1) spells out the educational implications of the DCT hy-pothesis, 2) summarizes the contrasting mainstream assumptions, and 3) reviews educational research explicitly related to DCT.

The important practical aspect of the DCT developmental analysis is its stress on the early development of the nonverbal system as the foundation for later cognitive skills that include language as well. The early development is based on sensorimotor experiences with concrete objects and events. It follows that cog-nitive growth depends on the richness of the early nonverbal experiences, increasingly associated with the language experience necessary for the development of the verbal side of a complete dual-coding mind. An important corollary is that cognitive growth will not be stimulated as effectively by a disproportionate early emphasis on language experience relative to nonverbal experience.

The early stage of the DCT analysis is consistent with general theoretical views and evidence on the effects of early experience on brain and behavioral development. The views are often traced to Hebb's (1949) suggestion that early visual experience is essential for the development of typical perception and promotes brain plasticity that facilitates learning and memory later on. These views influenced animal and human research in the 1950s and1960s, which showed that enriched early experience induced physiological and anatomical brain changes and also improved learning and memory. The experience-induced brain changes, however, also occurred even in adult rats and humans. Moreover, they are domain-specific so that, for example, early musical experience produces growth in brain areas involved in musical skills. Also relevant is the research by Ericsson (1996) and his colleagues that early and sustained deliberate practice is necessary for high-level performance skills in various nonverbal as well as verbal domains. Such results suggest that enriched experience is responsible for the formation of specific nonverbal cognitive representations, such as Hebbian cell assemblies or DCT imagens, but there is no direct evidence for such interpretations.

Earlier (Paivio, 1986), I concluded similarly that the evidence is unclear on the stronger DCT hypothesis that the growth of the verbal system depends on the richness of a nonverbal base. This is still the case, although there is some agreement on the general hypothesis. For example, McCune suggested that "dynamic event word meanings based on prelinguistic cognition further provide the meanings observed in verbs of early sentences" (2006, p. 233), and Neuman (2001) emphasized the role of knowledge in early literacy. Somewhat paradoxically, McCune (2006) also proposed that prelinguistic cognition is "nonconceptual, with children dependent on language [dynamic event words] to mold this . . . early cognition toward concepts" (p. 233). The ambiguity apparently hinges on a distinction between meanings and concepts, which we need not consider.

The contrasting emphasis on the primacy of language experience in education programs in western countries can be seen even in programs designed especially for socially disadvantaged children. For example, the Head Start educational programs for preschoolers from low-income families in the United States have always focused on literacy, language, and numeracy skills. In their research review, Barnett and Hustedt (2005) find mixed support for lasting benefits in subsequent school achievement and only modest improvement in children's development. For example, early increases in intelligence quotient (IQ) score typically fade out over time. The "modest" nature of improvements could also reflect the language emphasis of the programs. As noted in the final public address by the late Michael Pressley, there is a similar emphasis in the No Child Left Behind (NCLB) Act (PL 107-110), which "favors teaching phonemic awareness, phonics, fluency, vocabulary, and comprehension strategies, with basically no mention of anything else" (Pressley, 2006). He questioned whether there is an effective classroom in the United States that focused so heavily on those skills and suggested that "it would help if efforts were made to ensure that targeted preschoolers experience the cultural activities that provide conversational opportunities for many advantaged parents and preschoolers, such as trips to zoos, museums, shows, bookstores—and even quality toy stores!" (pp. 7–8). From the DCT perspective, this recommendation emphasizes experiences that particularly stimulate growth of the nonverbal side of dual coding systems.

As evidence for his recommendation, Pressley referred to a widely cited study by Campbell and Ramey (1994). Black infants were provided with an 8-hour-per-day intervention involving exercises designed to enhance perceptual motor as well as cognitive and language skills. The intervention resulted in significant and lasting gains in IQ. For example, 87% of the children exposed to the intervention had IQ scores in the normal range at age 12 as compared with 57% of control children.

Next, consider instructional variables and principles specifically relevant to DCT. As mentioned previously, participants in experiments can be prompted to use imagery and dual coding variables effectively in memory and other cognitive tasks. Can such variables be similarly helpful in general and remedial school settings? Early educators certainly thought so, and modern educational research justifies their recommendations. More specifically, the evidence supports the DCT prescriptive principles of fostering the development of verbal and nonverbal systems by concretizing abstract verbal information on the one hand and verbalizing to concrete information on the other. I summarize the main conclusions in regard to literacy and other skills that follow from comprehensive reviews of the research literature (Paivio, 2007; Sadoski & Paivio, 2001) and focusing in more detail on specific studies that are especially pertinent to the theme of this book.

Reading Skills

Beginning readers learn to read concrete words by sight much faster when the words are accompanied by referent pictures than when paired only with their pronunciations. Concrete verbal material enhances reading comprehension and recall in children and adults. Concrete advance organizers (e.g., brief written texts read prior to other texts) improve comprehension and recall of instructional text. Such results presumably reflect the various contributions of concreteness-evoked imagery and dual coding to the meaningfulness, memorability, and retrievability of information in text.

Instructing learners to form images during reading further enhances reading comprehension and vocabulary learning. Combining pictures, mental imagery, and verbal elaboration is even more effective in promoting understanding and learning from text by students ranging from grade school to university level. For example, consistent with DCT, Purnell and Solman (1991) reported additive effects of text and illustrations on the comprehension of technical material by high school students. On the basis of such results, Mayer (1999) made the following recommendations about multimedia learning: 1) use words and pictures rather than words alone, 2) present pictures and corresponding words or narrations close together in space or time, 3) minimize extraneous (irrelevant) details, and 4) present words as speech rather than on-screen text in animations (presumably to minimize modality-specific interference). These recommendations accord with the practical implications of DCT.

Written Composition

The use of concreteness, imagery, and dual coding makes students' writing more readable and memorable (cf. Hillocks, 1986). Such verbal associative techniques as listing relevant words that could be used in writing about a topic and practice combining sentences improve such features as organization and syntactic fluency of writing.

Remedial Literacy Education

Methods that implicate dual coding principles have been used in remedial education for learning difficulties. The methods can all be classified as augmentative aids in that they supplement traditional classroom teaching methods. All make use of nonverbal stimuli and some encourage use of imagery. Remediation has traditionally focused on decoding because readers must be able to recognize printed words before they can understand their meaning. Decoding ability is measured by tests that require reading words or naming letters aloud. Comprehension tests require understanding what words and text mean. It is relevant that decoding and comprehension are not highly correlated. Statistically, the respective tests cluster under two different factors (with subcategories within each). A striking example of dissociation of the two abilities is that some people with Asperger syndrome are "hyperlexics" who can read aloud extraordinarily well and yet not understand what they are reading.

Lindamood-Bell Learning Processes is a private remedial education company that developed reading programs that fit well with DCT (e.g., Lindamood, Bell, & Lindamood, 1997). Phonemic awareness is taught by associating phonemes with motor acts, pictures of the mouth, and descriptive labels (e.g., "lip poppers" for /p/ and /b/). The positions of the phonemes in words and longer sequences are taught using colored blocks. Comprehension is taught through a program of visualizing and verbalizing that is explicitly related to DCT (Bell, 1991). Instruction entails progressive build-up of imagery to larger and larger text segments—words, phrases, sentences, texts—with learners being encouraged to describe their images in increasing detail. Higher-order comprehension involved in inference, prediction, and evaluation is dealt with through imagination and verbal elaboration. This instructional technique thus teaches learners how to concretize text using imagery and dual coding as they read.

The strongest evidence for the efficacy of the Lindamood-Bell approach comes from a multischool augmentative intervention program that particularly emphasized visualization–verbalization procedures. The intervention dramatically raised the reading performance of students in Grades 3, 4, and 5 of low reading achievement schools in the Pueblo School District in Colorado so that the schools eventually outperformed other comparable Colorado schools in tests of reading (Sadoski & Willson, 2006). Figure 11.2 shows the improvement over years for students who started in Grade 3, thus demonstrating that DCT-related instructional techniques are effective with 8-year-olds, the upper range of the population targeted in this book. In clinical settings, visualization–verbalization has been used successfully to improve various reading test scores with children as young as 6 years (Nanci Bell, personal communication, August 2006.)

Mathematics

Clark and Campbell (1991) used dual coding mechanisms to develop a general theory of number processing. The theory emphasizes the concrete basis of number concepts and the roles of associative mechanisms and imagery in performing numerical operations. The basic dual coding processes have long been used in teaching arithmetic. Children first learn to name numerals and then their meanings by associating them with groups of objects or their pictures. They learn addition, subtraction, and multiplication concretely by adding marbles to a pile or taking them from it. They literally *calculate,* which derives from the Latin root

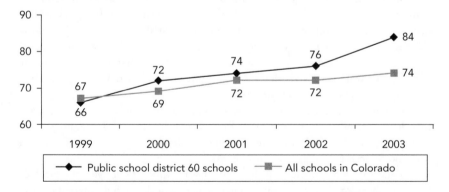

Figure 11.2. Reading performance test scores over 4 years for students in Pueblo School District 60 in the state of Colorado who, in Grade 3, started a multischool augmentative reading intervention program using the Lindamood-Bell Learning Processes programs. Their growth curve significantly exceeds that of students in other comparable Colorado schools (Sadoski & Willson, 2006). (*Note:* Based on data that are publicly available from the State of Colorado and Pueblo School District 60.)

that refers to small stones used in reckoning on an abacus. They learn corresponding verbal number associations by rote memorization of addition, subtraction, and multiplication tables. Productive extensions to large numbers and columns of numbers require the further operation of carrying products and so forth. Learning fractions builds on an understanding of division, similarly acquired by concrete examples translated into verbal and/or numerical operations. All of these skills entail development of increasingly long and varied representations (logogens) for number names and operators (rapid production of *two times three equals six* implies activation of a corresponding sentence-length logogen) as well as imagens of numerals and operators. Rods of different lengths and colors (Cuisenaire & Gattegno, 1954) have been used for teaching addition, subtraction, fractions, and so forth because they represent abstract relations and yet can be easily manipulated and imaged by children. Algebra is made easier by transforming equations into geometric shapes. In sum, effective mathematical education relies on appropriate concretization of abstract symbols and relations (Skemp, 1987).

Mathematician John Mighton (2003) started an educational charity called Junior Undiscovered Math Prodigies (JUMP) for elementary school students who had experienced difficulty learning mathematics in their schools. The program involves systematic concretization of mathematical concepts and operations, many of which (e.g., use of pie charts and box diagrams) are familiar to all teachers. What is different in the JUMP program is that they are used systematically so that every student masters the operations as applied to one problem before moving to more complex ones. Anecdotal evidence shows that individuals and whole classes of students classified as slow learners excelled in mathematics following the JUMP intervention. More formal studies of the program are presently in the works.

In addition to its remedial reading programs already described, Lindamood-Bell Learning Processes has developed a remedial mathematics program (Tuley & Bell, 1997). The program is similar to JUMP in its emphasis on concretization of mathematical operations and concepts. It differs from JUMP in that it teaches children how to use visualization (mental imagery) to represent numbers and operations. The program proceeds from 1) concrete experience using number lines, cubes, and the like, to 2) imaging the entities and operations, to 3) computation. The steps are depicted as a "math ladder," with imaging numerals at the lowest rung and fractions at the top. Learners climb the steps at their own pace. As in the case of JUMP, much anecdotal evidence supports the effectiveness of the Lindamood-Bell Learning Processes math program.

CONCLUSION

Education applications of DCT call for more systematic research on effects of dual coding variables at different age levels. Evidence is especially lacking on the importance of richness of early nonverbal experience on the development of language and cognition in general. Systematic observations and experiments should provide information on the number and variety of objects and events with which the child interacts and relate these to cognitive skills that presumably reflect growth in the "imagen family" (i.e., imagens of different modalities). Direct detection of imagery skills would be possible in infants less than a year old using such tasks as visual exploration of spatial transformations (Lew, Foster, Bremner, Slavin, & Green, 2005). The effects of early nonverbal experience on the development of vocabulary and other language skills could be similarly studied more systematically than has been the case thus far. Direct evidence that imagery and dual coding mediate effects at this early language stage would require adaptations of such tasks as selecting a named object from an array (analogues of picture vocabulary tests) or searching for an absent named object. One could also explore how early children begin to show evidence of more complex cooperative interplay of verbal and nonverbal systems, as in the visualization–verbalization effects already demonstrated with school-age children.

REFERENCES

Barnett, W.S., & Hustedt, J.T. (2005). Head Start's lasting benefits. *Infants & Young Children, 18*, 16–24.

Begg, I. (1972). Recall of meaningful phrases. *Journal of Verbal Learning and Verbal Behavior, 11*, 431–439.

Bell, N. (1991). *Visualizing and verbalizing for language comprehension and thinking.* Paso Robles, CA: NBI Publications.

Campanella, T. (1602). *The city of the sun.* Retrieved February 22, 2004, from http://www.levity.com/alchemy/citysun.html

Campbell, F.A., & Ramey, C.T. (1994). Effects of early intervention on intellectual and academic achievement: A follow-up study of children from low-income families. *Child Development, 65*, 684–698.

Clark, J.M., & Campbell, J. (1991). Integrated versus modular theories of number skills and acalculia. *Brain and Cognition, 17*, 204–239.

Clark, J.M., & Paivio, A. (1991). Dual coding theory and education. *Educational Psychology Review, 3*, 149–210.

Comenius, J.A. (1896). *The great didactic.* London: Adam & Charles Black.

Cuisenaire, G., & Gattegno, G. (1954). *Numbers in colour.* London: Heinemann.

Dilley, M.G., & Paivio, A. (1968). Pictures and words as stimulus and response items in paired-associate learning in young children. *Journal of Experimental Psychology, 6*, 231–240.

Ericsson, K.A. (Ed.). (1996). *The road to excellence: The acquisition of expert performance in the arts and sciences, sports and games.* Mahwah, NJ: Lawrence Erlbaum Associates.

Hebb, D.O. (1949). *The organization of behavior.* New York: John Wiley & Sons.

Hillocks, G., Jr. (1986). *Research on written composition: New directions for teaching.* Urbana, IL: ERIC Clearinghouse on Reading and Communication Skills and the National Conference on Research in English.

Lew, A.R., Foster, K.A., Bremner, J.G., Slavin, S., & Green, M. (2005). Detection of geometric, but not topological, spatial transformations in 6- to 12-month-old infants in a visual exploration paradigm. *Developmental Psychobiology, 47*, 31–42.

Lindamood, P., Bell, N., & Lindamood, P. (1997). Sensory-cognitive factors in the controversy over reading instruction. *Journal of Developmental Disorders, 1*, 143–182.

Mayer, R.E. (1999). Research-based principles for the design of instructional messages: The case of multimedia explanations. *Document Design, 1*, 7–20.

McCune, L. (2006). Dynamic event words: From common cognition to varied linguistic expression. *First Language, 26*, 233–255.

Mighton, J. (2003). *The myth of ability: Nurturing mathematical talent in every child.* Toronto: House of Anansi Press.

Moeser, S.D., & Bregman, A.S. (1973). Imagery and language acquisition. *Journal of Verbal Learning and Verbal Behavior, 12*, 91–98.

Neuman, S.B. (2001). The role of knowledge in early literacy. *Reading Research Quarterly, 36*, 468–475.

No Child Left Behind Act of 2001, PL 107-110, 115 Stat. 1425, 20 U.S.C. §§ 6301 *et seq.*

Paivio, A. (1965). Abstractness, imagery, and meaningfulness in paired-associate learning. *Journal of Verbal Learning and Verbal Behavior, 4*, 32–38.

Paivio, A. (1971). *Imagery and verbal processes.* New York: Holt, Rinehart, and Winston.

Paivio, A. (1975). Coding distinctions and repetition effects in memory. In G.H. Bower (Ed.), *The psychology of learning and motivation* (Vol. 9, pp. 29–41). New York: Academic Press.

Paivio, A. (1986). *Mental representations: A dual coding approach.* New York: Oxford University Press.

Paivio, A. (2007). *Mind and its evolution: A dual coding theoretical interpretation.* Mahwah, NJ: Lawrence Erlbaum Associates.

Paivio, A., & Lambert, W. (1981). Dual coding and bilingual memory. *Journal of Verbal Learning & Verbal Behavior, 20*, 532–539.

Piaget, J. (1993). *John Amos Comenius.* Retrieved February 29, 2004, from http/www.ibe. unesco.org/publicationsThinkersPdc/comeniuse.pdf

Pressley, M. (2006, April). *What the future of reading research could be.* Paper presented at the International Reading Association's Reading Research 2006, Chicago.

Purnell, K.N., & Solman, R.T (1991). The influence of technical illustrations on students' comprehension of geography. *Reading Research Quarterly, 26*, 277–299.

Richardson, J.T.E. (2003). Dual coding versus relational processing in memory for concrete and abstract words. *European Journal of Cognitive Psychology, 15*, 481–50l.

Rossi, P. (2000). (with S. Clucas, Trans.). *Logic and the art of memory: The quest for a universal language.* Chicago: University of Chicago Press.

Sadoski, M. (1985). The natural use of imagery in story comprehension and recall: Replication and extension: *Reading Research Quarterly, 20*, 658-667.

Sadoski, M., & Paivio, A. (2001). *Imagery and text: A dual coding theory of reading and writing.* Mahwah, NJ: Lawrence Erlbaum Associates.

Sadoski, M., & Willson, V.L. (2006). Effects of a theoretically-based large scale reading intervention in a multicultural urban school district. *American Educational Research Journal, 43*, 137–154.

Skemp, R.R. (1987). *The psychology of learning mathematics.* Hillsdale, NJ: Lawrence Erlbaum Associates.

Strømnes, F.J. (2006). *The fall of the word and the rise of the mental model: A reinterpretation of the recent research on the use of language and spatial cognition.* Frankfurt-am Main, Germany: Peter Lang Publishing.

Thompson, V., & Paivio, A. (1994). Memory for pictures and sounds: Independence of auditory and visual codes. *Canadian Journal of Experimental Psychology, 48*, 380–398.

Tuley, K., & Bell, N. (1997). *On cloud nine: Visualizing and verbalizing for math.* San Luis Obispo, CA: Gander Publishing.

Yates, (1966). *The art of memory.* London: Routledge & Kegan Paul.

12

Success for All, Embedded Multimedia, and the Teaching–Learning Orchestra

Robert E. Slavin, Nancy A. Madden, and Bette Chambers

Every year, 4 million children enter our nation's kindergartens. These children are bright, curious, and highly motivated. They expect to succeed in school and are eager to do so. As time goes on, however, many of these children fall by the wayside. Some had poor preparation at home or in preschool and are already at risk. Some will fail to learn to read in the early years. Some will succeed in the early years but fail in the upper-elementary or secondary grades as learning demands increase. Some will fail due to motivational or behavior problems. By high school, only a fraction of those bright, eager kindergartners is still succeeding and fully engaged as learners.

The winnowing process from kindergarten to middle school happens in all communities, but it is most relentless for the children of the poor. At each developmental hurdle, children who are disadvantaged are more likely to fail, and there are fewer forms of rescue if they do.

Since 1980, the academic performance of poor and minority children has been largely stagnant. On the 2005 National Assessment of Educational Progress (NAEP), reading performance of fourth and eighth graders was almost identical to what it was in 1980, and although mathematics performance had risen, substantial gaps still existed between poor and nonpoor children.

This chapter was written under funding from the Institute of Education Sciences (Grant No. R305A040082). However, any opinions expressed are those of the author and do not necessarily represent IES positions or policies.

Since the early 1980s, the dominant approach to education reform has been to increase levels of accountability. Accountability is important in focusing attention on the outcomes of education, not just the inputs; however, increasing accountability alone is not an effective approach. To increase achievement, we need to improve the programs and practices used every day by teachers at all levels. This, in turn, requires a focus on research and development to create and rigorously evaluate new approaches capable of making a substantial difference in student outcomes and then establish policies that encourage educators to use programs and practices with strong evidence of effectiveness. This chapter discusses the concept of evidence-based reform, describes the history and future plans of the Success for All comprehensive reform model and embedded multimedia as an example of evidence-based reform in practice, and proposes new research on instructional designs to meet the needs of all students.

EVIDENCE-BASED REFORM

Imagine that each year, every hospital in America received a rating based on its success rate with 100 key types of operations and that hospitals with low success rates would be subject to various sanctions until they met adequate yearly progress goals in each area. Now imagine further that at the same time, funding for medical research was slashed by 90% and the Food and Drug Administration (FDA) was abolished!

This situation roughly describes the condition of education. Accountability may or may not be a good idea for hospitals, but what drives progress in medicine is not accountability, it is research and development (R&D) and policies (e.g., those enforced by the FDA) that ensure that the results of high-quality research are immediately consequential for practice. In education, there is plenty of accountability, but investment in R&D is miniscule compared with that in medicine, agriculture, technology, or other successful fields. Furthermore, when rigorous research does validate educational programs, there is little incentive for schools to use them, or to stop using programs found to be ineffective.

The role of evidence is increasing in education but only at the margins. The Comprehensive School Reform legislation in the late 1990s provided funding for "proven, comprehensive" school reforms, but the "proven" part was soon forgotten. The No Child Left Behind Act of 2001 (PL 107-110), and especially Reading First, made constant reference to programs "based on scientifically based research," but Reading First ended up instead with more than 95% of funded schools using traditional basal textbooks lacking evidence of effectiveness. The Institute of Education Sciences of the U.S. Department of Education has been funding many more high-quality evaluations of practical programs, and it has established the What Works Clearinghouse, which is intended to review scientific research on educational programs. Eventually, evidence will be the engine that drives educational reform, as it is in so many other fields, but we are far from that situation today.

Success for All: Evidence-Based Reform in Practice

One example that illustrates both the potential and the pitfalls of evidence-based reform in practice is Success for All, a comprehensive reform model for elementary and middle schools focused primarily on reading. Begun in 1987, Success for All was designed from the outset to assemble practices that had been validated in research into a coherent approach to schoolwide reform (see Slavin, Madden, & Datnow, 2007). For example, the program makes extensive use of effective forms of cooperative learning (Slavin, Hurley, & Chamberlain, 2001; Slavin, 1995); proactive classroom management and a rapid pace of instruction (Evertson, Emmer, & Worsham, 2003); systematic, synthetic phonics in the early grades (Adams, 1990); and metacognitive reading comprehension skills in the upper-elementary and middle grades (Pressley, 2003). It uses one-to-one tutoring for struggling students (Wasik & Slavin, 1993); frequent, curriculum-based assessment (Fuchs, Fuchs, Hamlett, & Stecker, 1991); and a cross-grade grouping strategy called the Joplin Plan (Gutiérrez & Slavin, 1992). Each school has an onsite facilitator who uses coaching strategies adapted from Joyce and Showers (1995). Each of these elements was selected for the model after a careful and continuous review of scientific research in each area.

After the program itself was assembled and implemented, it was evaluated in more than 50 experimental-control comparisons, 30 of which were third-party evaluations, and a national, randomized evaluation in 35 schools found positive effects on reading outcomes (Borman et al., 2007). Reviews of research on comprehensive school reform have uniformly concluded that Success for All is one of just two programs with the strongest evidence of effectiveness (the other is Direct Instruction) (Borman, Hewes, Overman, & Brown, 2003; Comprehensive School Reform Quality Center [CSRQ], 2005; Herman, 1999). A longitudinal study followed Baltimore students in five Success for All and five control elementary schools to eighth grade, when they had been out of the program for at least 3 years. Former Success for All students were still significantly higher in reading achievement and were far less likely to have been retained or assigned to special education (Borman & Hewes, 2003).

Success for All has been widely disseminated. In 2007–2008, it was in about 1,200 elementary and middle schools in 47 states, serving mostly high-poverty Title I urban and rural schools. It is generally used in the highest-poverty schools in a given district rather than districtwide, but it is used throughout a few districts, including Kansas City, Missouri; Hartford, Connecticut; Lawrence, Massachusetts; and Long Branch, New Jersey.

Embedded Multimedia and Computer-Assisted Tutoring

The research on Success for All finds the program to be highly effective on average, but there remains great variation in outcomes among schools due to variations in quality and completeness of implementation (see Nunnery et al., 1996). Since 2001, the nonprofit Success for All Foundation has been working on applications of technology intended to make the outcomes of Success for All both larger and more reliable.

The essential concept behind these applications is the use of technology to enhance the performance of teachers and tutors, not to replace them. This "lesson-embedded technology" has two forms: 1) *embedded multimedia,* which refers to video[1] segments threaded into teachers' lessons, used to give students a clear mental image of the concepts being taught, and 2) *computer-assisted tutoring,* which refers to computer software designed to help a human tutor work with struggling children, providing assessment, multimedia content, scaffolded practice activities, record keeping, lesson planning, and professional development.

A key attribute of lesson-embedded technology is the intention to help the teacher or tutor do a better job of teaching rather than substituting for the human teacher. In fact, one explicit purpose of lesson-embedded technology is ongoing professional development for the teacher. The idea is that by showing *students* content and processes every day, *teachers* are also seeing the content and processes and are receiving constant reinforcement of ideas they learned about in workshops. For example, in lessons involving cooperative learning, embedded multimedia can show cooperative groups working effectively on many objectives and in many contexts, clarifying for teachers as well as students exactly what students are expected to be doing in cooperative groups. The video also models a playful but task-oriented affective tone within cooperative groups and a focus on giving groupmates elaborated explanations rather than just answers (Webb & Palincsar, 1996). Similarly, embedded multimedia can show actors or puppets modeling use of metacognitive skills, talking through their thinking or problem-solving processes, or modeling creativity. Video threaded into daily lessons and tutoring sessions models the content in a compelling and pedagogically valid way, but more than this, it gives both students and teachers daily visual models of how to effectively play their respective roles.

Seen as professional development, lesson-embedded technology solves a key problem of transfer from the developer of a classroom or tutoring program to the children who experience it. Traditional professional development resembles the children's game Telephone or Whispering Down the Lane, in which a message is garbled as it is passed from person to person. Developers train trainers who work with teachers who teach children, and the original message is diluted at each point of transmission, as illustrated in Figure 12.1. Lesson-embedded technology permits developers to send a clear and consistent message to trainers, teachers, and students. This does not replace workshops, coaching, teacher's learning communities, or other forms of professional development, but it is likely to maintain the integrity and effectiveness of the entire process.

---

[1]The term *video* is used to refer to content on VHS, DVD, or CD.

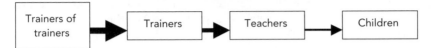

Traditional professional development

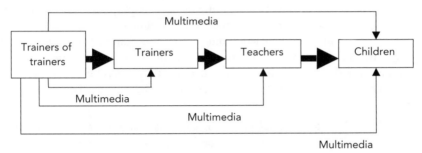

Embedded multimedia professional development

Figure 12.1. Embedded multimedia professional development.

Beyond the professional development aspects of lesson-embedded technology, the direct message to students takes advantage of powerful cognitive effects of linked visual and auditory instruction. Mayer (2001) and his colleagues have demonstrated in dozens of experiments that combining visual content (still pictures or video) with text or auditory content greatly increases learning and retention. This work builds on Paivio's (Clark & Paivio, 1991) dual coding theory, which holds that content learned in two memory systems is retained better than content learned in only one. Furthermore, each memory system has limits in terms of how much it can handle at any given time, so use of linked visual and auditory material "offloads" memory requirements from the auditory system, which is usually overloaded in classroom instruction, to the less overloaded visual system (Mayer & Moreno, 2003). In particular, research is increasingly finding that animations closely linked to text or auditory instruction greatly increase learning and retention (Hoeffler & Leutner, 2006). Neuman's (2006) theory of synergy in multimedia postulates that different media enhance different cognitive strategies, which together support comprehension.

Research on Lesson-Embedded Technology

Three year-long randomized experiments have evaluated outcomes of lesson-embedded technology in first-grade reading. One evaluated embedded multimedia, one computer-assisted tutoring, and one a combination of the two. These are described in the following sections.

Success for All with Embedded Multimedia (Reading Reels)

A study of embedded multimedia was carried out by Chambers, Cheung, Gifford, Madden, and Slavin (2006). First graders in 10 high-poverty, Success for All schools in Hartford, Connecticut, were randomly assigned to use either the Success for All beginning reading program with the embedded multimedia or the standard Success for All beginning reading instruction.

The multimedia content consisted of 30-second to 3-minute skits embedded within the teachers' daily 90-minute lessons. No additional time was added to the lessons to accommodate the multimedia. The purpose of the multimedia content was to directly present to students compelling demonstrations of key elements of beginning reading: letter sounds, sound-blending strategies, and vocabulary. In addition, it was hoped that by showing multimedia content in class, teachers would have constant reinforcement of effective teaching strategies.

The multimedia material, called Reading Reels, includes the following elements.

The Animated Alphabet   Animations teach and reinforce sound–symbol relationships. For example, the animation introducing the /d/ sound features a dinosaur in the shape of a lowercase *d* in a cave, with drops of water dripping on his head. Each drop makes a /d/ sound. After a few drops, the dinosaur roars and the water stops dripping. The pairing of the memorable images, the letter sound, and the letter shape give students many mental pathways to link the letter with its sound.

The Sound and the Furry   Brief skits, using Success for All puppet characters, model the word-blending process, phonemic awareness, spelling, fluency, reading strategies, and cooperative learning routines. For example, a puppet sees a sign that says, "Watch out for stick." He sounds out the word *stick* phonetically. Then, he notices a stick, which he picks up. The stick sticks to his fur, and in trying to get it off he bites it—and then realizes he's in real trouble. More than a hundred such vignettes illustrate sound-blending strategies from simple consonant-vowel-consonant words to multisyllable words.

Word Plays   Live action multimedia skits dramatize important vocabulary concepts from the Success for All beginning reading texts. These skits are particularly designed to help English language learners build the specific vocabulary for the books they will be reading. For example, when children are about to read a story called *A Trip to the Inca Kingdom*, they first see a skit that introduces words such as *coast, llamas, volcanoes,* and *messengers*.

Between the Lions   Puppet skits and animations from the award-winning PBS program *Between the Lions* help teach phonemic awareness, sound–symbol correspondence, and sound blending.

Findings   The pretests were the Peabody Picture Vocabulary Test (PPVT; Dunn & Dunn, 1997) and the Word Identification subtest from the Woodcock Reading Mastery Test–Revised (WRMT-R; Woodcock, 1987). The posttests included the reading fluency test from the Dynamic Indicators of Basic

Early Literacy Skills (DIBELS; Good & Kaminski, 2002) and three scales from the WRMT-R: Word Identification, Word Attack, and Passage Comprehension.

Analysis using hierarchical linear modeling (HLM) showed that the experimental group scored significantly higher than the control group on the Word Attack subtest ($ES = +0.47$). Although the experimental group also scored higher than the control group on Word ID ($ES = +0.23$), Passage Comparison ($ES = +0.20$), and DIBELS ($ES = +0.29$), these differences were not statistically significant in the HLM analysis.

The results partially support the expectation that the addition of embedded multimedia content to a beginning reading program would enhance children's reading achievement. Using a conservative HLM analysis, only one of the four outcome measures, Word Attack, showed significant experimental–control differences, but this is in line with theoretical expectations. Three of the four multimedia segments dealt primarily with letter sounds and sound blending, which are key components of Word Attack.

Computer-Assisted Tutoring (Alphie's Alley)   The Chambers and colleagues (in press) study was undertaken to determine the independent effects of the Alphie's Alley computer-assisted tutoring model. It used random assignment of tutored children within schools to receive tutoring with or without Alphie's Alley. The study took place in 25 Success for All schools located in eight states throughout the United States. In each school, the lowest 40% of first graders on curriculum-based measures were identified as potentially eligible for tutoring and randomly assigned to participate in either Alphie's Alley or control tutoring. The tutors themselves were randomly assigned to either use Alphie's Alley or to continue their usual tutoring strategies, as specified in the Success for All program.

Participants were 412 low-achieving first graders who received tutoring. Twenty-three percent of all tutors were certified teachers, and seventy-seven percent were paraprofessionals.

The tutoring activities in both conditions covered the following skills: phonemic awareness, concepts about print, letter skills, sight words, vocabulary, tracking, fluency, comprehension, and writing. Students in both conditions who experienced difficulties in reading were assigned to daily 20-minute one-to-one tutoring sessions. In the control condition, tutors used paper and pencil activities. In the experimental group, tutors used Alphie's Alley, the computer-assisted tutoring program designed specifically to align with the Success for All curriculum. The use of the technology was the only difference between the groups.

The Alphie's Alley program has four components: assessment, planning, computer activities, and embedded professional development to support implementation.

Assessment   Alphie's Alley assesses children's reading strengths and difficulties in the areas of phonemic awareness, phonics, fluency, and comprehension. It communicates this information on an assessment report for each student, continuously updating information relevant to the student's progress.

Planning   The program suggests a 2-week tutoring plan based on the child's assessment. From the tutoring plan, the student and tutor choose a goal for the student to focus on each week.

Computer Activities   Students work on Alphie's Alley computer activities specifically designed to reinforce skills taught in their core reading program. In some activities, students respond directly on the computer. If they cannot produce a correct answer, the computer gives them progressive scaffolding until they can reach the right answer. In other activities, the student responds to the tutor, who records whether the student's response was correct or not, and then the computer provides scaffolding. Sample activities that students encounter are as follows:

1. *Letter identification and writing*—The computer gives a sound, and the student must select or type a letter or letter combination that makes that sound.

2. *Auditory blending and segmenting*—The computer presents sounds for words, which the student blends into a word for the tutor, or the student breaks down simple words into separate sounds.

3. *Word-level blending*—The computer displays a word, and the student uses sound blending to decode it to the tutor.

4. *Spelling*—The computer says a word (or, at higher levels, a sentence), and the student types it.

5. *Tracking and fluency*—The student reads a storybook on the computer to the tutor using an arrow key to track word by word. The tutor notes errors, and the computer computes words correct per minute.

6. *Comprehension*—The computer displays questions about the stories and graphic organizers, which the student completes.

Embedded Professional Development to Support Implementation
Alphie's Alley offers performance support for tutors in the form of video vignettes and written suggestions on how to help remediate students' particular problems.

Findings   Students were administered scales from the Woodcock-Johnson III Tests of Achievement (Letter-Word Identification [pre- and posttest], Word Attack [posttest]) (Woodcock, McGrew, & Mather, 2000) and the Gray Oral Reading Test, Fourth Edition (GORT) (Fluency and Comprehension [posttest]; Weiderhold & Bryant, 2001). Implementation fidelity of both the regular Success for All tutoring and Alphie's Alley tutoring was rated on a three-point scale: fully implementing, partially implementing, and poorly implementing.

Implementation was variable. Tutors in 13 schools, teaching 203 students (49% of the student sample), were rated as "fully implementing." Those in 9 schools were rated as "partially implementing," and 3 schools were rated as "poorly implementing." Separate analyses by implementation rating showed no program impacts for partial and poor implementers; however, for fully implementing schools, results were generally positive.

Using analyses of covariance, significant positive effects on three of the four independent measures were found, with effect sizes and p-values as follows: Woodcock Letter–Word Identification: $ES = +0.45$, $F(2, 203) = 12.77$, $p < .001$; Woodcock Word Attack: $ES = +0.31$, $F(2, 203) = 3.76$, $p < .05$; and GORT Fluency: $ES = +0.23$, $F(2, 203) = 3.87$, $p < .05$. There were no significant differences on GORT Comprehension ($ES = +0.05$, n.s.).

This finding suggests that when implemented with fidelity, integrating technology to enhance the work of human tutors can lead to greater reading impacts than those likely to be achieved by tutors alone. Over time, tutors using the tool are likely to come to resemble the high implementers who achieved excellent outcomes in the first year.

Combining Embedded Multimedia and Computer-Assisted Tutoring

A third study evaluating the effects of embedded multimedia was carried out by Chambers and colleagues (in press). This study used random assignment of individual first graders to conditions. Low-achieving students were assigned to receive tutoring with or without computer-assisted support and embedded multimedia. Students who did not qualify for tutoring were randomly assigned to embedded multimedia or control conditions within Success for All schools.

The study took place in two large, multitrack, year-round schools that had been implementing Success for All for several years. On entry into first grade, 159 children in the two schools were assigned at random to one of four tracks. The tracks were then randomly assigned to treatments (technology or no technology). Within the sample, the 60 lowest-achieving students received tutoring. The remaining 99 students were the participants for the multimedia-only study.

In the experimental group, all students were instructed in reading using Success for All with embedded multimedia (Reading Reels), and, for the tutored students, computer-assisted tutoring (Alphie's Alley), as described previously. Students in the control treatment experienced Success for All without any multimedia content. Students were pre- and posttested on the Letter–Word Identification scale of the Woodcock-Johnson III Tests of Achievement and posttested on the Word Attack scale in addition to the GORT.

On analyses of covariance, controlling for Letter–Word Identification pretests, tutored first graders who received both technology enhancements scored significantly higher on all four measures (median $ES = +0.53$). Nontutored students who experienced just the embedded multimedia scored significantly higher than nontutored control students on two measures (median $ES = +0.27$). The results suggest that using technology to enhance rather than replace teacher instruction may accelerate children's learning.

The results of these three studies on lesson-embedded technology justify optimism about the potential of technology to play a different role in education, one of enhancing rather than replacing teachers' lessons. Threading multimedia content throughout class lessons and tutoring sessions appears to help make concepts clear and memorable to children, taking advantage of the well-established finding that linked visual and auditory content is retained better than either type of content alone.

The effects of the computer-assisted tutoring in these studies provide more positive support for the use of computers in teaching reading than reviews of computer-aided instruction have generally found (Kulik, 2003). Perhaps the role of assistant to the tutor, rather than a replacement for the tutor, might be a more effective application of the technology.

Other Applications of Lesson-Embedded Technology

Three additional applications of lesson-embedded technology are in development and are being evaluated in large-scale experiments.

Writing Wings   Writing Wings (Slavin, Madden, Chambers, & Haxby, in press) is a creative writing program for Grades 3–5 based on a writing process model (Calkins, 1983; Graves, 1983; Harris & Graham, 1996). Its major focus is cooperative learning, with students working in four-member teams to help each other plan, draft, revise, edit, and "publish" compositions in many genres. The Success for All Foundation is developing embedded multimedia to accompany Writing Wings, primarily to model the cooperative learning process and metacognitive writing skills for students and teachers. Two series of videos are being produced. The *Write-On Dudes* shows a four-puppet team and their human teacher working through the writing process with narrative, factual, and persuasive samples; business letters; newspaper articles; and other genres. Each 5- to 8-minute vignette models teacher instruction, and then a pair of puppets focuses on a particular writing problem. Each puppet character has his or her own characteristic problem: one thinks she has nothing to say, one is excessively verbose, one is poorly organized, and one writes nothing but facts without description. The puppets work with each other and their offbeat teacher, Ms. Inkwell, to overcome their problems in many contexts.

The Language Mechanics is a series of 3- to 5-minute vignettes in which actors humorously explain parts of speech, complete sentences, subject–verb agreement, commas, apostrophes, quotation marks, and other issues of writing mechanics. Writing Wings with embedded multimedia is being evaluated in a randomized experiment involving 25 schools nationwide.

Reading for Knowledge   Reading for Knowledge is a program designed to teach reading of informational texts. It is an adaptation of the Success for All Reading Wings program (Slavin et al., in press). In it, students see live-action vignettes of about 10–15 minutes that illustrate metacognitive reading strategies such as summarization, clarification, prediction, questioning, and comprehension monitoring (Pressley, 2003). For example, a group of students visiting Africa find themselves having to write a summary of a report on leopards that an absent-minded naturalist forgot to complete. The dialogue is designed to model the thinking processes that go into writing summaries as the students debate what to include and what to exclude and how to phrase their summary. A randomized evaluation of Reading for Knowledge is under way.

Team Alphie   Drawing on the dual coding and heightened student engagement of Alphie's Alley, the individualized computer-assisted tutoring program, Team Alphie, adds the power of cooperative learning. In Team Alphie, struggling readers who read at the same level work in pairs to complete practice activities on the computer. They take turns checking each other's accuracy. When the pair has reached mastery, a flag goes up on their computer screen notifying the teacher that the students are ready to have their mastery verified. The computer tracks the students' progress and presents them with activities at their level of functioning. Three to five pairs of students work together in half-hour sessions with a teacher who monitors partners working on the computer, verifies students' mastery of skills, and reteaches concepts when necessary.

INSTRUCTIONAL DESIGN AND EVIDENCE-BASED REFORM

Research on Success for All and on its extensions into lesson-embedded technology are examples of approaches that have potential to fundamentally change education. Other examples include comprehensive school-reform models (CSRQ, 2005; Borman et al., 2003), especially those with extensive student materials, such as Direct Instruction (Adams & Engelmann, 1996). From the perspective of effective uses of technology, the concept of lesson-embedded technology appears to have potential in creating more effective instructional and tutoring environments for children. Studies of technology applications have overwhelmingly evaluated computer-assisted instruction models that supplement classroom instruction but have little role for the teacher. Although such applications have modest benefits in mathematics (Kulik, 2003; Slavin & Lake, in press), they have few if any effects on reading (Kulik, 2003). Trailing-edge video technology appears to have particular promise for helping teachers do a more effective job in the classroom, but all sorts of technology—computers, interactive whiteboards, and so forth—need to be designed into the fabric of classroom instruction, not just used to provide occasional supplements.

Success for All, lesson-embedded technology, and other forms of systematic instructional design have transformative potential because they are replicable across a broad range of circumstances. If national educational policies began to encourage schools to adopt programs with strong evidence of effectiveness, there could be an enormous demand for programs in every subject and at every grade level. More importantly, building on many developments in technology, multimedia, instruction, cognition, and comprehensive school reform, we could begin a process of R&D, evaluation, and dissemination of effective programs that could create a dynamic for progress in education capable of progressively solving its longstanding problems. The remainder of this chapter discusses some ideas about how instructional designs of the future might creatively unite many technologies and pedagogies to increase student achievement.

Teaching–Learning Orchestra

In the classroom of the future, teachers might play a role such as that of the conductor of an orchestra (except that they would also be virtuoso performers), calling on a variety of human and technology "instruments" to accomplish lesson objectives. Computers, multimedia, and other technology might be infused in the lesson structure at points where their strengths add instructional value, but the teacher would teach the main lesson and lead the instructional sequence. Cooperative learning groups, or pairs of children, would also play a major role in each lesson, providing each other effective practice, one-to-one feedback, elaborated explanations, and motivation. The teacher/conductor would call on each of these "instruments," be they technology or human, to accomplish tasks for which each is best suited.

Imagine, for example, classrooms in which all children have wireless keypads linked to a computer on the teacher's desk and a large video screen is available at all times. Students could be seated in small teams that receive recognition based on the learning of all team members. Multimedia content would be readily available to help the teacher explain or model content, skills, and processes.

In any didactic lesson in any subject, there is a set of functions that must be fulfilled (see, e.g., Slavin, 2006):

- Orient students to the lesson.
- Present a conceptual overview.
- Solidify understanding.
- Ask questions for clarification and initial assessment.
- Provide opportunities for practice.
- Assess students' understanding.
- Reteach if necessary.
- Reassess if necessary.
- Provide feedback to students on their progress.

Embedded technology could play a role at each stage in the lesson. The teacher/conductor has an entire orchestra of human and technological instruments to convey the lesson content and ensure that all students master it, with each instrument used where it is the optimal solution to a particular lesson function, as illustrated in the following examples.

1. Orient students to the lesson—*teacher*

Teachers have the relationships with students and may be best suited to explaining why a given lesson is important, exciting, and worth learning.

2. Present a conceptual overview—*video*

For many lesson objectives, video could be the ideal medium for initial explanation. Well-designed video can present compelling images, graphics, skits, demonstrations, and so forth, not to teach the lesson but to kick it off in the right direction, using paired visual and auditory content that is likely to be comprehensible, memorable, and motivating.

3. Solidify understanding, and ask questions for clarification and initial assessment—*teacher, teams*

After a well-designed, lesson-embedded video begins a lesson, the teacher might review the key ideas and begin to ask questions of students. Rather than only calling on selected volunteers, teachers might pose questions, including questions preloaded on the computer and shown on the video screen, that students answer on their keypads. The teacher would immediately see a color-coded graphic that summarizes the percentage of students who have the right idea and indicates common errors. Immediately, in the flow of the lesson, the teacher could use this information to decide to reteach a difficult concept or to skip forward if the content appears too easy. The computer could give advice on this strategy, but the teacher would make the pacing decision.

Frequently, the teacher might ask students to discuss answers within their teams using a procedure called "Think-Pair-Share," in which students work in pairs to discuss a question and then the teacher calls on students at random to represent their pairs. Alternatively, teachers could use "numbered heads together" (Kagan, 2001), in which students practice together to prepare all team members on a given concept and then one student is chosen at random to respond for the group. This ensures that students focus their time working with teammates on explaining ideas to each other rather than just giving answers (see Webb & Palincsar, 1996).

4. Provide opportunities for practice—*teams*

After the lesson has been presented, students need an opportunity to master the lesson's content. Cooperative teams are the right format for this lesson function. Four-member teams might be given electronic or paper worksheets with which to practice. Their goal is to ensure that every team member can answer similar questions independently, so they have to work with each other to explain lesson content and to assess each other's understanding. Teams receive recognition (e.g., certificates) based on their success, as measured by the sum of independent assessment that follows teamwork. Team members may also receive a small bonus on their grades if their teams do well.

5. Assess students' understanding—*computer*

Questions preloaded on the computer might assess students' mastery of the lesson objective. Students use their keypads to take brief quizzes. At this point, team members may not help one another. Immediately, the teacher knows whether the class has reached a sufficient level of mastery and either moves on to the next lesson, reteaches to the whole class, or identifies a subgroup that will need additional assistance.

6.   Reteach and reassess if necessary—*teacher, computer*

In reteaching, the entire cycle may be repeated, beginning with the video content, or video material specifically for reteaching may be available, or the teacher may informally reteach.

 For situations in which a subgroup needs additional help, computerized remedial units may be designed to target the specific objective and to be used individually, in small groups with a teacher, or individually with a tutor as appropriate to the content and resources.

7.   Provide feedback to students on their progress—*teacher, team, computer*

The teacher, team, and computer all have roles to play in providing feedback to students. The computer can provide instant, positive, and consistent feedback for the young reader. This feedback is done by providing scores on activities and assessments immediately upon completion. Students receive rewards for achievement in the form of entertaining animations. For example, in Team Alphie, when team members answer questions correctly, they contribute points to the creation of a virtual team train. When the group achieves mastery of the activity, they view a race between their train and a computer-generated train.

 During teamwork, students are motivated to provide feedback to each other and reinforce each other for learning content, in part because the group receives rewards based on the improvement of every team member. Of course, the most important vehicle for feedback is the teacher who listens to children, gives them feedback, and most important, forms human relationships with them.

 Beyond the lesson itself, computers would be used to help teachers prepare for each lesson. A general structure, graphics, videos, PowerPoint presentations, practice items, and assessments would all be preloaded on the computer for a given lesson but could be supplemented or modified by the teacher in advance or skipped over or reviewed in the course of lesson presentation. Preparation materials might include explanations of key lesson objectives or pedagogical principles as well as videos of expert teachers teaching key parts of the lesson or of other demonstrations to help with difficult issues likely to come up, as exist in the Alphie's Alley computer-assisted tutoring software (Chambers, Abrami, et al., 2006).

 The Teaching–Learning Orchestra lesson structure would obviously be different for less didactic lessons, such as the teaching of creative writing or nonroutine problem solving in mathematics, and the length of the lessons may be quite different depending on whether the content lends itself to many brief lessons or a smaller number of lengthy ones. Furthermore, there may be many ways different from these to integrate teachers, cooperative teams, video, computers, and other technology to best effect. The point, however, is that there appears to be much to gain from integrated lesson design, using the best of the entire orchestra of possibilities a teacher might have available to teach each lesson.

CONCLUSION

The best hope for significant and lasting changes in education is the implementation of policies that favor the use of programs with strong evidence of effectiveness and the development of programs of R&D capable of designing, rigorously evaluating, and disseminating proven programs. Once this evidence-based reform dynamic takes hold, educational programs and material will constantly be improved and student outcomes will improve, just as progressive change in medicine, agriculture, and technology constantly makes old solutions obsolete and improves outcomes for all of society.

This chapter describes a program of R&D that serves as one example of evidence-based reform, beginning with the Success for All comprehensive school-reform model and continuing with embedded multimedia, computer-assisted tutoring, and other lesson-embedded technology. It outlines a vision for the lesson of the future, in which the teacher serves as the conductor of an "orchestra" of human and technological "instruments": his or her own instruction, cooperative learning teams, embedded multimedia, computerized lesson elements, on-the-spot assessments, and so forth. There is an enormous amount of work to be done to capture the potential of technology and skilled teachers working together to enhance achievement, but the evidence and experience we have to date suggests that this is an avenue that could lead to major improvements in the practice of education for all students.

The research on Success for All and embedded multimedia provides one demonstration, among many others, that the achievement of disadvantaged and minority children can be meaningfully accelerated using replicable methods. Many reformers (see Luce & Thompson, 2005) have identified schools and districts that routinely produce high achievement among disadvantaged students, and such information helps to dispel the myth that these children cannot be taught to high standards. Real progress, however, depends on being able to intentionally introduce effective practices into high-poverty schools on a broad scale. When we have programs known from rigorous research to reliably improve student achievement, it becomes both possible and imperative to use this information to transform children's educational experiences.

As an analogy, when Edward Jenner observed that milkmaids rarely got smallpox, that was interesting. When he showed that those who got cowpox did not get smallpox, that was promising. But when he deliberately infected healthy people with cowpox and this prevented smallpox, that was revolutionary. In education, we have long known a great deal about effective educational practices and have long identified successful teachers and schools for disadvantaged children, but we are now learning how to intervene on a scale that matters to use this information to benefit millions of at-risk children.

Long ago, Ron Edmonds stated, "We can, whenever and wherever we choose, successfully teach all children whose schooling is of interest to us" (1979). As rigorous experimental research continues to identify effective programs and practices known to work in disadvantaged schools, Edmonds's proposition becomes more pressing. If we know how to improve all children's learning, how can we continue not to do so?

REFERENCES

Adams, G.L., & Engelmann, S. (1996). *Research on Direct Instruction: 25 years beyond DISTAR*. Seattle: Educational Achievement Systems.

Adams, M.J. (1990). *Beginning to read: Thinking and learning about print*. Cambridge, MA: MIT Press.

Borman, G., & Hewes, G. (2003). Long-term effects and cost effectiveness of Success for All. *Educational Evaluation and Policy Analysis, 24*(2), 243–266.

Borman, G.D., Hewes, G.M., Overman, L.T., & Brown, S. (2003). Comprehensive school reform and achievement: A meta-analysis. *Review of Educational Research, 73*(2), 125–230.

Borman, G., Slavin, R.E., Cheung, A., Chamberlain, A., Madden, N.A., & Chambers, B. (2007). Final reading outcomes of the national randomized field trial of Success for All. *American Educational Research Journal, 44*(3), 701–731.

Calkins, L.M. (1983). *Lessons from a child: On the teaching and learning of writings*. Exeter, NH: Heinemann.

Chambers, B., Abrami, P.C., Tucker, B.J., Slavin, R.E., Madden, N.A., Cheung, A., et al. (in press). Computer-assisted tutoring in Success for All: Reading outcomes for first graders. *Journal of Research on Educational Effectiveness.*

Chambers, B., Cheung, A., Gifford, R., Madden, N., & Slavin, R.E. (2006). Achievement effects of embedded multimedia in a Success for All reading program. *Journal of Educational Psychology, 98,* 232–237.

Chambers, B., Slavin, R.E., Madden, N.A., Abrami, P.C., Tucker, B.J., Cheung, A., et al. (in press). Technology infusion in Success for All: Reading outcomes for first graders. *Elementary School Journal.*

Clark, J.M., & Paivio, A. (1991). Dual coding theory and education. *Educational Psychology Review, 3*(3), 149–210.

Comprehensive School Reform Quality Center. (2005). *CSRQ Center report on elementary school comprehensive school reform models*. Washington, DC: American Institutes for Research.

Dunn, L., & Dunn, L. (1997). *Peabody Picture Vocabulary Test–Third Edition*. Circle Pines, MI: American Guidance System.

Edmonds, R. (1979). Effective schools for the urban poor. *Educational Leadership, 37*(1), 15–24.

Everston, C.M., Emmer, E.T., & Worsham, M.E. (2003). *Classroom management for elementary teachers* (6th ed.). Boston: Allyn & Bacon.

Fuchs, L.S., Fuchs, D., Hamlett, C.L., & Stecker, P.M. (1991). Effects of curriculum-based measurement and consultation on teacher planning and student achievement in mathematics operations. *American Educational Research Journal, 28*(3), 617–641.

Good, R.H., & Kaminski, R.A. (Eds.). (2002). *Dynamic Indicators of Basic Early Literacy Skills* (6th ed.). Eugene, OR: Institute for Development of Educational Achievement. Also available online at http://dibels.uoregon.edu

Graves, D. (1983). *Writing: Teachers and children at work.* Exeter, NH: Heinemann.

Gutiérrez, R., & Slavin, R.E. (1992). Achievement effects of the nongraded elementary school: A best-evidence synthesis. *Review of Educational Research, 62,* 333–376.

Harris, K.R., & Graham, S. (1996). *Making the writing process work: Strategies for composition and self-regulation.* Cambridge, MA: Brookline.

Herman, R. (1999). *An educator's guide to schoolwide reform.* Arlington, VA: Educational Research Service.

Hoeffler, T., & Leutner, D. (2006). *Instructional animation versus static picture: A meta-analysis.* Poster presented at the annual meeting of the American Educational Research Association, San Francisco.

Joyce, B.R., & Showers, B. (1995). *Student achievement through staff development.* White Plains, NY: Longman.

Kagan, S. (2001). Teaching for character and community. *Educational Leadership, 59*(2), 50–55.

Kulik, J.A. (2003). *Effects of using instructional technology in elementary and secondary schools: What controlled evaluation studies say* (SRI Project Number P10446.001). Arlington, VA: SRI International.

Luce, T., & Thompson, L. (2005). *Do what works: How proven practices can improve America's public schools.* Dallas, TX: Ascent Education Press.

Mayer, R.E. (2001). *Multimedia learning.* New York: Cambridge University Press.

Mayer, R.E., & Moreno, R. (2003). Nine ways to reduce cognitive load in multimedia learning. *Educational Psychologist, 38*(1), 43–52.

National Assessment of Educational Progress. (2005). *The nation's report card.* Washington, DC: National Center for Education Statistics.

Neuman, S. (2006, April). *Why multimedia?* Paper presented to the Academy Colloquium, Amsterdam, The Netherlands.

No Child Left Behind Act of 2001, PL 107-110, 115 Stat. 1425, 20 U.S.C. §§ 6301 *et seq.*

Nunnery, J., Ross, S., Smith, L., Slavin, R., Hunter, P., & Stubbs, J. (1996, April). *An assessment of Success for All program configuration effects on the reading achievement of at-risk first-grade students.* Paper presented at the annual meeting of the American Educational Research Association, New York.

Pressley, M. (2003). Psychology of literacy and literacy instruction. In W.M. Reynolds & G.E. Miller (Eds.), *Handbook of psychology* (Vol. 7, pp. 333–356). Hoboken, NJ: Wiley.

Slavin, R.E. (1995). *Cooperative learning: Theory, research, and practice* (2nd ed.). Boston: Allyn & Bacon.

Slavin, R.E. (2006). *Educational psychology: Theory and practice* (8th ed.). Boston: Allyn & Bacon.

Slavin, R.E., Hurley, E.A., & Chamberlain, A.M. (2001). Cooperative learning in schools. In N.J. Smelser & P.B. Baltes (Eds.), *International encyclopedia of the social and behavioral sciences* (pp. 2756–2761). Oxford, England: Pergamon.

Slavin, R.E., & Lake, C. (in press). Effective programs in elementary mathematics: A best-evidence synthesis. *Review of Educational Research.*

Slavin, R.E., Madden, N.A., Chambers, B., & Haxby, B. (in press). *Two million children: Success for All.* Thousand Oaks, CA: Corwin.

Slavin, R.E., Madden, N.A., & Datnow, A. (2007). Research in, research out: The role of research in the development and scale-up of Success for All. In S. Fuhrman, D. Cohen, & F. Mosher (Eds.), *The state of education policy research* (pp. 261–280). Mahwah, NJ: Lawrence Erlbaum Associates.

Wasik, B.A., & Slavin, R.E. (1993). Preventing early reading failure with one-to-one tutoring: A review of five programs. *Reading Research Quarterly, 28,* 178–200.

Webb, N.M., & Palincsar, A.S. (1996). Group processes in the classroom. In D.C. Berliner & R.C. Calfee (Eds.), *Handbook of educational psychology.* New York: Simon & Schuster Macmillan.

Weiderholt, J.L., & Bryant, B.R. (2001). *Gray Oral Reading Test: GORT 4.* Austin, TX: PRO-ED.

Woodcock, R.W. (1987). *Woodcock Reading Mastery Test–Revised.* Circle Pines, MN: American Guidance Service.

Woodcock, R.W., McGrew, K.S., & Mather, N. (2000). *Woodcock-Johnson III Tests of Achievement.* Itasca, IL: Riverside.

III

How Technology Can Make a Difference

Susan B. Neuman

Section III contains chapters on innovations in technology and how technological supports can scaffold children's learning for higher reading achievement. Each of these chapters builds on the important design principles in the previous section and extends them by describing how speech recognition technology, television, and other digital assets can improve the achievements of students whose growth has languished beyond the very basics of reading instruction.

Adriana G. Bus and her colleagues at Leiden University in the Netherlands take up this challenge in Chapter 13 by demonstrating the power of "living" books for reading improvement. In a series of experiments, they report that stories with multimedia additions are more successful in holding children's attention and lead to greater language and greater comprehension for at-risk children.

In Chapter 14, Marilyn Jager Adams raises an important paradox: If the ability to read independently and frequently is critical to becoming a better reader, then how can we support those who struggle in reading, comprehend little, and are reluctant to read? Her answer is to use effective technology to essentially "bootstrap" domain-specific knowledge to provide better learner supports in schools and other settings. Chapters 14 and 15 emphasize how this bootstrapping might work for learning from television and digital media.

In Chapter 15, Heather L. Kirkorian and Daniel R. Anderson show how well-designed, curriculum-based children's television programs can teach and support children's reading development. They describe some of the principles that underlie quality programs and how these principles can be implemented to create higher-quality educational media that supports literacy development.

In Chapter 16, Sandra L. Calvert focuses on the uses of visual and auditory production features—sometimes described as *formal features*—to instruct and teach children even as they are being entertained. Features such as action, sound effects, and singing can be used effectively to orient children to content and build knowledge of literacy skills. Together, these chapters describe how informational technologies can be used to influence literacy, both in its traditional verbal form as well as its increasingly interactive forms.

Kathleen A. Roskos in Chapter 17 brings us back to the classroom. In the tradition of ecological psychology, she describes how environments in schools and classrooms can "coerce" more effective learning opportunities. Educational intervention can be enhanced by partitioning the physical space in coherent ways, using signage intentionally, and placing a variety and complexity of material resources, which supports stronger, richer, deeper student learning.

What these chapters in Section III make clear is that when we recognize children's needs and tailor instruction using specific design principles to better to meet these needs, students are able to succeed and achieve literacy outcomes at higher levels than ever before.

13

Design Features in Living Books and Their Effects on Young Children's Vocabulary

Adriana G. Bus, Maria T. de Jong,
Marian J.A.J. Verhallen, and Verna A.C. van der Kooy-Hofland

Because children from impoverished backgrounds often receive less language stimulation at home than children from nonimpoverished backgrounds, they are at heightened risk for poor academic readiness and achievement. They often are deprived of shared book reading—an activity that fosters literacy development in a unique way. A wealth of studies show that books are a powerful tool in the process of becoming literate, probably because they bring children into contact with a particular type of language (e.g., Bus, 2001; Bus, van IJzendoorn, & Pellegrini, 1995; Frijters, Barron, & Brunello, 2000; Sénéchal, LeFevre, Thomas, & Daley, 1998). Books tell stories using words and phrases that rarely occur in other language situations; think of phrases such as *for all it's worth, a soft slant of wind, the sun is high in the sky,* and so forth.

As we enter a new technological era, picture storybooks are made available in a digitized format that preserves all of the relevant qualities of the print version, such as a narrative and illustrations, but adds numerous additional features. We have begun to test whether children benefit from the digitized versions of storybooks available through a plethora of new media (e.g., Internet, television). We want to find out whether and how electronic books could remedy some limitations of traditional paper storybooks without spoiling children's pleasure in stories. We are interested in their potential contribution to interventions that intend

Preparation of this chapter was supported by an award (411-02-506) from the Netherlands Organization for Scientific Research (NWO) to Adriana G. Bus.

to call a halt to the depressing cycle of poor environments creating poor school performance.

Good examples of digitized picture storybooks that retain all print book qualities but simultaneously add new features are plentiful, even for the youngest children. *Nijntje, Maisy,* and *Musti,* all popular book series for the very young and originally only available as picture storybooks, are broadcasted by Dutch educational television, on sale as DVDs (which are often much cheaper than the original print books), or accessible through the Internet. Because even the youngest children are spending increasing amounts of time with screen media at the expense of time spent reading books independently or with adults (Rideout, Vandewater, & Wartella, 2003; Zeijl, Crone, Wiefferink, Keuzekamp, & Reijneveld, 2005), we would like to determine whether these alternate forms of picture storybooks have the potential to increase story and text comprehension.

Because books usually are viewed as static objects consisting of fixed words on pages, it is only logical that research so far has mainly focused on how adults' comments and nonverbal support scaffold children's text comprehension. Now that picture storybooks are available in digital—or "living"—versions, it is important to explore the effects of digital books, especially when parents are less likely to read several times per week to their child. In this chapter, we explore evidence that some electronic stories, available through a plethora of new media, have additional features that act as intermediaries between child and story text, especially in groups lagging behind in language proficiency.

It is unlikely that digital storybooks will replicate entirely the adult–child interactions that occur when reading print-based books. For example, electronic stories do not provide a venue for focused language exchange, enabling responses to children's language and thinking and providing exposure to the adult language (e.g., Raikes et al., 2006). Researchers, however, have suggested that additional features of digital storybooks such as film, music, and sound may have potency to serve as "electronic scaffolds" to support children's text understanding and memorization of words and phrases (e.g., Bus, de Jong, & Verhallen, 2006; McKenna, 1998).

Thus far, the main focus of research on living books has been on—according to de Jong and Bus (2003)—the most common multimedia additions: iconic features such as hidden animations and animated illustrations. So far there is a paucity of research testing effects of so-called *computer assistants,* stand-ins for adults who now and then appear on the screen to ask questions or provide help. Such additions to the next generation of living books may make the books not only cognitively but also emotionally more rewarding. In line with our previous research of book sharing (Bus, 2001; Bus & van IJzendoorn, 1988, 1995, 1997; Bus, Belsky, van IJzendoorn, & Crnic, 1997), it is imaginable that a computer assistant who interacts with the child may neutralize the absence of intimacy in encounters with living books.

PICTORIAL AND ICONIC FEATURES AS OBSTRUCTIONS OF NARRATIVE COMPREHENSION

Many exemplars of the first-generation digitalized picture storybooks typically provided unrelated interactive animations that could be accessed by clicking on parts of the pictures accompanying the text. We came across such hidden animations in about 60% of all living books produced in the years 1998–2002 (de Jong & Bus, 2003). For instance, the digitized version of Mercer Mayer's *Grandma and Me* (1994)—one of the first living stories ever available—includes animations hidden in the illustrations in addition to animated pictures synchronized with the oral text. When the cursor changes, you can click the mouse, which results in surprises: singing flowers, a dancing picture on the wall, or columns with ants marching over the screen. We can imagine that such additions may add to children's motivation and interest in hearing the story over and over; however, it is also imaginable that such additions distract children from the story. Because these features may encourage children to think of the story as a game, they may in turn interfere with the children's comprehension of the story (see Bolter, 1998; Labbo & Reinking, 1999; Leu, 2000).

We explored effects of such additions to living books by observing how children interact with the Dutch-spoken Janosch series and testing effects of repeated encounters with these electronic books (de Jong & Bus, 2004). Just like in *Grandma and Me,* there are many visual and sound effects hidden in most screens that can be found by moving the cursor over the illustrations. For instance, when Tiger (Janosch, 1986) is having an x-ray taken during an examination by a physician, a click on the light bulb above the x-ray machine makes the physician pick up the bulb and eat it, with crackling sounds to accentuate the action. A click on the omnipresent Tiger Duck in the same story makes a spring between the head and tail stretch out as far as it can, then recoil to unite the body parts again. A content analysis of about 50 living books that were on the market in the Netherlands between 1995 and 2002 revealed that only a small percentage of these hidden animations (9.4%) were congruent with the narrative (de Jong & Bus, 2003). One of the rare examples of a congruent animation can be found in the same scene at the physician's: an x-ray picture appears when we click on Tiger, probably an effective way to illustrate what the outcome is when a person is x-rayed. Such additions may add to children's understanding of complex words in the story text.

In a large-scale study based on the Janosch series, we found evidence that the presence of such animations diverts children's attention from the text. Similar to what Labbo and Kuhn (2000) observed, the hidden animations were so attractive to young children that they loaded about six animations on each screen of the story. We did not, however, find evidence for the suggestion by James (1999), based on four case studies, that young children are so completely infatuated with these hidden animations that they rarely finish navigating through the complete story. Even though our participants had a choice—playing with these optional hidden animations or listening to the text—they continued listening to the story, probably because simultaneous film images of the story appeared. Most participants preferred to hear the complete story more than once.

We also did not find support for the hypothesis that understanding of the text decreases when children trifle with the hidden animations (de Jong & Bus, 2004), a result that matches findings reported by Ricci and Beale (2002). After 12 sessions with the electronic storybooks, children's comprehension was at about the same level as when the story was read to the children the same number of times. This result differs from Labbo and Kuhn's (2000) hypothesis that children's text understanding will lag behind when incongruent animations embedded in the pictures guide children's attention away from the storyline. They noticed that Roberto, a kindergarten child with a basic concept of stories and story features, often lapsed into passive viewing when the special features in the electronic book were inconsistent with the story. He seemed to enjoy the hidden animations, but this affective motivation did not lead to increased understanding of the story.

ANIMATED ILLUSTRATIONS AS INCENTIVES FOR STORY AND TEXT COMPREHENSION

The *Maisy* episodes available on television and DVD are very similar to the *Maisy* books by Lucy Cousins; they each contain stories about breakfast, baking cookies, and cleaning up the house. The difference between the television show and the storybooks is that in the television show, static illustrations are transformed into film images, music is added to enhance or support impressions, and pictures are completed with relevant sounds (child's voices, a mooing cow, falling drops). For instance, the first illustration in the Maisy book *Badje* [Maisy's Pool] (1999) shows Maisy and her friend Tallulah sitting in the grass lethargic from the heat. The text tells that they are warm. By adding motion, sound, and music, the DVD version of this same story strengthens the impression that Maisy and Tallulah are warm. In the initial scene, Maisy and Tallulah are chasing each other but with visibly decreasing enthusiasm. Their voices sound dull in an increasing degree until Tallulah, worn out by the heat, collapses. The fading music supports the impression evoked by these images: It is too warm to chase each other.

As suggested by various authors (e.g., Calvert, Huston, Watkins, & Wright, 1982; Neuman, 1997), additional features of multimedia stories such as motion and camera work (zooms, cuts, and pans) may supply children with sources of information that act as mediators between the children and text. Because few contemporary children do not have access to a television or computer, most have learned how to process film information—the grammar of cuts, pans, zooms, and edits—into their final interpretation of a story (Robinson & Mackey, 2003). These additional features may be profitable because they enable the learner to fill gaps in text comprehension (Mayer & Moreno, 1998). Because children hold verbal and nonverbal representations in their working memory at the same time, they are able to build referential connections between, for example, seeing how the water flows away through a hole in the bath and the text telling that the bath leaks (Paivio, 1986). Sharp and colleagues (1995) found corroboration for the hypothesis that short stories accompanied by a helpful video framework supported 6-year-old children's story recall and interpretation more than stories accompanied by mainly static images. In examining third graders' recall and inferential abilities, Neuman (1989) found that students who watched a multimedia story recalled more story elements than students exposed to only one medium. These results with young children, however, could not be replicated with older and more advanced pupils. Results from Neuman's (1992) study examining the influence of different media presentations on fifth graders' inferences about two mystery stories did not support the hypothesis that multimedia stories supported learning more than printed stories. Both media elicited similar story-processing strategies.

We hypothesize, therefore, that older children may have greater imaginative skills and background knowledge, allowing them to reconstruct story images and create verbal representations from text without an additional set of processing tools (Pressley, Cariglia-Bull, Deane, & Schneider, 1987). Multimedia may be especially profitable when print book-reading experiences are out of children's reach in traditional verbal settings because children's language proficiency lags behind and there are too many gaps in understanding to fill by guessing at the story meaning and the language (Sharp et al., 1995). In line with this hypothesis, a study by Uchikoshi (2005) found positive relationships between viewing book-based television shows and language and literacy outcomes in groups of kindergarten children learning English as a second language.

One of our experiments that included 135 three-year-olds, mainly from families at risk, tested effects of repeated encounters with *Maisy* stories (Bus & de Jong, 2006). In one group, we alternated a static version of a Maisy story with an animated version of the same story, thus imitating what often happens in daily life. For example, children may watch a *Maisy* television program at home and then have the same story, in book format, read to them in preschool. In the other group, the examiner shared the *Maisy* books with individual children. Afterward, we tested these 3-year-old children's knowledge of complex words and phrases such as *milking the cow, starving, clearing away the mess, right on time, piles of shopping, on the inside, on the outside,* and other words and phrases that are more complex than those typically heard in daily communication at this young age. We found that alternating reading the static story with viewing a multimedia version of the same story produced higher scores on questions about the story's core vocabulary than did the static condition alone, suggesting that the additional features of multimedia stories acted as mediators between the children and the story text.

In the same vein, we carried out a series of experiments at schools in the inner city of The Hague—which is mainly populated by immigrant families—testing the ability of book-based animated stories, when well designed and produced, to have positive effects on young viewers' narrative comprehension and language skills (Verhallen & Bus, 2007; Verhallen, Bus, & de Jong, 2006). In the first study, two versions of the same book were presented on the computer; however, one version included static images and the other included multimedia additions (e.g., cinematic techniques such as zooms, pans, cuts, and sound effects). The main character in this story, a witch, has a problem: Because her house and everything in it, including the cat, is black, she often stumbles over the cat. The multimedia version often adds to the static version of the book; for example, the camera may zoom in on the facial expressions of the witch, thereby emphasizing her emotional responses simultaneously named in the story text.

We concluded that in a group of 5-year-old participants, all of whom were learning Dutch as a second language and were from low-educated families, living books seem to provide a framework for understanding stories and remembering linguistic information, a result that matches our findings with the 3-year-olds. Children profited more from repeated encounters with the multimedia storybook, which was indicated by more complete retellings. Furthermore, after four repetitions lasting 24 minutes, children had learned seven new words in the multimedia situation (12%–14% of the words we suspected children would not know)—twice as many as the average number (three or four) they learned with static pictures. In other words, new processing tools such as motion and camera work help to convey content instead of diverting attention from the story or the language. Note that these results were found in groups of kindergarten children who, in comparison to their peers, lag behind in language proficiency and are at great risk of developing a reading problem at school. We expect less pronounced results in average groups due to the fact that those children are less dependent on scaffolding for understanding the story text.

TEMPORAL CONTIGUITY

One of our earlier studies (de Jong & Bus, 2002) showed that outcomes of experiments are different when the animated pictures are not contiguous with the narration. While exploring the effects of *P.B. Beer is jarig* [P.B. Bear's Birthday Party] (Davis, 1996), one of the first living books available in the Netherlands, we discovered that when children were given a choice of several options, pictorial and iconic options were chosen at the expense of listening to the story text (de Jong & Bus, 2002). In the living book *P.B. Bear's Birthday Party*, children have a choice—listen to the text or watch the animated illustration—but they cannot do both at the same time. The text about P.B. Bear, the main character, going to the bathroom to wash his face after he woke up is disconnected from the animated illustration showing P.B. Bear washing up. The designers decided not to synchronize the oral text with the animated illustration but, rather, with visual changes in the print. By highlighting the print while it was spoken they expected to strengthen children's awareness of letter–sound relationships.

We noticed that the iconic mode of electronic books (clicking on illustrations and icons) attract 4- to 5-year-olds' attention at the expense of reading the full page and text fragments (see Greenfield et al., 1996). After six 15-minute sessions, the difference in the number of readings was dramatic. Most children in the electronic story condition heard no more than about half of the text one and a half to two and a half times. In the regular book-reading condition, the complete story was read to the children six times. As a result, most participants in the living book condition did not memorize many words and phrases from the verbatim text. When an adult took advantage of the same amount of time, six sessions each lasting 15 minutes, to read the print book version to the children, the children made much more progress in text comprehension. In other words, the availability of animated acts of story events including motion, music, and appropriate sounds interferes with the narrative when these options are not linked to the narrative text and children have free play. If animations are available in addition to the narration and children have a choice to either watch the animation or listen to the text, most 4- and 5-year-old children prefer the iconic information at the expense of the narration.

Therefore, presenting animations congruent with the narration simultaneously rather than successively may be of overriding importance in guiding children (Mayer & Moreno, 1998). Or, put differently, it is not just the synergy of various information sources that supports text comprehension (Neuman, 1997); effects also depend on temporal contiguity of various verbal and nonverbal information sources. To explain these results, we hypothesized that film images draw attention selectively to contiguous content, thereby helping children with many gaps in text understanding to select picture information relevant for processing the story text (Greenfield et al., 1996; James, 1999; Kamil, Intrator, & Kim, 2000). When there are many gaps in children's understanding of the story text, we can imagine that a reduced information load as a result of multimedia guidance may help children to figure out the meaning of unknown words and phrases and to memorize those words and phrases after repeatedly experiencing images simultaneous with the narration. Features such as motion, zooms, cuts, and pans provide children with an additional guide in selecting the important or central content of the images that relate to the text, just as a spotlight on a stage tells the audience where to look. These features probably limit the overload of information offered by illustrations with numerous irrelevant details. As the two different classes of information—one specialized for information concerning nonverbal objects and events and the other for dealing with language—are fine-tuned, they may support and expand each other in conveying the same content even more than picture storybooks (Paivio, 1986). Children with a low level of language proficiency who are unfamiliar with 10% or more of the story vocabulary may benefit especially from multimedia additions because they are more in need of additional support (Verhallen et al., 2006).

REPETITION: A NECESSARY PREREQUISITE

When there are gaps in children's understanding of the language used in stories, repetition may be especially indispensable for understanding and memorizing unfamiliar vocabulary and grammatical structures (e.g., Sulzby, 1985). There are surprisingly few book-reading studies that test obvious questions. For example, do young children get bored after a few repetitions of the same story, as may become manifest by decreased attentional arousal, thereby bringing learning to a halt? Or, do they stay attentive even after several repetitions, resulting in acquiring new language? Most important for the questions raised in this chapter, do living books have more potencies to keep children interested even after several repetitions of the same story? To answer these questions, we tested how immigrant kindergarten children with a comparatively low proficiency in the language of schooling—an increasing part of the school population not only in the Netherlands but all over the world—respond to repetition of age-appropriate picture storybooks with and without multimedia additions.

Studies of children watching television suggest that children are more inclined to continue investing mental effort in programs when their appraisals of coping options are high. That is, when given a choice between watching television and playing, children are more inclined to focus their eyes on the screen when information matches their level and they expect to benefit from their efforts (e.g., Anderson & Lorch, 1983; Bickham, Wright, & Huston, 2001; Crawley, Anderson, Wilder, Williams, & Santomero, 1999; Huston & Wright, 1983). In line with this *active theory,* we may expect that children only benefit from repetition of stories when their appraisals of their coping options are high. If children are lacking support in understanding a story, their aversive systems may become active after a few repetitions, and they may become less and less inclined to continue their efforts to understand the story text. This theory may explain our previous finding that children with low language proficiency benefited more from repeated encounters with multimedia stories than from repeated encounters with picture storybooks without additional multimedia information sources (Verhallen et al., 2006). We therefore expect that when story text is difficult for young children, their attentional arousal may decrease when the story is repeated several times without providing additional sources of information that enable them to derive the meaning of words and phrases from the context. By contrast, with the provision of additional information, as is available in some digitized picture storybooks, they may continue to invest mental effort, thus benefiting more from repeated encounters with the story. In other words, repetition is not by definition annoying or profitable but only on condition that children's appraisals of coping options are high.

Alternatively, it is hypothesized that arousal increases in response to attention-catching features in multimedia stories. A wealth of studies in the domain of mediated communication such as television and advertising support the idea that features of new media such as motion, music, and sound elicit more psychophysiological arousal (e.g., Lang, 2006). For instance, according to *motion effect theories*, an inherent preference for moving objects is manifested in physiological changes such as a decrease in heart rate, increase in skin conductance of electricity when external stimuli are presented, and changes in brain electrical activity (Sundar & Kalyanaraman, 2004). As a consequence of more immersive mediated experiences such as compelling tunes and engaging scenes, multimedia stories may preserve more psychophysiological arousal in response to the affective and motivational intensity of the stimuli even after repeated encounters with the same story (Lang, 2006). This alternative model therefore predicts an overall higher level of attentional arousal in response to the affective and motivational intensity of the stimuli in multimedia stories; however, according to this model, it is not very likely that such arousal mediates learning from multimedia stories.

EFFECTS OF BOOK CHARACTERISTICS ON ATTENTIONAL AROUSAL

In line with the active theory, we expected that children's attentional arousal would decrease when a story was repeated on several occasions without additional sources of information. Children may continue to invest mental effort when there are additional sources of information that enable them to derive the meaning of words and phrases, thus promoting their learning from repeated encounters with the story. In other words, we tried to find evidence that repetition is only boring or unprofitable when children do not get sufficient support in understanding the story text. Similar to numerous studies of television and advertising but different from what typically occurs in studies of book reading or watching educational television programs, we assessed psychophysiological activity as an indicator of attention (Ravaja, 2004). We measured electrodermal reactivity because this measure is known to increase when children concentrate on activities such as doing mental arithmetic problems (Dawson, Schell, & Filion, 2000; Pecchinenda & Smith, 1996; Ravaja, 2004).

Verhallen and Bus (2007) found evidence that multimedia stories are more likely than stories with static pictures to retain attentional or motivational arousal over sessions. The skin conductance was registered every 500 msec by applying a constant voltage (0.5V) to electrodes placed on the palmar surfaces of the medial phalanges of the second and third finger of the nondominant hand. To code the data, we developed a computer program to assess the number of changes in skin conductance of at least .02 micro Siemens. When a multimedia story was presented four times, the average number of 6 skin conductance responses per minute in Session 2 slightly increased to an average number of 7 skin conductance responses per minute in Session 4, a score far beyond the score of 1–3 responses per minute in a state of rest (Dawson et al., 2000). By contrast, arousal level gradually decreased from an average score of 7 skin conductance responses per minute in Session 2 to a score of 4 per minute in the fourth session when a story with just static pictures was repeated time after time. This meant that in the group that was read to from the static story, attentional arousal had fallen back to a level statistically significantly lower than the group that was read to from the multimedia story. The statistically significant decrease in arousal after three repetitions we observed for the static story may indicate that aversive systems become active earlier when the book is static, thus reducing the chance that children benefit from repeated encounters with the same story. Multimedia stories, by contrast, retain their appeal for at least four repetitions, which suggests that they are more eligible for supporting continuation of attentional or motivational activation (Lang, 2006).

Another unique result of this study is that a sustained level of arousal mediates the relationship between multimedia additions and text comprehension. This indicates that an external characteristic variable such as the availability of multimedia takes an internal meaning by sustaining children's attentional arousal. There is strong evidence for the theory that attentional arousal elicited by multiple deliveries of information plays an essential role in the causal chain of learning from electronic stories. The children in the multimedia condition may have retained a higher arousal level because they experienced this version as more redundant and therefore supportive than children in the static condition. Consequently, they may have continued their efforts to improve text comprehension, thereby memorizing more words and phrases. Children invest more mental effort in using or processing what they see and hear when they perceive the story as more redundant and comprehensible (Crawley et al., 1999), the final result being that they memorize more information from the program. When, by contrast, only static illustrations were available and children's perception was more dependent on text comprehension, aversive systems became active earlier. Note that these results are found in groups of kindergarten children who, in comparison with their peers, lag behind in language proficiency and are at great risk for developing a reading problem at school. We expect less pronounced results in groups of typical learners due to the fact that they are less dependent on scaffolding for understanding the story text.

When designing new living books, it is important to take into account that the added value of multimedia stories is not just that they are a new form of media; rather, the important factor is the ability of the story representation to retain attentional arousal while children explore the story. For this reason, the quality of multimedia stories has to comply with the strictest requirements. When designing multimedia stories, the story content and not the entertainment value should be the main source of inspiration. Furthermore, in the context of reviewed research, it should be a priority to make the story understandable by adding redundancy and not to add features explaining separate words and phrases.

CONCLUSION

Teachers and parents are inclined to mistakenly characterize living books as an "easy" medium, suggesting that they require less mental investment by children than print books, which, by contrast, are assumed to activate children's minds

(Salomon, 1984). Our finding that living books, more so than the static versions of the same books, can keep children aroused even after the umpteenth time that they hear the story opposes this assumption. We also did not find evidence supporting another preconception; namely, that attention-catching motion pictures dispel attention for language. Children's text understanding benefited more from multimedia stories than from static stories, a result that we were able to replicate several times. These misrepresentations of the effects of digitized stories keep teachers and other caregivers from introducing living books despite an expanding number of computers available in classrooms.

We should also take into account that—according to a series of seminal studies that tested when and how additional media such as motion, sound, and music affect learning—not all electronic stories are equally supportive of text understanding. We observed negative effects for lapsed time between narration and corresponding animations and animations that were incongruent with the story (de Jong & Bus, 2002; Labbo & Kuhn, 2000). Such features divert children's attention from the story text and decrease the number of readings of text in favor of iconic and pictorial explorations. By contrast, congruent animations presented simultaneously, rather than successively, with corresponding narration by using animation, zooms, cuts, and pans, seem to promote learning from repeated encounters with the story (Calvert et al., 1982; de Jong & Bus, 2002, 2004; Neuman, 1997; Verhallen et al., 2006). Our research so far also suggests that children with a low level of language proficiency who are unfamiliar with 10% or more of the story vocabulary benefit the most from such principles, probably because they are most susceptible for differences in the quality of scaffolds (Verhallen et al., 2006).

Based on our results so far, we hypothesize that attentional arousal is one of the mechanisms by which external characteristic variables, such as combining animated pictures with the narrative, may take on internal psychological meaning. We used psychophysiological measures to determine that stories with multimedia additions are more successful in holding children's attention when stories are repeated several times. Aversion becomes manifest at an earlier session when stories only include static pictures. The results match with *the active model* that was developed to explain learning from television viewing (Anderson & Lorch, 1983; Bickham et al., 2001; Huston & Wright, 1983): Children invest more mental effort in using or processing what they see and hear when they perceive the program as more comprehensible (Crawley et al., 1999) and redundant, the final result being that they memorize the program better and learn more. Because a static storybook provides little support to fill in gaps in children's text understanding, children's appraisals of their own ability to comprehend a story decrease; as a result, they learn less and less from repeated encounters with the story. We expect that outcomes would be less pronounced in groups of typical learners, as they are less dependent on scaffolds in understanding the story text.

Our findings indicate that digital storybooks should be considered assets rather than problems, providing kindergarten children who, in comparison to their peers, lag behind in language proficiency and are at great risk of developing a reading problem at school new chances to advance their language skills (Tyner, 1998). Children profit from a synergistic intervention, especially when they have few background experiences to help them understand a storyline and derive the meaning of unfamiliar words and sentences from additional information sources. More precisely, when children have limited proficiency in the language of instruction—a situation that is becoming more and more common all over the world—additional iconic information may help to convey story content and story language, just as adult–child interactions do during book reading. Well-designed book-based programs on television and Internet sites that include multimedia might be a great way to promote at-risk children's story understanding and linguistic skills at home and in school.

REFERENCES

Anderson, D.R., & Lorch, E.P. (1983). Looking at television action or reaction? In J. Bryant & D.R. Anderson (Eds.), *Children's understanding of television: Research on attention and comprehension* (pp. 1–33). New York: Academic Press.

Bickham, D.S., Wright, J.C., & Huston, A.C. (2001). Attention, comprehension, and the educational influences of television. In D.G. Singer & J.L Singer (Eds.), *Handbook of children and the media* (pp. 101–120). Thousand Oaks, CA: Sage Publications.

Bolter, J.D. (1998). Hypertext and the question of visual literacy. In D. Reinking, M.C. McKenna, L.D. Labbo, & R.D. Kieffer (Eds.), *Handbook of literacy and technology: Transformations in a post-typographic world* (pp. 3–13). Mahwah, NJ: Lawrence Erlbaum Associates.

Bus, A.G. (2001). Early book reading in the family: A route to literacy. In S. Neuman & D. Dickinson (Eds.), *Handbook on research in early literacy* (pp. 179–191). New York: Guilford Press.

Bus, A.G., Belsky, J., van IJzendoorn, M.H., & Crnic, K. (1997). Attachment, and bookreading patterns: A study of mothers, fathers and their toddlers. *Early Childhood Research Quarterly, 12,* 75–90.

Bus, A.G., & de Jong, M.T. (2006, March). The promise of printed and multimedia stories for children at-risk. In A. Panagiotopoulou & M. Wintermeyer, *Bildung schafft Gerechtigkeit—durch Forderung von Literalitat? Erkenntnisse und Erfahrungen aus vier europaischen Landern.* Frankfurt am Main, Germany: DGfE-Kongress.

Bus, A.G., de Jong, M.T., & Verhallen, M.J.A.J. (2006). CD-ROM talking books: A way to enhance early literacy. In D. Reinking, M.C. McKenna, L.D. Labbo, & R.D. Kieffer (Eds.), *International handbook of literacy and technology* (Vol. 2, pp. 129–144). Mahwah, NJ: Lawrence Erlbaum Associates.

Bus, A.G., & van IJzendoorn, M.H. (1988). Mother–child interactions, attachment, and emergent literacy: A cross-sectional study. *Child Development, 59,* 1262–1272.

Bus, A.G., & van IJzendoorn, M.H. (1995). Mothers reading to their three-year-olds: The role of mother–child attachment security in becoming literate. *Reading Research Quarterly, 30,* 998–1015.

Bus, A.G., & van IJzendoorn, M.H. (1997). Affective dimension of mother–infant picturebook reading. *Journal of School Psychology, 35,* 47–60.

Bus, A.G., van IJzendoorn, M.H., & Pellegrini, A.D. (1995). Storybook reading makes for success in learning to read. A meta-analysis on intergenerational transmission of literacy. *Review of Educational Research, 65,* 1–21.

Calvert, S.L., Huston, A.C., Watkins, B.A., & Wright, J.C. (1982). The relation between selective attention to television forms and children's comprehension of content. *Child Development, 53,* 601–610.

Cousins, L. (Writer/director). (1999). Badje [Maisy's Pool] [motion picture]. In *Muis bedtijd en andere verhaaltjes* [Maisy bedtime and other stories]. Benelux: Universal Pictures.

Crawley, A.M., Anderson, D.R., Wilder, A., Williams, M., & Santomero, A. (1999). Effects of repeated exposures to a single episode of the television program Blue's Clues on the viewing behaviors and comprehension of preschool children. *Journal of Educational Psychology, 91,* 630–637.

Davis, L. (1996). *P.B. is jarig* [P.B. Bear's Birthday Party]. Nieuwegein: Bombilla/VNU Interactive Media.

Dawson, M.D., Schell, A.M., & Filion, D.L. (2000). The electrodermal system. In J.T. Cacioppo, L.G. Tassinary, & G.G. Berntson, *Handbook of psychophysiology* (pp. 200–223). Cambridge: Cambridge University Press.

de Jong, M.T., & Bus, A.G. (2002). Quality of book-reading matters for emergent readers: An experiment with the same book in a regular or electronic format. *Journal of Educational Psychology, 94,* 145–155.

de Jong, M.T., & Bus, A.G. (2003). How well suited are electronic books to supporting literacy? *Journal of Early Childhood Literacy, 3,* 147–164.

de Jong, M.T., & Bus, A.G. (2004). The efficacy of electronic books in fostering kindergarten children's emergent story understanding. *Reading Research Quarterly, 39,* 378–393.

Frijters, J.C., Barron, R.W., & Brunello, M. (2000). Direct or mediated influences of home literacy and literacy interest on prereaders' oral vocabulary and early written language skill. *Journal of Educational Psychology, 92,* 466–477.

Greenfield, P.M., Camaioni, L., Ercolani, P., Weiss, L., Lauber, B.A., & Perucchini, P. (1996). Cognitive socialization by computer games in two cultures: Inductive discovery or mastery of an iconic code? In I.E. Sigel (Series Ed.) & P.M. Greenfield & R.R. Cocking (Vol. Eds.), *Advances in applied developmental psychology: Vol.11. Interacting with video* (pp.141–167). Norwood, NJ: Ablex.

Huston, A., & Wright, J. (1983). Children's processing of television: The informative functions of formal features. In J. Bryant & D.R. Anderson (Eds.), *Children's understanding of television: Research on attention and comprehension* (pp. 35–68). New York: Academic Press.

James, R. (1999). Navigating CD-ROMs: An exploration of children reading interactive narratives. *Children's Literature in Education, 30,* 47–63.

Janosch (1986). *Ik maak je weer beter, zei Beer* [I'll make you well again, said the bear]. Brussels, Belgium: Casterman.

Kamil, M.L., Intrator, S.M., & Kim, H.S. (2000). The effects of other technologies on literacy and literacy learning. In M.L. Kamil, P.B. Mosenthal, P.D. Pearson, & R. Barr (Eds.), *Handbook of reading research* (Vol. 3, pp. 771–788). Mahwah, NJ: Lawrence Erlbaum Associates.

Labbo, L.D., & Kuhn, M.R. (2000). Weaving chains of affect and cognition: A young child's understanding of CD-ROM talking books. *Journal of Literacy Research, 32,* 187–210.

Labbo, L.D., & Reinking, D. (1999). Negotiating the multiple realities of technology in literacy research and instruction. *Reading Research Quarterly, 34,* 478–492.

Lang, A. (2006). Using the limited capacity model of motivated mediated message processing (LC4MP) to design effective cancer communication messages. *Journal of Communication, 56,* 57–80.

Leu, D.J. (2000). Literacy and technology: Deictic consequences for literacy education in an information age. In M.L. Kamil, P.B. Mosenthal, P.D. Pearson, & R. Barr (Eds.), *Handbook of reading research* (Vol. 3, pp. 743–770). Mahwah, NJ: Lawrence Erlbaum Associates.

Mayer, M. (1994). *Just grandma and me.* Novoto, CA: Broderbund.

Mayer, R.E., & Moreno, R. (1998). A split-attention effect in multimedia learning: Evidence for dual processing systems in working memory. *Journal of Educational Psychology, 90,* 312–320.

McKenna, M.C. (1998). Electronic texts and the transformation of beginning reading. In D. Reinking, M.C. McKenna, L.D. Labbo, & R.D. Kieffer (Eds.), *Handbook of literacy and technology: Transformations in a posttypographic world* (pp. 45–59). Mahwah, NJ: Lawrence Erlbaum Associates.

Neuman, S.B. (1989). The impact of different media on children's story comprehension. *Reading Research and Instruction, 28,* 38–47.

Neuman, S.B. (1992). Is learning from media distinctive? Examining children's inferencing strategies. *American Educational Research Journal, 29,* 119–140.

Neuman, S.B. (1997). Television as a learning environment: A theory of synergy. In J. Flood, S. Brice Heath, & D. Lapp (Eds.), *Handbook of research on teaching literacy through the communicative and visual arts* (pp. 15–30). New York: Simon & Schuster.

Paivio, A. (1986). *Mental representations. A dual coding approach.* Oxford: Oxford University Press.

Pecchinenda, A., & Smith, C.A. (1996). The affective significance of skin conductance activity during a difficult problem-solving task. *Cognition and Emotion, 10,* 481–503.

Pressley, M., Cariglia-Bull, T., Deane, S., & Schneider, W. (1987). Short-term memory, verbal competence, and age as predictors of imagery instructional effectiveness. *Journal of Experimental Child Psychology, 43,* 194–211.

Raikes, H., Pan, B.A., Luze, G., Tamis-LeMonde, C.S., Brooks-Gunn, J., Banks Tarullo, J.C., et al. (2006). Mother–child bookreading in low-income families: Correlates and outcomes during the first three years of life. *Child Development, 77,* 924–953.

Ravaja, N. (2004). Contributions of psychophysiology to media research: Review and recommendations. *Media Psychology, 6,* 193–235.

Ricci, C.M., & Beal, C.R. (2002). The effect of interactive media on children's story memory. *Journal of Educational Psychology, 94,* 138–144.

Rideout, V.J., Vandewater, E.A., & Wartella, E.A. (2003). *Zero to six: Electronic media in the lives of infants, toddlers and preschoolers.* Menlo Park, CA: Henry J. Kaiser Family Foundation.

Robinson, M., & Mackey, M. (2003). Film and television. In N. Hall, J. Larson, & J. Marsh (Eds.), *Handbook of early childhood literacy* (pp. 126–141). London: Sage Publications.

Salomon, G. (1984). Television is "easy" and print is "tough": The differential investment of mental effort as a function of perceptions and attributions. *Journal of Educational Psychology, 76,* 647–658.

Sénéchal, M., LeFevre, J.A., Thomas, E.M., & Daley, K.E. (1998). Knowledge of storybooks as a predictor of young children's vocabulary. *Journal of Educational Psychology, 88,* 520–536.

Sharp, D.L.M., Bransford, J.D., Goldman, S.R., Risko, V.J., Kinzer, C.K., & Vye, N.J. (1995). Dynamic visual support for story comprehension and mental model building by young, at-risk children. *Educational Technology Research and Development, 43,* 25–40.

Sulzby, E. (1985). Children's emergent reading of favorite storybooks: A developmental study. *Reading Research Quarterly, 20,* 458–481.

Sundar, S.S., & Kalyanaraman, S. (2004). Arousal, memory, and impression-formation effects of animation speed in web advertising. *Journal of Advertising, 33*(1), 7–17.

Tyner, K. (1998). *Literacy in a digital world: Teaching and learning in the age of information.* Mahwah, NJ: Lawrence Erlbaum Associates.

Uchikoshi, Y. (2005). Narrative development in bilingual kindergartners: Can Arthur help? *Developmental Psychology, 41,* 464–478.

Verhallen, M.J.A.J., & Bus, A.G. (2007). *Exploring the relationship between repeated readings of a storybook, attentional arousal, and vocabulary learning in young children at-risk.*

Verhallen, M.J.A.J., Bus, A.G., & de Jong, M.T. (2006). The promise of multimedia stories for kindergarten children at risk. *Journal of Educational Psychology, 98,* 410–419.

Zeijl, E., Crone, M., Wiefferink, K., Keuzenkamp, S., & Reijneveld, M. (2005). *Kinderen in Nederland* [Children in the Netherlands]. Den Haag: SCP-publication 2005/4.

14

The Limits of the
Self-Teaching Hypothesis

Marilyn Jager Adams

The National Assessment of Educational Progress (NAEP), or Nation's Report Card, was designed to monitor the academic attainment of our nation's school children. In this, its core purpose is to provide the information needed to ensure that all children, regardless of background or region, receive full educational opportunity. Toward that end, the outcomes of the NAEP are divided into three broad performance categories: *proficient*, corresponding to solid grade-level performance; *advanced*, corresponding to superior performance; and *basic*, indicating partial mastery of the knowledge and skills required for grade-level lessons and learning. Although the NAEP was conceived in the 1960s, it was not until the early 1990s that the funding, policy, and technology came together to return useful information about our nation's progress. The first usefully large-scale assessment in reading was administered in 1992, and the results stunned the nation.

The big surprise of the 1992 NAEP (Mullis, Campbell, & Farstrup, 1993) was not that merely 25% of tested fourth graders demonstrated reading at or above grade level (i.e., *proficient* and *advanced*). The big surprise of the 1992 NAEP was that the scores of fully 40% of tested fourth graders, nationwide, fell below the *basic* category; among children of poverty, 80% fell below *basic*. Given that 8% of students in the test sample were deemed incapable of taking the test for reasons of limited English proficiency or special educational profiles, the implication was that nearly half of our nation's students lacked the minimal knowledge and skills required for grade-level learning.

The 1992 NAEP told us that our schools were failing. Most especially, they were failing those very children who depend most of all on school for their formal education—those very children for whom public education was principally instituted.

The United States has traditionally taken great pride in its system of public education. In "the land of opportunity," education is "the key to opportunity." It was nearly impossible to believe that the NAEP scores accurately reflected the productivity of our nation's schools. A strong suspicion was that these results were anomalous—that they represented a local perturbation, a local downturn in a larger, longer-term backdrop of greater educational success. To be sure, this was only a hypothesis or, perhaps, a hope. Because 1992 was the first well-sampled, large-scale, state-by-state administration of the reading NAEP, it was impossible to know for sure. Yet, when the outcomes of the 1994 reading NAEP (Campbell, Donahue, Reese, & Phillips, 1996) proved still worse, many minds were made up.

Surely some dire educational malady was causing a precipitous drop in our school children's reading achievement, and the major suspect was the whole language philosophy that was then sweeping the nation and that adamantly rejected the value of teaching children the alphabetic basics. Therefore, state after state announced reading reform initiatives for students in kindergarten through third grade. A central goal of these initiatives was to reinstate direct, systematic instruction of the alphabetic basics, including knowledge of letters and letter–sound correspondences, phonemic awareness, and phonics.

The renewed emphasis on early alphabetic instruction was well founded. Weaknesses at school entry in alphabetic basics, especially letter knowledge and phonemic awareness, were found to be strong predictors of reading difficulties across the elementary-school years (e.g., Vellutino et al., 1996; Wagner et al., 1997). Indeed, researchers had found first graders' end-of-year ability to decode or sound out words to predict 40% of the variance in their reading comprehension in secondary school (Foorman, Francis, Fletcher, Schatschneider, & Mehta, 1998). Furthermore, weaknesses in phonological decoding and phonemic awareness are characteristic of students with severe reading delay among both students with dyslexia and "garden variety" poor readers (e.g., Fletcher et al., 1994; Shankweiler et al., 1995; Stanovich & Siegel, 1994). Meanwhile, new computational and imaging technologies were enabling cognitive psychologists and neuroscientists to probe the dynamics of reading ever more deeply, both affirming and clarifying the integral dependence of fluent, productive reading on deep and ready knowledge of spelling–sound correspondences (see Adams, 1990; Harm & Seidenberg, 1999; Pugh et al., 1996).

Coupled with such research, certain educational implications were equally clear. First, reading acquisition depends fundamentally on knowledge and understanding of the alphabetic basics. Second, many children failed to develop such knowledge and understandings on their own. Third, there was every indication that classroom instruction could make a significant difference. Method comparison studies had shown over and over that providing beginning readers with explicit, well-organized instruction in phonics is of special value toward helping them learn to read (Adams, 1990; Chall, 1967; Pflaum, Walberg, Karegianes, & Rasher, 1980; National Institute of Child Health and Human Development

[NICHD], 2000; National Research Council, 1998). In addition, the research literature offered a growing body of demonstrations that engaging children in activities designed to develop phonemic awareness hastens phonics and spelling acquisition (see Adams, Trieman, & Pressley, 1997; NICHD, 2000). Again, then, the renewed emphasis on early alphabetic instruction was well founded.

Yet, there was a wishful side of this initiative, too. Research had shown that, at least in large number statistics, the reading achievement of students who had not caught on by the end of first grade tended never to catch up (Carter, 1984). To what extent could reading failure be eliminated by ensuring all children a proper start? Research had shown problems with phonemic awareness and phonics to be the signature of reading disability. By failing to teach these basics, had we effectively caused an epidemic of reading disability? Research had shown that reading comprehension, through the middle grades (Juel, 1994) and even through high school (Foorman, Francis, Shaywitz, Shaywitz, & Fletcher, 1997), was strongly predicted by students' ability to decode at the end of Grade 1. If first graders were taught to decode, would their comprehension grow in response? Could the tide be reversed by securing phonemic awareness and phonics at the outset? After all, the great advantage of an alphabetic system is held to be that it enables readers to identify any printed word provided they know how to translate its spelling to speech sounds (e.g., Flesch, 1955; Share, 1995). Taught well, then, phonics should in turn enable students to acquire new words they encounter in print all by themselves through self-teaching. By extension, the effective value of concentrating on solid, early phonics instruction might be expected to snowball, compounding itself over time, growing in impact with each successive year in school.

To be sure, the extreme version of the fix-it-through-phonics notion was more than one could hope for. In logical terms, it was highly tenuous conjecture. The proposition "If no phonics, then problems" holds only that phonics is *necessary* for reading growth. Its converse, "If phonics, then no problems," would follow only given the untenable condition that phonics is both *necessary* and *sufficient* for reading growth.

On the other hand, the question of how much and in what ways an emphasis on phonics instruction would reduce reading difficulties, was wholly legitimate. An invaluable aspect of the K–3 reading initiatives is that it has offered a large and realistically complex implementation base to examine the impact and the limitations of such emphasis with respect to both students and literacy goals. Better still, to the extent that the K–3 initiatives have done their job, our educational system is in position both to identify and, with the basics in place, to productively address continuing needs. The remainder of this chapter addresses these issues.

IMPACT OF THE K–3 READING INITIATIVES

The results of the 2005 reading NAEP (Perie, Grigg, & Donahue, 2005) are shown in Figure 14.1 alongside those from 1992 (Campbell et al., 1996). As

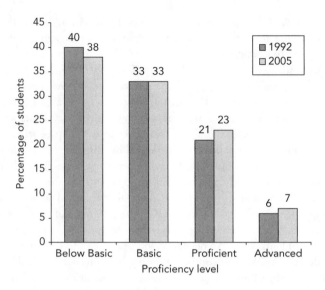

Figure 14.1. Reading proficiency for fourth-grade, public school students as measured by the 1992 (Mullis, Campbell, & Farstrup, 1993) and 2005 (Perie, Grigg, & Donahue, 2005) National Assessment of Educational Progress in reading.

shown, the reading achievement of fourth graders has increased. Relative to 1992, fewer children scored below *basic,* and more scored at or above *proficient* or grade level in 2005. These gains, however, are not statistically significant, much less anything close to what was hoped for or needed. In mathematics, by contrast, the NAEP scores have increased much more dramatically and the achievement gap has narrowed significantly over the same period of time (Perie, Grigg, & Dion, 2006), despite the fact that the reading reform was higher in priority, implementation guidance, and monitoring. Indeed, the math gains suggest that reform emphasis in itself can produce significant increases in student learning, which, in turn, raises the question of why the reading initiatives have not worked better. To approach this issue, let us turn to test outcomes from two of the states that were among the earliest in implementing primary-grade reading reforms.

CALIFORNIA READING INITIATIVE

The 1992 NAEP reading results were troubling for all states, but especially for California (see Mullis et al., 1993). Basing expectations on size alone, California, with one eighth of the country's population, should have ranked in the middle of the distribution. Instead, the reading performance of 52% of California's fourth graders fell below *basic,* thus tying for last in the nation among states. This was despite the fact that California's exclusion rate was the highest in the country; 14%

of its students were deemed incapable of participation in the assessment as compared with a median across states of 6%. By 1994, the NAEP showed California to have fallen further, with 56% of its children performing below *basic* proficiency.

Led by lifelong political activist Marion Joseph, California responded aggressively. The whole language curriculum was identified as the major cause of its educational maladies. And, indeed, California does appear to have been more deeply immersed in whole language than most: In the teacher questionnaire portion of the 1992 NAEP, 69% of California's teachers indicated *heavy* (as compared with *moderate* or *little or no*) emphasis on whole language; across the other states, the median response for *heavy* was 40%. In addition, 52% of California's teachers indicated little or no reliance on phonics; the median response from the other states was 33%.

A reading task force was convened in 1995 and was soon followed by new laws, a new framework, new standards, new teacher certification requirements, new professional development programs, a statewide program of student testing, and a new textbook adoption. Although California's framework and standards are broad and rigorous, spanning all grades and addressing the range of language and literary challenges, the reform to date has focused principally on securing the alphabetic basics, especially among students in kindergarten through Grade 3.

The data in Table 14.1 present the National Percentile Rank (NPR) scores for California's second through fifth graders on the Stanford Achievement Test Series, Ninth Edition (Stanford 9; Harcourt Brace, 1996), a norm-referenced test of reading achievement as reported by the California Department of Education (2007). The scores extend from the 1997–1998 school year, which is when the state's reading initiative began, through the 2001–2002 school year, after which the state changed assessments and English proficiency criteria, thus making continued comparisons difficult. The questions in consideration are

1. Did the initiative significantly and positively affect students' reading growth?

2. Did the initiative result in significant narrowing of the achievement gap?

3. Did the impact of the initiative strengthen as the children progressed through successive years of schooling?

Table 14.1. Average National Percentile Rank (NPR) score on the Stanford 9 achievement test for all tested California students in Grades 2–11 from academic years 1997–1998 to 2001–2002

School year	Grades									
	2	3	4	5	6	7	8	9	10	11
1997–1998	39	36	40	40	43	41	44	34	32	37
1998–1999	43	40	42	41	45	43	46	34	32	36
1999–2000	48	44	45	44	47	45	47	36	33	37
2000–2001	50	46	47	45	48	46	48	35	33	37
2001–2002	52	47	50	46	49	46	48	35	33	38

In examining Table 14.1, the reader is asked first to turn his or her attention to the primary grades, as it was on these grades that California's reading initiative was principally focused. As shown, the performance of the second graders grew consistently, year after year, from 39% in 1997–1998 to 52% in 2001–2002. For third graders, the pattern is similar. To this extent, it would seem that California's reading initiative has indeed been quite positive, at least in the primary grades as measured statewide by the Stanford 9 test. Let us therefore turn to the other two issues: Has the impact of the reading initiative extended to needier students? And, have its benefits endured or, better yet, increased beyond the primary grades?

Table 14.2 presents the NPR scores on the Stanford 9 for students of Limited English Proficiency (LEP). Inasmuch as this is the only less-advantaged subgroup that California reported separately across these years, it is used here to consider the impact of the initiative on the achievement gap. The size of California's LEP subgroup grew from 20% of the tested population in 1997–1998 to nearly 25% in 2001–2002. For 2nd grade, the growth was from 25% to 35%; for 11th grade, it was from 11% to 14%. (California Department of Education, 2007).

In Table 14.2, as in Table 14.1, the impact of California's K–3 reading initiative is plainly visible. For Grade 2 LEP students, Stanford 9 scores grew consistently, year after year, from 19% in 1997–1998 to 34% in 2001–2002. The gain is substantial and, at least in terms of raw percentile scores, quite comparable to that evident in the school population overall. Nevertheless, the LEP students remain behind throughout the school years. Why?

One glaring contrast between the scores of the LEP students and the overall population is in the initial levels of literacy achievement. As discussed in Chapters 1 and 9, children's preschool language and literacy experience exerts long and strong influence on their scholastic achievement. In terms of background, most of California's LEP students are Hispanic (85%) and most, especially among the Hispanic population, are poor. Hispanic children have been shown to be less likely than others to attend preschool at all, and those who do have been shown to attend for fewer years and in centers of lower quality than their non-Hispanic peers

Table 14.2. Average National Percentile Rank (NPR) score on the Stanford 9 achievement test for California's Limited English Proficient (LEP) students in Grades 2–11 from academic years 1997–1998 to 2001–2002

School year	Grades									
	2	3	4	5	6	7	8	9	10	11
1997–1998	19	14	15	14	16	12	15	10	8	10
1998–1999	23	18	17	16	18	14	17	11	9	11
1999–2000	28	21	20	17	19	15	18	12	9	11
2000–2001	31	23	21	18	20	16	19	12	9	11
2001–2002	34	26	24	20	21	17	19	12	9	11

(Rumberger & Tran, 2006). With interest in narrowing the achievement gap, then, a strong implication would seem to be that California is in dire need of better preschool support in complement to its K–3 reading initiative.

The third hope undergirding the K–3 reading initiatives was that solid alphabetic instruction at the outset of students' schooling would continue to accelerate children's reading growth beyond the primary years. To consider this outcome, the reader is asked to examine the diagonals in Tables 14.1 and 14.2. The cohort that was in Grade 2 in 1997–1998 was in Grade 3 in 1998–1999, Grade 4 in 1999–2000, and so forth. Inasmuch as each successive cohort remains stronger across grades than the one preceding it, the increments in the Grade 2 scores appear both real and enduring. Conversely, the scores show little sign of increase across grade levels in either table. If there exists some slight acceleration across grades for the population overall (Table 14.1), it appears the same for all cohorts, including those who were in Grade 2 prior to 1997–1998 when the initiative began. For the LEP students (Table 14.2), this pattern is only starker. The scores of each cohort in the LEP subgroup appear remarkably constant from grade to grade, not dwindling with development but not growing substantially either.

California has not yet created a system for monitoring LEP transitions statewide. Nevertheless, gross statistics tell us that new students account for a small minority (4.5%) of the LEP enrollment and that the annual rate of transition to Fluent English Proficient designation has been between 6% and 9% across these years. For each cohort, the net LEP enrollment declines by about 1% per school year. This low transition rate is despite the fact that upward of 45% of LEP students score at transition levels on the California English Language Development Test (CELDT, http://celdt.cde.ca.gov/). It is also despite the fact that the majority of California's LEP enrollees (85%) were born in the United States (Jepsen & de Alth, 2005; Tafoya, 2002) and about one third live in homes in which English is the dominant language (Rumberger, 2007). In Grade 6, more than half of the LEP enrollees have been going to school in the same district since kindergarten, and by Grade 10 more than half have been enrolled in U.S. schools for at least 10 years, about one third of whom have been enrolled in the same district since kindergarten (Hill, 2004; Wise et al., 2006). Holding district factors constant, Jespen and de Alth (2005) found the best predictor of reclassification for LEP students is not performance on the CELDT but, instead, performance on the English Language Arts section of California Standards Test (http://www. cde.ca.gov/ta/).[1]

---

[1]California requires completion of a Home Language Survey for all students upon school entry. If the parent's response to this survey indicates that a language other than English was the child's first language and continues to be the child's predominant language at home, then the CELDT must be administered within 30 days of admission. Redesignation as *Fluent English Proficient* requires performance at the *advanced* level on the CELDT, performance on the California Standards Test in English-Language Arts that meets the *basic* cut-point, a recommendation for redesignation by the child's teacher, and approval by his or her parents.

The LEP population should, in principle, be a high turnover sample. To the extent this were so, one could not expect mean test scores to increase across grades. Yet, as just described, available statistics indicate that California's LEP students are rarely transitioned to Fluent English Proficient status. More daunting, the statistics suggest that these students' English language designation may be less of an impediment to their literacy growth than their literacy growth is an impediment to their English language designation. Whatever it is that these children need, the schools are failing to provide it.

In any case, the California Department of Education (2007) added score breakouts to its assessment reports for several other groups in 1999. As for the overall population and the LEP subgroup, the Grade 2 scores of each of these groups of students increased substantially between 1999 and 2002: Economically Disadvantaged increased from 29% to 39%, Not Economically Disadvantaged from 56% to 68%, and English Only and Fluent English Proficient from 53% to 61%. Moreover, for each of these groups, the overall pattern is the same: The impact of the initiative on primary-grade test performance is visible; the magnitude of the impact increases consistently across successive implementation years of the initiative; and the relative benefit evident in the Grade 2 scores persists across ensuing school years. Equally, however, there is little evidence for any group that the reading initiative has brought any benefits above and beyond those registered by second grade.

In summary, though positive and promising, California's efforts have not yet been sufficient either to bring the majority of students up to grade-level expectations or to close the achievement gap appreciably. On one end of the developmental continuum, California's test scores underscore the need for more and better preschool support, especially for less affluent and language-minority students. On the other, the data force the question of what else California's schools can or should do to build on or complement the benefits sown in the primary grades.

FLORIDA READING INITIATIVE

Although the NAEP is handy for gauging the relative educational progress of states and student groups nationally, it is too general to be useful to the separate states for evaluating specifics of their curricular scope and sequence or its delivery. Similarly, though norm-referenced assessments such as the Stanford 9 are useful for gauging students' relative standings, they shed little light on specific strengths and weaknesses. Part of the reading reform initiative has therefore been one of urging the separate states to implement criterion-referenced assessments tied to explicit grade-by-grade learning frameworks. As one of the "first-generation" accountability states (Lee, 2006), Florida was among the first to have a criterion-referenced assessment firmly in place and aligned with its framework, the Sunshine State Standards.

The outcomes of the criterion-referenced part of the Florida Comprehensive Achievement Test (FCAT) are reported in terms of five broad performance levels. Levels 3, 4, and 5 are meant to correspond to adequate, solid, and advanced grade-level performance, roughly equivalent to report card grades of *C, B,* and *A,* respectively. Levels 2 and 1 signify below–grade-level performance, corresponding roughly to report card grades of *D* and *F.*

Between 2001, when Florida began reporting these scores, and 2006, the percentage of Level 1 students in mathematics has shrunk considerably, having dropped from 21% to 12% for 3rd graders and from 20% to 15% for 10th graders (Florida Department of Education, 2007). For reading, in contrast, the results are mixed. For reading, the percentage of 3rd graders scoring within Level 1 has fallen from 27% to 14% since 2001. Because Florida's 3rd graders must score within Level 2, at a minimum, to be promoted to 4th grade, this is good. It also suggests that, like California, Florida has made significant progress in strengthening primary-grade reading instruction. Among 10th graders, however, the percentage scoring within Level 1 in reading has risen from 31% to 38%. Because 10th graders must score within Level 2 to be eligible for a high school diploma, this is not good. It also suggests that, like California, Florida is struggling with approaches to effectively support the literacy growth of students in the middle grades and higher. Florida's promotion and graduation hurdles were intended as incentives, but until they are within reach they may instead be obstacles for many students. Although Florida's 10th graders may repeat the test multiple times, many instead opt to drop out of school. Florida's graduation rate is estimated at 53%, ranking 50th in the nation (Orfield, Losen, Wald, & Swanson, 2004).

ANALYSIS OF PERFORMANCE ON THE FLORIDA COMPREHENSIVE ACHIEVEMENT TEST

In the interest of learning how to improve this situation, a team led by the Florida Center for Reading Research compared student performance on the FCAT to several componential measures of reading, cognitive, and linguistic abilities (Schatschneider et al., 2004). The student sample included 200 students in each of 3rd, 7th, and 10th grades, selected to be representative of the Florida reading demographic. In complement to the FCAT, the researchers assessed 1) verbal knowledge and reasoning using the Wechsler Intelligence Scale for Children (WISC; Wechsler, 1991) Vocabulary and Similarities tests plus listening comprehension on FCAT passages; 2) oral reading fluency using grade-level texts from the Gray Oral Reading Test (Wiederholt & Bryant, 1992) plus passages from the FCAT; 3) decoding efficiency, speed, and accuracy using the sight word and pseudoword lists of the Test of Word Reading Efficiency (TOWRE; Torgesen, Wagner, & Rashotte, 1999); 4) nonverbal reasoning using the WISC Matrix Reasoning and Block Design, and 5) working memory using listening and reading span tests.

To examine the relative contribution of these components, a dominance analysis was conducted for each grade. For the 3rd graders, the best predictor of overall FCAT performance was oral reading fluency, accounting for 55% of the variance overall and 17% of unique variance (i.e., variance unshared by the other assessments). The second strongest factor for the 3rd graders was verbal knowledge and reasoning, accounting for 47% of the FCAT variance overall and contributing 7% of unique variance. By 7th grade, the explanatory power attributable to fluency differences (43% overall and 8% unique) was slightly upstaged by verbal knowledge and reasoning (51% overall and 10% unique). By 10th grade, verbal knowledge and reasoning was by far the best predictor of FCAT scores, picking up 52% of the overall and 15% of the unique variance. At this point, the contribution of fluency had fallen to 32% of the overall and only 7% of the unique variance.

Phonemic-decoding scores were not reported separately by the research team because they were found to correlate so strongly with the fluency measures as to add little additional information. Nevertheless, compared with national norms, the average phonemic-decoding score of Florida's Level 1 3rd graders was at the 26th percentile, suggesting that, for most, phonics was not the core impediment to reading growth. By comparison, the fluency scores of the Level 1 students fell beneath the 10th percentile at every grade level. Specifically, the average reading fluency of the Level 1 students was at the 6th percentile for 3rd graders, the 7th percentile for 7th graders, and the 8th percentile for 10th graders. In addition, the Level 1 students' verbal knowledge and reasoning percentiles dropped from the 42nd percentile in 3rd grade to the 34th and 30th percentiles in the 7th and 10th grades, respectively. The causes of this decline, suggest Schatschneider et al. (2004), are most likely rooted in the inability or unwillingness of the Level 1 students to read as extensively as their more proficient peers.

ANALYZING THE CAUSES OF DYSFLUENCY

Provoked by their team's analysis of the FCAT data (Schatschneider et al., 2004), Torgesen and Hudson (2006) decided to reanalyze the fluency performance of five other groups of students from whom they had collected assessment data over the years. Two of the groups of students were 10- to 12-year-olds who had participated in intensive reading remediation study with a special emphasis on phonics and decoding; the students had been selected for the study because their reading was well below grade level at the outset. The third and fourth groups were composed of students who had been identified as being at risk in kindergarten and first grade and had participated in intensive prevention studies, again with an emphasis on phonics. For one of these groups, the intervention had been conducted in first grade, and the follow-up data were collected at the end of second grade. For the other, the intervention had extended from kindergarten through second grade and the follow-up data were collected at the end of fourth grade.

The fifth group of students was composed of a cross section of fifth graders, spanning the range of reading abilities.

The measures against which the students' fluency performance were analyzed included 1) nonword decoding efficiency, 2) sight-word reading efficiency, 3) vocabulary size, and 4) naming speed for digits. In every one of the groups, the majority of the fluency variance (67%–83%) was explained by sight-word reading efficiency. Above and beyond sight words, the contribution of vocabulary was significant among the most proficient readers, reminiscent of the shift from fluency to verbal knowledge and reasoning in Schatschneider et al.'s (2004) analysis of Florida's FCAT scores (see also Jenkins, Fuchs, van den Broek, Espin, & Deno, 2003). Beyond sight words and vocabulary, decoding efficiency added no more than 2% of additional predictive power.

PHONICS IS NECESSARY BUT NOT SUFFICIENT

First, and very importantly: Do the data just reviewed suggest that proficient decoding does not matter? The answer to this question is a categorical, emphatic *no*. Consistent with the larger literature, the Florida analyses show that nonword decoding, in itself, was strongly correlated with the children's fluency. What they add, however, is that by the middle grades, nonword decoding was also very strongly correlated with the children's sight-word facility, which in turn was a better predictor of their fluency. To couch this in familiar terms, think about your own reading. Sometimes the mature reader pauses to sound out an unfamiliar word but not very often. Instead, the sight, sound, and meaning of the vast majority of the words on a page seem to pop to mind at a glance. These words are sight words, and the instantaneity with which they are recognized is due to the completeness with which their spellings, sounds, and meanings are represented and interconnected in the reader's memory.

Indeed, mature readers are generally able to read off never-before-seen words with remarkably little effort—so little, in fact, that if the word is in the reader's speaking or listening vocabulary, he or she may never even notice that it has never before been seen. This capacity to read novel words easily is called *decoding automaticity*. Decoding automaticity is rooted in the reader's cumulative knowledge of spelling patterns and their mappings to speech correspondences; in effect, this complex of knowledge provides a support structure by which nearly every new word is partly learned already.

Although the most obvious benefit of having learned to decode may be that it enables readers to sound out the occasional unknown word they encounter in print, it is not the most important benefit beyond the beginning stages. Instead, the most pervasive and invaluable benefit of phonics is that, through experience, it creates the infrastructure in memory that enables readers to identify new words with ease and to retain them distinctly and enduringly as sight words. Phonics provides the infrastructure for acquiring sight words, and, reciprocally, the acquisition of many, many sight words enriches that infrastructure and affords decoding automaticity.

Thus, through research with Israeli students, Share (1999, 2004) has shown that—provided the child successfully identifies the word—just a few exposures of a new word in the course of reading leave a detailed trace in memory. For example, Share (2004) showed that even a single, correctly decoded encounter in the course of reading a story generally enabled third graders to distinguish the new word from alternatives with similar spellings or identical pronunciations and to spell it with impressive accuracy when probed several days or even weeks later. A related study by Share and Shalev (2004) indicates that the principal reason that poor and dyslexic readers retain fewer new words from reading is simply that they are less likely to identify them correctly while reading.

Cunningham and her colleagues have replicated these effects in English with first graders (Cunningham, 2006) and second graders (Cunningham, Perry, Stanovich, & Share, 2002). Before engaging children in the reading task, Cunningham and colleagues measured their prior orthographic or, essentially, sight-word knowledge through three different tasks: One presented conventionally and oddly spelled nonwords (e.g., *fage vs. fayj*), asking which looked more like a real word; another asked the children to discern real words from homophonically spelled nonwords (e.g., *take vs. taik*); the third presented two real, homophonic words and asked the children to select between them based on meaning (e.g., "Which is a flower?" *rose vs. rows*). The results of both of these studies show the children's prior orthographic knowledge to be a strong predictor of the likelihood that they would decode the target words correctly while reading and, beyond that, of how well they would retain the words even having identified them correctly during reading.

The implication is that, even given equal amounts of reading, ease or likelihood of learning sight words through reading increases directly with the number of sight words the student already possesses. Relative to children with a smaller sight-word repertoire, those with larger sight-word repertoire will be more likely read novel words correctly and to retain them when they do. Left to their own devices, by comparison, children who have acquired less sight-word knowledge will be less likely to read novel words correctly and will remember them less well even if they do. Happily, sight-word acquisition can be productively supported through practices in which students are encouraged to try to do their best to identify new words while reading and are corrected when they fail (e.g., Ehri & Saltmarsh, 1995; Reitsma, 1983, 1989; Manis, 1985). Do note, however, the latter is not self-teaching; it is teaching.

Cunningham and colleagues (2002) also found that their young readers identified the target words with significantly more success (84% vs. 67%) when the words appeared in meaningful context rather than unmeaningful (scrambled) context (see also Jenkins et al., 2003; Nation & Snowling, 1998). The mechanism by which this happens is presumably that the cogent context primes the target word from the inside out, assisting the reader in constructing or selecting its correct pronunciation (see Gorfein, 2001). Yet, priming necessarily depends as much on the familiarity of the word to be read as it does on the coherence or comprehensibility of the context.

The implication is that, even given equal amounts of reading, the likelihood of independently acquiring new sight words from reading must also increase directly with the child's vocabulary. Relative to children with weaker language and vocabulary knowledge, children with stronger language and vocabulary knowledge will be more likely to acquire new sight words while reading for the simple reason that they are more likely to identify them correctly on encounter. Conversely, children with weaker language and vocabularies will be less likely to identify and, therefore to retain, new words they encounter while reading. Furthermore, because meaningfulness or lexical familiarity should contribute more associative glue to the just-read word, the retention of new words also depends on knowing (and thinking of) their meanings (see Berends & Reitsma, 2006). Even further, as the bonds between orthography and meaning strengthen, they begin to work synergistically with the word-perception processes, the result being that decoding and word recognition are both faster and more accurate when the words to be identified are embedded in meaningful context. This is so not only among mature readers (see Gorfein, 2001) but also among typically developing grade-school readers (e.g., Cunningham et al., 2002; Jenkins et al., 2003; Nation & Snowling, 1998).

Vocabulary is thus very important for sight-word acquisition; yet, it is still more important to understanding and learning. After all, in the decontextualized world of text, it is principally through their words and wordings that authors convey their intended meaning and message. To the extent that students cannot understand the words of a passage, they must equally forfeit its intended meaning. In keeping with this, long- and well-established (e.g., Thorndike, 1973) vocabulary knowledge is a strong predictor of students' reading comprehension.

Why, then, should vocabulary be such an obstacle to reading development for students who, like so many of those in California, demonstrate basically good English language competence? A major reason is that, in its range of topics and its need for precision and clarity, written text makes use of far more words than most oral language situations. Nation and Waring (1997) estimated that only 4,000 basic word families account for 97% of oral language. By comparison, estimates of the number of words in the reading materials of contemporary adults (British National Corpus, 2007) or U.S. school children (Carroll, Davies, & Richman, 1971) exceed half a million. Counting only base words (e.g., only one word for such word sets as *represent, representing, representation,* and *misrepresent*), Nagy and Anderson (1984) estimated that the number of distinctly meaningful words expected of the average 12th grader may actually be closer to 40,000, but still, that's 10 times more than needed for—or available to be learned from—typical oral discourse.

The implication is that children who seemingly possess full and agile oral language competence may or may not possess the vocabulary required by their books; ordinary, spoken language exchanges do not offer opportunity for gauging students' reading vocabulary. More importantly, spoken language experience does not offer students opportunity to acquire the kind of the vocabulary required for becoming a reader. The kind of language and vocabulary on which comprehension of written text depends can only be gained through experience with written texts.

Moreover, the magnitude of the vocabulary challenge involved in becoming a reader is immense. Even if, beginning in 1st grade and continuing through 12th grade, classrooms consistently taught—and students perfectly retained—20 vocabulary words each and every week, the vocabulary gain would equal only 8,640 words in total (20 words × 36 weeks of school × 12 years), many times fewer than what is required. Such considerations have led some scholars to conclude that the only feasible means by which students might acquire the vocabulary needed for reading is by inferring their meanings from context in the course of reading (see Nagy, Herman, & Anderson, 1985).

The actual probability of learning the meaning of any new word through reading is quite small in any case (Nagy, Anderson, & Herman, 1987; Schatz & Baldwin, 1986) and smaller still when the text is challenging for the student. Summarizing his own work, Anderson (1996) reported, "The overall likelihood [of learning the meaning of new words through reading] ranged from better than 1 in 10 when children were reading easy narratives to near zero when they were reading difficult expositions" (p. 61). Comparisons of narrative and expository texts show that the vocabulary demands of the latter are significantly more challenging. Not only do expository texts contain more rare words per page, but the meanings of those words tend to be more specific and information-laden (Biber, 1988; Gardner, 2004). Yet, in the middle grades and higher, expository texts become the primary resource for learning.

But here is another Catch-22. The prospect of inferring a word's meaning from context depends on understanding the context itself, and research shows that adequate comprehension of a text depends on understanding at least 98% of its running words (Betts, 1946; Carver, 1994; Hu & Nation, 2000; Laufer, 1988). Consistent with this, the strength of students' vocabulary predicts the likelihood of learning a word from context (Daneman & Green, 1986; Herman, Anderson, Pearson, & Nagy, 1987; Shefelbine, 1990; Sternberg & Powell, 1983), the probability of correctly inferring a new word's meaning from context (Morrison, 1996; Nassaji, 2004), and both the amount and nature of reasoning that is evidenced when they are asked to do so (Calvo, Estevez, & Dowens, 2003; Nassaji, 2004). Even when students are told the meaning of a new word, their prior vocabulary strength predicts the likelihood that they will retain it (Biemiller & Boote, 2006; Jenkins, Stein, & Wysocki, 1984; Robbins & Ehri, 1994). Nevertheless, supplying the meaning of an unknown word in the course of reading at the moment when needed is a singularly helpful means of anchoring it in the student's memory (e.g., Jenkins, Matlock, & Slocum, 1989; also see NICHD, 2000). But, again, the latter is not self-teaching; it is teaching.

The implication is that, even given equal amounts of reading, children with stronger vocabularies will acquire more new words along the way. Relative to students with stronger language and vocabulary skills, those with weaker vocabulary skills are less likely to understand the wordings of their text, less likely to be able to infer the meanings of unfamiliar words from context, and less likely to retain the meanings of whatever words they might glean or be told. Thus, vocabulary strength is a potent predictor of students' reading comprehension from the middle grades and higher. Moreover, weak English vocabulary is characteristic of children from high-poverty neighborhoods.

MAKING SELF-TEACHING POSSIBLE THROUGH TEACHING

In summary, solid working knowledge of phonics and the inclination or discipline to use that knowledge while reading is imperative for good literacy growth. Phonics enables students to translate the print on the page into language and, therewith, to process it through their prior knowledge. Phonics is therefore necessary. The problem is that phonics is not sufficient: To the extent that the student lacks the prior knowledge—be it orthographic, lexical, semantic, linguistic, or conceptual—that the text presumes, the output of the decoding process cannot be fully received, interpreted, or retained. The dilemma is that, beyond phonics, the balance of what is required for reading is principally available only through exposure to text and ideally through reading itself.

The challenge is thus twofold. First, how can children be led to read as much as they need? Second, how can they be ensured the assistance that they need to understand and learn productively while reading? In mulling these questions, bear in mind that, given the goals of developing new sight-words and new vocabulary, the texts students need most to read must offer some challenge, representing instructional rather than independent reading levels.

As reported by the National Reading Panel (NICHD, 2000), the single best practice for moving students beyond the basics is what the panelists termed *guided oral reading*. Guided oral reading occurs when a child reads and rereads texts aloud alongside a helpful adult. Why is guided oral reading so helpful? Among other reasons, there are two that are arguably critical. First, the adult provides an audience and partner, thus keeping the child attentive and on task. Second, the adult helps. When words are difficult or misread, the adult assists and corrects. When meanings are unknown, the adult supplies them. When the text is too presumptuous, the adult elaborates and provides background knowledge. When the text presents important (or interesting or funny) information, the adult draws attention to it, helping the child to enjoy and reflect on it, too. When the child reads splendidly, the adult is appreciative. Because listeners know exactly where the child is in the text, they can choose optimal moments to probe understanding, to elicit predictions, or to invite reflection or discussion. As documented by the National Reading Panel, such read-aloud sessions promote not just fluency but also word recognition, comprehension, and full-scale reading scores. Note, too, that many of the most effective practices for developing vocabulary and comprehension strategies also rest on read-aloud dynamics (see NICHD, 2000).

Evidence suggests that just a few minutes a week of such one-to-one reading generally makes a big difference in a child's reading growth (Adams, 2006). As such, home reading practices may well be the principal factor underlying the achievement gap. For example, many parents make it a mission to ask their children to sit down and read aloud with them across the primary grades. Moving into the middle grades, many parents share-read chapter books with their children. If concerned about their child's reading progress, many parents hire a private tutor who works with their child once or twice a week, spending maybe half the time on guided oral reading. When the school assigns reports to the children, many parents partner with their children to mull over topics and choose and explore suitable resources from the library. When tests are scheduled on the school agenda, many parents strongly encourage their children to study and even take time to study with them.

Indeed, these sorts of literary help are commonly available in the educated home. Unfortunately, there are also many children whose parents cannot, do not, or do not even know that they are expected to provide such support. If one-to-one supported reading practice is so invaluable, then how are these children to get it?

The National Reading Panel (NICHD, 2000) urges all teachers to make more time for guided oral reading. This urging is well and good, but, realistically, schools are not able to offer much one-to-one reading support for reasons of the very structure of the classroom. For example, for a teacher to read just 10 minutes per day with each of 25 children in a classroom would require more than 4 hours per day—assuming zero transition time and provided that each of the 24 unattended children in the classroom behave themselves perfectly for the duration. Indeed, research affirms that one-to-one reading opportunities are generally both rare and brief, whether in the general education classroom (McIntosh, Vaughn, Schumm, Haager, & Lee, 1993; Moody, Vaughn, & Schumm, 1997) or in special education classrooms (Vaughn, Levy, Coleman, & Bos, 2002; Vaughn, Moody, & Schumm, 1998). Furthermore, by all indications, the amount of classroom time spent reading is even less in poorer schools and with poorer readers (Allington, 1983, 1989; Birman et al., 1987).

To what extent can the reading achievement gap between America's have and have-not students be explained in terms of the likelihood that somebody at home reads with them? To what extent might the reading and learning of the student body at large be accelerated if, somehow, our schools were able to find the capacity to offer every child the benefits of guided oral reading? It is not *only* reading that is at stake, either; students' entire education depends so heavily on reading. The NAEP indicates that only 29% of fourth graders and 32% of eighth graders are at or above grade level in science. Similarly, the percentages for fourth and eighth graders, respectively, are only 34% and 22% in civics; and only 18% and 17% in U.S. history (Grigg, Lauko, & Brockway, 2006; Lee & Weiss, 2007; Lutkus & Weiss, 2007). To what extent would our students' dismal achievement in history, science, and math rise if somehow our schools were able to give students the one-to-one tutelage needed to truly read and to actively understand their content-area texts?

TECHNOLOGY FOR GUIDED ORAL READING SUPPORT

With these issues in focus, I worked intensely with a number of colleagues from the mid-1990s to 2007, first at BBN Technologies and then at a start-up company called Soliloquy Learning, Inc. (no longer in existence), on developing a technological solution to this problem. Specifically, our efforts focused on harnessing speech recognition so as to give the computer "ears." The goals of this technology are 1) to offer students the oral reading opportunities and guidance they need to learn through reading and 2) to provide teachers with the assistance and information they need to closely monitor and guide their students' growth.

In many ways, our initial applications[2] with this technology were modeled on conventional "living books." As with conventional living books, the text and illustrations are presented to the student on a computer monitor. The student can click on any individual word to hear it pronounced. If the student is unsure of the word's meaning, the glossary offers (i.e., reads aloud) the word's context-appropriate definition, a usage sentence, and a graphic where possible. The student may also click a button to hear all or any part of the text expressively read aloud by a professional narrator. In addition, the software presents comprehension questions, which serve both to motivate and to assess the student's understanding.

Because of the speech recognizer, however, this software has a distinct advantage relative to the conventional living book. Specifically, as the student reads, the software "listens." When the student struggles, it provides help right then and there. The software continually evaluates the nature and significance of miscues. It instantly highlights any words deemed problematic, requesting that the student reread them before moving on.

If the student continues to struggle, the software pronounces the word aloud, requiring the student to repeat it and to continue reading from there. Meanwhile, the software keeps meticulous records of what and how well the student has read, including fluency, comprehension, and a list of all words that warrant review. All such information is sent to the teacher's site on the network,

---

[2]Soliloquy Learning, Inc., developed two programs of its own: *Soliloquy Learning Elementary Anthology* and *Soliloquy Learning Science and Social Studies Library*. In addition, it produced a number of packages for other publishers, including *Insights Reading Fluency* (Charlesbridge Publishing); *QuickReads* (Pearson Learning Group); *Reading Fluency Coach* (Scott Foresman); and *Rapid Reading Assistant* (Harcourt U.K.).

where it can be compiled in whatever way the teacher finds useful (e.g., individually, by group, by classroom, by grade, per day, per title).

The software also archives audio recordings of the students' readings. Each audio recording is tied to the relevant text, which, in turn, is color coded to show segments of difficulty. The software instructs the student to review all color-coded segments of the text before rereading. The color coding is also intended to make it easer for teachers to decide which parts of the readings warrant their attention for purposes of guiding instruction; they need only scan their students' network reports for the color coding and then click and listen. Another way to think about the software's record-keeping is that, in effect, it tattletales. In consequence, when students are assigned to work with it, they are induced to spend their time well, thus freeing the teacher to work with groups or individuals, addressing their specific needs and interests.

The initial versions of the software were specifically designed to provide the kind of guided oral reading that is needed to advance students from novice to intermediate reading status. Field trials with the software have affirmed that, through its use, children's reading fluency does indeed increase. For example, in a study with second through fifth graders in inclusive classrooms who read with the system for approximately 20 half-hour sessions, the fluency gain was equal to an effect size of 0.33 as compared with their in-school controls and 0.90 as compared with national norms (Adams & Sullivan-Hall, in preparation).

Unfortunately, we have also ascertained that many intermediate students blithely progress through their texts at a respectable clip but with little or no evident effort to understand what they are reading. Fluency is necessary for productive reading; however, like phonics, it is not sufficient. That is, when a child is unable to read a text with reasonable speed and accuracy, comprehension is precluded. The converse, however, does not follow: Reading quickly and accurately does not ensure comprehension; comprehension requires thoughtful attention in itself.

With the goal of directing students' active attention to meaning, message, and vocabulary, we began to work on what we think of as our "second generation" of software. This effort is fairly straightforward, technologically. We inserted "invisible triggers" in the software to present comprehension questions at critical junctures in the text. Because the students cannot see a question before it pops up, it is not possible for them to just read the question and grope through the text for the answer. Nor can the students tell by looking at the text where the questions are lurking. Instead, thanks again to the speech recognizer, the questions simply present themselves when the student has read to the appropriate point in the text. The questions are focused on terms or issues that must be understood by the reader for the next section of the text to make sense. For this reason, the software requires the student to answer each question correctly before moving on. The questions are in an open-book format and can always be answered by looking back at what has just been read. However, kids are very impatient people. Because they cannot tell when a question will pop up, they quickly learn that the most efficient way to beat the system is to think *while* they are reading, just in case.

With the help of my colleague, Patti Sullivan-Hall, we methodically structured the reading material. Soliloquy Learning's Science and Social Studies Library includes 150 nonfiction selections. All selections are authentic (not simplified), as they are intended to offer the student supported immersion in the vocabulary, language, information, and modes of thought that characterize their domains. Most are adaptations of material published by the Cobblestone Magazine family. The readings are organized into 16 topical units corresponding to core topics in the national science and social studies frameworks. Within units, key vocabulary appears and reappears in different contexts while key concepts and arguments are visited, recalled, and revisited, ever more deeply or from a slightly different vantage point. In this design, the goal is to multiply the benefits of reading and rereading beyond the bounds of any specific text. Our objective is to maximize the likelihood that by the time the students are done with a unit, new knowledge and the words that describe it should be indelibly theirs.

The speech recognizer manages the trigger points; through the speech recognizer, the software knows exactly where the student is in the text at any point in time. Meanwhile, the trigger points are nothing more than calls to the computer. In the science and social studies curriculum, the computer responds to these calls by presenting questions. It might just as well respond by presenting interactive graphics (e.g., show the starting point of the Lewis and Clark Expedition), sound effects (e.g., a whale song plays when alluded to in the text), or instructive video clips (e.g., the sun causing night and day on a rotating earth; a tsunami from formation to landfall; a time-lapsed chicken embryo). In similar spirit, we yearned to turn our attention to math word problems. We are unspeakably sad that Soliloquy Learning is gone. We try to comfort ourselves with the knowledge that we proved that, contrary to the proclamations of many, such technology really is wholly feasible, and we showed that, even in its infancy, it is also wholly worthwhile. It is our deepest hope that others will develop it further in our wake.

CONCLUSION

Although the K–3 reading initiatives have significantly improved the achievement of students in the primary grades, growth has languished in the middle and upper grades. Available test results suggest that our schools are doing a good job teaching the basics to most children; however, research concurs that the basics are not enough.

Beyond the basics and whether the focus is fluency, vocabulary, or knowledge (Cunningham & Stanovich, 1997; Stanovich, 1993), the most important activity for developing literacy is that of inducing students to read independently. Yet, when a text is difficult for children, they comprehend and learn little and tire quickly. Thus, until students are able to read with independence, the most important activity for developing literacy is that of reading alongside them, one to one. Unfortunately, given the teacher–student ratio of the typical classroom, sufficient provision of individual, guided oral reading sessions with due frequency is simply not possible. It is our belief that technology such as that discussed in this chapter offers great promise toward multiplying the productivity of the classroom so as to ensure ample, affordable, one-to-one reading and learning support for every student.

REFERENCES

Adams, M.J. (1990). *Beginning to read: Thinking and learning about print.* Cambridge, MA: The MIT Press.

Adams, M.J. (2006). The promise of automatic speech recognition for fostering literacy growth in children and adults. In M. McKenna, L. Labbo, R. Kieffer, & D. Reinking (Eds.), *Handbook of literacy and technology* (Vol. 2, pp. 109–128). Mahwah, NJ: Lawrence Erlbaum Associates.

Adams, M.J., Trieman, R., & Pressley, M. (1997). Reading, writing, and literacy. In I. Sigel & A. Renninger (Eds.), *Mussen's handbook of child psychology, Vol. 4: Child psychology in practice* (pp. 275–356). New York: Wiley.

Allington, R.L. (1983). The reading instruction provided readers of different reading abilities. *Elementary School Journal, 83,* 95–107.

Allington, R.L. (1989). Coherence or chaos? Qualitative dimensions of the literacy instruction provided low-achievement children. In A. Gartner & D. Lipsky (Eds.), *Beyond separate education.* Baltimore: Paul H. Brookes Publishing Co.

Anderson, R.C. (1996). Research foundations to support wide reading. In V. Greaney (Ed.), *Promoting reading in developing countries* (pp. 55–77). Newark, DE: International Reading Association.

Berends, I.E., & Reitsma, P. (2006). Addressing semantics promotes the development of reading fluency. *Applied Psycholinguistics, 27,* 247–265.

Betts, E.A. (1946). *Foundations of reading instruction.* New York: American Book Co.

Biber, D. (1988). *Variation across speech and writing.* Cambridge, UK: Cambridge University Press.

Biemiller, A., & Boote, C. (2006). An effective method for building meaning vocabulary in primary grades. *Journal of Educational Psychology, 98*(1), 44–62.

Birman, B.F., Orland, M.E., Jung, R.K., Anson, R.J., Garcia, G.N., Moore, M.T., et al. (1987). *The current operation of the Chapter 1 program: Final report from the National Assessment of Chapter 1.* Washington, DC: Government Printing Office.

British National Corpus, Version 3 (BNC XML Edition). (2007). Distributed by Oxford University Computing Services on behalf of the BNC Consortium; http://www.nat corp.ox.ac.uk/

California Department of Education. (2007). *Standardized testing and reporting (STAR) results.* Retrieved June 2007 from http://star.cde.ca.gov/

Calvo, M.G., Estevez, A., & Dowens, M.G. (2003). Time course of elaborative inferences in reading as a function of prior vocabulary knowledge. *Learning and Instruction, 13*(6), 611–631.

Campbell, J.R., Donahue, P.L., Reese, C.M., & Phillips, G.W. (1996). *NAEP 1994 reading report card for the nation and the states* (NCES 95-045). U.S. Department of Education, National Center for Education Statistics. Washington, DC: U.S. Government Printing Office.

Carroll, J.B., Davies, P., & Richman, B. (1971). *The American Heritage word frequency book*. Boston: Houghton Mifflin.

Carter, L.G. (1984). The sustaining effects study of compensatory and elementary education. *Educational Researcher, 13*(7), 4–13.

Carver, R.P. (1994). Percentage of unknown vocabulary words in text as a function of the relative difficulty of the text: Implications for instruction. *Journal of Reading Behavior, 26*, 413–437.

Chall, J.S. (1967). *Learning to read: The great debate*. New York: McGraw-Hill.

Cunningham, A.E. (2006). Accounting for children's orthographic learning while reading text: Do children self-teach? *Journal of Experimental Child Psychology, 95*, 56–77.

Cunningham, A.E., Perry, K.E., Stanovich, K.E., & Share, D.L. (2002). Orthographic learning during reading: Examining the role of self-teaching. *Journal of Experimental Child Psychology, 82*, 733–740.

Cunningham, A.E., & Stanovich, K.E. (1997). Early reading acquisition and its relation to reading experience and ability 10 years later. *Developmental Psychology, 33*(6), 934–945.

Daneman, M., & Green, I. (1986). Individual differences in comprehending and producing words in context. *Journal of Memory and Language, 25*, 1–18.

Ehri, L.C., & Saltmarsh, I. (1995). Beginning readers outperform older disabled readers in learning to read words by sight. *Reading and Writing: An Interdisciplinary Journal, 7*, 295–326.

Flesch, R. (1955). *Why Johnny can't read*. New York: Harper and Row.

Fletcher, J.M., Shaywitz, S.E., Shankweiler, D.P., Katz, L., Liberman, I.Y., Stuebing, K.K., et al. (1994). Cognitive profiles of reading disability: Comparisons of discrepancy and low achievement definitions. *Journal of Educational Psychology, 86*, 6–23.

Florida Department of Education. (2007). *Florida Comprehensive Assessment Test, scores, reports & searchable FCAT database*. Retrieved March 24, 2007, from http://fcat.fldoe.org/

Foorman, B.R., Francis, D.J., Fletcher, J.M., Schatschneider, C., & Mehta, P. (1998). The role of instruction in learning to read: Preventing reading failure in at-risk children. *Journal of Educational Psychology, 90*, 37–55.

Foorman, B.R., Francis, D.J, Shaywitz, S.E., Shaywitz, B.A., & Fletcher, J.M. (1997). The case for early reading interventions. In B. Blachman (Ed.), *Foundations of reading acquisition and dyslexia: Implications for early intervention* (pp. 243–264). Mahwah, NJ: Lawrence Erlbaum Associates.

Gardner, D. (2004). Vocabulary input through extensive reading: A comparison of words found in children's narrative and expository reading materials. *Applied Linguistics, 25*(1), 1–37.

Gorfein, D. (2001). *On the consequences of meaning selection: Perspectives on resolving lexical ambiguity*. Washington, DC: American Psychological Association.

Grigg, W., Lauko, M., & Brockway, D. (2006). *The nation's report card: Science 2005* (NCES 2006-466). U.S. Department of Education, National Center for Education Statistics. Washington, DC: U.S. Government Printing Office.

Harcourt Brace. (1996). *Stanford Achievement Test* (9th ed.). San Antonio, TX: Author.

Harm, M., & Seidenberg, M.S. (1999). Reading acquisition, phonology, and dyslexia: Insights from a connectionist model. *Psychological Review, 106*, 491–528.

Herman, P.A., Anderson, R.C., Pearson, P.D., & Nagy, W.E. (1987). Incidental acquisition of word meaning from expositions with varied text features. *Reading Research Quarterly, 22*, 263–264.

Hill, E.G. (2004). *A look at the progress of English language learner students*. Sacramento, CA: Legislative Analyst's Office.

Hu, M., & Nation, P. (2000). Unknown vocabulary density and reading comprehension. *Reading in a Foreign Language, 13*(1), 403–430.

Jenkins, J.R., Fuchs, L.S., van den Broek, P., Espin, C., & Deno, S.L. (2003). Sources of individual differences in reading comprehension and reading fluency. *Journal of Educational Psychology, 95*(4), 719–729.

Jenkins, J.R., Matlock, B., & Slocum, T.A. (1989). Two approaches to vocabulary instruction: The teaching of individual word meanings and practice in deriving word meaning from context. *Reading Research Quarterly, 24*(2), 215–235

Jenkins, J.R., Stein, M.L., & Wysocki, K. (1984). Learning vocabulary through reading. *American Educational Research Journal, 21*(4), 767–787.

Jepsen, C., & de Alth, S. (2005). *English learners in California schools.* San Francisco: Public Policy Institute.

Juel, C. (1994). *Learning to read and write in one elementary school.* New York: Springer-Verlag.

Laufer, B. (1988). What percentage of text-lexis is essential for comprehension. In C. Lauren & M. Nordmann (Eds.), *Special language: From humans to thinking machines* (pp. 316–323). Clevedon, UK: Multilingual Matters.

Lee, J. (2006). *Tracking achievement gaps and assessing the impact of NCLB on the gaps: An in-depth look into national and state reading and math outcome trends.* Cambridge, MA: The Civil Rights Project at Harvard University.

Lee, J., & Weiss, A.R. (2007). *The Nation's report card: U.S. History 2006* (NCES-2007-474). U.S. Department of Education, National Center for Education Statistics. Washington, DC: U.S. Government Printing Office.

Lutkus, A.D., & Weiss, A.R. (2007). *The Nation's report card: Civics 2006* (NCES-2007-476). U.S. Department of Education, National Center for Education Statistics. Washington, DC: U.S. Government Printing Office.

Manis, F.R. (1985). Acquisition of word identification skills in normal and disabled readers. *Journal of Educational Psychology, 77*, 78–90.

McIntosh, R., Vaughn, S., Schumm, J., Haager, D., & Lee, O. (1993). Observations of students with learning disabilities in general education classroom. *Exceptional Children, 60*, 249–261.

Moody, S.W., Vaughn, S., & Schumm, J.S. (1997). Instructional grouping for reading: Teachers' views. *Remedial and Special Education, 18*(6), 347–356.

Morrison, L. (1996). Talking about words: A study of French as a second language learners' lexical inferencing procedures. *Canadian Modern Language Review, 53*, 41–75.

Mullis, I.V.S., Campbell, J.R., & Farstrup, A.E. (1993). *NAEP 1992 reading report card for the nation and the states: Data from the national and trial state assessments.* U.S. Department of Education, National Center for Education Statistics. Washington, DC: U.S. Government Printing Office.

Nagy, W.E., & Anderson, R.C. (1984). How many words are there in printed school English? *Reading Research Quarterly, 19*(3), 304–330.

Nagy, W.E., Anderson, R.C., & Herman, P. (1987). Learning word meanings from context during normal reading. *American Educational Research Journal, 24*, 237–270.

Nagy, W.E., Herman, P., & Anderson, R.C. (1985). Learning words from context. *Reading Research Quarterly, 20*, 233–253.

Nassaji, H. (2004). The relationship between depth of vocabulary knowledge and L2 learners' lexical inferencing strategy use and success. *The Canadian Modern Language Review, 61*(1), 107–134

Nation, K., & Snowling, M.J. (1998). Individual differences in contextual facilitation: Evidence from dyslexia and poor reading comprehension. *Child Development, 69*(4), 996–1011.

Nation, P., & Waring, R. (1997). Vocabulary size, text coverage, and word lists. In N. Schmitt & M. McCarthy (Eds.), *Vocabulary: Description, acquisition, and pedagogy* (pp. 6–19). Cambridge, UK: Cambridge University Press.

National Institute of Child Health and Human Development. (2000). *Report of the National Reading Panel. Teaching children to read: An evidence-based assessment of the scientific research literature on reading and its implications for reading instruction: Reports of the subgroups* (NIH Publication No. 00-4754). Washington, DC: U.S. Government Printing Office.

National Research Council, Committee on Preventing Reading Difficulties. (1998). *Preventing reading difficulties in young children.* Washington, DC: National Academies Press.

Orfield, G., Losen, D., Wald, J., & Swanson, C. (2004). *Losing our future: How minority youth are being left behind by the graduation rate crises.* Cambridge, MA: The Civil Rights Project at Harvard University.

Perie, M., Grigg, W., & Donahue, P. (2005). *The nation's report card: Reading 2005* (NCES 2006-451). U.S. Department of Education, National Center for Education Statistics. Washington, DC: U.S. Government Printing Office.

Perie, M., Grigg, W.E., & Dion, G.S. (2006). *The nation's report card: Mathematics 2005* (NCES 2006453). U.S. Department of Education, National Center for Education Statistics. Washington, DC: U.S. Government Printing Office.

Pflaum, S.W., Walberg, H.J., Karegianes, M.L., & Rasher, S.P. (1980). Reading instruction: A quantitative analysis. *Educational Researcher, 9*, 12–18.

Pugh, K.R., Shaywitz, B.A., Shaywitz, S.E., Constable, R.T., Skudlarski, P., Fulbright, R.K., et al. (1996). Cerebral organization. *Brain, 119*(4), 1221–1238.

Reitsma, P. (1983). Printed word learning in beginning readers. *Journal of Experimental Child Psychology, 36*, 321–339.

Reitsma, P. (1989). Orthographic memory and learning to read. In P.G. Aaron & R.M. Joshi (Eds.), *Reading and writing disorders in different orthographic systems* (pp. 51–73). Dordrecht, NE/Norwell, MA: Kluwer Academic.

Robbins, C., & Ehri, L.C. (1994). Reading storybooks to kindergartners helps them learn new vocabulary words. *Journal of Educational Psychology, 86*, 54–64.

Rumberger, R.W. (2007). Lagging behind: Linguistic minorities educational progress during elementary school. *UC Linguistic Minority Research Institute News, 16*(2), 1–3.

Rumberger, R.W., & Tran, L. (2006). *Preschool participation and the cognitive and social development of language minority students.* Santa Barbara, CA: UC Minority Research Institute.

Schatschneider, C., Buck, J., Torgesen, J.K., Wagner, R.K., Hassler, L. Hecht, S., et al. (2004). *A multivariate study of factors that contribute to individual differences in performance on the Florida Comprehensive Reading Assessment Test.* Tallahassee: Florida Center for Reading Research, Florida State University.

Schatz, E.K., & Baldwin, R.S. (1986). Context clues are unreliable predictors of word meanings. *Reading Research Quarterly, 21*(4), 439–445.

Shankweiler, D., Crain, S., Katz, L., Fowler, A.E., Liberman, A.M., Brady, S.A., et al. (1995). Cognitive profiles of reading-disabled children: Comparison of language skills in phonology, morphology, and syntax. *Psychological Science, 6*, 149–156.

Share, D. (1995). Phonological recoding and self-teaching: Sine qua non of reading acquisition. *Cognition, 55*(2), 151–218.

Share, D., & Shalev, C. (2004). Self-teaching in normal and disabled readers. *Reading and Writing: An Interdisciplinary Journal, 17*, 769–800.

Share, D.L. (1999). Phonological recoding and orthographic learning: A direct test of the self-teaching hypothesis. *Journal of Experimental Child Psychology, 72*, 95–129.

Share, D.L. (2004). Orthographic learning at a glance: On the time course and developmental onset of self-teaching. *Journal of Experimental Child Psychology, 87*, 267–298.

Shefelbine, J. (1990). Student factors related to variability in learning word meanings from context. *Journal of Reading Behavior, 22*, 71–97.

Stanovich, K.E. (1993). Does reading make you smarter: Literacy and the development of verbal intelligence. In H. Reese (Ed.), *Advances in child development and behavior* (Vol. 24, pp. 133–180). San Diego: Academic Press.

Stanovich, K.E., & Siegel, L.S. (1994). Phenotypic performance profile of children with reading disabilities: A regression-based test of the phonological-core variable-difference model. *Journal of Educational Psychology, 86*, 24–53.

Sternberg, R., & Powell, J.S. (1983). Comprehending verbal comprehension. *American Psychologist, 38*(8), 878–893.

Tafoya, S.M. (2002). The linguistic landscape of California. *California Counts, 3*(4), 1–14.

Thorndike, R.L. (1973). *Reading comprehension education in fifteen countries: An empirical study.* New York: Wiley.

Torgesen, J.K., & Hudson, R.F. (2006). Reading fluency: Critical issues for struggling readers. In S.J. Samuels & A. Farstrup (Eds.), *Reading fluency: The forgotten dimension of reading success* (pp. 130–158). Newark, DE: International Reading Association.

Torgesen, J.K., Wagner, R.K., & Rashotte, C.A. (1994). Longitudinal studies of phonological processing and reading. *Journal of Learning Disabilities, 27*(5), 276–286.

Torgesen, J.K., Wagner, R.K., & Rashotte, C. (1999). *Test of word reading efficiency.* Austin, TX: PRO-ED.

Vaughn, S., Levy, S., Coleman, M., & Bos, C.S. (2002). Reading instruction for students with LD and EBD: A synthesis of observation studies. *Journal of Special Education, 36*, 2–15.

Vaughn, S., Moody, S., & Schumm, J.S. (1998). Broken promises: Reading instruction in the resource room. *Exceptional Children, 64*, 211–226.

Vellutino, F., Scanlon, D.M., Sipay, E., Small, S., Pratt, A., Chen, R., et al. (1996). Cognitive profiles of difficult-to-remediate and readily remediated poor readers: Early intervention as a vehicle for distinguishing between cognitive and experiential deficits as basic causes of specific reading disability. *Journal of Educational Psychology, 88*, 601–838.

Wagner, R.K., Torgesen, J.K., Rashotte, C.A., Hecht, S.A., Barker, T.A., Burgess, S.R., et al. (1997). Changing relations between phonological processing abilities and word-level reading as children develop from beginning to skilled readers: A 5-year longitudinal study. *Developmental Psychology, 33*(3), 568–479.

Wechsler, D. (1991). *Wechsler Intelligence Scale for Children* (3rd ed.). San Antonio, TX: Harcourt Assessment.

Wiederholt, J.R., & Bryant, B.R. (1992). *Gray Oral Reading Test* (3rd ed.). Austin, TX: PRO-ED.

Wise, L.L., Becker, D.E., Butler, F.L., Schantz, L.B., Bao, H., Sun, S., et al. (2006). *Independent evaluation of the California High School Exit Exam (CAHSEE): 2006 evaluation report.* Alexandria, VA: Human Resources Research Organization.

15

Television and Learning

Heather L. Kirkorian and Daniel R. Anderson

What do children do when they are not in school? Children from prosperous circumstances are likely to spend much of their time in scheduled activities including organized after-school programs, sports, music lessons, and reading and writing groups among other things. Summertime is often organized around camps or summer programs centered on nature and the environment, computer skills, arts and hobbies, or physical outdoor skills. Above all, most of these activities are structured and disciplined and involve teaching and learning. Parents, who are typically college educated, often encourage reading as the primary form of media use. As these children become older, of course, more time is devoted to increasingly challenging homework assignments, music practice, sports practice, and other activities. In the life of the prosperous American child, little time is typically left for purely discretionary and entertainment activities such as television viewing and computer game use, although Internet use and other use of computer technology increase for both academic and social purposes. Concerns popularly expressed about these children are that they have become overscheduled, stressed, and hurried (e.g., Rosenfeld & Wise, 2000). Whatever the validity of these concerns, it is clear that such children collectively excel academically, socially, and in life's larger pursuits.

Children living in poverty face far different circumstances. For many reasons, relatively few of the structured activities available to children from prosperous families are available to children living in poverty. Frequently, as a result of parent employment, parental permissiveness, or other circumstances, children of poverty have a great deal of free time. Even when these children are given demanding duties such as caring for younger siblings, they do so at home without adult-imposed structured activities. Consequently, media, especially television, fills much of their free time. Analyses of television use have repeatedly found that children living in poverty spend vastly greater amounts of time with television than children from more fortunate circumstances (for review, see Comstock & Paik, 1991).

In the 1960s, Joan Ganz Cooney had the fundamental insight that this time spent with television did not have to be time wasted. If television programs could be created to be truly educational as well as entertaining, attractive, and able to compete with purely entertainment programs, then television could be a powerful tool for educational intervention (Cooney, 1966). With the help of foundation and government funding, Cooney created Children's Television Workshop (now Sesame Workshop) and the historic television program *Sesame Street*. This program became successful in gaining large audiences of targeted preschoolers and over the years fostered the realization that television programs could be both educational and successful (in both audience and commercial profit). Consequently, today there are many educational television programs on both public and commercial networks. Unlike *Sesame Street*, however, few of these programs are specifically designed as educational interventions for children living in poverty.

Well-designed, curriculum-based children's television programs teach the intended lessons (for a review of research, see Fisch, 2004). For example, studies of *Sesame Street* have shown that viewers learn the intended lessons, are better prepared for school than are nonviewers, and ultimately get better grades in high school English, science, and math. As high school students, those who viewed *Sesame Street* as preschoolers reported more leisure book reading and were able to name more book titles and authors of books read in the last year than were nonviewers (Anderson, Huston, Schmitt, Linebarger, & Wright, 2001).

When *Sesame Street* was created, there was very little research on which to draw, and many elements of program design were guesses informed by formative research utilizing small convenience samples of preschoolers (Lesser, 1972). An initial and continuing goal was to develop useful principles clarifying how and why children pay attention to television. It was understood that children would not learn from the program if they did not pay attention. Moreover, any program that does not hold children's attention will not be selected over other competing programs. In the early 1970s, the second author of this chapter, Anderson, became interested in children's attention to television as part of a general interest in attention and ultimately devoted his career to the problem. Over the years, many useful principles emerged from his and others' research and became guiding principles not only for the ongoing production of *Sesame Street* but a whole new generation of preschool educational television programs, for example, *Blue's Clues* (Anderson, 2004). In this chapter, we describe some of these principles and discuss how they can be implemented in the creation of educational media for preschool children.

MEASURING ATTENTION

At any given moment an individual may potentially be bombarded by a welter of sights, sounds, smells, tastes, touches, emotions, internal sensations, thoughts, and memories. Attention is the process of selecting some aspect of these internal and external stimuli to be the focus of conscious awareness. Once a source of stimulation is selected, be it television or anything else, attention is maintained for some period of time and then shifted, either deliberately and appropriately or because the person becomes distracted by a novel source of stimulation or loses interest in the source. As a psychological process, attention is a surprisingly deep subject and is studied in many different ways. Research on children's television viewing, however, has primarily used "looks" at the screen as the main indicator of attention. In the typical study, videotapes of children are coded for the onsets and offsets of looking at the screen. These records of look onsets and terminations can be synchronized with frame-by-frame coding of the content of the television show. In this way, looking can be precisely related to the presence or absence of particular program features or types of content. Although there have been some field studies that record television viewing as it naturally occurs in homes, most studies of looking take place in laboratory settings. In such laboratory studies, efforts are usually made to imitate a natural viewing situation using comfortably furnished rooms with a variety of age-appropriate toys available. A goal in these studies is to create situations in which, like at home, other behaviors besides television viewing are possible so that children do not look at the television all of the time it is on.

Recognizing that the intensity of attention can vary, even as a child maintains looking at the screen, another category of research focuses on investment of cognitive resources, or the depth of attentional engagement, using a variety of behavioral and physiological measures. These have also been used in research with children and will be discussed later. A detailed review of research on attention to television, including adult studies, may be found in Anderson and Kirkorian (2006).

LOOKING AT TELEVISION

Although they are not usually aware of it, most viewers, including adults, look at and away from the screen 120 to 150 times per hour on average (e.g., Anderson & Levin, 1976; Burns & Anderson, 1993). In a quantitative analysis of research, Richards and Anderson (2004) reported that look length distributions are surprisingly similar in infants, children, and adults and are similar across many individuals. Distributions are lognormal so that there are many short looks less than a few seconds in duration and relatively few long looks that can last several minutes or more. In effect, attention to television consists of many brief episodes along with some of very long duration. It should be noted that in homes, viewers frequently engage in alternative activities along with watching television; most viewers have something to do besides watching television. Children may play with toys or each other, and adults may read, do chores, and talk on the telephone (Schmitt, Woolf & Anderson, 2003). Much of our research with children has been directed at why looks at television begin, why they are maintained, and why they end. Understanding the principles behind looking at television is key to making an effective television program.

Despite similarities in look distributions, there are large differences with age in how much viewers look and what they look at. For example, Anderson, Lorch, Field, Collins, and Nathan (1986) examined television viewing in children and adults in their homes as recorded by video over 10-day periods. Given that an individual was present in the viewing room with the television set in use, there was a sharp increase in the percentage of time spent looking at the screen from infancy through the preschool years, after which attention slowly increased with age, peaked around age 12, and then decreased somewhat in adults. Men looked at the screen more of the time than did women, although both watched less than children between the ages of 6 and 17 years. Similar increases in looking at television from 1 to 4 years were reported by parents and also observed in laboratory studies (e.g., Anderson & Levin, 1976). The increase in attention to television with age clearly reflects increased comprehension of television programs. As they grow older, children pay attention to a greater variety of program content so that by about 6 years of age, many children begin to watch substantial amounts of television intended for adults (action-adventure shows, situation comedies, variety shows, game shows, sports, and the like; Schmitt, Anderson, & Collins, 1999).

It should be noted that our studies repeatedly found that infants' and toddlers' attention to television was very low, which makes sense in the context of comprehension. Since the mid-1990s, however, videos and programs have been produced exclusively for this audience. Little is known about the nature of infant and toddler attention to these new media, but work by Barr and colleagues (2003) and by our research group (Pempek et al., 2008) suggests that attention in very young children can be quite high to videos produced for them. There are also huge individual differences in television watching, with some very young children paying little attention and others seemingly engrossed. We will discuss infant and toddler attention later, but it should be noted that the American Academy of Pediatrics (1999) recommends that infants younger than 2 years of age not watch television at all.

THEORIES OF CHILDREN'S ATTENTION TO TELEVISION

Until the 1980s, there was only an implicit theory of attention to television and that was the notion that television viewing, particularly in young children, was largely reactive and passively controlled by attention-eliciting features of the program (e.g., violent action, sound effects). Singer (1980) formalized this theory and proposed that television uniformly elicits orienting responses in children. According to Singer, the "busyness" of television leads to a sensory bombardment, thus preventing viewers from gaining any useful information from the program. Similar views have been proposed by others (e.g., Healy, 1990).

Other theories of attention to television focus on content of the program rather than ubiquitous effects of the medium as a whole. Anderson and Lorch (1983) viewed attention to television as primarily in service of the viewers' cognitive processing of content. In this theory, attention to television is largely driven by the viewers' understanding of the content and reflects the viewers' cognitive level and experience with television. This theory incorporates form and content of the program, individual characteristics of the viewer, and nature of the viewing environment as predictors of attention. These topics will be considered in greater detail later in this chapter.

Other approaches are more developmental in nature. For instance, Huston and Wright (1983) proposed a theory of the development of attention to television from infancy that distinguished between perceptually salient and informative formal features. Huston and Wright defined *formal features* generally as any characteristic of television that can be deployed across a wide range of content, such as camera techniques and sound effects. *Perceptually salient features* include movement, sound effects, and rapid pacing, whereas *informative features* include dialogue and narration. In the Huston and Wright model, attention in very young children is initially drawn to perceptually salient formal features but, with age and experience, viewers habituate to these and differentially attend to informative features that are necessary for understanding the story. It is important to note that these categories are not necessarily exclusive. For example, perceptually salient formal features that are paired with comprehensible or otherwise interesting content may initially elicit an automatic orienting response but eventually elicit attention because of their association with meaningful content (e.g., Calvert, Huston, Watkins, & Wright, 1982; Valkenburg & Vroone, 2004). Research with infants indicates that the transition to attention driven by informative features and understanding occurs around the second birthday (Pempek et al., 2008). The influence of formal features on visual attention to television is described in detail in the next section. An understanding of the use of formal features to guide attention is essential in producing effective educational television (Anderson, 2004).

FORMAL FEATURES

Several studies have documented the relationship of formal features to looking at the screen in preschool children. Attention increases in response to some attributes (sound effects, child voices, peculiar voices, movement, animation, female and child characters, fast music) and decreases with others (male characters, extended zoom shots, slow music). Furthermore, many of these relationships increase with age (Alwitt, Anderson, Lorch, & Levin, 1980; Anderson & Levin, 1976; Levin & Anderson, 1976; Schmitt et al., 1999; Wartella & Ettema, 1974). The authors proposed that these relationships of television program features to attention are due to a form of media literacy: learned associations between specific features and types of content. For example, child actors are associated with child-directed content, whereas adult men are relatively more common on adult programs such as newscasts. The finding that relationships between many formal features and attention increase with age supports this conclusion. There are some exceptions: movement and shot changes are positively related to attention across the age span. These particular features may function both as elicitors of orienting responses and as learned cues to important new content.

Some features have mixed effects. For example, content boundaries (as between a program and a commercial or between two different types of content in a magazine-format program) end looks in attentive viewers and elicit looks from inattentive viewers (Alwitt et al., 1980). A key finding is that auditory attributes are particularly crucial in eliciting looks from inattentive viewers. This is extremely important in getting viewers to fully attend to content that is crucial for comprehending the intended lesson. Strategic use of formal features, both auditory and visual, has been a key factor in the success of programs such as *Blue's Clues* and *Dora the Explorer* as well as *Sesame Street* (Anderson, 2004). Together the research indicates that formal features are important in guiding children's attention to the screen but that effects differ among features. Some features have the effect of gaining attention (e.g., movement, sound effects), whereas others terminate or suppress attention (e.g., extended zoom shots, adult male voices). Moreover, children's attention to television may depend on interactive effects of form, content, and viewer characteristics such as age (Schmitt et al., 1999). In addition, some research indicates that these same features are important in guiding attention to interactive, computer-based content (Moore & Calvert, 2000).

Children also learn that formal features come in "packages" that signal different kinds of content. This is likely critical in initial program choice when the children are "surfing" through the many channels that may be available. For instance, Huston and colleagues (1981) found that daytime educational programs were more likely to use informative (i.e., able to convey content) and reflective (e.g., repetition, slow to moderate action) features whereas Saturday-morning cartoons relied more heavily on salient features (e.g., fast action). This research group later demonstrated that children readily learn these relationships with television viewing experience, differentiating between those intended for adults and children (Campbell, Wright, & Huston, 1987) and for girls and boys (Huston, Greer, Wright, Welch, & Ross, 1984).

In an unpublished study that we did for Children's Television Workshop in the late 1970s, Elizabeth Lorch and this chapter's second author, Daniel Anderson, compared equal numbers of African American 3- and 5-year-olds to European American 3- and 5-year-olds. Compared with the European American children, the African American children were collectively from much lower socioeconomic circumstances. We did detailed analyses of the children's attention to the formal features discussed previously as well as to all the individual characters appearing on *Sesame Street* at that time. In no case did we find that there were differences between these groups of children in attention to the formal features or to the characters. The African American children paid the same amount of attention to the same features as their European American peers. This lack of difference even held for black versus white human characters on the program. To our knowledge, no other studies have made these comparisons. We regret that these data were at the time considered proprietary and were never published. Nevertheless, at least for preschoolers, there are no important racial or socioeconomic differences in the attentional response to formal features and character types.

CONTENT

Many books and magazine articles have emphasized the mesmerizing power of television to hold children's attention. Usually, these discussions have emphasized the role of formal features such as scene change and movement in repeatedly eliciting orienting responses (e.g., Healy, 1990; Singer, 1980; Winn, 1977). In fact, children are quite selective in what they view, and content is a far greater determinant than form of whether children will watch. For example, several studies have directly assessed the role of program comprehensibility, a key aspect of content. Anderson, Lorch, Field, and Sanders (1981) found that 3- and 5-year-olds looked more during *Sesame Street* segments containing dialogue with immediate referents (i.e., objects that were concretely present on screen) than those containing nonimmediate referents (i.e., off-screen or abstract subjects). Dialogue with concrete referents should in general be more understandable to young children than more abstract dialogue. Both age groups paid substantially more attention to segments with concrete dialogue, indicating the importance of understanding in driving attention to television. In a second study, comprehensibility was experimentally manipulated by creating segments of *Sesame Street* with distortions in dialogue (i.e., Greek dubbing or backwards speech) or canonical sequence of events (i.e., randomly ordered shots). The only difference between the distorted segments and the original segments is that the distorted segments are harder to understand. Two-, three-and-a-half-, and five-year-old children paid substantially less attention to these comprehensibility-distorted segments than to the same segments when they were undistorted. In fact, many of the children spontaneously commented that the television was broken or that they wanted to change the channel. A major point is made by this study: A producer cannot hold children's attention through a lot of sound effects and camera tricks. The fundamental reason that children watch television is because they appreciate interesting and entertaining content.

This comprehensibility effect has been replicated by other research groups (Lorch & Castle, 1997; Pingree, 1986). That said, a much milder manipulation of comprehensibility failed to yield differences in attention in one study. Campbell and colleagues (1987) varied sentence complexity and abstractness of messages and found only small and nonsignificant reductions in attention with more difficult dialogue as compared with simpler dialogue. When the varied results on the effects of comprehensibility are taken together, it is clear that there must at least be the promise of understandable content conveyed by the television program. If children perceive the program to be incomprehensible, they stop paying attention.

If content is king—if it is the essential foundation of a successful children's television program—then we should see that children pay much greater attention at home to some kinds of content as compared with others. So, it is not surprising that children pay more attention to children's programs than they do to adult programs, as found from 10 days of videotaped viewing at home by Schmitt and colleagues (1999). In a direct test of whether content or formal features are the primary determinants of attention, Schmitt and colleagues (2003) found that children pay more attention to children's programs than they do to commercials directed at children. This finding is particularly telling insofar as commercials are produced with a far greater density of formal features than are children's or adults' television programs. This further confirms that children's attention to television is driven to a much greater extent by content than by formal features.

The second author of this chapter, Anderson, has done extensive consulting with producers of educational television. He has often found that producers are surprised at how important content is as a determinant of attention. Every piece of his advice to producers emphasizes the cognitive processing load induced on children by every decision concerning editing, transitions, and the use of formal features. All of these decisions must be made with respect to clarifying and conveying the meaning of the content. They should not be used as cheap tricks to elicit and maintain attention.

Rapid shot and scene changes, for example, induce an increased cognitive processing load on young children that makes it harder for them to comprehend the ongoing content. Imagine a simple establishment shot of a building in daytime followed by a cut to a shot of an interior room. An adult viewer readily assumes that the room is inside the building and that it is still daytime. Although most 4-year-olds understand this type of filmic montage, some become confused by such transitions (Smith, Anderson, & Fischer, 1985). To understand that comprehending video montage is computationally demanding, it should be recognized that adults employ 17 distinct regions of the cerebral cortex to understand straightforward action scenes from movies (Anderson, Fite, Petrovich, & Hirsch, 2006). As many of these areas of the cortex are slow to mature, it is clear that the task of making sense of edited video is in fact challenging for a young child. Although formal features can indeed briefly enhance attention, they also represent cues to the meaning of the content and often are the very means of conveying that content. Watching television is not like looking through a window; children learn how to watch and interpret television over years of experience. This brings us to children younger than the age of 2 years.

DEVELOPMENTAL CONSIDERATIONS

At this point, it is not clear to what degree infants and toddlers comprehend television or even whether comprehensibility is a major driver of looking at television as it is in older children. It has been theorized that very young children's attention to television is predominantly driven by dynamically changing, salient visual features in contrast to content-driven attention in older children (Anderson & Pempek, 2005; Huston & Wright, 1983, 1989).

Some research indicates that at the very least, infants integrate audio and video information when looking at a program insofar as they look more at a program with congruent audio and video as compared with video with a soundtrack taken from a different program (Hollenbeck & Slaby, 1979). In a study by Richards and Cronise (2000), however, older (18–24 months) but not younger (6–12 months) infants looked more at a meaningful program than a computer-generated audiovisual stimulus. Similarly, Pempek and colleagues (2008) reported that 18- and 24-month-olds looked longer at normal than distorted segments (random shots or backward dialogue) of *Teletubbies*, replicating the comprehensibility effect found for older children, but that 6- and 12-month-old infants did not discriminate between comprehensible and incomprehensible segments of the program. We have also found that there are substantially different patterns of eye movements during periods of attention, indicating that infants' looking is driven by different program characteristics than that of older children (Kirkorian, 2008). Taken together, the findings thus far support the hypothesis that infants' attention to television is driven by salient stimulus features of television rather than by content.

Together, these results suggest a qualitative difference from older children in attention to television over the first few years of life. It is not yet clear that sequential and linguistic comprehensibility of the program matters to infants, at least until about 18 months of age. Anderson and Pempek (2005) refer to this developmental shift as a video deficit in very young children. At this point the best hypothesis is that infants pay attention to television in a reactive manner driven by salient formal features, much as hypothesized by Huston and Wright (1983). The educational value of videos produced for infants and toddlers is, therefore, dubious.

OTHER MODERATORS OF ATTENTION TO TELEVISION

In considering children age 2 years and older, other factors in addition to form and comprehensibility of content determine whether children will pay attention to a program. These include repetition of and familiarity with the content and characteristics of the situation and viewer. These topics will be discussed next as examples of moderators of attention to television.

Repetition and Familiarity

Every parent of young children has observed that some recorded programs or movies get watched repeatedly. Anderson observed this with his 3-year-old daughter, who watched the *Blue's Clues* pilot 14 times by herself and then 3 more times with friends. Crawley, Anderson, Wilder, Williams, and Santomero (1999) formally investigated repetition of *Blue's Clues* with 3- to 5-year-old children. Attention remained at high levels across five viewings. Only 5-year-old boys demonstrated any decrease in looking. Unpublished research by the producers of *Dora the Explorer* revealed exactly the same effects of repetition with that program (Christine Ricci, Director of Research, personal communication). When considering entertainment and educational content separately, Crawley and colleagues found that attention remained consistent during entertainment content across the five repetitions, whereas educational content initially received more attention and then gradually decreased to match attention to entertainment content by the fourth day of viewing. The authors concluded that the educational content was initially more cognitively demanding than the entertainment content, therefore receiving more quiet attention, and that the decrease with repetition reflects learning. Corresponding with the decrease in attention, however, overt and enthusiastic interactions with the program steadily increased with repetition (shouting out answers to questions; pointing at the screen, saying, "That one!" or "There it is!"; dancing). It should be noted that comprehension and learning from television programs goes up substantially with repetition (Crawley et al., 1999; Skouteris & Kelly, 2006). In particular, far transfer of concepts from *Blue's Clues* (i.e., transfer of learning to related but not identical problems) increased with repetition (Crawley et al., 1999; for an extended review of transfer of learning from television see Fisch, Kirkorian, & Anderson, 2005).

In a study of very young children, Barr and colleagues (2003) measured infants' attention to baby videos at home. They reported that attention was higher for familiar videos than for unfamiliar ones, demonstrating that infants have very high tolerance for and perhaps even appreciation of repetition. These findings fail to support Singer's (1980) prediction that attention quickly habituates because attention to television is driven primarily by novelty. In contrast, increased comprehensibility and predictability of content may be an important factor driving attention to television in infants and even in preschoolers. No study has examined the effects of program repetition in children older than preschoolers, but parents report that repeated viewing decreases as children get older (Mares, 1998). It is our guess that older children are considerably less interested in repetition than are infants and preschoolers.

Viewing Situation and Task Demands

Attention to television is at least partly determined by the immediate context in addition to the television program itself. For example, Lorch, Anderson, and Levin (1979) demonstrated that reducing opportunities for an alternative activity (i.e., toy play) had the effect of doubling attention to the television. This finding has been replicated in studies by Lorch and colleagues (2004). It is interesting that children appear to develop significant multitasking strategies for watching television. When preschool children play with toys while the television is on, they selectively attend to those portions of the program that are most important for comprehension of the content (Lorch et al., 1979).

Viewing can also be influenced by social context. Anderson, Lorch, Smith, Bradford, and Levin (1981) demonstrated that look initiation, look termination, orientation to a distractor, and overt television-related behavior (e.g., laughing, talking about the show, pointing at the screen, dancing) were significantly more likely to occur when a coviewing peer had just exhibited that behavior. Other researchers have also found that attention within coviewing pairs is more similar than is attention between pairs (Huston et al., 1984). Clearly, television viewing can be a significant social activity for children, which has both good and bad implications for the producer. If a show works, social viewers will be more attentive and interactive than isolated viewers; if the show does not work well, some children will lose attention, engaging in activities other than viewing, and their peers will follow.

Finally, attention to television can vary as a function of a viewer's goals in watching television. For example, Field and Anderson (1985) found that attention and self-rated mental effort in 5- and 9-year-olds was higher if they were told that they would be tested following the segment as compared with children instructed simply to watch the program. Thus, children at least as young as age 5 can vary the amount of attention they invest in viewing a program as a function of perceived task difficulty.

Individual Differences

There can be large differences among individuals in how much attention is paid to any given television program. As already noted, some of these differences reflect cognitive maturity and comprehension, which in turn depends on general development and prior experiences. Some studies suggest that individual differences in self-concept influence attention to television. Most of these studies focus on the gender of the viewer. For instance, Slaby and Frey (1975) demonstrated that young boys paid more attention to adult male characters than to female characters if they had achieved gender constancy (i.e., the realization that gender is a stable characteristic of oneself that is not influenced by superficial changes such as hairstyle or clothing). Luecke-Aleksa, Anderson, Collins, and Schmitt (1995), in analysis of attention to television at home, replicated this finding. Girls, in contrast, looked more at female characters regardless of whether they had achieved gender constancy. Moreover, both boys and girls who had achieved gender constancy tended to watch different programs than same-age children who had not achieved gender constancy. Girls watched more children's programs while boys shifted more of their viewing to action and sports programs that were more adult-oriented. Linebarger and Chernin (2005) replicated the gender constancy effect in an eye-tracking study. They observed same-sex preferences in visual fixations of gender-constant children when both a male and female were on screen simultaneously.

Some research demonstrates that child viewers are more likely to look at child characters than at adult characters (Schmitt et al., 1999), but research on other demographic variables such as race and socioeconomic status is limited to overall television exposure or program choice rather than direct measures of visual attention during television viewing. For example, children in minority families watch more television overall than do children in white families (e.g., Bickham et al., 2003; Brown & Pardun, 2004), and television viewing is typically negatively related to parent education (e.g., Anand & Krosnick, 2005), as we noted at the beginning of this chapter. Moreover, school-age children and young adolescents prefer to watch programs featuring characters with similar racial backgrounds (e.g., Brown & Pardun, 2004; O'Connor, Brooks-Gunn, & Graber, 2000). In particular, black children are generally loyal to a few shows with predominantly black casts, whereas white children's preferences are more widely spread across more programs with predominantly white casts (Brown & Pardun, 2004). As we have noted early in this chapter, however, we did not observe differences in attention to black and white characters with African American and European American preschoolers, who may have far less awareness of race than do older children.

ATTENTIONAL INERTIA

Effective television does not just hold attention, it can become completely absorbing. The popular literature on children and television is replete with accounts of young children staring at the screen for long periods, seemingly inured to distraction. Research has verified this phenomenon, which is called *attentional inertia* (Anderson, Alwitt, Lorch, & Levin, 1979). Several lines of research have found that engagement with the program generally deepens as time spent looking at the screen progresses; that is, viewers become increasingly absorbed the longer they continually maintain looking at the television.

Attentional inertia has been found across a broad age range, from infants to adults (for a detailed review, see Richards & Anderson, 2004). Physiological and behavioral research converges in support of the hypothesis that cognitive engagement increases as time into a single look progresses. Richards and Cronise (2000) reported that heart rate in 6- to 24-month-olds suddenly and sharply decreased at the beginning of a look at television, followed by a constant and gradual decrease until just before look termination, at which point heart rate returned to baseline. A variety of psychophysiological experiments have found that decelerated heart rate over the course of a look is indicative of progressively engaged attention. Consistent with this hypothesis, increased look length is also associated with other measures of cognitive engagement, such as decreased distractibility (e.g., Anderson, Choi, & Lorch, 1987; Richards & Turner, 2001) and increased reaction time to orient toward a distractor or to respond in a secondary task (e.g., Anderson et al., 1987; Lorch & Castle, 1997).

Research on comprehension and recall of program content also supports the hypothesis of a positive association between look length and cognitive engagement. For example, Burns and Anderson (1993) found that recognition memory was better for video clips that were initially presented in the later part of long looks (i.e., after 15 seconds of steady looking) than during short looks or the first part of long looks (i.e., before 15 seconds elapsed); recall in the latter two categories did not differ. Elizabeth Lorch and her colleagues have found that attentional inertia strengthens inferential activities that allow connected comprehension of different parts of narrative television programs (Lorch et al., 2004; Lorch, Milich, Astrin, & Berthiaume, 2006); children with attention-deficit/hyperactivity disorder not only show reduced attentional inertia but also are less likely to achieve connected comprehension of these television programs. These findings highlight the importance of sustained attention for learning from television.

Attentional inertia does vary with respect to content. For example, attentional inertia in children older than 18 months is stronger for comprehensible than for incomprehensible material (Richards & Anderson, 2004). Moreover, Hawkins and colleagues (Hawkins, Tapper, Bruce, & Pingree, 1995; Hawkins et al., 2002) examined the effect of content on the strength of attentional inertia more thoroughly in adults and found that the effect of inertia in maintaining attention across a boundary increased as a function of the degree to which the content in the two segments was causally related (Hawkins et al., 1995). Furthermore, they found that inertia is stronger in holding attention across a change in content for commercial-to-program boundaries than for program-to-commercial boundaries, suggesting that viewers' expectations about upcoming content are important (Hawkins et al., 2002). In contrast to the popular view of engaged attention to television as mesmerized mindlessness (e.g., Healy, 1990; Singer, 1980; Winn, 1977), it is the state in which learning from television occurs in depth.

CONCLUSION

Children of poverty watch television, and television is one clear route of educational intervention. Although television may be of little educational value to advantaged children, the evidence is that television viewing is associated with increased achievement for low-income children (e.g., Comstock & Paik, 1991). Educational television that is specifically designed to educate children who have fewer outside resources and activities is successful in better preparing them for school (Zill, 2001).

In thinking about designing educational television for children of poverty, or for any children, there is a clear bottom line. First and foremost, what drives children's attention to television is the content. If the content is interesting and engaging, children will attend even if the show is nothing more than a sequence of black-and-white stills with actor voiceovers. This *animatic* technique is used by the producers of programs such as *Dora the Explorer* to test the comprehensibility and entertainment value of a script. The second author of this chapter (Anderson) has seen preschool children, including children from very poor neighborhoods in New York, raptly viewing and interacting with such animatics. The animatics are almost completely devoid of motion, music, sound effects, and other formal features; nevertheless, if they convey a good story, they receive nearly as much attention and enthusiastic interaction as a completed episode. One cannot, through clever postproduction and "sweetening," make a program attention-worthy if the content is not compelling to children.

It should be clear from this review that research on attention to television overwhelmingly supports a content-based approach for children at least as young as 2 years of age. This does not mean that dynamic video and audio production techniques are irrelevant. Children have brief and consistent attentional responses to visual and auditory changes and to features such as movement, especially if they have been inattentive when these features occur. Moreover, a certain visual and auditory dynamism (e.g., musical underscores) adds important arousal and emotional qualities to a program. In addition, children learn that formal features have roles in conveying content and that they may signal aspects of content such as whether it is intended for children. Understanding the research, sophisticated producers have developed programs, such as *Blue's Clues*, that carefully deploy formal features to ensure attention during portions of the content that are key to learning (Anderson, 2004). The judicious use of principles to elicit and maintain children's attention combined with engaging educational content can foster the sustained focused attention that accommodates deeper cognitive processing of program material. This can have the short-term consequence of children learning the particular content being taught but over time can also foster formal education itself (Anderson et al., 2001).

This emphasis on content means the producer must know and understand the audience. The producer must also understand that a program must be targeted to a particular developmental level insofar as comprehension is so critical to the success of the program. If television is produced specifically as an educational intervention for children at risk, the producer must come to understand the developmental level, knowledge, language, and experiences of the children in the projected audience. This is essential in order to produce content that is interesting, entertaining, and above all understandable to these children.

As a cautionary comment, there have been reports from several correlational studies that watching television is associated with later deficits in attention (Christakis, Zimmerman, DiGuiseppe, & McCarty, 2004; Landhuis, Poulton, Welch, & Hancox, 2007). This may cause some hesitation in thinking about whether to use television as a source of educational intervention in children who may be vulnerable to development of poor attentional skills. It is not yet clear from this research whether television in fact plays a causal role in the association, although the authors of these studies speculate that it does. Alternative possibilities are many. For example, parents of children with attentional problems may encourage their children to watch television because it is a situation in which these children become more quiet and attentive. If, in fact, television does have a causal influence on attentional skills, it is of the greatest importance to determine the underlying mechanism of influence. For example, is there something about the way attention is paid to television that is inimical to the development of attention in other domains? In fact, there is research that indicates that television can actually be used to teach and enhance attentional skills (e.g., Salomon, 1979; for a more recent review, see Kirkorian, Anderson, & Wartella, 2008). It is far too soon to jump to conclusions about television's role in affecting attention development itself.

In our view, television is an ideal and likely very cost-effective means of educational intervention in the lives of poor children. Although a given hour of many alternative activities (e.g., parent reading to child, music lessons, organized athletics) may be more valuable to the child than any given hour of television viewing, it is not realistic to think that children of poverty will anytime soon replace their large amounts of television viewing with such activities. Television can have a powerful and positive influence on education, as the research on *Sesame Street* has shown. It behooves us to strive to make much, if not all, television watched by economically disadvantaged children a powerful and positive influence on their educational and social development.

REFERENCES

Alwitt, L.F., Anderson, D.R., Lorch, E.P., & Levin, S.R. (1980). Preschool children's visual attention to attributes of television. *Human Communication Research, 7,* 52–67.

American Academy of Pediatrics, Committee on Public Education. (1999). Media education. *Pediatrics, 104,* 341–342.

Anand, S., & Krosnick, J.A. (2005). Demographic predictors of media use among infants, toddlers, and preschoolers. *American Behavioral Scientist, 48,* 539–561.

Anderson, D.R. (2004). Watching children watch television and the creation of *Blue's Clues.* In H. Hendershot (Ed.), *Nickelodeon nation: The history, politics, and economics of America's only TV channel for kids* (pp. 241–268). New York: New York University Press.

Anderson, D.R., Alwitt, L.F., Lorch, E.P., & Levin, S.R. (1979). Watching children watch television. In G. Hale & M. Lewis (Eds.), *Attention and cognitive development* (pp. 331–361). New York: Plenum.

Anderson, D.R., Choi, H.P., & Lorch, E.P. (1987). Attentional inertia reduces distractibility during young children's television viewing. *Child Development, 58,* 798–806.

Anderson, D.R., Fite, K.V., Petrovich, N., & Hirsch, J. (2006). Cortical activation while watching video montage: An fMRI study. *Media Psychology, 8,* 7–24.

Anderson, D.R., Huston, A.C., Schmitt, K.L., Linebarger, D.L., & Wright, J.C. (2001). Early childhood television viewing and adolescent behavior. *Monographs of the Society for Research in Child Development, 68*(Serial No. 264), 1–143.

Anderson, D.R., & Kirkorian, H.L. (2006). Attention and television. In J. Bryant & P. Vorderer (Eds.), *The psychology of entertainment* (pp. 35–54). Mahwah, NJ: Lawrence Erlbaum Associates.

Anderson, D.R., & Levin, S.R. (1976). Young children's attention to Sesame Street. *Child Development, 47,* 806–811.

Anderson, D.R., & Lorch, E.P. (1983). Looking at television: Action or reaction? In J. Bryant & D.R. Anderson (Eds.), *Children's understanding of TV: Research on attention and comprehension* (pp. 1–34). New York: Academic Press.

Anderson, D.R., Lorch, E.P., Field, D.E., Collins, P.A., & Nathan, J.G. (1986). Television viewing at home: Age trends in visual attention and time with TV. *Child Development, 57*, 1024–1033.

Anderson, D.R., Lorch, E.P., Field, D.E., & Sanders, J. (1981). The effect of television program comprehensibility on preschool children's visual attention to television. *Child Development, 52*, 151–157.

Anderson, D.R., Lorch, E.P., Smith, R., Bradford, R., & Levin, S.R. (1981). The effects of peer presence on preschool children's television viewing behavior. *Developmental Psychology, 17*, 446–453.

Anderson, D.R., & Pempek, T.A. (2005). Television and very young children. *American Behavioral Scientist, 48*, 505–522.

Barr, R., Chavez, M., Fujimoto, M., Garcia, A., Muentener, P., & Strait, C. (2003, April). *Television exposure during infancy: Patterns of viewing, attention, and interaction.* Poster presented at the biennial meeting of the Society for Research in Child Development, Tampa, FL.

Bickham, D.S., Vandewater, E.A., Huston, A.C., Lee, J.H., Caplovitz, A.G., & Wright, J.C. (2003). Predictors of children's electronic media use: An examination of three ethnic groups. *Media Psychology, 5*, 107–137.

Brown, J.D., & Pardun, C.J. (2004). Little in common: Racial and gender differences in adolescents' television diets. *Journal of Broadcasting and Electronic Media, 48*, 266–278.

Burns, J.J., & Anderson, D.R. (1993). Attentional inertia and recognition memory in adult television viewing. *Communication Research, 20*, 777–799.

Calvert, S.L., Huston, A.C., Watkins, B.A., & Wright, J.C. (1982). The relation between selective attention to television forms and children's comprehension of content. *Child Development, 53*, 601–610.

Campbell, T.A., Wright, J.C., & Huston, A.C. (1987). Form cues and content difficulty as determinants of children's cognitive processing of televised educational messages. *Journal of Experimental Child Psychology, 43*, 311–327.

Christakis, D.A., Zimmerman, F.J., DiGuiseppe, D.L., & McCarty, C.A. (2004). Early television exposure and subsequent attentional problems in children. *Pediatrics, 113*, 708–713.

Comstock, G., & Paik, H. (1991). *Television and the American child.* San Diego: Academic Press.

Cooney, J.G. (1966). *The potential uses of television in preschool education: A report to the Carnegie Corporation of New York.* New York: Carnegie Corporation.

Crawley, A.M., Anderson, D.R., Wilder, A., Williams, M., & Santomero, A. (1999). Effects of repeated exposures to a single episode of the television program *Blue's Clues* on the viewing behaviors and comprehension of preschool children. *Journal of Educational Psychology, 91*, 630–637.

Field, D.E., & Anderson, D.R. (1985). Instruction and modality effects on children's television attention and comprehension. *Journal of Educational Psychology, 77*, 91–100.

Fisch, S.M. (2004). *Children's learning from educational television: Sesame Street and beyond.* Mahwah, NJ: Lawrence Erlbaum Associates.

Fisch, S.M., Kirkorian, H.L., & Anderson, D.R. (2005) Transfer of learning in informal education: The case of television. In J.P. Mestre (Ed.), *Transfer of learning from a modern multidisciplinary perspective* (pp. 371–393). Greenwich, CT: Information Age Publishing.

Hawkins, R.P., Pingree, S., Hitchon, J.B., Gilligan, E., Kahlor, L., Gorham, B.W., et al. (2002). What holds attention to television? *Communication Research, 29*, 3–30.

Hawkins, R.P., Tapper, J., Bruce, L., & Pingree, S. (1995). Strategic and non-strategic explanations for attentional inertia. *Communication Research, 22,* 188–206.

Healy, J. (1990). *Endangered minds: Why our children don't think.* New York: Simon & Schuster.

Hollenbeck, A., & Slaby, R. (1979). Infant visual responses to television. *Child Development, 50,* 41–45.

Huston, A.C., Greer, D., Wright, J.C., Welch, R., & Ross, R. (1984). Children's comprehension of televised formal features with masculine and feminine connotations. *Developmental Psychology, 20,* 707–716.

Huston, A.C., & Wright, J.C. (1983). Children's processing of television: The informative functions of formal features. In J. Bryant & D.R. Anderson (Eds.), *Children's understanding of television: Research on attention and comprehension* (pp. 35–68). San Diego: Academic Press.

Huston, A.C., & Wright, J.C. (1989). The forms of television and the child viewer. In G. Comstock (Ed.), *Public communication and behavior* (Vol. 2, pp. 103–158). San Diego: Academic Press.

Huston, A.C., Wright, J.C., Wartella, E., Rice, M.L., Watkins, B.A., Campbell, T., et al. (1981). Communicating more than content: Formal features of children's television programs. *Journal of Communication, 31*(3), 32–48.

Kirkorian, H.L. (2008). Age differences in eye movements during video viewing (Doctoral dissertation, University of Massachusetts-Amherst, 2007). *Dissertations Abstracts International, 68,* 4865.

Kirkorian, H.L., Anderson, D.R., & Wartella, E. (2008). Media and young children's learning. *Future of Children, 18,* 63–86.

Landhuis, C.E., Poulton, R., Welch, D., & Hancox, R.J. (2007). Does childhood television viewing lead to attention problems in adolescence? Results from a prospective longitudinal study. *Pediatrics, 120,* 532–537.

Lesser, G.S. (1972). Learning, teaching, and television production for children: The experience of *Sesame Street. Harvard Educational Review, 42,* 232–272.

Levin, S.R., & Anderson, D.R. (1976). The development of attention. *Journal of Communication, 26*(2), 126–135.

Linebarger, D., & Chernin, A.R. (2005, May). *Gender differences in young children's eye movements while watching television.* Paper presented at the annual meeting of the International Communications Association, New York.

Lorch, E.P., Anderson, D.R., & Levin, S.R. (1979). The relationship of visual attention and comprehension of television by preschool children. *Child Development, 50,* 722–727.

Lorch, E.P., & Castle, V.J. (1997). Preschool children's attention to television: Visual attention and probe response times. *Journal of Experimental Child Psychology, 66,* 111–127.

Lorch, E.P., Eastham, D., Milich, R., Lemberger, C.C., Sanchez, R.P., & Welsh, R. (2004). Difficulties in comprehending causal relations among children with ADHD: The role of attentional engagement. *Journal of Abnormal Psychology, 113,* 56–63.

Lorch, E.P., Milich, R., Astrin, C.C., & Berthiaume, K.S. (2006). Cognitive engagement and story comprehension in typically developing children and children with ADHD from preschool through elementary school. *Developmental Psychology, 42,* 1206–1219.

Luecke-Aleksa, D., Anderson, D.R., Collins, P.A., & Schmitt, K.L. (1995). Gender constancy and television viewing. *Developmental Psychology, 31,* 773–780.

Mares, M.L. (1998). Children's use of VCRs. *Annals of the American Academy of Political and Social Science, 557,* 120–131.

Moore, M., & Calvert, S.L. (2000). Vocabulary acquisition for children with autism: Teacher or computer instruction. *Journal of Autism and Developmental Disorders, 30,* 359–362.

O'Connor, L.A., Brooks-Gunn, J., & Graber, J. (2000). Black and white girls' racial preferences in media and peer choices and the role of socialization for black girls. *Journal of Family Psychology, 14,* 510–521.

Pempek, T.A., Kirkorian, H.L., Stevens, M., Lund, A.F., Richards, J.E., & Anderson, D.R. (2008, March). *Video comprehensibility and attention in very young children.* Poster session presented at the biannual International Conference on Infant Studies, Vancouver, BC.

Pingree, S. (1986). Children's activity and television comprehensibility. *Communication Research, 13,* 239–256.

Richards, J.E., & Anderson, D.R. (2004). Attentional inertia in children's extended looking at television. In R.V. Kail (Ed.), *Advances in child development and behavior* (Vol. 32, pp. 163–212). San Diego: Academic Press.

Richards, J.E., & Cronise, K. (2000). Extended visual fixation in the early preschool years: Look duration, heart rate changes, and attentional inertia. *Child Development, 71,* 602–620.

Richards, J.E., & Turner, E.D. (2001). Distractibility during the extended viewing of television during the early preschool years. *Child Development, 68,* 963–972.

Rosenfeld, A., & Wise, N. (2000). *The over-scheduled child: Avoiding the hyper-parenting trap.* New York: St. Martin's Press.

Salomon, G. (1979). *Interaction of media, cognition, and learning.* San Francisco: Jossey-Bass.

Schmitt, K.L., Anderson, D.R., & Collins, P.A. (1999). Form and content: Looking at visual features of television. *Developmental Psychology, 35,* 1156–1167.

Schmitt, K.L., Woolf, K.D., & Anderson, D.R. (2003). Viewing the viewers: Viewing behaviors by children and adults during television programs and commercials. *Journal of Communication, 53,* 265–281.

Singer, J.L. (1980). The power and limits of television: A cognitive-affective analyses. In P. Tannenbaum (Ed.), *The entertainment function of television* (pp. 31–66). Mahwah, NJ: Lawrence Erlbaum Associates.

Skouteris, H., & Kelly, L. (2006). Repeated-viewing and co-viewing of an animated video: An examination of factors that impact on young children's comprehension of video content. *Australian Journal of Early Childhood, 31,* 22–30.

Slaby, R.G., & Frey, K.S. (1975). Development of gender constancy and selective attention to same-sex models. *Developmental Psychology, 46,* 849–856.

Smith, R., Anderson, D.R., & Fischer, C. (1985). Young children's comprehension of montage. *Child Development, 56,* 962–971.

Valkenburg, P.M., & Vroone, M. (2004). Developmental changes in infants' and toddlers' attention to television entertainment. *Communication Research, 31,* 288–311.

Wartella, E., & Ettema, J.S. (1974). A cognitive developmental study of children's attention to television commercials. *Communication Research, 1,* 69–88.

Winn, M. (1977). *The plug-in drug.* New York: Viking Press.

Zill, N. (2001). Does *Sesame Street* enhance school readiness?: Evidence from a national survey of children. In S.M. Fisch & R.T. Truglio (Eds.), *"G" is for "growing": Thirty years of research on children and Sesame Street* (pp. 115–130). Mahwah, NJ: Lawrence Erlbaum Associates.

16

Maximizing Informal Learning from Digital Technologies

Sandra L. Calvert

When Americans think of literacy, they generally think of children's ability to read and write words. This kind of literacy is indeed an important way to become a well-versed citizen in the information age (Neuman, Copple, & Bredekamp, 2000). However, often neglected and even diminished in importance are visual/iconic and musical/echoic modes of thinking, which tend to be prominent in the information technologies that comprise children's daily lives (Calvert, 1999). Visual and nonverbal auditory icons are also a legitimate mode of thinking, one that is undervalued and underused to reach children who do not readily understand the abstract verbal symbols that are required for success in school settings.

Media use a rich display of visual and auditory production features, known as *formal features,* that can readily be used to instruct and teach children even as they are being entertained (Calvert, 1999). In particular, formal features such as action, sound effects, and singing can be used as scaffolds, building bridges between how a child thinks at particular points in development to the knowledge to be learned.

Little is known about how children come to understand and become literate in the use of these media symbols that pervade their daily lives. Nor do we understand enough about how visual and nonlinguistic auditory symbols provide links to words in ways that can enhance or diminish literacy. Yet, African American and Latino children, who are often economically disadvantaged, are more likely to live in homes that are television dominated—where nonverbal, visual forms are prominent modes of experience—than are their Caucasian peers

This chapter is based on a paper titled *Production Features as Scaffolds for Children's Learning: Lessons for Instructional Design,* presented by Sandra Calvert at Pathways to Literacy Achievement for High Poverty Children: A Ready to Learn Research Agenda, October 1, 2006, Ann Arbor, Michigan.

(Roberts, Foehr, & Rideout, 2005). Not only do children who live in lower-income families view more television than those who live in higher-income families, but they are also more dependent on educational media for learning skills that are needed to succeed in school (Huston et al., 1992; St. Peters, Fitch, Huston, Wright, & Eakins, 1991). Therefore, it is important that we understand how minority youth come to read the "grammar" of the media.

My point is a simple one that has important educational implications for minority youth: television viewing is often blamed for poor literacy skills, yet there is rich potential for television to enhance literacy skills as well, particularly for children who grow up in lower-income households. By focusing on forms of thought that ethnic minority children typically use in their daily lives—which tend to be visual, nonverbal, and musical in nature (Heath, 1989; Roberts et al., 2005)—scaffolds can be created to words that may facilitate African American and Latino children's literacy.

Two major lines of research and thought are pursued in this chapter. The first involves how formal features can be used to facilitate children's learning and understanding of verbal material, a more traditional kind of literacy. In this area, I focus on the role that formal features can play as scaffolds for children's verbal learning. The second line of thought and research involves how children come to understand the unique codes of media as a symbol system in its own right. Because ethnic minority children are heavy users of both television and music, it is particularly important that we come to understand how formal features can be used to facilitate their literacy skills. I then discuss implications of formal feature use for effective instructional design.

FORMAL FEATURES

Formal features are audiovisual production features that structure, mark, and represent content (Huston & Wright, 1983). They are the grammar of audiovisual media (Calvert, 1999). As seen in Table 16.1, these features at a macro level involve *action* (physical movement) and *pace* (the rate of scene and character change). At a micro level, these features include visual camera techniques such as *pans* in which objects are followed in a continuous sweeping motion, *zooms* to close-ups or away from objects, *fades* in which the screen goes black, *dissolves* in which one object appears on top of another, *cuts* from one point of view to another, and *visual special effects* in which the physical rules of reality are violated. Auditory micro features include *sound effects* in which loud noises occur; character *vocalizations* of unusual nonspeech sounds; *music* that is either in the *foreground* (prominent) or *background* (with dialogue); *singing* (music and language combined); *laugh track* (off-screen audience laughs); *dialogue* by *adults* (adults speakers), *children* (child speakers), or *nonhumans* (e.g., animals characters in cartoons); and *narration* (one person speaks and explains the story). Being able to decode and "read" these features is the essence of being a literate user of information technologies.

Table 16.1.   Taxonomy of formal features

Features	Definitions
Macro features	
Action	Amount of movement
Pace	Rate of scene and character change
Visual micro features	
Cuts	Camera technique involving quick shifts in visual perspective
Zooms	Continuous camera technique moving the lens toward or away from an object or scene
Fades	Camera technique that goes to black
Dissolves	Camera technique that makes the edges of the scene blurry as a new image emerges
Pans and trucks	Camera technique in which objects or events are followed continuously on a horizontal or vertical plane
Visual special effects	Camera techniques such as trick photography, freeze frames, and fast motion
Auditory micro features	
Foreground music	Loud music with no dialogue
Background music	Music with dialogue
Vocalizations	Nonspeech noises
Sound effects	Unusual prominent audio effects (e.g., zip!)
Laugh track	Audible laughing by an off-screen audience
Child dialogue	Child speech
Adult dialogue	Adult speech
Nonhuman dialogue	Speech by an animal character or other nonhuman character
Narration	Speech by one individual, typically explaining on-screen events
Singing	Music and lyrics combined

Formal features vary in *perceptual salience,* that is, in their attention-getting properties. Perceptual salience involves stimulus properties such as movement, contrast, change, incongruity, and complexity, which are likely to have survival value for our species (Berlyne, 1960). Applied to information technologies, macro features such as action (movement) and rapid pacing (change and complexity) and visual and auditory micro features such as character vocalizations, sound effects, visual special effects, and frequent camera cuts (incongruity, change, contrast) have been classified as perceptually salient. By contrast, features such as adult dialogue, child dialogue, and narration, although potentially carrying the most informative linguistic content, are in and of themselves low in salience (see Calvert, Huston, Watkins, & Wright, 1982).

The linguistic features of adult dialogue, child dialogue, and narration have considerable potential to foster children's interest in and sensitivity to oral language. If words are written on the screen, literacy skills can also be promoted.

However, the varying salience of different features used to present content in information technologies creates a challenge: How do you get children to pay attention to and process language when there are so many other more interesting features to attract and hold their attention? In many media interfaces, the answer lies in the judicious pairing of other features—action, sound effects, character vocalizations, and singing—with written and spoken language. These features are maximally effective as a learning tool when they dovetail with the cognitive skills that children bring to bear on information at different points in development.

FORMAL FEATURES AS SCAFFOLDS FOR CHILDREN'S LEARNING

Vygotsky (1978) argued that young children need scaffolds, or bridges, that link what children currently know and understand to knowledge that is just beyond their realm of understanding. His approach focused on verbal, linguistic ways of learning, particularly the bridges that parents build between what their child knows and the knowledge to be learned. Just as knowledge may be more or less available to children during certain developmental time frames, so too are children's abilities to process certain symbol systems. According to Bruner, Olver, and Greenfield (1968), very young children think in enactive, motoric modes followed by visual iconic and finally abstract symbolic verbal modes. These modes of thinking can be activated and enhanced by using certain production features in a presentation, thus providing scaffolds to improve the effectiveness of informal instructional learning environments, including those presented in a linguistic format. Although less understood than the verbal scaffolds presented by parents, one thesis developed here is that formal features can also serve as scaffolds for children's learning.

Features as Early Elicitors of Imitation and Enactive Ways of Thought

Thinking with the body can readily be observed in infants' and young children's imitation of the many live adults and symbolic models that they view. Meltzoff (1988) demonstrated that even infants can imitate actions portrayed on a video, though the presentation had to involve contingent replies to what the infant did. These early imitative activities activate the mirror neuron system in which infants learn to understand by copying others' movements (Meltzoff, 2002).

We examined songs as ways to promote early learning by creating a scaffold between children's actions (i.e., enactive rehearsal) and the lyrics of the song (Calvert & Goodman, 1999). Toddlers either sang songs or sang the songs while displaying actions that conveyed the meaning of the song. For instance, they either sang *I'm a Little Teapot* and tipped their bodies over and "poured out" the tea or they just sang the song. The toddlers who used enactive ways of rehearsing the song lyrics subsequently understood the meaning of the song better than those who simply sang it without the aid of motor rehearsal. Put another way, the motor behaviors provided a scaffold, that is, a link, to the meaning of the song lyrics.

Similar findings occurred when preschool-age children were exposed to an episode of *Dora the Explorer* in which we manipulated the interactive prompts that get children to act out content (Calvert, Strong, Jacobs, & Conger, 2007). In the original version, Dora asks children to do things with her such as climb the ladder to rescue Benny the Bull, thereby eliciting imitative actions from her verbal prompts. We manipulated this prosocial, educational story so that children were exposed to either 1) a control version in which there was no interaction and an adult sat at the back of the room; 2) a control observational version in which the adult sat beside the child while viewing; 3) a participatory version in which the adult interacted with Dora and the child could do so or not; and 4) an interactive version in which the program paused and the child had to use a computer to move the program to the next point. Children from Latino backgrounds, who tended to come from Head Start programs, were compared with their Caucasian peers who came from middle-class backgrounds. After viewing, children answered a verbal multiple-choice test. We found that the more children participated with Dora, the better they understood the central story content.

In homes where verbal discussion may not be a priority, such as low-income African American homes (see Heath, 1989), having an animated character "look" at children through a camera lens, ask questions of viewers, and engage children in program-related activities and discussion can potentially improve children's learning of educational program content. Perhaps television characters can serve the same function as an interactive adult, thereby providing scaffolds for children's learning in low-income households. Although the middle-class Caucasian children understood the content better than the lower-income Latino children did, Latina girls who were in the interactive condition understood the central story content better than the Latina girls in the observational condition (Calvert et al., 2007).

Action as a Mode of Thought

Preschool-age children often think in a visual, iconic mode (Bruner et al., 1968). Action or movement can enhance or disrupt children's learning of content, be it presented on a television or a computer (Calvert, 1999).

The classic study of children's learning from television was conducted by Hayes and Birnbaum (1980). In the study, they showed preschool-age children original intact programs or altered programs that had the sound track of one program combined with the visual track of another program. In mismatched conditions, children remembered the visual track over the verbal track. This outcome became known as the visual superiority effect: Children remember the visual track at the expense of the auditory track.

In our early work (Calvert et al., 1982), we wondered if the visual superiority effect was really because of the perceptually salient character actions. Moreover, because action and dialogue are similar to iconic and symbolic modes of thought, we believed that action could facilitate children's learning, particularly at young ages when the predominant mode of thinking is more iconic than at subsequent points in development. By contrast, we expected that dialogue alone, a nonsalient form, would be of more benefit to older children. In our initial correlational study, preschool and kindergarten students and third to fourth graders viewed an episode of *Fat Albert and the Cosby Kids*, a prosocial cartoon featuring a cast of animated African American boys and their live African American host, Bill Cosby. We had previously scored the formal features of that program, including the character action. We later linked children's attentional patterns to the program and their comprehension of program content to those features.

Children remembered the central plot-relevant content better when the language had been paired with action rather than when the central content was only spoken. These findings were true of the older as well as the younger children. In fact, the youngest children who understood the program best did not attend when Bill Cosby was speaking, presumably because his narrative comments occurred during low-action sequences and were incomprehensible, so they stopped looking. Our results suggested beneficial effects of action through the middle childhood years (Calvert et al., 1982). Similarly, 4- and 7–year-olds reproduced the actions more than the language of characters when they heard or viewed a story (Gibbons, Anderson, Smith, Field, & Fischer, 1986).

Lawler (1982), who was creating computer worlds during this same time frame, was able to improve his 2-year-old daughter's literacy skills by building vocabulary words into a program which put information on a visual beach scene. For an object to appear on the beach, his daughter Peggy had to key in the word. For instance, if she keyed in the word *pony*, a pony appeared on her beach. In other words, she had control of making events happen. Lawler created what became known as intrinsically interesting learning environments.

In subsequent experimental studies, my colleagues and I decided to examine the role of various formal production features in creating intrinsically interesting learning environments. In our first study (Calvert, Watson, Brinkley, & Bordeaux, 1989), we created a game called *Park World* in which objects were programmed to appear with or without action and with or without sound effects. Six different groups contained four objects each (e.g., the group *vehicles* contained car, truck, plane, and train), for a total of 24 objects. Four versions of *Park World* were created to examine the effects of movement and sound effects independently of the specific object. For example, across the four versions of *Park World*, the car appeared moving with sound effects, moving without sound effects, nonmoving with sound effects, and nonmoving with no sound effects. Kindergarten-age children listened to the same story about *Park World* for four days as the experimenter keyed in the objects. Each day, children selected objects to go in their park from the six sets and keyed in those object names. Children chose more objects that moved than those that were stationary to go into their park. On the fifth day, we asked children to tell us all of the objects that were in *Park World*. Objects that moved were more likely to be recalled than those that were stationary. The findings suggested the importance of action for remembering information.

In our next study (Calvert, Watson, Brinkley & Penny, 1990), we randomly selected a version of *Park World* and added a voice synthesizer to speak the object names, creating what became known as *Talk World*. The action was retained. Here we became particularly interested in how to link action and language to improve children's recall of content. Children heard the story only one time in this version and were then asked to tell us the names of all the objects that they could remember from *Talk World*. This time we compared good and poor readers in kindergarten and second grade. There were no effects for kindergartners who were not yet reading; however, poor readers in the second grade recalled just as many objects as the good readers when the objects moved. By contrast, good readers recalled more objects than poor readers when the objects were stationary. The results suggested the beneficial effects of action for poor readers, as action basically provided a scaffold for children's verbal recall of object names.

Rehearsal is a mechanism that enhances children's learning of educational content. Following Salomon's (1974) ideas of activating (i.e., calling upon) versus supplanting (i.e., providing) cognitive skills, I (Calvert, 1991) modified how the story was presented in *Talk World*. In the verbal label condition, we continued to read the words (i.e., supplantation condition). In the no label condition, rather than reading the targeted words, we now paused (i.e., activation condition). Objects still moved or were stationary. Preschoolers' and kindergartners' spontaneous production and subsequent recall of objects was then examined. Children in the no label condition were far more likely to produce the names of targeted words, particularly when the objects also moved. For both age groups, using action and verbal labels together facilitated recall better than having no action or no label. The kindergarteners' recall was most likely to benefit from having both verbal labels and action presented simultaneously, suggesting that they were able to integrate the different forms of presentation better than the preschoolers did. Here, then, we see beneficial effects of action as a scaffold for language for both rehearsal and memory of content.

Children with developmental disabilities such as autism often are challenged when learning language, in part because they are more interested in machines than in the human interactions that are a major context for language development (Baron-Cohen, Wheelwright, Lawson, Griffin, & Hill, 2002). Computers, therefore, are a potentially useful mechanical device for teaching language to children with autism. To examine the potential of production features in a computer scenario for children with autism, Monique Moore and I created a scenario in which children could learn words that were associated with moving objects on a computer display. The Lovaas method, in which children are taught to pay attention to an adult to facilitate language acquisition, was used in conjunction with the computer program or alone as the control condition. After instruction, children were asked if they wanted to play outside or keep playing on the computer. We also assessed their verbal learning. Preschool children who had autism were more motivated to continue playing the computer game and learned more nouns when they had been instructed via the computer than by the Lovaas method alone (Moore & Calvert, 2000).

In summary, although visual content can interfere with children's recall of verbal content when a mismatch occurs between the verbal and visual content, action generally helps children understand verbal content when these two forms present consistent information. Beneficial effects occur whether the content is presented via television or computer interfaces. Action seems particularly helpful for children who are young, who do not read well, and who have developmental disabilities such as autism. Even though older children get better at processing words without some kind of visual scaffold, action can still benefit children's learning well into middle childhood. Latino children benefit from programs designed to elicit interaction from them.

Singing for Verbatim Recall

Singing is a reflective feature that combines lyrics with music (Huston et al., 1981). Although educators have often thought that singing is a useful way to improve learning, the scaffold that it provides to language offers a bridge to verbatim memory, not to comprehension of content.

School House Rock was an instructional series designed to teach children history, science, mathematics, and English. Short vignettes of approximately 3 minutes presented animated bits with singing to accentuate the message. In our first study of *School House Rock* (Calvert & Tart, 1993), we examined a vignette about the Preamble to the U.S. Constitution. College students were compared in conditions in which the Preamble was either spoken or sung. Immediate and long-term recall of the words to the Preamble was assessed after several viewings. Students who had seen the sung version of the Preamble recalled more of the words in the exact original order than those who had seen the spoken version of the vignette. The results linked repeated exposure to a sung vignette to very good short-term and long-term memory of words.

In a subsequent study (Calvert, 2001), I examined a history vignette from *School House Rock* about the Revolutionary War. The conditions varied the use of a visual or a nonvisual track and the use of a sung or a spoken audio track. This time, children viewed the vignette only once. Contrary to prediction, children understood the spoken track better than the sung track. Although unexpected, these findings dovetailed nicely with an intriguing finding from our Preamble study: Words were sometimes substituted in students' renditions of the Preamble that did not preserve the original meaning of the Preamble. For example, one person in the singing condition wrote "to ensure the blessings of liberty to ourselves and our *prosperity*" rather than "to ensure the blessings of liberty to ourselves and our *posterity.*" These findings suggested some problems in using singing to teach information that went deeper than superficial memorization of the lyrics.

"I'm Just a Bill," another *School House Rock* history vignette, described how a bill goes through the process of becoming a law. I manipulated how much children were exposed to this vignette (Calvert, 2001). Specifically, third graders and college students were exposed to the vignette in its original spoken and sung soundtrack either once or four times. After the final exposure, verbatim recall, verbal sequencing of how a bill becomes a law, and comprehension of the content was assessed. The repetition condition increased all students' verbatim recall and verbal sequencing of content but not their recognition of the important story content. When asked what a bill was, one child told us that a bill was "something that you pay."

Taken together, the findings suggest that singing provides an excellent and durable way to rehearse and remember content in a verbatim form; however, if you want to improve comprehension of the message, speaking the same content is the best way to improve memory. These findings support Craik and Lockhart's (1972) levels of processing theory in which content can be processed at a superficial level without a deeper understanding of the meaning of that content. It appears that singing, unless accompanied by enactive rehearsal such as what we did with *I'm a Little Teapot*, is a superficial learning technique, whereas the use of language without singing is more likely to receive deeper processing. Thus, although singing provides scaffolds to verbal content, its effectiveness as an instructional feature depends on the kind of lesson to be learned. A challenge for instructional design is to create additional scaffolds between language and songs that can yield deeper processing of the content. One such possibility may be to use rap, a musical form that is popular in African American culture that combines spoken language with a rhythmic presentation.

Parsing Content: Sound Effects and Vocalizations as Markers of Important Content

In addition to serving as a mode in which to represent content, formal production features can parse and mark content for further processing, thereby providing a scaffold to the verbal linguistic content that follows. Our early naturalistic study of *Fat Albert and the Cosby Kids* was the first place that we documented this beneficial effect (Calvert et al., 1982). In the episode that we studied, Fat Albert would say, "Hey, Hey, Hey, I've got something to say." Then, he would say important verbal content that helped children understand the story. Children who selectively attended the most immediately after character vocalizations (in this case, Fat Albert's "Hey, Hey, Hey") understood the central story content the best. We hypothesized that children initially attend to vocalizations because of their perceptually salient qualities. Even after children were familiar with vocalizations, we argued that these perceptually salient audio features still captured attention and elicited active processing because the vocalizations had become a learned signal that was associated with important story content.

In subsequent experimental studies, we manipulated sound effects inserted at key scene transitions to see if it helped children understand the central plot-relevant content of the narrative. In one study, we found that sound effects inserted at three key scene changes increased kindergartners', but not third and fourth graders', recognition of the implicit, central plot-relevant content (Calvert & Gersh, 1987). The older children in the study understood the central content, but the younger children needed the sound as a scaffold (Calvert & Gersh, 1987).

In a follow-up study in which we varied how rapidly the scenes and characters changed, we found that sound effects worked best for the rapidly paced program (Calvert & Scott, 1989). Specifically, young children were more likely to selectively attend to scene changes in the rapidly paced program when sound effects were present, not absent. Moreover, selective attention at these key program transitions predicted kindergartners' comprehension of the content. Older children, by contrast, did not need the sound effects for comprehension of the rapidly paced program. Research indicates that infants begin to integrate sound effects with target actions at about 1 year of age (Somander, Garcia, Miller, & Barr, 2005).

Taken together, the results suggest the value of sound effects as a way to draw attention to key program content that can then lead to temporal integration of the plot line. Put another way, sound effects and character vocalizations can help children build a scaffold to link important program transitions and fill in the gaps when they are viewing television programs. The effectiveness of these salient features to guide attention occurs very early in development.

DOES LITERACY INVOLVE MORE THAN READING AND WRITING TEXT IN THE INFORMATION AGE?

Our traditions as a species are deeply rooted in our creation of and use of written language, an aspect of thinking that makes us unique from other species. Written words as a mode of cultural transmission became dominant when the printing press emerged, allowing that aspect of thought to be widely disseminated with ease (Calvert, 1999). We now live in a world where we not only can view other people's thoughts through production practices such as flashbacks in time, but we can also create and transmit our visual realities through devices such as cameras or drawings that we interface with computers. In these ways, newer technologies allow us to communicate with one another in visual as well as in musical and written forms of thought. Little is known about how we come to understand and use nonverbal symbols even though they comprise much of what children experience in their daily lives.

Take a feature such as a camera zoom versus a camera cut. The camera zoom provides focus; it simulates how one uses one's eyes to learn information. A camera zoom moves into a close-up of an object, modeling the skill of whole to part or vice versa (Salomon, 1974). By contrast, camera cuts call upon viewers to fill in the gap of going from part to whole. Salomon's classic research (1974) demonstrated that young preschool-age children benefited the most after exposure to a camera zoom, which supplanted (i.e., provided) the cognitive skill for them, whereas older children benefited the most from viewing a camera cut, which activated that cognitive skill, calling upon the children to produce the activity of going from part to whole themselves.

Camera dissolves are a media convention that generally represent a shift in time, including major time changes such as flashbacks. Although the dissolve does not have a direct link to how we use our eyes, it is a representation that is easier to understand than a camera cut when conveying a flashback. For instance, Calvert (1988) found that kindergartners and first graders were much more likely to understand that a flashback had taken place when a dreamy dissolve rather than an abrupt camera cut had occurred between the scene transitions. Although fourth and fifth graders were less dependent on the camera cut for comprehension of the time change, even they understood the camera dissolve best. How children come to understand camera dissolves and cuts is unknown.

IMPLICATIONS FOR INSTRUCTIONAL DESIGN

As can be seen from the empirical research, production features provide a vast array of options to provide scaffolds for motor, verbal, visual, and sequential ways of learning. Pauses and prompts that are built into a program can elicit active processing from very young children who interact with the characters and content, thereby yielding enactive ways of remembering content and imitative displays of that learning. Action provides a visual mode to represent content that can facilitate but also disrupt memory of linguistic information, depending on how those scaffolds are built between these two symbol systems. Singing provides a reflective way of processing words, though it can stay superficial unless enactive bridges are built to elicit deeper processing of the content. Sound effects and character vocalizations elicit attention and facilitate processing of central and sequentially presented content though they can be distracting if they do not match the ecology of the visual presentation.

One interesting design challenge is how to facilitate children's attention to, and learning of, written rather than oral words presented in screen media. I have observed poorly designed interfaces in which the action is being presented at the same time that the written words are appearing on screen. The goal of the design is to get children to read, but the presentation is probably drawing attention away from the words and to the moving images. The solution may well be to have the words appear while a still image is on screen and then have the images move after the words are read and written. If the words are appearing as they are being read, the moving words should elicit attention and processing, thereby improving literacy. Faces are also distracting because children tend to look at the person rather than the words on the screen. *The Electric Company*, a 1970s educational television program designed to enhance literacy skills, dealt with this design issue by having two faces appear sideways and in shadow, thereby facilitating attention to written words that were blended on the screen rather than to the faces.

As an instructional design feature, singing has the educational benefit of preserving a verbatim memory of events that can be accessed for very long periods of time. The design challenge of singing is to get children and even adults to think more deeply about the content so that they not only remember the lyrics but understand the message. Fortunately, words can be processed at any time so that information is available if listeners are prompted or motivated to think about the underlying message. At young ages, enacting the lyrics helps children get the right message (Calvert & Goodman, 1999), and repeating the song helps enhance verbatim memory of the content (Calvert & Tart, 1993). Although we have not studied singing that is accompanied by written words, that approach may be helpful for yielding deeper processing at older ages, as may the use of rap.

As instructional design features, vocalizations can readily elicit children's visual attention, thereby providing a bridge to the significant program content that improves learning. Perceptually salient sounds are a good ecological fit when embedded within rapidly paced television programs (Calvert & Scott, 1989). They are most useful at very young ages in terms of plot comprehension, but they elicit attention and processing at many developmental time frames, starting in infancy and continuing at least through middle childhood (Somander et al., 2005; Calvert et al., 1982). Sound effects are easily integrated into previous productions, which we often did during our studies, making them a very cost effective way to improve the instructional effectiveness of existing programs.

CONCLUSION

Children spend much of their daily lives with screen media. At this point, television is still the dominant medium in children's homes, particularly those from African American and Latino families who live in television-centered homes (Rideout & Hamel, 2006; Roberts et al., 2005). Children from these ethnic minority groups also tend to be less successful in school than their Caucasian peers.

Much has been done via programs such as *Sesame Street* to improve the educational outcomes of low-income children (Fisch & Truglio, 2001). More could be done to facilitate learning television content through the judicious use of production features. For instance, music is a very popular form of presentation in African American and Latino culture (Roberts et al., 2005). Musical forms, such as rap, could be used to teach verbal academic lessons to African American children in a form that is interesting and relevant to their culture. Parents who talk to their children facilitate language development, but many minority children come from homes that are not overly talkative (Heath, 1989). In these cases, productions can be crafted to elicit active participation, including verbal discussion with the characters. Although the future promises to be a more interactive one, our research indicates that similar design principles apply to computer as well as television platforms.

In the 21st century, which is dominated by visual and digital media, it is timely to think about how our information technologies are influencing literacy, both in its traditional verbal form as well as in its visual, musical, and increasingly interactive form. The judicious use of formal features as scaffolds to the content and to the form of children's thought are essential to the creation of well-designed instructional platforms and to our understanding of what literacy entails in the 21st century.

REFERENCES

Baron-Cohen, S., Wheelwright, S., Lawson, J., Griffin, R., & Hill, J. (2002). The exact mind: Empathizing and systematizing in autism spectrum conditions. In U. Goswami (Ed.), *Blackwell handbook of childhood cognitive development* (pp. 491–508). Malden, MA: Blackwell.

Berlyne, D.E. (1960). *Conflict, curiosity, and arousal.* New York: McGraw Hill.

Bruner, J.S., Olver, R.R., & Greenfield, P.M. (1968). *Studies in cognitive growth.* New York: Wiley.

Calvert, S.L. (1988). Television production feature effects on children's comprehension of time. *Journal of Applied Developmental Psychology, 9,* 263–273.

Calvert, S.L. (1991). Presentational features for young children's production and recall of information. *Journal of Applied Developmental Psychology, 12,* 367–378.

Calvert, S.L. (1999). *Children's journeys through the information age.* Boston: McGraw Hill.

Calvert, S.L. (2001). Impact of televised songs on children's and young adults' memory of educational content. *Media Psychology, 3,* 325–342.

Calvert, S.L., & Gersh, T.L. (1987). The selective use of sound effects and visual inserts for children's television story comprehension. *Journal of Applied Developmental Psychology, 8,* 363–375.

Calvert, S.L., & Goodman, T. (1999, April). *Enactive rehearsal for young children's comprehension of songs.* Poster presented at the biennial meeting of the Society for Research in Child Development, Albuquerque, NM.

Calvert, S.L., Huston, A.C., Watkins, B.A., & Wright, J.C. (1982). The relation between selective attention to television forms and children's comprehension of content. *Child Development, 53,* 601–610.

Calvert, S.L., & Scott, M.C. (1989). Sound effects for children's comprehension of fast-paced television content. *Journal of Broadcasting and Electronic Media, 33,* 233–246.

Calvert, S.L., Strong, B.L., Jacobs, E.L., & Conger, E.E. (2007). Interaction and participation for young Hispanic and Caucasian girls' and boys' learning of media content. *Media Psychology, 9,* 431–445.

Calvert, S.L., & Tart, M. (1993). Song versus prose forms for student's very long-term, long-term, and short-term verbatim recall. *Journal of Applied Developmental Psychology, 14,* 245–260.

Calvert, S.L., Watson, J.A., Brinkley, V., & Bordeaux, B. (1989). Computer presentational features for young children's preferential selection and recall of information. *Journal of Educational Computing Research, 5,* 35–49.

Calvert, S.L., Watson, J.A., Brinkley, V., & Penny, J. (1990). Computer presentational features for poor readers' recall of information. *Journal of Educational Computing Research, 6,* 287–298.

Craik, F., & Lockhart, R. (1972). Levels of processing: A framework for memory research. *Journal of Verbal Learning and Verbal Behavior, 11,* 521–533.

Fisch, S., & Truglio, R. (2001). *G is for Growing: Thirty years of research on children and Sesame Street.* Mahwah, NJ: Lawrence Erlbaum Associates.

Gibbons, J., Anderson, D.R., Smith, R., Field, D.E., & Fischer, C. (1986). Young children's recall and reconstruction of audio and audiovisual material. *Child Development, 57,* 1014–1023.

Hayes, D., & Birnbaum, D. (1980). Preschoolers' retention of televised events: Is a picture worth a thousand words? *Developmental Psychology, 16,* 410–416.

Heath, S. (1989). Oral and literate traditions among black Americans living in poverty. *American Psychologist, 44,* 367–373.

Huston, A.C., Donnerstein, E., Fairchild, H., Feshbach, N., Katz, P., Murray, J., et al. (1992). *Big world, small screen.* Lincoln, NE: University of Nebraska Press.

Huston, A.C., & Wright, J.C. (1983). The informative functions of formal features. In J. Bryant & D.R. Anderson (Eds.), *Children's understanding of television: Research on attention and comprehension* (pp. 35–68). New York: Academic Press.

Huston, A.C., Wright, J.C., Wartella, E., Rice, M.L., Watkins, B.A., Campbell, T., et al. (1981). Communicating more than content: Formal features of children's television programs. *Journal of Communication, 31,* 32–48.

Lawler, R.W. (1982). Designing computer-based microworlds. *Byte,* 138–160.

Meltzoff, A.N. (1988). Imitation of televised models by infants. *Child Development, 59,* 1221–1229.

Meltzoff, A.N. (2002). Imitation as a mechanism of social cognition: Origins of empathy, theory of mind, and the representation of action. In U. Goswami (Ed.), *Blackwell handbook of childhood cognitive development* (pp. 6–25). Malden, MA: Blackwell.

Moore, M., & Calvert, S.L. (2000). Vocabulary acquisition for children with autism: Teacher or computer instruction. *Journal of Autism and Developmental Disorders, 30,* 359–362.

Neuman, S.B., Copple, C., & Bredekamp, S. (2000). *Learning to read and write: Developmentally appropriate practices for young children.* Washington, DC: National Association for the Education of Young Children.

Rideout, V.J., & Hamel, E. (2006). *The media family: Electronic media in the lives of infants, toddlers, preschoolers and their parents.* Menlo Park, CA: Kaiser Family Foundation.

Roberts, D., Foehr, U., & Rideout, V. (2005, March). *Generation M: Media in the lives of 8–18 year-olds.* Menlo Park, CA: The Henry J. Kaiser Foundation.

Salomon, G. (1974). Internalization of filmic schematic operations in interaction with learners' aptitudes. *Journal of Educational Psychology, 66,* 499–511.

St. Peters, M., Fitch, M., Huston, A.C., Wright, J.C., & Eakins, D. (1991). Television and families: What do young children watch with their families? *Child Development, 62,* 1409–1423.

Somanader, M., Garcia, A., Miller, N., & Barr, R. (2005). *Effects of sound effects and music on imitation from television during infancy.* Paper presented at the Society for Research on Child Development, Atlanta, GA.

Vygotsky, L.S. (1978). *Mind in society: The development of higher psychological processes.* Cambridge: Harvard University Press.

17

The Benefits of Going Green

Kathleen A. Roskos

Research supports strong ties between the quality of the physical environment and students' learning at school. Too often, however, the environmental quality of the classroom remains a backdrop for learning rather than an integral part of the learning process. The design knowledge we have is not effectively translated to practice, and, as a result, the physical environment is often neglected as a critical factor in improving instructional effectiveness. Although there is a large body of research linking health and productivity with specific school environment factors (e.g., air quality), a large majority of schools are not designed to create healthy, productive study and learning environments. Nowhere is this more pronounced than in the numerous poor neighborhood schools to which thousands and thousands of teachers and children go every day. Such neglect takes its toll, hidden in the form of sick days, absenteeism, slower learning, lower test performance, and loss of motivation (Kats, 2006). As global attention turns to creating a healthier, safer, more energy-efficient world, we need to look at the local schools in our own backyards and reassess the tremendous impact of the physical school environment on student learning.

Organizing the physical environments of schools and classrooms for stronger, richer, deeper student learning is rooted in design knowledge—matters of relational space, the person–object interface, multi-sensory experience, sense of community and identity, and what designers term the *ecology of the artificial* (Ceppi & Zini, 1998), or the built environment of the school created and constructed by its own participants. This body of knowledge, however, is neither well known nor well understood by most educators whose primary concerns, understandably, are with assessment, curriculum, and instruction. At best, architectural and design concepts are tangential in educators' professional education and often narrowly construed in relation to the comfort, safety, and aesthetics of the classroom environment. In a world that is becoming increasingly media-saturated and hyperconnected, however, educators need to create more dynamic learning environments that are continuous, relevant, adaptive, agile, rich in information, and responsive to students' learning needs. To do this, they need design knowledge and a new *strategy of attention* (respect, appreciation, alertness) toward the physical environment as a resource in creating rich, complex, supportive environments for student learning. This chapter takes up these topics in hopes of stimulating new thoughts, fresh ideas, and a new appreciation for the ecology of the artificial.

The chapter is divided into four main parts. Part one—the "green" part—briefly discusses achieving standards of environmental quality in the construction and maintenance of schools and the classrooms they house. Parts two and three—the smart and deep learning sections of this chapter—survey the research base on the person–environment relationship as it pertains to the physical environment and what it means for learning at school. Part four describes a curricular framework that organizes environment design knowledge for educator preparation and professional development. This part outlines the usable design knowledge educators need for optimizing the physical environment for teaching and learning.

"GREENING" SCHOOL DESIGN

Each day, about 60 million students, teachers, and staff spend a considerable portion of their waking hours in schools (American Architects Foundation [AAF], 2006). Said another way, about 20% of America goes to school every day. In total, students will spend an estimated 20,000 hours of their lives in school environments (Gump, 1987). This is a lot of time spent *living* in schools and classrooms, some of which are in terrible shape. According to the U.S. General Accounting Office (1995), more than a quarter of all students (an estimated 14 million) attend schools considered below standard or dangerous, and almost two thirds of schools have building features (e.g., air conditioning) that are in need of extensive feature updates or repair. In about 15,000 of America's schools, the very air, in fact, is unfit to breathe (American Federation of Teachers, 2004). Such grim statistics, however, cannot convey the human toll of "what it means to a child [living in poverty] to leave his often hellish home and go to a school—his hope for a transcendent future—that is literally falling apart" (Kozol, 1991, p. 100). For children who are poor, going to schools in terrible shape only adds insult to injury.

Why is the environmental quality of many schools so poor? There are no simple answers for a host of historical and economic reasons, but there are some insights from an ancient architectural truth: The built environment carries with it the beliefs and goals of its creators. Rooted in Puritan principles of the 1700s, most American schools were built not to optimize health and comfort (or even learning) but rather to achieve a minimum level of shelter at the lowest possible cost. To learn, after all, was to suffer. Even now into the 21st century, very few schools are designed with the specific objective of creating high-grade learning environments despite the fact that school buildings represent the largest construction sector in the United States—$80 billion in 2006–2008.

Also true to its Puritan roots, schools are mostly a local matter and thus vulnerable to the chronic shortage of funds found in most school systems. Many school buildings and the classrooms therein suffer from inadequate maintenance and the degradation of basic systems such as ventilation, air quality, and lighting quality as well as poor control over pollutants (e.g., cleaning materials). Few states regulate indoor air quality or ventilation systems, and even fewer allocate sufficiently for upkeep of school facilities or new construction (too often done "on the cheap"). Driven by economies of scale and standardization, today's schools meet basic building codes, but many do not provide comfortable, productive, and healthy instructional environments for students and teachers (Advocacy Center for Children's Educational Success with Standards, 2004).

Times are changing, though. Conventional school design, welded to the past, is being challenged by a vigorous, new movement to design "green schools." Going green—a fresh design concept—means a *strategy of attention* to more day lighting, less toxic materials, improved ventilation and acoustics, better light quality, and improved air quality in schools and classrooms. According to Kats (2006), it costs about 2% more to build green schools, but the health and learning benefits are enormous. Based on a substantial data set (Loftness et al., 2002; Turner Construction, 2005), student productivity and test achievement showed a 3%–5% improvement in green schools; 70% of green schools reported reduced student absenteeism and improved student performance; and green schools increased overall school quality and competitiveness in attracting and retaining high-quality teachers. Greening the schools, as the data suggest, pays off many-fold: financially by reducing operations and maintenance costs; environmentally by conserving energy and water, not to mention reducing harmful carbon dioxide emissions; and humanly, as illustrated by improved student health, test scores, and faculty retention.

To build momentum for healthy high-performance school buildings, the U.S. Green Building Council for K–12 schools and higher education buildings developed a rating system referred to as Leadership in Energy and Environmental Design (LEED) for Schools Rating System. LEED for Schools is a "nutritional label" for green, healthy schools, providing third-party verification that a school building was designed and is operating the way it was intended to be. LEED for Schools certification emphasizes the following:

- Classroom acoustics
- Master planning
- Indoor air quality
- Mold prevention
- Energy efficiency
- Water conservation

LEED-certified schools across the country consistently demonstrate benefits in energy cost savings, emissions reduction, water conservation, and health gains for students and teachers.

As places, schools are significant in people's lives. Built by human hands, schools also shape the people who "live" in them everyday. In this shaping process, the school's physical environment has no small part. More or less, it can be healthy, safe, engaging, supporting, and stimulating for teachers and students alike. From a large body of research on building performance in school and out, we are learning that the environmental quality of most schools is not optimal, even in the best of neighborhoods. Built to code for times past, school design must change for times to come, growing green in an age of sustainability.

DESIGNING "SMARTER" CLASSROOMS

At school, the classroom is the designated place for learning. Here students gather, sit, and work together and alone in pursuit of knowledge. It is a multisensory place influenced by the shape of spaces within it, functional organization, and a host of sensory perceptions (e.g., light, color, acoustics, microclimatic conditions, tactile effects). The students see, touch, hear, and feel—the classroom's sensory richness is the foundation of investigation and discovery, research and cognition, and self-learning. Four research syntheses benchmark what we know about the influence of the classroom physical environment on students' learning. Summarized next in historical order, these studies show steady progress toward "smarter" classroom design that is diversified, stimulating, and welcoming and where each student belongs but also has spaces for privacy and pause.

Consolidating scattered reports across the education literature and divergent strands from different disciplines in the last decades of the 20th century, Weinstein (1979) identified the effects of specific environmental variables (e.g., noise, light, temperature) and ecological niche factors (e.g. density, furniture arrangements) on student learning. Evidence showed little impact of the classroom physical environment on student achievement but considerable impact on student behaviors and attitudes. Following the inferential trail of this finding, Weinstein proposed that more positive attitudes and behaviors may eventually result in more academic achievement. Greater student engagement, she reasoned, affords more opportunity to learn from instruction and to sustain it—a logic borne out in studies of attendance, test scores, and overall student performance gains linked to building attributes (Schneider, 2002). Weinstein's compilation also helped to establish quality indicators in the basic categories of health and safety, the ambient environment, and the instructional environment that provided the basis for classroom environment rating scales (e.g., the Early Childhood Environment Rating Scale; Harms & Clifford, 1980) still in use today.

About two decades later, Moore (2001), in a comprehensive research review, cited a number of physical environment factors in the early childhood setting that yield developmental gains, such as size, density, noise, retreats, activity settings, and modified open plans. Moreover, the synthesis showed that the interactive effects of physical environment factors and social factors—socioeconomic status of participants in the setting, teacher style, and program philosophy—may be mutually reinforcing in the physical design, such that the whole is greater than the sum of its parts. Well-defined activity settings, for example, combined with an open classroom style led to more child engagement and thus more opportunity to learn from experiences. Moore's review also identified three categories of design principles that could be used in preparing the early childhood environment for learning: 1) a neighborhood hub model for facilities where the school or center is the "hub" of the surrounding neighborhood; 2) home as the metaphor for spatial organization with welcoming entries, smaller spaces for work and play, places for privacy, and so forth; and 3) provision of outdoor activity space for extending classroom activities, for play and for exercise.

Around the same time, Fisher (2000) conducted a thorough review of the empirical research to determine how educational spaces should be configured to support student achievement. Descriptive studies cited a host of influential design factors: amount of space, openness of space, sense of identity, flexibility, and levels of privacy to name a few. The search, however, yielded no body of scientifically rigorous studies demonstrating environmental effects that might inform design configurations, except for two intriguing exceptions.

First, evidence showed strong causal links between the quality and amount of science equipment and furniture in labs and the quality of student's behavioral and learning outcomes. Well-equipped and artfully arranged science labs, it appears, create *relational space*, that is to say, integrated space, that enables links between specialized activities and ways of thinking. Relational space is not only rich in information but also in opportunities to interpret and represent it with new understanding. The critical design point gleaned is the potential power of relational space for connecting activity, ways of thinking, and fields of knowledge.

Second, evidence pointed to building aesthetics—scale, color schemes, transitional spaces, the incidence of views and vistas, and circulation patterns—as influential in student learning. Fisher (2000) concluded that more research is needed to pinpoint these aesthetics–learning relationships for purposes of informing design trends and specifications in classroom design. Research outside the field of education, however, is also relevant here, augmenting evidence of the effects of the classroom environment on teaching and learning. For example, large-scale health effect studies of worker-controlled temperature and ventilation in 107 European buildings found significantly reduced absenteeism and increased productivity compared with a control group (Heerwagen, 2002). In a review of 1,500 studies relating building attributes such as lighting, the Building Investment Decision Support (BIDS) program found that better environmental design correlates with increases in individual well-being and productivity (Loftness, Hartkopf, & Gurtekin, 2002); good lighting, in fact, has consistently been found to improve student test scores and reduce off-task behavior (Lemasters, 1997).

Faced with a massive need for school design renewal, the AAF, with the support of Knowledge Works Foundation, examined the body of quantitative and qualitative research on school design amassed since the 1990s (AAF, 2006). Augmenting this information with interview, focus group, and forum data from school design stakeholders around the country, the AAF made eight recommendations, listed in Table 17.1, that synthesized school design research and architectural thought. Introduced at the National Summit on School Design in the fall of 2005, the 70-page report constitutes the most up-to-date knowledge base on research-based principles of educational environment design (Lackney, 2003).

What do these principles, the fruits of decades of research, tell us about designing better, smarter classrooms into the future? The design lessons are as follows:

1.   There is the growing recognition that learning is on the move, expanding beyond the classroom walls and finding new venues: computers, iPods, cell phones, television, digital cameras, and Smart Boards. Classroom design must respond to this new reality, providing flexible spaces for active learning that reach out to the world through easy access to new technologies.

2.   Learning thrives in small places that foster small-group interactions, support relationships and attachments, and offer retreats and niches. The standard classroom is hard-pressed to provide these kinds of spaces and should be reconfigured around the imagery and scale of the home. Details such as welcoming entries, lofts, small alcoves, project areas, and enclosed yards proportion the classroom into a smaller, more intimate learning environment that promotes and sustains interaction.

3.   Learning is nurtured in healthy, safe places. These days, the growing crisis of obesity in children and youth along with a growing population of students with asthma and allergies raise new urgent health concerns about the environmental quality of the classroom environment. Environmentally sensitive indoor designs (light, air, sound quality) and better-planned outdoor learning environments that mirror indoor learning maximize year-round uses for vigorous activity, and instill a sense of pride in students about their schools should be high-priority items in classroom renovation and in new school construction.

Table 17.1.   National Summit on School Design recommendations

Design schools to support a variety of learning styles.
Enhance learning by integrating technology.
Foster "small schools" culture.
Support neighborhood schools.
Create schools as centers of the community.
Engage public in the planning process.
Make healthy, comfortable, flexible learning spaces.
Consider nontraditional options for school facilities and classrooms.

Source: Lackney (2003).

DEEP LEARNING SPACES

It's one thing to argue for greener, smarter classrooms based on research evidence and to raise consciousness, if not inspire passion, for change in the design of school as *a place*. It is quite another to educate for change that results in well-designed classroom places—not hand-me-down, ad-hoc places—that hold real meaning for teachers and students. This requires a search for a new epistemology of classroom design that sheds old architectural views and revitalizes physical space as a constituent, formative element in students' learning paths and processes. It can begin with a body of knowledge organized around two fundamental principles:

1.   The classroom environment supports teaching and learning.
2.   The classroom environment is safe and healthy.

Each of these principles consists of essential concepts and processes that activate design knowledge and move it toward creating deep learning spaces where teachers and students work, play, communicate, and live well.

Supporting Teaching and Learning

A growing body of educational design research points to *home* as the template for organizing physical space at all scales (e.g., building, classroom, activity center) (Crumpacker, 1995; Moore, Lane, Hill, Cohen, & McGinty, 1979). The imagery and scale of home can be used to provide welcoming entryways, to structure just-right spaces for activity, to create enclosed "backyards," and to display cultural items from the neighborhoods where students live. Appropriately scaled, homelike elements (e.g., walls, hallways, proximity between spaces, room proportion) support compact, mixed-use, easily walkable instructional areas that communicate a sense of harmony and control. A prime example is the main "street" of the School of the Future, a collaborative project between the Philadelphia School District and Microsoft Corporation (see http://www.microsoft.com/education/demos/schooloffuture/index.html). The street corridor is the social spine of the facility, connecting all major spaces and activities on the first two floors of the three-story facility. Finishes, such as benches and foliage, bring an outdoor atmosphere to this socially active space. Architectural proportioning at the human scale of *home* fosters student engagement in the learning environment at all ages. Most pronounced, perhaps, is the evidence that the design features of *home* reduce stress in young children, creating a sense of comfort that helps them to concentrate on learning. Feeling at ease, they are also more apt to explore events and materials around them, thus widening their range of experience.

Size is a fundamental design concept. A large body of research demonstrates that the amount of classroom space per student is a powerful determinant of environmental quality (Moore, 2001; Moore & Lackney, 1994). Crowding thwarts attention to learning and leads to aggression (Loo, 1972). Optimal instructional space should allow for 12–16 learners in preprimary and primary grades, 16–20 learners in the middle school, and 20–24 learners in secondary school grade levels (Lackney, 2003).

Adequate amount of space is especially important for young children just developing their social skills in a peer group. Because young children's communication skills are rudimentary, their sociocognitive skills are stretched to the maximum in social situations, often triggering peer conflict as well as personal stress. More space allows shy children or those having difficulties adjusting to the group to keep peers at a distance and to explore parts of the classroom where they are less socially exposed. Debunking the 35-square-foot myth as a sufficient amount of classroom space, research indicates that 48–54 square feet of accessible play space per child is required to minimize children's stress levels (Legendre, 2003; van Liempd, 1998). This specification also permits the construction of privacy niches in the environment found to support positive social behaviors and to reduce aggression (Smith, 1974).

For older children, class size research indicates a social and physical link to achievement—perhaps attributable to reductions in spatial density and crowding—which in turn affords higher-quality student–teacher interactions over time. Smaller class sizes are especially beneficial for students attending inner-city schools, where studies show "smaller is better" for improving reading and mathematics achievement (Achilles, 1992). Design research also suggests that a variety of adjoining learning spaces and arrangements works best in schools. Smaller yet connected spaces that ensure visual openness yet adequate acoustical barriers allow for small-group work and also can be further divided for individual, self-directed learning. When it comes to raw space, in sum, the operative principle is optimal size (square footage) for students to gather, work, and play in a variety of learning groups and spaces.

Raw space is a basic necessity, but it is not sufficient for ensuring environmental quality in classroom design. Still needed are well-defined, resource-rich activity areas that stimulate students' active engagement with subject matter concepts and skills and literate thinking. Research converges on the fact that small spaces for activity that accommodate 2–5 students increase engagement, exploration, and social interaction between students and between teachers and students (Kantrowitz & Evans, 2004; Moore, 1986; Smith & Connolly, 1986). An adequate number of activity areas (i.e., ratio of students to number of activity areas) ensures more time spent in constructive work, less off-task behavior, increased use of learning materials, and more substantive talk. As students learn to navigate different activity areas, they also develop self-regulation skills needed to make transitions from one activity to another, to pay attention, and to stay on task. Overall, well-defined activity areas demand cognitive engagement over random behavior and aimless wandering or daydreaming in the setting.

Some research also describes what to put in activity areas so as to up the ante for learning (Kounin & Sherman, 1979; Kritchevsky, Prescott, & Walling, 1969).

Two interrelated design concepts are critical: *variety* and *complexity of material re-sources*. *Variety* relates to amount to do; it is important to ensure that there are different kinds of activities available to attract students. For young learners, research suggests at least two activity areas per student for variety; that is, about five areas for a class of 15 students, given three to four students rotating among the areas in a 45- to 60-minute time block. *Complexity* has to do with the cognitive demand that materials require to hold and challenge students' attention in activity. More complex materials have multiple uses and multiple parts, making them more compelling, provided they are well matched to children's developmental levels. When activity areas are designed for variety and cognitive demand, students pursue new activities, persist with an activity, self-monitor their progress, and express genuine satisfaction with what they are doing.

Treating the physical environment as a *three-dimensional textbook* is another important design concept in creating a supportive learning environment. Architecturally, this involves creating studio-like spaces where students can pursue longer-term projects and collaborate as well as study on their own. General classrooms in the School of the Future, for example, have moveable walls for creating bigger instruction spaces as well as special project rooms in between two rooms that can be used for individual or group work. In early childhood classrooms, Gelman and Brenneman (2004) reported the benefits of creating a "coherent, embedded environment" for young children's mathematical and scientific cognitive development. They found that including a science place for engaging in science topics over an extended period of time, along with proper tools such as science notebooks, helped children to build mental structures of science concepts, such as the characteristics of a living thing.

Environment as a *three-dimensional textbook* also means weaving together virtual and physical learning spaces to encourage the use of technology in pursuing ideas and problem solving. A technology hub centrally located in the classroom environment where digital (e.g., cameras), audio, video, and computer (e.g., laptops) resources are consolidated for easy access yet are portable for students' use (Butterfield, 1999) may be optimal. A premier example, the Interactive Learning Center in the School of the Future is designed for students, faculty, and the community. It not only contains a technology lab equipped with wireless and hard-wire connections but also a literacy nook designed as a small-group discussion space with informal seating. In addition, the technology lab contains a student production and copy room, a conference room, and a circulation desk for managing materials.

Proper signage and wall function truly make the environment a *three-dimensional textbook* worth reading. Wall space should be used to "teach on the walls" when possible (e.g., use of Smart Boards) and to document learning experiences that occur in the classroom. Students' work, charts, poems, language experience stories, and content-oriented murals should dominate the wall space. Wall space, however, should not be cluttered and noisy with information. Rather, it should include sufficient white space to foreground images and text for easy access and reading. Along with personal cubbies, message boards, word walls, storage areas, and posted directions, walls can also contain interactive activities, such as plasma screens for information, mini museums, sorting tasks, and scribble space, all of which include signs and labels.

Ensuring Safe and Healthy Classrooms

At all building scales, cleanliness, accessibility, and material safety are the very basics of an appropriate physical environment for teachers and students. Studies show the negative effects of too much noise (interior and exterior) on cognitive development (Cohen, Glass, & Singer, 1973; Wachs, 1976); architects argue for "fresh-air architecture" that ensures proper ventilation and air flow (Loftness et al., 2002); and designers recommend creating lightscapes that contain variations in intensity, differences in color, and possibilities for filtering and enriching light (Ceppi & Zini, 1998).

Teachers have some measure of influence and control over these factors of the physical environment but only to a point. They are not the final arbiters of maintenance, entry/exit construction, or materials purchasing nor are they necessarily acoustic and lighting experts. What they can manipulate, however, are the design concepts of boundaries, pathways, and the immediate outdoor learning environment to ensure safe, healthy places for active learning.

The arrangement of the classroom environment is rooted in the design concept of *boundaries* (i.e., the mapping of physical space). How the physical space is partitioned influences student motivation, activity, and social interaction. Research has looked at this design problem from two perspectives: defining person space (desks, cubbies, retreats) and defining functional space (instruction, meeting, activity). For older children, space is typically partitioned into islands of person space interspersed among row-and-column or clustered seating arrangements. For younger children, physical space is generally divided into clearly defined person space (cubbies) and functional areas for whole-group time and small-group activity centers. Early childhood classrooms require additional design factors: clearly delineating activity areas, locating areas close to materials needed for activity, separating incompatible activities, making areas visually accessible, and providing spatial options for privacy. Boundaries can double as display and storage areas and need not be permanent. Physical dividers (e.g., book shelves) as well as visual dividers (e.g., mobiles; rugs) can be used. Clear boundaries protect student projects, small-group work, and privacy and thus support self-regulatory skills of paying attention and concentration.

Pathways create circulation patterns that hold potential for learning and social interaction. Ideally, these routes should provide a clear line of sight but also detour around activity areas to allow gentle transitions between activity areas. Meandering pathways with forks and *T*s encourage browsing and observing others' activity in getting from Point A to Point B. Conversely, for issues of safety, pathways must be designed to ensure visual supervision and should avoid long, unbroken corridors. Most of all, pathways should not lead into dead space where students get stuck and distracted in counterproductive activities. Dead space is created when activity areas are arranged around the perimeter of the room, leaving a large, open area in the center. Effective use of meandering pathways in classroom design can encourage positive social behaviors yet ensure proper supervision and safety.

An increasingly important concept in classroom design is creating learning spaces outside that mirror learning spaces inside. Childhood is a key period for promoting physical activity—the bedrock of cognitive development. Sufficient space for developing and practicing basic movement patterns (walking, running, galloping, jumping, hopping, skipping, throwing, catching, kicking, balancing) is essential if young children are to develop the advanced motor coordination skills they need for literacy. Outdoor space should be located on the south side of buildings to catch as much sun and light as possible. To maximize outdoor activity year round, easy-to-assemble materials should be used to create microclimates that protect from cold winds and from extreme sun.

The *outdoor learning environment* should be designed to not only promote physical activity but also to serve as a laboratory for exploratory learning not possible indoors (e.g., gardens). Outdoor areas can be modeled after backyards and can include resource-rich activity areas that provide for diverse learning activities—not just gross motor physical activities but also fantasy play and nature investigations. The need for well-planned outdoor learning environments cannot be overemphasized—especially in light of the growing need for more physically active students—and should be well integrated with indoor classroom design. Physical education facilities in middle and high schools, for example, should have direct access to playing fields, biking trails, in-line skating tracks, jogging paths, and outdoor leadership activities (e.g., hiking).

CONCLUSION

Today's teacher must ask—more urgently than ever before—what kind of space helps students learn. How do I shape physical space into a place where my students learn together about the real world and about possible worlds; where they discover the uses of their minds, imagination, materials, and new technologies; and where they feel well, productive, energized and safe. To ask is to first become design conscious and in turn an active designer of optimal learning environments for instruction and community building. The curriculum outlined in Table 17.2 offers a basic framework for developing the educator's design knowledge toward the goal of continuous, relevant, and adaptive classroom environments.

In Table 17.2, the column labeled *Aims* captures the new vision of environmental design for learning at all scholastic levels (AAF, 2006). Essential knowl-

Table 17.2. Environment design curriculum framework

	Content	
Aims	Principles	Concepts
Active learning beyond school walls Learning environments on a human scale	Support teaching and learning	Scale of home Size of space per child Activity areas for learning Space as three-dimensional textbook
Healthy, safe places for learning	Provide healthy and safe environments	Boundaries Pathways Outdoor space

edge about the *ecology of the artificial* or built environment is summarized in the *Content* column, representing basic design concepts needed to create learner-centered, knowledge-centered, assessment-centered, and community-centered classroom environments (Bransford, Brown, & Cocking, 2000). The curriculum framework is a simple structure in the complex effort to reconceptualize and re-organize school architecture and design toward a new meaning of physical space in teaching and learning.

"To start with," Malaguzzi wrote, "there is the environment" (Edwards, Gandini, & Forman, 1998, p. 64)—a topic not often addressed in educational reform, scientifically based reading research, closing the achievement gap, or changing the odds for students in poverty. Yet, we all did or still do inhabit schools with all our senses, and millions of future teachers and students will do the same. The physical spaces of school can be in tune with and attentive to students' biological abilities, affording possibilities for expressing and developing all their genetic equipment. Or not. *Not,* however, is unacceptable in light of what we know about the educational environment and its influences on student learning and well-being. Students have the right to learn in schools and classrooms that are healthy, well maintained, and pleasant. Teachers have the right to teach there. To live well in school, "the spaces, materials, colors, light, microclimate, and furnishings must be direct and integral participants in the great alchemy of growing within a [learning] community" (Vecchi, 1998, p. 135). For this to happen, educators need to develop a more informed strategy of attention; they need to become more knowledgeable if they are to shape the physical space of the classroom for deep learning.

REFERENCES

Achilles, C.M. (1992). *The effect of school size on student achievement and the interaction of small classes and school size on student achievement.* Unpublished manuscript, University of North Carolina–Greensboro, Department of Educational Administration.

Advocacy Center for Children's Educational Success with Standards. (2004, Winter). Public school facilities: Providing environments that sustain learning [Electronic version]. *ACCESS Quarterly, 4*(1), 1, 4.

American Architects Foundation. (2006, June 12). *New report sets direction for school design in 21st century: Target joins Great Schools by Design initiative.* Retrieved September 2006 from http://www.archfoundation.org/aaf/aaf/News.36.htm

American Federation of Teachers. (2004, April). *An environment for learning.* Retrieved May 2007 from http://www.aft.org/presscenter/speeches-columns/wws/2004/WWS_0404.pdf

Bransford, J., Brown, A., & Cocking, R. (Eds.). (2000). *How people learn: Brain, mind, experience and school.* Washington, DC: National Academies Press.

Butterfield, E. (1999). *School renovation and the importance of maintenance: Q & A with Charles Boney, Jr.* Retrieved August 2006 from www.designshare.com/Research/Boney/renovation1.htm

Ceppi, G., & Zini, M. (1998). *Children, spaces, relations: Meta-project for an environment for young children.* Milan, Italy: Domus Academy Research Center.

Cohen, U., Glass, D.C., & Singer, J.E. (1973). Apartment noise, auditory discrimination, and reading ability in children. *Journal of Experimental Social Psychology, 9,* 407–422.

Crumpacker, S.S. (1995). Using cultural information to create schools that work. In A. Meek (Ed.), *Designing places for learning* (pp. 31–42). Alexandria, VA: Association for Supervision and Curriculum Development.

Edwards, C., Gandini, L., & Forman, G. (1998). *The hundred languages of children: The Reggio Emilia approach-advanced reflections* (2nd ed.). Greenwich, CT: Ablex Publishing.

Fisher, K. (2000). Building better outcomes: The impact of school infrastructure on student outcomes and behaviour. *Schooling Issues Digest.* Australia: Commonwealth Department of Education, Training and Youth Affairs.

Gelman, S., & Brenneman, K. (2004). Pathways to science for young children. *Early Childhood Research Quarterly, 19,* 151–158.

Gump, P. (1987). School and classroom environments. In I. Altman & J.F. Wohlwill (Eds.), *Handbook of environmental psychology* (pp. 131–174). New York: Plenum Press.

Harms, T., & Clifford, R.M. (1980). *Early childhood environment rating scale.* New York: Teachers College Press.

Heerwagen, J. (2002, July). Sustainable design can be an asset to the bottom line. *Environment Design & Construction.* Retrieved May 2007 from http://www.edcmag.com/CDA/Archives/fb077b7338697010VgnVCM100000f93

Kantrowitz, E.J., & Evans, G. (2004). The relation between the ratio of children per activity area and off-task behavior and type of play in day care centers. *Environment and Behavior, 36*(4), 541–557.

Kats, G. (2006, October). *Greening America's schools: Costs and benefits. A Capital E Report.* Retrieved May 2007 from http://www.cap-e.com/

Kounin, J.S., & Sherman, L.W. (1979). School environments as behavior settings. *Theory Into Practice, 18*(3), 145–151.

Kozol, J. (1991). *Savage inequalities.* New York: Crown Publishers.

Kritchevsky, S., Prescott, E., & Walling, L. (1969). *Planning environments for young children: Physical space.* Washington, DC: National Association for Education of Young Children.

Lackney, J.A. (2003). *33 principles of educational design.* School Design Research Studio. Retrieved August 2006 from http://schoolstudio.engr.wisc.edu/33principles.html

Legendre, A. (2003). Environmental features influencing toddlers' bioemotional reactions in day care centers. *Environment and Behavior, 35,* 523–549.

Lemasters, L.K. (1997). A synthesis of studies pertaining to facilities, student achievement and student outcomes. *VA Polytechnic.* [Cited in Schneider, http://www.edfacilities.org]

Loftness, V, Hartkopf, V., & Gurtekin, B, (2002). *Building investment decisions support (BIDS): Cost benefit tool to promote high performance components, flexible infrastructures, and systems integration for sustainable commercial buildings and productive organizations.* Retrieved May 2007 from www.aia.org/SiteObjects/files/BIDS_color.pdf

Loo, C. (1972). The effects of spatial density on the social behavior of children. *Journal of Applied Psychology, 2*(4), 372–381.

Moore, G.T. (1986). Effects of the spatial definition of behavior settings on children's behaviors: A quasi-experimental field study. *Journal of Environmental Psychology, 6*(3), 205–231.

Moore, G.T. (2001, June). *Children, young people and their environments.* Keynote address at the Fourth Child and Family Policy Conference, Dunedin, NZ.

Moore, G.T, & Lackney, J.A. (1994). *Educational facilities for the twenty-first century: Research analysis and design patterns* (Report R94-1). Milwaukee: University of Wisconsin–Milwaukee, School of Architecture and Urban Planning.

Moore, G.T., Lane, C.G., Hill, A.B., Cohen, U., & McGinty, T. (1979). *Recommendations for child care centers* (Report No. R79-2). Milwaukee: University of Wisconsin–Milwaukee, Center for Architecture & Urban Planning Research.

Schneider, M. (2002). *Do school facilities affect academic outcomes?* Retrieved May 2007 From http://www.edfacilities.org/pubs/outcomes.pdf

Smith, P. (1974). Aspects of the playgroup environment. In D. Canter & T. Lee (Eds.), *Proceedings of the conference: Psychology and the built environment.* London: Architectural Press.

Smith, P.K., & Connolly, K.J. (1986). Experimental studies on the preschool environment: The Sheffield Project. *Advances in Early Childhood Education and Day Care, 4,* 27–66.

Turner Construction. (2005). *Turner Construction green buildings survey.* Retrieved May 2007 from http://www.turnerconstruction.com/greenbuildings

U.S. General Accounting Office. (1995). *School facilities: America's schools not designed or equipped for 21st century* (GAO Report No. HEHS-95-95). Washington, DC: Author. (ERIC Document Reproduction Service No. D383056)

van Liempd, I. (1998). Unpublished findings from research conducted by AKTA Bureau of Research and advice on the use of space in the Netherlands.

Vecchi, V. (1998). What kind of space for living well in school? In G. Ceppi & M. Zini (Eds.), *Children, spaces, relations: Meta-project for an environment for young children.* Modena, Italy: Grafiche Rebecchi Ceccarelli.

Wachs, T.D. (1976). Utilization of a Piagetian approach in the investigation of early experience effects: A research strategy and some illustrative data. *Merrill-Palmer Quarterly, 22,* 11–30.

Weinstein, C.S. (1979). The physical environment of the school: A review of the research. *Review of Educational Research, 49*(4), 577–610.

Index

Page numbers followed by *f, t,* and *n* indicate figures, tables, and footnotes, respectively.